THE QUESTION OF GOD
IN HEIDEGGER'S PHENOMENOLOGY

Northwestern University
Studies in Phenomenology
and
Existential Philosophy

THE
QUESTION OF GOD
IN
HEIDEGGER'S
PHENOMENOLOGY

George Kovacs

Northwestern University Press
Evanston, Illinois

Northwestern University Press
Evanston, Illinois 60201

Printed in the United States of America

Library of Congress Cataloging-in-Publication Data

Kovacs, George, 1935–
    The question of God in Heidegger's phenomenology / George Kovacs.
        p.   cm.—(Northwestern University studies in phenomenology
    and existential philosophy.)
    Includes bibliographical references.
    ISBN 0-8101-0850-X.—ISBN 0-8101-0851-8 (pbk.)
    1. God—History of doctrines—20th century. 2. Heidegger, Martin,
1889–1976—Contributions in concept of God. I. Title. II. Series:
Northwestern University studies in phenomenology & existential
philosophy.
BT102.H425K68   1989
211'.092—dc20   89-37027
                                                                      CIP

To My Parents, and to Alexis,
with Thankfulness
and Love

Contents

CONTENTS

List of Symbols Used

This list includes all the symbols used for Heidegger's writings. The abbreviation "Ga." followed by a number (in parentheses after the title) indicates the number of volume in the *Gesamtausgabe*.

AM *Aristoteles, Metaphysik IX 1–3: Vom Wesen und Wirklichkeit der Kraft* (Ga. 33)

BE *Beiträge zur Philosophie: Vom Ereignis* (Ga. 65)

BP *Zur Bestimmung der Philosophie. 1: Die Idee der Philosophie und das Weltanschauungsproblem. 2: Phänomenologie und transcendentale Wertphilosophie* (Ga. 56/57)

ED *Aus der Erfahrung des Denkens*

EDG *Aus der Erfahrung des Denkens* (Ga. 13)

EM *Einführung in die Metaphysik*

F *Der Feldweg*

FD *Die Frage nach dem Ding: Zu Kants Lehre von den transzendentalen Grundsätzen*

FS *Frühe Schriften* (Ga. 1)

G *Gelassenheit*

GB *Grundbegriffe* (Ga. 51)

GM *Die Grundbegriffe der Metaphysik: Welt-Endlichkeit-Einsamkeit* (Ga. 29/30)

GL *Grundfragen der Philosophie: Ausgewählte "Probleme" der "Logik"* (Ga. 45)

GP *Die Grundprobleme der Phänomenologie* (Ga. 24)

H *Heraklit. 1: Der Anfang des abendländischen Denkens (Heraklit). 2: Logik: Heraklits Lehre vom Logos* (Ga. 55)

HA *Hölderlins Hymne "Andenken"* (Ga. 52)

HB *Über den Humanismus*

HD *Erläuterungen zu Hölderlins Dichtung*

HF *Hebel—der Hausfreund*

HH *Hölderlins Hymnen "Germanien" und "Der Rhein"* (Ga. 39)

HI *Hölderlins Hymne "Der Ister"* (Ga. 53)

HP *Hegels Phänomenologie des Geistes* (Ga. 32)

HS *Heraklit* (with Eugen Fink)

HW *Holzwege*

IH *"Only a God Can Save Us: Der Spiegel's* Interview with Martin Heidegger"

ID *Identität und Differenz*

KM *Kant und das Problem der Metaphysik*

KS *Kants These über das Sein*

KV *"La fin de la philosophie et la tâche de la pensée"* (in *Kierkegaard vivant*)

LW *Logik: Die Frage nach der Wahrheit* (Ga. 21)

ML *Metaphysische Anfangsgründe der Logik im Ausgang von Leibniz* (Ga. 26)

N *Nietzsche* (2 vols.: N, 1 and N, 2)

OH *Ontolgie: Hermeneutik der Faktizität* (Ga. 63)

P *Parmenides* (Ga. 54)

PA *Phänomenologische Interpretationen zu Aristoteles: Einführung in die phänomenologische Forschung* (Ga. 61)

PK *Phänomenologische Interpretation von Kants Kritik der reinen Vernunft* (Ga. 25)

PT *Phänomenologie und Theologie*

PW *Platons Lehre von der Wahrheit*

PZ *Prolegomena zur Geschichte des Zeitbegriffs* (Ga. 20)

SA *Schellings Abhandlung über das Wesen der menschlichen Freiheit (1809)*

SD *Zur Sache des Denkens*

SF *Zur Seinsfrage*

SG *Der Satz vom Grund*

SZ *Sein und Zeit*

SZG *Sein und Zeit* (Ga. 2)

TK *Die Technik und die Kehre*

US *Unterwegs zur Sprache*

VA *Vorträge und Aufsätze* (3 parts: VA, 1; VA, 2; VA, 3)

VS *Vier Seminare*

W *Wegmarken*

WD *Was heisst Denken?*

WF *Vom Wesen der menschlichen Freiheit: Einleitung in die Philosophie* (Ga. 31)

WG *Vom Wesen des Grundes*

WM *Was ist Metaphysik?*

WP *Was ist das—die Philosophie?*

WW *Vom Wesen der Wahrheit*

WWP *Vom Wesen der Wahrheit: Zu Platons Höhlengleichnis und Theätet* (Ga. 34)

Preface

> Denken ist die Einschränkung
> auf einen Gedanken, der einst
> wie ein Stern am Himmel der
> Welt stehen bleibt. (ED, p. 7)

The guiding star of Heidegger's pathway of thought is the question of Being, the thinking of the ontological difference. This profound unity of the experience of thinking leads to a new understanding of human existence, of freedom, of language, of history, and, on the whole, of the nature and task of philosophy. The "new" understanding of many "old" problems is rendered possible precisely through the originality and the unity of the ontological problematic as a whole. Heidegger, indeed, is the philosopher of Being in an epoch that is marked by the forgetfulness of Being, by the thoughtlessness about the root of beings in Being, by the turning away from the sense of wonder that there are beings at all and not rather nothing.

The unity and the richness of the themes of Heidegger's thought suggest the possibility of asking these questions: Is there a "place" for the problem of God in Heidegger's philosophy? What is the meaning of the question of God in Heidegger's phenomenology? What is the function of the word *God* in his way of thinking? It may be surprising that in the title of this study there is an indication of the presence of the question of God in Heidegger's thinking, in his meditations on the question of Being. However, this "in" should be understood as a foreshadowing of the research and not as a preestablished ground for the coming reflections. In the same way, the problem of God is meant to be a problem, a philosophical rethinking of the question of God that is wider and deeper than the commonly understood dilemma of theism and atheism. The main task of this investigation is to discern the meaning of the question of God in Heidegger's thinking, that is, in the context of the ontological meditation.

The methodology (the "how") of this study is governed by the demands of its task; it is geared to analyze and thus to understand the question of God from within Heidegger's thinking according to his published writings, in the light of the question of Being. This investigation, therefore, begins with an objective analysis of Heidegger's thought. It includes a close examination of all his works (in the German original) with special attention to the (direct as well as indirect) references to the problem of God. Many themes and insights of his philosophy have an immediate relationship to the problem of God (for example, the World, truth, meaning of existence). It is interesting to notice that, in a way, quite often Heidegger says "more" about God when he speaks "less" about him directly.

Through the analysis of his thought, then, it becomes possible to discover a philosophical attitude toward the problem of God and to grasp the reasons for it. This research makes it clear that Heidegger's thought implies an indifference toward theism and atheism, that it goes beyond the dilemma of theism and atheism; it shows that the question of God acquires a new focus and meaning in (especially) his phenomenology. In the final analysis, this study contributes to the comprehensive and systematic grasp of Heidegger's position on the question of God; it includes critical reflections and raises some crucial questions on the nature as well as on the "place" of God in his way of thinking.

The dialogue (the method of thinking) with Heidegger's writings leads to unearthing the (three) main phases (dimensions) of his development of the question of God and to pursuing the questioning even further than Heidegger. It is crucial to examine more closely the works that are more essential for understanding his considerations of the problem of God. However, the analysis of this problem became so extensive and the pertinent material so vast that it was necessary to focus and limit the final presentation of this research to the philosophical (thematic as well as systematic) aspects of the issue at hand. These reflections, therefore, are different (in nature and task) from the theological and psychological appropriations of his thought as well as from the merely historical (genetic) accounts of his views on God.

This study, then, is not a chronological summary or review of the ideas on God in Heidegger's works even though the writings examined fit into a chronological (genetic) order; it is, rather, a thematic and a systematic analysis of the nature as well as of the ramifications of the question of God in Heidegger's way of thinking, in the "constellation" of the comprehension of Being.

What are the main steps and accomplishments of this investigation? They may be described briefly, according to the order of exposition (indicated by the Contents), as follows.

Part 1 considers some aspects of Heidegger's philosophy and shows their connection with as well as their implications for a possible reflection on the problem of God. It includes an introduction to the nature of the question of God in Heidegger's thinking and represents a preview of the ramifications of this problematic. The main purpose of this part, however, is to indicate that there *is* a question of God in Heidegger's phenomenology, that there is a "place" for the idea of God in his thinking. It emphasizes the way the question of God comes about within the thinking of Being, that the thinking of the ontological difference implies a rethinking of the metaphysical problem of God. These initial reflections move with a measured space in order to allow for a gradual immersion into Heidegger's philosophy; they help the grasping of the way, especially by those who may not have tried it far enough.

Part 2 investigates key insights of SZ; it examines comprehensively those themes of the existential analytic that have a relationship to the problem of God. Its purpose is to discern the *first phase* of the question of God in

Heidegger's thinking. This phase is described as a process of demythologization, as a critical and questioning reexamination of the "storytelling," causal, metaphysical approach to the problem of God. The critical perspective of SZ, however, is neither theistic nor atheistic; it unearths the background and the ontological inadequacy of the causal explanation of God. SZ does not intend to nor can it give a final answer to the God-question; in the final analysis, it leaves open the possibility of the relation of human existence to God. The existential analysis represents a this-worldly understanding of the World and of human reality; the critical attitude toward and the transformation of the traditional approach to the problem of God ought to be understood as the results of the existential, phenomenological analysis. All that can be found in SZ about the problem of God is part of the ontological nature of the inquiry; the examination of the Being-question (a reawakening of it) by means of the analysis of existence (There-being) implies a rethinking of the God-question. This is the reason for the presence of the phenomenological problem of God in the early Heidegger; this problem, however, remains undeveloped in SZ.

Part 3 distinguishes two more phases of the development of the question of God in Heidegger's thinking. The examination of the questioning attitude in Heidegger's works that followed SZ (the Kant studies, WM, WW, WG, PW, EM, and HD) discloses the *second phase* of the question of God; it is described as that of questioning, as the recognition of the question of God as a genuine, meaningful question after the separation of the question of Being from the question of God. This second phase is also characterized by the indifference of the ontological questioning toward the question of God. This indifference, together with the other elements of the radical depth of the questioning, however, in the light of the analysis of seminal writings of the later Heidegger (TK, HB, WP, VA, ID, BE), leads to the discernment of the *third* and final *phase* of the question of God in his thought, to a new way of thinking about the notion as well as about the entire question of God. This final phase is described in Part 3, Chapter 18; it analyzes

the nature as well as the boundaries (and the limitations) of this new perspective on the question of God.
These reflections, then, show that the term *demythologization* (the often "destructive" criticism) is not the last
but only the first term describing Heidegger's position
on God, that the critical attitude prepares the ground
for dealing with the question of God as a question and
even for a new way of thinking about God. The meditation on the question of Being (as well as on the essence
of truth and on language), on the unfolding of the ontological difference (relating beings to Being and grasping them from the horizon of Being), does shed some
new light on the difference between Being and God (on
the theological difference) and not only on the difference between Being and beings (on the ontological difference). What is the difference (after the recognition
of the demythologization) between God and beings in
light of the ontological difference? What is the essence
of the theological difference from the ontological perspective (that is, as the difference between Being and
God)? What is the nature of the theological difference
from the ontic perspective (that is, as the difference
between beings and God)? Heidegger responds to these
questions by emphasizing the theological indifference
of the ontological difference (thus by unearthing the
question of God as a question) and by remaining open
toward and intimating a possible new way of thinking
the meaning of the word *God* in the light of the meaning
of Being. The rethinking of the meaning of Being,
then, does not sweep away but rather reawakens the
sense of wonder about God.

Part 4 is based on those writings of Heidegger that
had already become available for the first time in the *Gesamtausgabe*, the complete edition of all his writings (still in
progress); it analyzes and reflects on key issues (the nature
of philosophy and atheism, the meaning of transcendence, World, creation, the "other") that define and make
more clear his position on the question of God. Though
these writings were also referred to in the preceding
parts, they deserve distinct, separate investigation for
methodological as well as for thematic reasons. Many of

these works (mostly university lecture courses at Marburg and Freiburg) confirm with additional (historical) background and even further *clarify* the three phases (dimensions) of the question of God. Their examination also leads to the discovery of the need to think not only with but also *further* than Heidegger, to continue the questioning about Being and about God even beyond his pathway of thought.

Part 5 describes the nature and the ramifications of the question of God in Heidegger's thinking (its "place" and function in his philosophy, the three phases, perspective and significance). It emphasizes the main accomplishments and unearths the boundaries as well as the limitations of (and raises some crucial questions about) his approach to the question of God. The final conclusion of this research, then, is not a closure but the *opening up* of new (more) questioning that is free to go even further than Heidegger's position on God and Being, that is, ultimately, on the "matter" (*Sache*) of thinking.

All translations in this study, unless otherwise noted, are mine; the original text is included in the Notes. All emphases, unless otherwise indicated, are those of the author of the text in question. Comprehensive information about Heidegger's works (chronology of writing and publication, dates of university lecture courses) is included in the Bibliography. The symbols used for Heidegger's writings are listed immediately after the Contents.

At the completion of this work, I remember thoughtfully those who contributed to my journey of thought. I am most thankful to Professor Martin Heidegger for his works and encouragement; they opened up new possibilities of thinking in my search for the meaning of Being and in my struggle with the question of God. It was at the University of Louvain, during my student years there, that my interest in phenomenology found its sense of direction; I am grateful to all my professors at the Higher Institute of Philosophy, especially to Professors Albert Dondeyne and Alphonse De Waelhens, for the ideals of scholarship and learning they have shown me by example and teaching. I thank Professor Samuel IJsseling, director of the Husserl Archives at Louvain, for making available to me the resources of this international center of research in phenomenology. I express my thanks to Florida International University (Miami, Florida) for the granting of a sabbatical for research and writing. I am thankful to Northwestern University Press for the interest in this research, and to its readers and editors for their thoughtful work with the manuscript.

It is with deep gratitude, joy, and love that I remember my parents; they taught me the love of knowledge and wisdom. The completion of this work would not have been possible without the love, patience, and understanding I received in abundance from my wife, Margaret, and children, Christina, Erica, and Marta.

The concluding of this investigation, then, is not an ending; it is, rather, a "homecoming," a "turning" to the roots, to the source of new beginnings.

PART   1

SOME ASPECTS OF HEIDEGGER'S THINKING AND THE PROBLEM OF GOD

1

Thinking and Being

The pathway of thinking is the most difficult one to find and to go on for man. The difficulty is the result of the strange experience of thinking, because the pathway of thinking leads to something that is closest to us, and, therefore, its horizon is wider than a mere glance would indicate. The way leading to the "near" is the way of thinking that offers an advancing to meaningful thought (*Nachdenken*) and allows at the same time a running forward to the situation of thoughtlessness (*Gedankenlosigkeit*).[1] This twofold possibility accounts for the difficulties and the challenges of the thinking-process. The historical struggle between the calculating-technical thinking (*das rechnende Denken*), proper to positive science, and the meditative-reflective thinking (*das besinnliche Denken*), proper to philosophy, mirrors the basic potentialities of man as a thinking being.[2]

An open-minded view of the history of the different kinds of thinking (scientific, philosophical; metaphysical, ontological; theoretical, existential; pragmatic, artistic) can prepare and lead the way toward the disclosure of the essence of thinking itself. The clarification of the true nature of thinking becomes difficult, however, because the clarifying view is very often dominated by a preview and as such is the product of previous, already established, and "taken-for-granted" understandings of the nature of thinking itself. The practice of thinking, nevertheless, ought to be free of the narrow and distorted views of the nature of human thinking. The rediscovery of the essence of thinking begins with the liberating return to the phenomenon of thinking itself (phenomenological reduction) that makes it possible to raise the right and basic questions regarding the nature of thinking.

What is the original essence of thinking? What is its structure? What calls forth thinking? How does the thinking process come about? What is the source of a thought? These are some of the key issues leading into the mainstream of Heidegger's philosophy. Thinking (*Denken*), as he understands it, becomes like a response to a call (demand), a listening to a speaking, an attitude of openness and faithful attentiveness, an act of genuine remembrance, a profound thankfulness (*der eigentliche Dank, das andenkende Denken, Andenken*).[3] The experience of the multidimensionality of thinking is a preparation for the discovery of thinking as an event and appropriation of Being (*Ereignis des Seins*), because thinking is the "thinking of Being" (*Denken des Seins*).[4]

The closeness of the thinking-process to man and the nearness of the to-be-thought-of to thinking remain unthought, but not forgotten; the very familiarity with thinking and speaking as indispensable elements of daily living accounts for this. What could be more taken for granted than the fact that man is a thinking, reasoning, living being? The ever developing sophistication of the so-called laws of thinking and of the psychological analysis of the faculty of thinking seems to assure man's dominion and clarity in the realm of reasoning-reflecting-thinking. However, this same closeness to thinking and the familiarity with the laws of thinking through logic become obstacles to the authentic thinking-process. We often speak about the different kinds of thinking but rarely raise a question about thinking itself, about thinking as such. The horizon of thought is preestablished and already presupposed. This same horizon allows for the varying perspectives of physical, mathematical, and philosophical ways of viewing-thinking.

Closeness, familiarity, and self-evidence belong to the phenomenological presentation of thinking. In the phenomenology of Heidegger thinking is understood as the thinking of Being. The closeness, familiarity, and self-evidence of thinking have their own foundation in the closeness, familiarity, and self-disclosure of the meaning of Being. Apparently, nothing is closer, more familiar, or more obvious for us than the fact that we say of something that it *is*. The universally accepted understanding of *is*, a kind of cataloged meaning, answers all questions about the meaning of *is*. Being, the fact that something *is*, appears in thinking as a general affirmation of the reality of beings. Being *as* a question, Being *as* something problematic, is not thought of, and even this eschewal or neglect of questioning is forgotten as we are warned in all the writings of Heidegger. If the history of philosophy is understood in the light of the thinking-process, and if the meaningfulness of the question about Being is discovered, then a new era of history is dawning. Thus, according to Heidegger's phenomenology, we are coming definitively to the end-time of philosophy and, therefore, can await the daybreak of authentic thinking. When philosophy, considered as the Western tradition of metaphysics, comes to its end, to its final consummation, *then* the task of thinking can begin.[5] The ending is not to be considered as final point or terminus, but as a condition of a new start toward a future destiny of thinking and Being. This ending is the consummation of an entire historical process in the Western world and the sign of our times. It is indeed, to put it more exactly in Heidegger's terminology, a preparation for the coming manifestation and appropriation of Being according to its historical destiny or epochal mittence (*Geschick des Seins, Epoche des Seins—das epochale Wesen seines Geschickes, Epoche des Seinsgeschickes*).[6] The preparation and the readiness indicate that Being needs man for its revelation and preservation in the historical process. The readiness becomes a reality through the new way of thinking, through the essential and meditative thinking that goes back to the very foundation of thought and thus engages in the dialogue with the historical tradition as part of the historical destiny (mittence) of Being. The new, meditative, and thinking thinking, however, is described by Heidegger as a new appropriation (interpretation) and not as a destruction of the tradition of Western philosophy. In an interview in 1966 (published in 1976 after his death and according to his instructions) Heidegger explains his own philosophy as a rethinking of the tradition and remarks, "There is need for a rethinking which is to be carried out with the help of the European tradition and of a new appropriation of that tradition."[7] The transformation of Western thought means a return to the origin and calling of this same tradition. This new way of thinking, the meditative and listening thinking of Being, according to Heidegger's warning, cannot be the result of replacing our tradition by the acceptance of the Eastern experience of the world; it may come about only through a dialogue with the historical roots of the entire culture as the historical and universal destiny (*Weltgeschick*) of Being.

2

The Three Moments

T hinking and Being, the correlation of Being and thought as suggested by the terms *appropriation* and *mittence*, constitute the primordial themes of Heidegger's philosophy, of all his questioning meditations. His pre-philosophical experience appears as an attempt to recapture the original essence of thinking and Being. The description of the post-philosophical situation can be considered as an ideal phase in the history of Being. Philosophy, the metaphysical experience of thought in the tradition, is situated by Heidegger between the just-mentioned *pre* and the just-mentioned *post*. Philosophy is the history of thought as experienced between these two phases (events); it is characterized by the progressive falling away (going astray) from the true source of thought. Philosophy in the Western world is understood as metaphysics, and the whole history of this philosophy is a destiny (mittence) of Being; it represents a definite way of asking and thus understanding the question regarding the meaning of Being. The metaphysical interpretation of Being from the standpoint of Heidegger's phenomenology appears as the refusal to recognize the Being-question *as* a question. Keeping in mind this failure of Western philosophy, Heidegger sometimes even refuses to call his way of thinking a philosophy in order to indicate that he questions (rethinks) the very nature of philosophy and that he does not want his thought to be identified (at least not without some serious reservations) with the traditional (historical) notion of philosophy.[1] His task includes a confrontation with the great philosophers. Some aspects of his critique and especially the absence in his thought of a dialogue with several of the great traditions (for example, religious, Biblical) of thought, however, may seem to eclipse the comprehensive nature of his notion of essential thinking (*wesentliches Denken*). The meaning and the complexity of Heidegger's dialogue with and attitude toward the great philosophical systems cannot be rightly appreciated without situating them in the context of the problematic about Being. The historically documented meditations show us Heidegger's way of thinking and are not intended to analyze a past age or a past philosophical system. The three phases of thought cannot be identified entirely with three periods of history. They constitute the structure of Heidegger's way of thinking; they are the threefold movements or moments of his phenomenology. Certainly, they refer to periods of history, but they go beyond the commonly understood notion of history and elaborate an ontological comprehension of history as such. Because of the significance of these threefold historical dimensions or movements in Heidegger's thinking, they may be called simply three moments (constituent elements) of his thought. This term also calls attention to some similarities between Hegel's phenomenology of Spirit and Heidegger's thinking of Being.[2] Heidegger's reflections on Hegel are quite significant for the understanding of several issues in Heidegger, such as the nature of philosophy, finiteness and the infinite, knowledge, Being, God, truth, and history. Both these thinkers meditate on the nature of historical reality and understand human history as the unfolding of truth. They also agree on the need to understand the history of philosophy in a philosophical, ontological way. However, their final insights are quite divergent; their differences come from their differing conceptions of Being itself.[3] Nevertheless, Heidegger is interested in studying the philosophy of Hegel, and he calls attention to the fact that it was Hegel who first made the philosophical history of philosophy into an object of thought.[4] After this brief reference to the significance of the historical structure in Heidegger's way of thinking, each one of the three moments indicated can now be treated separately.

The *first* moment may be called the pre-philosophical moment. It includes the understanding of the nature and significance of the pre-philosophical experience of thinking. Historically, this moment is mirrored in the originality of the early Greek experience of Being. Heidegger's comprehensive analysis of and profound fascination with the insights of the pre-Socratic thinkers (such as Anaximander, Heraclitus, and Parmenides) represent much more than a mere historical curiosity or an appreciation of the early Greek mind and culture. He goes back to these great thinkers of the West in order to learn from their experience of the world, from their pre-metaphysical interpretation of Being. He examines their original way of thinking and shows that which has remained unthought and thus unsaid by them. The dialogue with their thought teaches the art of essential thinking and leads to the rethinking of their thought-experience. In this way, Heidegger tries to discover the primordial, pre-metaphysical thinking of nature, truth, Being, and human reality. This early experience of thought, despite all the vicissitudes of history, has remained the hidden source as well as the true heritage of the destiny of the Western world. The significance of the pre-philosophical moment consists in the pre-reflective, pre-metaphysical experience of nature and Being. Heidegger regards this early phase of the tradition as representing the cradle of authentic philosophizing. However, the ensuing interpretations of the early tradition by the great metaphysical systems, Heidegger claims, represent a distortion of and the falling away from the early heritage. Thus begins the history of metaphysical thinking.[5] The basic transformation of the original Greek experience started to take place in Plato and Aristotle, though in these great thinkers of the Western world there are still some living sparks of the early Greek discovery.

This pre-philosophical experience ought to be understood in the proper context of Heidegger's phenomenology and precisely in relationship to the evaluation of philosophy as metaphysics. The Greek experience of the world and its closeness to the manifestation of Being constitute quite a unique period in the history of thinking. This is the reason why Heidegger returns so often to this source of the Western world and hopes to recapture the originality of Greek thought in order to think more profoundly the un-thought of their experience. Because of this special significance of the Greeks for authentic philosophizing, Heidegger considers even the Greek language itself as a uniquely philosophical language in which, somehow, Being itself comes into words. To this way of thinking there is no other language like Greek, except German. Obviously, it is not necessary to accept this exclusive affirmation about the Greek or the German language. It may be shown that (at least) some other languages and traditions have similar qualities. Nevertheless, the importance of Greek philosophy remains because it is the source of the history of thinking in the Western world.

We come now to the *second* moment in Heidegger's phenomenology, and we may call it the philosophical or the metaphysical
moment. The significance of this moment is suggested by the notion
of the destruction of metaphysics, of the onto-theo-logical structure
of philosophy according to Heidegger's view of the history of philosophy after the early beginnings. Destruction leads to the right understanding of the tradition of philosophy; it is more than a mere
negative work of elimination. Destruction means the overcoming of
the old metaphysics and the discovery of a new metaphysics, of a new
understanding of Being. The positive aspect of the destruction is
emphasized by the later Heidegger.[6]

The history of philosophy is the history of the interpretations
of Being. For Heidegger, all philosophy in the West is ultimately
metaphysical in nature; it lacks the basic distinction between the question about particular beings (*Seiende*) and the question about Being
as such (*Sein*); it describes the nature and hierarchy of beings but
forgets the question about the meaning of Being, about the "is." Traditional metaphysics, Heidegger claims, simply identifies Being as
such with *a* particular (for example, the highest, the absolute) being
and thus explains it *as a* particular being. For Heidegger, Being is
not *a* being though it is the Being *of* beings at the same time. The
old metaphysics remains preoccupied with beings and thus forgets
the question of Being (obscures the ontological difference between
beings and Being), and thus the truth of Being remains hidden for
the metaphysical way of thinking. This is the most important characteristic, the basic nature, of all metaphysics and of the entire history
of Western philosophy. This foundational insight and radical criticism
regarding traditional metaphysics are emphasized by the early as well
as by the later Heidegger.[7] The question of Being as such is neither
an authentic nor a radical (questioning) question for the old metaphysics because this question is answered beforehand and the answer
appears as taken for granted even in the way in which this question
arises within the historical metaphysical view. The whole classical
metaphysical idea of the ground of all beings as one special being,
therefore, represents for Heidegger a failure of the true and radical
way of thinking, an evasion of the true questions about Being. This
way of looking at the history of philosophy is certainly a very critical
one and not every contemporary philosopher shares it, even with
reservations.[8] This evaluation of metaphysics, however, should not be
regarded as an immutable doctrine but rather as a new way and field
of questioning.

Philosophy as metaphysics advances toward its own

culminating end and perfection; Heidegger discovers this final moment of metaphysics in the philosophy of Nietzsche.[9] In a paradoxical manner, metaphysics prepares its own destruction because it produces at its highest influence the phenomenon of Nihilism. For this reason the Heideggerian meditation on Nihilism becomes a philosophical turning point. The second moment of Heidegger's phenomenology, considered as a whole, becomes significant more as the historical destiny of (sequence to) the pre-philosophical experience and not so much as a historical study or as a radically negative attitude toward the Western tradition. For an authentic understanding of Heidegger, in this context it is vital to see the progression of his way of thinking through the destruction-process as an overcoming (*Überwindung*), and not to focus merely on the target points of the attacks or accusations. This is what we should seek, leaving to the historian of philosophy the judgmental aspect of this reading of history. All that we need to retain is nothing more and nothing less than Heidegger's view of Western philosophy and history as metaphysics. The epochal mittence of Being, the event of Being, the destiny of Being, is discovered through this history. In the final analysis, these notions and their meanings belong to the mystery of history and human reality. What happens when metaphysics comes to its final culmination (*Vollendung*) in the form of Nihilism? If the metaphysical philosophy is submitted to the destruction-process, then what shall be the result of this destruction? Is there a new epochal mittence of Being to come about? If philosophy as metaphysics is unsuited for asking the true and radical questions about Being, then what is to be done in order to find a remedy for this basic failure? Is there any hope in the future? This series of questions leads us to the third moment or dimension of Heidegger's meditations.

The *third* moment of Heidegger's phenomenology is that of essential thinking as the hallmark of the post-philosophical era. The thinking of the ontological difference now comes to its full dimension and the meaning of Being becomes the center of all questioning. The problems of Time and Being are considered in a new light. It might be said that this third moment represents the original ambition of Heidegger's way of thinking, and that it is the anticipated, intended outcome (task, goal) of the first two moments of his phenomenology as a whole. Here again we are led into the mystery of Being and prepared for the next epochal mittence of Being; we still do not know when and how this shall come about. Our attitude ought to be that of expectation because we cannot force, by our own effort, the coming manifestation of Being. We can only stand and endure our destiny of remaining constantly in the lighting-process of Being (*Lichtung des Seins*).[10] The most important achievement should be the discovery of authentic thinking, the understanding of genuine remembrance (*Andenken*), the docility to the thinking-remembering as the thinking of Being. The most relevant feature of this phase is characterized by questioning and not so much by elaborating a doctrinal speculation. This fundamental situation of questioning is the meaning of authentic philosophizing for Heidegger.[11] For him questioning is the "devoutness of thinking"; it is the very structure of thinking itself.[12]

The three moments of Heidegger's phenomenology, in a way, represent for us some important aspects of his thought as a whole. We can see in them the structure of his meditations on varying philosophical problems leading always to the fundamental question about Being as the unique preoccupation worthy of all effort. No matter what Heidegger is speaking about, it is always his intention to arrive at the "original experience" that precedes the development of Western philosophy as metaphysics (the first moment); he then points out the change brought about in the history of Western philosophy as metaphysics (the second moment); finally, he leads us to a new experience of the "original experience" (the third moment). This is much more than a simple methodological procedure. This is, indeed, the approach to the question about Being; this is the coming about of the ontological difference. Here we have the only thought, the unique problematic of Heidegger.

Perhaps some other characteristic ideas and other relevant aspects of Heidegger's thinking should be pointed out, such as the nature of philosophy, the meaning of science, the different kinds of thinking, the pathway to authentic thinking, the essence of thinking, the meaning of language and its connection with thinking, the relation between thinking and poetizing, the meaning of truth and the rightly understood relativism, the problem of contingence, the essence of technology, the interpretation of history as the epochal mittence of Being, and the problem of the Holy and the Divine. Nevertheless, it should be recognized that a merely thematic view of Heidegger's thinking leads easily to a distorted view. Even a summary of this kind of philosophical meditation very quickly becomes meaningless and appears as a playing with abstract words or, at best, as a lifeless speculation. The most important thing to be learned from him is the rightly understood questioning and thinking. Thinking is a movement toward the "to-be-thought-of," a responding-obeying to an intimation. Thinking is always under way; it is always undergoing a new crisis. This is the key to the study of Heidegger's philosophy.

There are certainly many difficulties in understanding his language and grasping his seemingly strange and abstract ideas. Heidegger himself excuses the strangeness ("awkwardness," newness) of his own terminology and expressions in the introduction to *Sein und Zeit*.[13] As he says, we have no words or grammar when we are confronted with the difficult task of comprehending being in its Being. The difficulty of the problems treated is reflected in the newness of his terminology. Besides this, we should remember that for Heidegger language is not merely an instrument of communication, but is basically the coming of Being into words or, according to his somewhat mysterious expression, the "house of Being."[14] The so-called difficulty of terminology, therefore, is not so much an obstacle as a helpful warning against a superficial interpretation of his way of thinking.

3

The Eclipse
of the Problem
# of God

According to Heidegger, in the final analysis "each thinker thinks only one *unique* thought,"[1] comes to one foundational insight; the thinking of Being, the relationship between the truth of Being and essential thinking, is definitively such a unique, foundational thought of Heidegger. His phenomenology is a progressing meditation, a preparation for the manifestation of Being in its meaning and the coming about of the ontological difference. It is essential to grasp this unique and difficult thought in order to find the right context of this study, which is interested primarily in what is apparently only a partial question in Heidegger's way of thinking, namely the philosophical problem of God.

Through the somewhat schematic viewing of the ambitions of Heidegger's phenomenological thinking, nothing other than a preview of the rethinking methodology characterized by the sequence of the three moments is intended. This sequence or structure reveals some important aspects of Heidegger's phenomenology as a whole. The five terms of the preceding reflections—Thinking, Being, prephilosophical, metaphysical, and post-philosophical—can give us an orientation to the complex problematic of Heidegger's philosophy and help us to discover in it the right meaning of the problem of God.

In all philosophy we are confronted with the basic question about the meaning and the place of God in man's interpretation of the world and of himself. Prescinding here from the philosophy of religion and from the theological problem about God, the purely philosophical approach to this complex question can be studied. The history of philosophical systems contains the history of the struggle of the human mind in dealing with the questions regarding the existence, nature, and significance of God (or that of other forms of ultimate reality and meaning in life). The constant concern with the idea of God is a basic fact of universal history; human beings always ask questions about the religious dimension of life and reality, about the Holy, about the gods, about immortality and related issues. Philosophical questions are nourished by symbolic thought. The history of the so-called final explanation of all beings teaches us about the openness of the human mind toward the horizon of the divine. The study of the great myths, of the history of religions and even the phenomenon of areligiosity of our times speak of man's profound desire to find somewhere "the traces of the visible God in the world."[2]

Philosophical thinking has always tried to understand, analyze, and interpret the pre-philosophical image of God. The phenomenon of religion and the preoccupation of man with the divine have become part of human life: great thinkers have always taken seriously the problems involved in this human experience. The theistic or atheistic implications of a philosophical system at times were considered among the most important aspects of its evaluation, and, in a way, tests of its validity. This kind of discussion is very often guided by more than philosophical considerations. The judgment on this issue, however, is primarily a task for the historian. The fact that this kind of questioning exists even until today, however, calls for a serious reflection from the point of view of contemporary philosophy, especially from that of phenomenology.

Some might suppose that this kind of questioning and reflection was rewarding in the past simply because of the nature and limitations of earlier scientific knowledge. This impression can be strengthened, though its truth not necessarily proved, through the fact that the new sciences are taking over more successfully what were once the domains and tasks mainly of philosophy and theology. God's apparent withdrawal from the human world and, through man, his elimination from the physical and even from the human (and humanistic) sciences cannot be interpreted as philosophical shortsightedness.[3] The absence of a scientific affirmation of and concern with God, however, does not imply the elimination of the God-question from the human world of thinking. The new attitude of the sciences and of contemporary culture may be interpreted as a challenge to learn that the decisive aspect of the question of God is not scientific but rather philosophical in nature.

Here again we are faced with a new situation today. It seems that the phenomenological movement implies atheism according to some thinkers (such as Sartre) or, according to others, it leads to the attitude of indifference (neutrality) toward the problem of God based on philosophical considerations. A remark made by M. Merleau-Ponty is most expressive in this regard. He says: "It is interesting to note that today one no longer proves God's existence, like St. Thomas, St. Anselm or Descartes."[4] This seeming lack of concern with the problem of God is one of the features of contemporary philosophical thought. One of the most acceptable, not to say exclusive, ways of being concerned with this issue seems to be the speaking of the "where," namely of the philosophic or extra-philosophic character, of the problem of God. The discussion of this "where" is closely related to the phenomenological reflection on the possibility, nature, and meaning of metaphysics and of metaphysical thinking.[5] All these seemingly marginal references to the problem of God, and the lack of serious, comprehensive confrontation with this problem in the light of contemporary thought, reveal the need as well as the indigent nature of our times (dürftige Zeit)[6] and suggest an invitation to a new way of thinking, a movement toward a profound rethinking of the philosophical meaning of God. The extensive discussion of the Nietzschean idea about the "death of God" is a characteristic phenomenon of these times. The ambiguity of this expression, however, can produce a one-sided view of the complexity of this problem and eventually lead to a game of intellectual acrobatics and to an inadequate interpretation of the religious experience.

Therefore, it is not enough to say that there has always been discussion in philosophy about the question of God. Perhaps there have even been too many offhand references and facile solutions to this problem. It may happen that we are still far from asking even the right questions in this matter.

The first phase, therefore, of a serious study of the problem of God ought to be an objective study of the nature and function of philosophical thinking as such. On the other hand, to ask the God-question is a way of studying modern philosophy.[7] This viewpoint makes the demand and gives the stimulus to understand correctly the thought of a thinker. The second phase, in elaborating the God-question, is the analysis of a thinker's position in this matter as based upon the whole meaning of his philosophy. Only after the elaboration of these two phases shall a third one become possible, one that includes a critical confrontation with and an evaluation of the new rethinking experience.

Obviously, this way of philosophizing has its own difficulties because it presupposes a profound comprehension of the entire system elaborated by a thinker. This comprehension is indispensable in order to situate the God-question in its right place. If one proceeds by this way of thinking, then one may be able to discover a revealing continuity in the evolution of ideas and understand more meaningfully the present situation of philosophy. It may be said that from this point of view the problem of God is always located on the horizon of philosophical reflection. Precisely because this horizon is ultimate, it gives the impression of the progressive elimination of God from the field of rational knowledge and suggests a complete relativity of any affirmation about this problem. This judgment, however, is entangled in the certitude aspect of human knowledge according to the spirit of Cartesianism. If the God-question is one of the many questions that preoccupy man, the philosophical dimensions of this questioning cannot be excluded. To ask the question of God can be a meaningful way of examining philosophical thinking in all its implications. After all, the confrontation with this problem involves more than a secondary or accidental aspect of philosophy.

4

Four Groups
of Questions

The "where" of the question of God is conditioned by the nature of philosophical systems as well as by the originality of individual thinkers. The locations of these "wheres" are endemic to the history of philosophy. What is Heidegger's view of these "wheres"? Where is the "place" of the question of God in Heidegger's thinking? Is there a "place" for God in his phenomenology at all? These questions describe the focus of the main attention of these analyses of and reflections on the question of God in Heidegger; they are interested in thinking with Heidegger and, thus, in learning something about the nature and possibility of reflection on God. This investigation, therefore, is different from, though not without significance for, the examination of the theological "appropriations" (or at least applications) of Heidegger's thought;[1] it asks the God-question in Heidegger's phenomenology and tries to understand it from the inside of (within) this "system." This is the reason for emphasizing some aspects of his way of thinking and their relevance for (influence on) the problem of God in his thought. The recognition of the differentiating characteristics of his philosophy with regard to other forms of reflection and the awareness of his claim that philosophy as such is a special way of thinking contribute to the discovery in and with his thought of what may well be a new approach to the problem of God in its philosophical aspect.

The dialogue with Heidegger's views on the meaning of Being and authentic thinking, on his evaluation of the history of Western philosophy, based on the understanding of the radically questioning attitude of his mind, irrepressibly leads to the asking of certain groups of questions, such as the following four.

The *first* group of questions relates to the problem of metaphysics. Does the destruction (overcoming) of Western metaphysics include the elimination of the philosophical question about God? Is the problem of God meaningful only on the level of metaphysics, or, perhaps, may it be asked again in a new way after the destruction of metaphysics? If the comprehension of the meaning of Being is brought about through the quest for the roots of metaphysics, does this then imply a going beyond the theistically interpreted ground of all beings? Does the problem of God become irrelevant in the light of Heidegger's preoccupation with the comprehension of Being as Being? Does the idea of God considered as the source or the cause of all beings remain meaningful at all if we take seriously this new interpretation of Being? Is there any connection at all between the notion of Being (as understood by Heidegger) and the metaphysical concept of God? Does the question about the meaning of Being mean an overcoming of the problem of God on the level of philosophical thinking or a going beyond it? In order to prepare an answer to these questions, it is necessary to examine the meaning of Being and the problem of the ontological difference in Heidegger's phenomenology. Only in this context can one hope for an objective, genuine understanding of the references to the problem of God in Heidegger's thinking.

A *second* group of questions can be raised through a more thematical outlook. Why is it that Heidegger speaks of the gods, of the half-gods, of the divinity, of the Holy, of the Christian God, and of the messengers of the gods? What does he mean by these terms and expressions already heavily charged by tradition? Are these references only an occasion for him to continue the meditations on the ontological difference, or do they imply for him some particular relevance and meaning? This assortment of references invited some critics to see in Heidegger's phenomenology a theistic or an atheistic orientation toward the problem of God. The "where" of the God-question is not identical for all the interpreters of Heidegger's thought. The "where" of the God-question can be "located" only through an objective, comprehensive evaluation of all the references to this problem. To find this "where" is the primary intention of this study.

A *third* group of questions can be asked in light of Heidegger's interpretation of the essence of language. If language is not an instrument of domination in the hands of technological man but the coming of Being into words; if language means listening rather than simply talking; if it implies more attentive openness rather than the activity of the human faculty of communication; if thinking is authentic poetizing as Heidegger understands it; if the language of the poet is characterized by a mediative communication between the divines and the mortals; if language is obeying a command; *then* what is the significance of the poet's allusions and references to the divines, to the gods, to the semigods, and to God? Is revelation, then, the only source of meaningful discourse and speech on God? Does this idea of revelation have something in common with the idea of divine revelation affirmed by Christian theology? Can this new notion of language allow for and lead toward a genuine rethinking of the problem of God? These questions require a confrontation with the difficulties of the later Heidegger and help us to understand the silence and the sparseness of words about the problem of God.

The *fourth* group of questions is focused on the idea of atheism. Is there a phenomenological atheism in Heidegger's way of thinking (over) the problem of God? In what sense can he speak of overcoming the dilemma of theism and atheism? Is there a consistency in his position when he continually avoids the final answer? What are his objections against theism and atheism? Are there any developmental phases of the question of God in Heidegger's thinking? Is there something that we should discover regarding the problem of God in the light of Heidegger's phenomenology? What is the relationship between a philosophical meditation and the force and weight of personal conviction about the meaning of God? It is important to grasp the philosophical significance of the following attitudes toward the reality and meaning of God: indifference, agnosticism, uncertainty, lack of interest; affirmation, negation, ambiguity, undecidedness; openness, respect. What are the main reasons for adopting any of these attitudes? Which ones of these attitudes reflect most accurately Heidegger's thought? What is the nature of and what are the reasons for the indifference of the earlier Heidegger regarding a possible relatedness of human existence to God (*ein mögliches Sein zu Gott*)?[2] What is the meaning of the greater openness toward the idea of God in the later Heidegger? When these issues are analyzed, the main area of interest is in Heidegger's way of thinking insofar as it comes through in his published works. This kind of research, however, may not necessarily disclose his final personal convictions regarding all the dimensions of these issues.[3] It should not be forgotten that, in the final analysis, the philosophical interpretation of the God-question is only one of the manifold dimensions of this entire problem. A personal conviction can be more profound than a strictly philosophical insight: it requires a decision by the individual person as a whole.

This fourth group of questions shall receive an answer when the "where" of the Heideggerian God-question is taken into account. The problem of God in Heidegger's thinking is intimately related to the problem of the ontological difference. The "where" (the context and the level) of the God-question in Heidegger, therefore, is basically the ontological difference. The God-question in Heidegger's phenomenology can be spoken of insofar as this question is implied in the meditation on the ontological difference. Thus, for instance, there is an atheism in the earlier Heidegger only so far as this is implied in some way in the problematic of the ontological difference. It can be said at the same time that a philosophical theism is acceptable insofar as the questioning-process about the ontological difference does not eliminate metaphysics altogether, as such, and so far as the interpretation of the meaning of Being in the later Heidegger allows a new way of thinking (over) the problem of God.

5

The Heideggerian
Question
about God

The preceding four groups of questions indicate very clearly the connection that exists between Heidegger's phenomenology and the problem of God. This relationship can be discovered within Heidegger's way of thinking before any comparison with another philosophy. The remark made by W. J. Richardson is a revealing one in this regard. He says that he studied all the great themes of Heidegger's phenomenology and, nevertheless, Richardson resolutely avoided the problem of God. In order to explain this refusal to deal with this meaningful philosophical question he says: "This is not because there is nothing to say about God in Heidegger's thinking. On the contrary, it is because there is too much to say for it to be said merely by indirection."[1] Certainly, any serious study of the Heideggerian problem about God presupposes a thorough analysis of his thought as a whole; in this sense the reservation made by Richardson is a necessary one.

Perhaps there are too many references to God in Heidegger's works. If the total number of references to this problem were counted, we might be surprised to see how often and in how many ways the problem of God and the question about the Holy enter into the meditation on the ontological difference.[2] This situation not only makes the presupposed comprehension of this thinker's development necessary but requires, at the same time, a special concentration on the God-question as such and the capability to comprehend this particular question in light of the entire problematic about the meaning of Being. Such an enterprise can be successful only if it follows very closely the different phases of Heidegger's way of thinking. The God-question in Heidegger's philosophy is not a limited or an isolated problem, but in a certain sense it is the whole of his thought from an important point of view. When studying the works of Heidegger one can notice easily that a turning point in the elaboration of the Being-question implies a corresponding turning point in the way of dealing with the problem of God. In these cases not only are the references to the God-question multiplied, but the whole attitude toward this problem undergoes a change and becomes more articulate.

From rather negative reactions, qualified sometimes by his critics as a militant atheism, he comes through a "devaluation" of the metaphysical God to a rediscovery of the "wholly-otherness" of the truly divine God and to a new approach to the entire problem of God. The experiencing of the meaning of Being, the comprehension of Being, is somehow paralleled by the experiencing of God's presence or absence. In the later Heidegger there are many indications about the relationship that exists between the disposition of There-being (*Dasein*) (human existence) as a condition for the manifestation of Being (*Sein*) and the preparing-expectant attitude of the mortals (*die Sterblichen*) as a prerequisite element for a new coming of the divines (*die Göttlichen*). The ultimate problem will be to find the right way to interpret the Heideggerian notion of Being and to grasp its unclarified relationship to the notion of God. Obviously, this comes very close to the difficulty of how to understand the ontological difference. The decisive question can be formulated as follows: To what extent can one speak of a theological difference in Heidegger's thinking?[3] Whatever the answer to this question, whether a phenomenological theism or atheism is implied in the final interpretation of the ontological difference, the important point is that the problem of God appears in Heidegger's thought as a problem. This is a real question for him. O. Pöggeler, a most authoritative interpreter of Heidegger's way of thinking, indicates very clearly, "The God-question appears from the very beginning of Heidegger's pathway of thought."[4]

The convergence between the previous remark by Richardson and the opinion of Pöggeler confirms what has been said regarding the relevance of the problem of God in Heidegger's phenomenology.

Richardson speaks after an objective study of Heidegger's thought. By examining Heidegger's development, Pöggeler reaches a well-founded conclusion that points out the Christian overtones of the Heideggerian problematic. He indicates the main references to the problem of God in the different periods of Heidegger's thinking, and he is not afraid to show the background and the critical limitations of the interpretations involved. But even without consulting the studies of this great thinker's philosophy, it is enough to read some of his "smaller" works (such as *Identität und Differenz, Über den Humanismus, Vom Wesen des Grundes*) in order to discover in them the problem of God as the accompanying "shadow" of the problem of Being.[5]

There is another aspect of the Heideggerian question about God that one should keep in mind in order to grasp its real significance. This relevant aspect is that of going beyond the usual discussion opposing theism and atheism. If a study of the problem of God has as its main purpose only to demonstrate the possible affirmation or negation of God, then it is already situated outside the Heideggerian approach to this problem, in fact outside the whole Heideggerian way of thinking. Heidegger's overcoming of the dilemma of theism and atheism cannot be regarded as indifference or as lack of interest or as simple evasion of this complex problem in human life and thought. The apparent neutrality toward a decisive answer in this matter should be understood as the consequence of the questioning attitude. This attitude includes a serious preoccupation with the conditions that need to be prepared in order to ask the right question. Posing the right questions is much more important than the curiosity that fallaciously seeks a quick and ready answer.

Another element of Heidegger's apparent neutrality regarding the affirmation as well as the negation of God is the fact that it is not a theory as such but rather the description of an experience. It is the description of our times as characterized by the experience of the absence of the divine, by a basic undecidedness and ambiguity about God and about the gods (*Entgötterung*, "dedivinization," is the state of *Entscheidungslosigkeit*, of undecidedness about God).[6] This indifference of modern man toward the experiencing of the divine is a necessary outcome of his deafness to the voice of Being. Modern "technical" man is fascinated by the noise of machines and is inclined to take this noise for the voice of God. But the man who is able to listen to the intimation of Being and understand its language, the man who has this attentiveness and openmindedness, discovers the difficulty of discerning the speaking of the soul, of the world, and of God.[7] The meaning of these kinds of phenomenological meditations in the writings of the later Heidegger, and their seeming hesitations or doubts, should not be interpreted as expressions of a basic undecidedness from Heidegger's point of view (as some of his critics, such as K. Löwith, seem to suggest).[8] It should be understood, rather, as the experiencing of the situation of godlessness (*Gott-losigkeit*) in the context of the manifold history of Being. The meaning of godlessness consists not in a mere incredulity (*Ungläubigkeit*) or in a moral incapacity (*Unfähigkeit*) of man, but in something more fundamental, namely in the coming to pass of the history of Being itself, in a destiny (mittence) of Being (*ereignete Geschichte des Seins selbst*). Godlessness for Heidegger is an experience of the history of Being, a way of understanding an epochal mittence in the destiny of Being (*seinsgeschichtlich erfahrene Gott-losigkeit*).[9]

It follows from the preceding reflections that the history of Being constitutes the "where" of the Heideggerian problematic about God. This "where" is the key to any interpretation of Heidegger's thinking about the problem of God. Only from this context is it possible to grasp the significance of the God-question on the level of the ontological problematic and to see in it a possible new approach to this enduring philosophical question.

There is a long and slowly developing history of the problem of God in Heidegger's thinking. If the inaugural phase of questioning includes a "devaluation" of the metaphysical God, together with the expulsion of the remains of Christian, metaphysical theology from the realm of philosophy, this does not exclude the possibility of thinking philosophically the essence (*Wesen*) of God; it even intends to prepare a place for a renewed theology in the sense intuited by Luther.[10] The liberation from the power of the metaphysical God is meant to be much more than a mere liberation *from*; it is intended to be a liberation and a being free *for* the "divine God."[11] These indications found in SZ, ID, as well as other works of Heidegger become more relevant in the light of the ideas developed in HB, where we are told that the existential analysis of man's essence does not imply anything about the existence or the nonexistence of God.[12] We are reminded, therefore, that to see an atheism in the ontological interpretation of human existence (*Dasein*) as being-in-the World, and in the description of the relationship of the human being to the truth of Being, would be a misunderstanding of the entire problematic of Being.[13] The final phase of Heidegger's thinking takes the problem of God, like that of Being, as a question to be asked necessarily in the context of World and truth.[14] This is a new way of asking the God-question.

Finally, it should not be forgotten that Heidegger interprets the Nietzschean expression about the "death of God" as an outcry for the coming of the truly meaningful, divine God.[15] The death of the moralistic God is the great event in the final phase of Western philosophy when metaphysics comes to its own end-perfection and the phenomenon of Nihilism becomes universal. This is an event, a destiny of Being in its epochal mittence. The lecture courses on Nietzsche show us clearly how the authentic experiencing of Being, the preparation for the demands of Being, can include a preparation for the coming of the divine. The study of Nietzsche's thought is the "place" for Heidegger "where" he can meditate the power of Being and the interpretations of the ontological difference. He remains faithful to his original quest for the meaning of Being. He prefers to accept the mystery of Being rather than a quickly thought notion of God in the realm of philosophy.

6

Some New Aspects
of the
God-Question
in Heidegger

The problem of God in modern philosophy appears, in a way, as a central idea related to the problem of metaphysics. Almost every thinker talks about God in one way or another, because opinion in this matter seems to have a significant relevance for a philosophical orientation. The interest goes far beyond the affirmation or the negation of God. There is a process of evolution in the way one approaches this problem, the way one thinks the very idea of God, the way one understands God's relation to man and to the world. In spite of the variety of perspectives on this issue among individual philosophers, there is a continuity of thought from the historical point of view. Thus W. Schulz points out an evolution of thought that would lead from Nicolaus Cusanus to Heidegger's philosophy.[1] This continuity of thought itself is revealing because it clarifies and brings into the open the history of the problem of God as an enduring question. There is never a complete answer to the mind's questioning nor perfect fulfillment of the human expectation. A meaningful rethinking is at work in the new way of questioning and understanding. The fact of this continual unfolding does not necessarily imply a complete relativism, nor does it lead to thoughtlessness. It manifests, rather, the deep-rootedness of philosophical questioning about God. Indeed, it may be said that the problem of God is grounded upon a prephilosophical encounter with the horizons of human existence as a living presence in and to the world. The place of man in the world should be the starting-point for any philosophical consideration of the meaning of God. A phenomenological approach may well situate the "where" of the God-question in a "place" quite different from the one where traditional thinking used "to place" it. Is not the very discussion about the "where" already an indication of taking for granted a "somewhere" regarding the idea of God? The history of modern metaphysics, as W. Schulz suggests, constitutes a history of this "where."

What is Heidegger's relationship to the development of metaphysical thought as the history of the "where" of the question of God? The analysis of as well as the response to this question constitute an integral element of the discernment and understanding of the "where" of the question of God in Heidegger's way of thinking. W. Schulz rightly suggests that to ask the question of God is a way of philosophizing and that the approach to this question defines a certain way of philosophical thinking; the connection between them is surely a fact of history. The continuity of this connection, however, may not be strong enough to justify Schulz's claim that Heidegger's notion of Being (clearly not identical with God anymore) is only the radicalization of Nicolaus Cusanus's thought on God.[2] The issue at stake here is the nature (uniqueness and originality) of metaphysics; the background of Heidegger's criticism (for example, phenomenological) is indispensable for assessing the relationship between phenomenology and metaphysics, between Heidegger and the tradition. The awareness of this connection leads to certain questions: What are the differentiating characteristics of Heidegger's question of God? How does it differ from the approach of other thinkers? What is different and new in Heidegger's approach to the problem of God? These questions underlie the following reflections.

The traditional philosophical affirmation of the existence of God was considered a logical and necessary step in the light of the principle of causality. This affirmation of God's existence is part of metaphysics, especially for the scholastics. For Heidegger this metaphysics is onto-theo-logical; it interprets the Being of beings as the *causa sui*, as the metaphysical concept of God. The ontological problematic as developed by Heidegger inaugurates the destruction-process of this onto-theo-logical metaphysics. This destruction includes the devaluation of the metaphysical concept of God.[3] In this trend of thought the causal approach to the God-question is criticized and seems to become inadequate (if not even meaningless) in the light of the new interpretation of the World and of the meaning of Being. The metaphysical "why," the metaphysical causality, seems to be alien to the phenomenological understanding of the world. However, this devaluation of the causality approach does not necessarily need to imply a philosophical negation of God; it means only that the "where" of the God-question is not considered on the level of metaphysical causality. The "where" of the God-question is basically changed.

The meaning of this change, however, cannot be interpreted correctly without taking into account some basic notions and principles of phenomenology, such as intentionality, constitution, phenomenological reduction, transcendental consciousness, objectivity, and rationality. These notions of Husserl's phenomenology exercised a foundational influence on the entire phenomenological movement created by him and, at the same time, became a source of divergent interpretations and thus of new phenomenological orientations by his "disciples," such as Heidegger, M. Scheler, A. Pfänder, E. Minkowski, and M. Merleau-Ponty. The understanding of several basic insights of Husserl is necessary for the right appreciation of the thought of his "followers" as well as for the grasping of the phenomenological trend of thought. Heidegger's lecture courses at Marburg and Freiburg shed a new light on his indebtedness to and on his departure from Husserl's phenomenology; a better understanding of this relationship contributes to a more accurate interpretation of Heidegger's thought as a whole and of his approach to the question of God. Is there some Husserlian background to the Heideggerian question of God? This question raises several issues that are beyond the specific task of this study and, at the same time, presuppose the completion of the task at hand; in light of the thematic, comprehensive elaboration of the question of God in Heidegger's thinking, it shall become feasible to ask the question regarding the possible relationship to the Husserlian background and to a separately analyzed Husserlian question of God. In accordance with the task of this study, however, it is helpful to examine briefly some ideas of Husserl that are significant for the new approach to the question of God and identify the status of the question of God in his phenomenology, as well as his own personal conviction about this issue.

Husserl's very idea of phenomenology introduces a new perspective into philosophy and into the philosophical concern with the notion of God. Phenomenology, according to Husserl, is the method of research, the description of the primordial evidences of consciousness as encountering the realm of beings; it is the study of consciousness as intentional (related to the world) and of the world as intentionally constituted. Phenomenology, therefore, examines the realm of objectivity as it is given to consciousness and describes the ways consciousness intends, gives meaning to, or constitutes the object, the meaning of Being (*Seinssinn*). The study of consciousness in its entirety, as intentional and transcendental by nature, then, also becomes the analysis of objectivity. According to Husserl's description, phenomenology investigates "being as the correlate of consciousness, as something 'intended' after the manner of consciousness: as perceived, remembered, expected, represented" as well as "what consciousness 'means' . . . intends the objective . . . 'demonstrates' the objective as that which is 'validly,' 'really.' "[4] By the method of the phenomenological reduction, by a return to the phenomena, "to the things themselves" as they are given to consciousness as consciousness, phenomenology describes the foundational relationship between subjectivity (consciousness) and objectivity (being). This descriptive analysis is the result of pure, unprejudiced intuition of essences; it accepts nothing that does not measure up to the phenomenological ideal of essential intuition (experience).[5] Husserl defines the standard of phenomenology as descriptive analysis as follows: "*To claim nothing we cannot make essentially transparent to ourselves by reference to Consciousness* and on purely immanental lines."[6] Pure, transcendental consciousness cannot be disconnected by the phenomenological reduction; it is the residue of the reduction.[7] Transcendental subjectivity *is* the experience of the world; subjectivity is the correlate of objectivity (world). The meaning of the world is a given meaning (*Sinngebung*): a meaning given, constituted by the subject (consciousness). The constituting activity of subjectivity, however, is not idealistic; constitution is not creation. The world as the object gives, reveals itself, to the view of consciousness as the source of its meaning. "Consciousness is the necessary condition for the emergence of meaning and objects, but it does not create them."[8] This issue relates to the dilemma of realism and idealism; it shows the connection between phenomenology and the history of philosophy (metaphysics).

Whatever difficulties there might be in interpreting Husserl's phenomenology, the preceding considerations clearly indicate that Husserl's views of consciousness and constitution (basic notions of his entire system of thought) do not mean that he ought to reject the idea of God as the creator of the world and giver of meaning. Husserl's notion of the constituting activity of consciousness (intentional constitution) cannot be identified with the metaphysical principle of causality; it refers to the teleology and the structural unity of consciousness as giver and receiver of meaning. The constitution of the world by the subject is not creation. Husserl does not deny that the world constituted (known) by consciousness (by subjectivity) may be created by God as the absolute, ultimate consciousness as the traditional metaphysician would suggest. He simply says that reality (world, meaning, truth) cannot be grasped apart from the correlation to the thinker (subjectivity, consciousness); the meaning of the world for consciousness in some way must be constituted by consciousness. Husserl's concept of the world seems to remain indifferent toward the idea of God as creator of the world.⁹ This same attitude of indifference also characterizes the Heideggerian notion of the world according to the existential analysis.

Husserl's phenomenology, nevertheless, does include some concern with the philosophical question of God. In section fifty-eight of *Ideas* he speaks of the transcendence of God as "the polar opposite" of the transcendence of the world. The phenomenological reduction leads to the question about the "ground" (not the cause) of the constituting consciousness as the "source of possible and real values extending indefinitely." This concern with the "ground," Husserl continues in the same passage, gives (*erbringt*) "rational grounds (*Vernunftgründe*) for the existence of a 'divine' Being beyond the world" that transcends the world as well as "the 'absolute' Consciousness."¹⁰ Husserl concludes this remark by stating that this God would be "*an 'Absolute' in a totally different sense from the Absolute of Consciousness,* as on the other hand it would be a *transcendent in a totally different sense* from the transcendent in the sense of the world."¹¹ Because of this special nature of the transcendence and absoluteness of God, he disconnects or brackets this God from the field of phenomenology as the research of pure Consciousness. Thus he suspends and makes no judgment about God. In section fifty-one of *Ideas* Husserl claims that a "world-God" is impossible and that God as the "ultimate Absolute" cannot be immanent in experience (God's immanence in the absolute Consciousness cannot be understood as immanence "in the sense of Being as experience"). The manifestation of the transcendence of God is different from the constitution of thinglike realities. The principle of the Absolute can be found only in the Absolute through absolute reflection. Husserl rejects the use of the principle of causality and even the rational theological principle as representing a transcendence in the sense of world-transcendence. "Our immediate aim concerns not theology but phenomenology, however important the bearing of the latter on the former may indirectly be."[12] Therefore, Husserl does recognize a possible relationship between phenomenology and the question of God (theology). In section eighty-one of *Ideas* the question of the "ultimate Absolute" is raised again. Here it is said that the "transcendental Absolute" reached through the reduction is "not ultimate; it is something which in a certain profound and wholly unique sense constitutes itself, and has its primeval source in what is ultimately and truly absolute."[13] Whatever the final interpretation of this passage may be, it does indicate, especially in the light of the previously cited passages, that at least in some way Husserl's phenomenology does lead to the asking of the question of God, even if this question reaches the outmost limits of philosophical reflection. God is regarded by the father of phenomenology as the ultimate and the true Absolute, as the sufficient ground of all actuality and as the source of all values. According to Heidegger, the ground-question of metaphysics is, "Why (*warum*) are there beings at all and not rather nothing?"[14] For Husserl, as for Leibniz and Schelling, however, this question means, "What for (*wozu*) is all that is?"[15]

If there may be doubts about the exact nature and significance of the idea of God in Husserl's phenomenology, there is little ambiguity regarding his personal conviction on this issue. Husserl's entire lifework was a search for truth. His remarks and conversations during the last few years of his life indicate that he was convinced that genuine science as the phenomenological ideal of knowledge, in the final analysis, leads to God as the Absolute. Phenomenology, however, is not a doctrine but a method, a way that may lead back to God; phenomenology as such, nevertheless, is not a religious philosophy by itself. For this reason, Husserl remarked toward the end of his life that he was not a Christian philosopher and that he should not be viewed as such, not even after his death.[16] He thought that human life, in the final analysis, is a way leading to God and suggested that his philosophy tried to show this goal without the help of theology. He counted himself among those who earnestly seek God (*Gottsuchern*) and expressed his profound faith in God on several occasions before his death.

The preceding reflections indicate the extent and the nature of Husserl's concern with the question of God. They also suggest that there is some relationship between the status of the question of God in Husserl and the nature of the question of God in Heidegger. In the phenomenology of Husserl the comprehensive elaboration of the question of God and the problem of immortality are canceled out: "what is not intentionally constituted has already been denied any claim to being."[17] The phenomenological reduction implies for Husserl the suspension of the transcendence of God; he disconnects the elaboration of the notion of God from the field of phenomenological research. Husserl's ideal of philosophy as a rigorous and universal science cannot be understood without his views of constitution and rationality. Scientific, rigorous knowledge is the knowledge of essences; in the act of intentionality beings present (give) themselves to consciousness. To know being scientifically is to know its essence as a meaning (intention) presenting itself with absolute necessity to consciousness (meaning, the essence of being is constituted in reason). Therefore, a universal science of being is made possible by this constitution. Husserl is concerned not with the analysis of any subject (a factual subject would be only an example) but with what a subject must be (he describes the essence of consciousness). He reexamines the nature and delimits the field of causality; his phenomenology is not analyzing subjectivity as the adequate cause of what is constituted (constitution is intentional, not creation, not causal) but, rather, as the condition of possibility for the emergence of meaning and being (reality). Obviously, the idea of divine veracity (*veracitas*) is not considered here, and the basic attitude is faith (*Glaube*) in reason.[18] According to the phenomenological perspective, the truth of philosophy as a rigorous science is not founded on God, as Descartes would suggest, nor on the a priori conditions of possibility as in Kant, but on the immediate experience (intuition) of the evidence that guarantees the agreement (dialogical relationship) between man and the world. The proper philosophical act here means meditation (reflective analysis) and not merely syllogism. Therefore, the philosophical method itself is changed in phenomenology (in Husserl as well as in Heidegger). The abstract and purely conceptual mode of reasoning (through syllogisms and formal logic as the only laws of thinking), the argument based on the principle of causality, the notion of teleology, the interpretation of finiteness of human existence, the nature of values and of philosophical knowledge, and many other elements of the traditional affirmation of God in philosophy lose their power and decisiveness in the phenomenological question about God.

Heidegger as a phenomenologist seems to devalue, in the context of his concern with the question of God and the question of Being, some metaphysical notions and principles, such as the principle of causality. He does this in connection with the notion of the destruction of metaphysics. He rejects the metaphysical idea of God as based on the metaphysical principle of causality and shows the limitations of the metaphysical conceptualization of God's essence. This criticism, however, is not intended to be synonymous with a negation of God's existence and should not be regarded as a final refusal of the possibility of a philosophical approach to the problem of God. The main issue here is that the metaphysical God is not a truly divine God for Heidegger. The metaphysical approach to prove God's existence becomes a useless abstraction for him. The "where" of the God-question in Heidegger's phenomenology is changed; it is transferred from the level of metaphysical causality to the context of the ontological problematic, to the level of the meditations on the manifestations of Being. A new question regarding the problem of God is prepared, and the conditions of the right way of questioning are analyzed. It is not enough to say that the Cause-God as presented by Heidegger is the God only of a misconceived metaphysics, nor is it enough to point out that Heidegger is not an atheist.[19] All these claims might be readily admitted. However, the decisive point here consists in seeing this question in the light of the entire Heideggerian question of Being. Not the final answer itself, but the questioning-process is the key to the understanding of the nature of the question of God in phenomenology.

The preceding reflections give an idea of the change inaugurated through the phenomenological movement and can indicate already a possible new approach to philosophical discourse on the existence of God and on the meaning of religious transcendence. This new approach does not mean that there is always an explicit concern with a final response to the question of God in phenomenology as in the great philosophical systems. The God-question seems to become often irrelevant and thus not adequately analyzed from the point of view of phenomenology. Neutrality, however, is rarely the case in this matter. In many instances, the concern with the problem of God is expressed by way of criticism of some particular aspect of this issue rather than by a systematic elaboration. It is mainly by way of implication, indirect assumptions, and consequences that the problem of God appears in the work of many phenomenologists.

The question of God is not an immediate concern of phenomenology because phenomenology analyzes primarily man's understanding of himself and of the world. Some phenomenologists consider it irrelevant to the scope of phenomenology and thus they try to ignore it. Does this mean, then, that phenomenological thinking has nothing to contribute to this issue? Does phenomenology, indeed, remain entirely neutral and indifferent toward this problem? Phenomenology has much to say about the question of God. This "saying," however, very often takes the forms of criticism and questioning. Even the refusal to deal with this question is worthy of examination because it is the result of philosophical considerations. Sometimes a valid criticism is exaggerated or obscured by simplifying too much the object of critical analysis. How often is the genuine religious (for example, the Christian) idea of God misunderstood, misinterpreted, and misrepresented by Western philosophers (such as Sartre)? How many times is the God of the Biblical tradition identified with the God of scholastic metaphysics? The interpretation of a thinker's ideas ought to be protected against misrepresentations and misunderstandings. The interpretation of Heidegger's thought is no exception in this regard. At the same time the study of the Heideggerian God-question ought not to avoid a critical appraisal of his exposition of the Christian understanding of God. This appraisal becomes possible only in the light of the new approach that is characterized by a new kind of questioning and rethinking the whole problem of God. The references to this issue and its implications belong to the entire problem of the meaning of Being in Heidegger's thinking.

At first, it may be confusing that the study of the problem of God in Heidegger is not primarily interested in choosing between theism and atheism but rather in going beyond them. God appears in his works as a question and as the questioned. Here, again, we can notice another aspect of the change inaugurated by the phenomenological understanding of truth as non-concealment (*Unverborgenheit*, ἀλήθεια. This notion of truth is quite different from Descartes's, in which certitude is the basic characteristic of truth and God is considered as the absolute foundation of truth (*fundamentum absolutum et inconcussum veritatis*). This change marks a fundamental difference between Heidegger and traditional thinking. The historicity (*Geschichtlichkeit*) of truth for Heidegger is much more than an accidental or an external element to truth itself; it is its continual happening, its coming-to-pass. The traditional concept of truth as adequation (*adaequatio*), as conformity (*conformitas, Übereinstimmung*) between the intellect and things is inadequate; it cannot be taken for granted by phenomenology because it reflects only a very limited and even an ambiguous understanding of the essence (*Wesen*) of truth.[20] The idea of eternal truths remains outside the main concerns of the existential analysis of There-being (*Dasein*).[21] There-being is finite, and this finitude constitutes the horizon of philosophical meditation. The problem of possible eternity for There-being, the thinking of the eternity of God, and the possibility of revealed truth are neither examined nor decided by the existential analysis. All these seem to lie outside the phenomenological analysis of truth and knowing. The original nature of truth is not explained by the idea of truth as judgment (*Urteilswahrheit*); knowing cannot be defined merely as the certitude (*Gewissheit*) aspect of affirmation and negation. Original truth, the basic nature of truth, is a phenomenon of non-concealment, an event of Being in its epochal history.

These considerations indicate that the mainstream of phenomenological thinking introduces a serious crisis into the traditional (metaphysical) approach to the problem of God. Is it possible to find a new way of asking the philosophical question of God in the light of the phenomenological perspective on truth and reality? Is the question of God a meaningful question in phenomenology? Is there a "place" for the question of God in Heidegger's thinking? Is there a "place" for the philosophical concept of God in the early Heidegger's phenomenology? A careful analysis shows that Heidegger, after the existential analysis of There-being and with the development of the ontological difference, is progressing toward a new understanding of the meaning of Being and arriving at a position where he can ask again, and in a new way, the question of God. The destruction of metaphysics is not the destruction of the possibility for a new comprehension of what were metaphysical problems. A new way of asking the God-question and the new conditions of this asking can be discovered in Heidegger's thinking. As O. Pöggeler says about the later Heidegger: "Heidegger can ask again the God-question because, according to his experience, it is only the metaphysically thought essence of God that is refuted and not the divinity (*Gottheit*) of God."[22] Therefore, the possibility of a theology remains. The relation between There-being and God is spoken of by Heidegger often in a language that is more poetical than strictly phenomenological (philosophical) at a first glance. This new language is an important aspect of his thought regarding the question of Being as well as the question of God. This research shows that in the final analysis the Heideggerian interpretations of the idea of God can be grasped correctly only in the light of his comprehension of Being. The difference and the relationship between Being and God clearly express the new way of asking the God-question. The relationship between the concept of God and the notion of Being belongs to the most difficult and critical aspects of Heidegger's pathway of thought. The understanding of the difference between Being and God is the height, the "mountaintop," from which one is allowed to view the distance that separates the phenomenological notion (and problem) of God from the metaphysical idea (and function) of the highest being (*das höchste Seiende*).

The problem of faith, the question of divine revelation, the absence of the gods, the phenomenon of Nihilism, the place of atheism in the history of Being, the preparation of the conditions for a future manifestation of the true God, the discovery of the Holy, the problem of conviction and its relation to phenomenological meditation, the rightly understood relativism, the analysis of the present age as the destiny of Being, the epochal mittence of Being, the problem of modern technical science, authentic humanism—all these have implications for the problem of God and can be understood in the light of the Being-question. All the previously mentioned dimensions of the problem of God require an objective study of Heidegger's entire thought. The interpretation of his question of God begins here with the discovery of his way of thinking. To study the problem of God in Heidegger's thinking means to study his whole philosophy from this point of view. The real significance of the God-question will be discovered when it is understood in the context of the Being-question. The "place," the "where," of the Heideggerian question of God is the examination of the question of Being, the meditative thinking of the ontological difference.

Conclusion

The preceding reflections indicate clearly the relationship that exists between the philosophy of Heidegger and the problem of God. There *is* a place for the examination of the problem of God in Heidegger's phenomenology. This fact represents the initial finding as well as the first step of this study. The preceding considerations also indicate the nature as well as the "place" of the Heideggerian concern with the problem of God. The ontological difference, the core of Heidegger's phenomenology, implies a phenomenological problem of God; it constitutes the "where" of the question of God. There is a significant relationship between the understanding of the question of Being (in the light of the emphasis on the ontological difference) and the interpretation of the philosophical question of God. The thematic analysis of and the reflection on this basic relationship are the primary concerns and the main tasks of this research. The thematic, comprehensive examination of Heidegger's pathway of thinking, as this appears in his published works, yields the following conclusion: The thinking of the ontological difference and the question of Being imply a simultaneous rethinking of the entire philosophical problem of God.

Some will say that the Heideggerian problem of God constitutes an example of phenomenological atheism; others may look at it as the absence of God in this philosophy; and finally, there are those who see in it a theism. Here the difficulty can be seen again. When we speak of atheism or theism, according to the usual definitions of these terms, we are situating the problem on the level of onto-theological metaphysics; meanwhile, the Heideggerian God-question is located on the level of the ontological problematic. Certainly there is a relation to metaphysics, but the "where" of this problem, in the final analysis, is not a metaphysical one for Heidegger. This is the reason why it is preferable to speak of the phenomenological God-question or of a God-question simply, without the immediate reference to theism or atheism.

The following parts of this study develop the thematic analysis of, as well as a systematic reflection on, the main phases and dimensions of the question of God in Heidegger's thinking. The aim of these parts is not the survey of the history of this issue in Heidegger's development, but rather the thematic (and to some extent genetic) exploration of its structure and philosophical significance. Only a thematic and comprehensive analysis of the question of God as such can lead to the right appreciation of his views on theism and atheism and thus make possible a new way of thinking the philosophical problem of God. This research, therefore, differs from other studies that deal with the historical perspective or with some other limited aspects (such as the gods, the divine, the relationship between philosophy and theology) of the problem of God in Heidegger.[1] Several lecture courses by Heidegger at Marburg and Freiburg were published in the *Gesamtausgabe* beginning in 1975. These works enriched the comprehensive nature of this research; they strengthen and further clarify several insights of his writings published during his life. They add a new dimension to the understanding of Heidegger's thought as well as reinforce this analysis of his rethinking of the question of God.[2]

PART   2

A

DEMYTHOLOGIZATION

OF THE

PROBLEM OF GOD

The main purpose of Part 1 of this study was to show that there *is* a God-question in Heidegger's phenomenology as a whole. The reflections of Part 2 will go a step further in trying to understand the right meaning of the *first phase* of the Heideggerian question about God. They identify and designate this phase as that of *demythologization*.

Demythologization represents, in the context of SZ, a step toward the philosophical understanding of the question of Being as well as of the notion of God. Demythologizing is identical with "not telling a story (μῦϑόν)" about the origin of beings, that is, not reducing beings to another being when explaining the meaning of the Being of beings.[1] The "storytelling" ("mythological") explanation of beings, Heidegger insists, considers Being as a quality of beings. God as the origin or first cause of all beings, as the most perfect being, that is, the traditional metaphysical (philosophical) God, was a philosophical (ontological) explanation of beings; hence, the Being of beings was defined as being-created by God. Such an idea of God represents a "mythological" explanation of beings and, therefore, a "mythological" problem of God (that is, a "mythological" approach to the problem of God). Because of the ontological connotations of this idea of God, Heidegger cannot accept the traditional ("mythological") approach to the problem of God in the context of his ontology. He can only demythologize, leave aside, liberate from the "storytelling" perspective and explanation, the traditional approach to the problem of God in the context of his meditation on the question of Being. This is the reason for the critical attitude of the early Heidegger toward the philosophical problem of God. However, this demythologization, the divesting of the "storytelling" elements (purification), of the traditional approach calls for a rethinking of the problem of God and for a deeper understanding of the meaning of faith as the source of Christian existence.

The term *demythologization*, then, stands for the nature of the problem of God in the early phase of the development of Heidegger's thought; its attention is focused on the main thrust of the critical attitude toward the metaphysical approach to the affirmation of God. SZ does not destroy the idea of God: it merely unwraps, takes apart, and thus analyzes the structure of the "storytelling" ("mythologizing") perspective on God. For Heidegger, the explanation of beings by retrieving their origin to God as their cause represents a story about their origin as well as about God; the story of beings, then, leads to (in the final analysis ends and begins with) God as the source and cause of their story, of their reality and history. This explanation discovers God as the final account for the origin and nature (order, structure) of beings; God is the final (focal) and foundational (source) element ("chain") in telling the story (explanation) of beings; he is discovered as the highest being, as the "Being" of beings, as the final story (explanation) of all stories, events, and beings. Beings, however, according to Heidegger, may not be grasped in their Being merely by tracing (by telling a story, by explaining) them back to a final, ultimate being, because the ultimate being (God), even though the highest, is *still* (just) a being. The main issue, according to Heidegger, is, How is it that there are beings *at all* and not rather nothing? The "storytelling" explanation, then, does not tell the "whole story." It is not concerned with the question of Being as such, with the wonder of the "is," but merely adopts the highest being (God) as the final story (explanation). The question of Being, according to SZ, transcends the notion (and thus the question) of God.

The demythologization, however, is *not* a *destruction* of the idea and of the question of God; it is, much rather, a criticism of the use of "God" as a "story" about beings that short-circuits the question about the Being of all beings, about the meaning of the "is." Demythologization, then, is not atheism; it is an explanation of the inadequacy of the use of the notion of God for the elaboration of and as a response to the ontological (Being) question. The final result of this analysis of the "storytelling'" approach to the problem of God, therefore, is neither theistic nor atheistic but hermeneutical and ontological; it shows and critically reflects on the structure of the causal explanation that leads to God and, at the same time, falls short of distinguishing the notion of God as the highest being from the more far-reaching (transcendent) question of Being, of the ontological horizon. The phenomenological conclusion from the demythologization is not the destruction of the idea of God as the highest being but, rather, the foundation of the thought that the notion of the highest being may not be truly "high" (divine) enough to think most "highly" (divinely) of God. This thought remains an open question. The notion of the highest being as one of the particular beings, however, at least for Heidegger, is not "high" (ontological, deep, transcendent) enough to think the question of Being. The unfolding of the demythologization as the critical and, at the same time, nonideological analysis of the metaphysical explanation of the notion of God constitutes the first phase (a basic dimension) of Heidegger's thinking on the question of God. SZ and the earlier works of Heidegger belong to this first phase.

The attention of these considerations is focused on the following two questions: What is changed in the God-question through Heidegger's phenomenology? How does this change come about? Part 2 of this study, therefore, shows how the problem of God is being transformed and questioned from the point of view of the existential analysis.

The best way of studying this phase of the Heideggerian question of God is through a close examination of SZ. This basic work, in spite of its "incompleteness," is of foundational significance for the entire development of Heidegger's thought. Throughout his later works, especially where important areas of his thought recur, there will always be that Ariadne's thread, tying and sewing up that "ligne directrice" originating from his first major work.[2] His own words are the most indicative in this regard: "only by way of what Heidegger I has thought does one gain access to what is to-be-thought by Heidegger II. But (the thought of) Heidegger I becomes possible only if it is contained in Heidegger II."[3] It is crucial, therefore, to gather together (to re-collect) those remarks and aspects of the existential analysis of There-being that imply, in some way, any reference to the problem of God. This phase is the foundation of the problem of God in Heidegger's way of thinking. Here is the reason for the importance of the phenomenology of SZ. The question of God can be present in the thought of a thinker in many ways, and it should not be forgotten that an absence sometimes is a more effective way of "speaking" than a presence. There are questions that are more conspicuous by their absence than by their unquestioned presence. The God-question is precisely one of these questions.

The foundational role of SZ in the development of Heidegger's thought accounts for its central place in the following reflections. Its special significance transcends the fact that the name *God* is mentioned twenty-seven times and *divine* once.[4] If one pays attention to these references and situates them in the light of the Being-question, then it becomes possible to discover through them the first phase of the God-question (the demythologization). It is interesting to notice that often those references that do not speak directly of the problem of God are quite revealing. The following reflections, then, analyze the nature and the development of the first phase of the problem of God in Heidegger according to the thematic order of SZ.

7

There-being
and the
Absence of God:
The New Ontology

T he first pages of SZ introduce a clearly defined problematic and tell about the conditions of its elaboration. The most characteristic questions appear already in the beginning: What is really a being? What makes it really a being? What is the Being of a being? If a being is explained and determined by "telling a story" ("myth") about it, by claiming that it comes from or is created by another being, this means only a "mythological" ("storytelling") explanation.[1] This type of explanation consists in reducing a being to another being from which it has its origin. However, this causal explanation does not explain the Being of a being nor does it examine the meaning of Being. This explanation does not reflect the grasping of the question about Being itself; it does not answer the question regarding the Being of a being. What is a being? What makes a being really a being? The answer to these questions is simply transferred to another being (cause, origin) by the "storytelling" explanation; the answer is procrastinated, not given. What is the Being of a being? The mythological explanation does not answer this foundational question that underlies all the other questions. Instead of transferring the problem to another being (and delaying questioning), the answer should originate from the difference, from what is distinguishing Being from a (particular) being. The comprehension of Being, therefore, is not achieved in the discovery of beings. The explanation of Being through beings is situated in the perspectives of origin and causality. This is a "mythological" explanation in Heidegger's view. Therefore, the very question he is asking is a demythologizing one.

The discovery of Being is made possible by the right way of asking, by an authentic questioning. The questioned is not *a* being, but Being itself. How do we come to the discovery of Being? Through There-being (*Da-sein*), through the understanding of the "ultimate" structure of There-being. This is the way to Being (*Sein*) according to the phenomenology of SZ. The understanding of There-being is necessary in order to ask the Being-question. Why does this necessity or condition exist? Simply because questioning (*Fragen*) is not merely the exercise (application) of a human faculty, but is a mode or a way of Being (*Seinsart, Seinsmodus*) of a being.[2] It is a potentiality of There-being's Being (*Seinsmöglichkeit*): its way of "to-be" (Being). Because There-being is characterized by this exceptional potentiality of asking the Being-question, the elaboration of the question about the meaning of Being (*Sinn von Sein*) then requires a previous explication of *a* particular being (that is, There-being) from the point of view of its Being.[3] There-being, man as a special being, always has a relation to its (own) Being. There-being's "essence" is situated (lies, is) in its existence (*Existenz*), in its "drive-to-be" (*Zu-sein*).[4] This is what distinguishes There-being from other beings as mere entities (that is, *Vorhandenes*). There-being, man, is not simply a thing characterized by indifference toward its own "to-be." There-being cannot be considered as being like stones or stars, like things or mere entities discernible through their "what-ness" and having no relation to their "to-be" as a task (*Aufgabe*). There-being has its own way of "to-be" that is unlike an entity's way of "to-be" (*Vorhandensein*); it has its way of "to-be" as its own (*Jemeinigkeit*); it can "assume" or "lose" itself in its own Being (*Eigentlichkeit, Uneigentlichkeit*). There-being is characterized by existentiality (*Existenzialität*) and by comprehension of Being (*Seinsverständnis*) through the comprehending of its own Being. Therefore, there is the need first to understand man as There-being in order to ask the question about Being. Man as a questioning being is the way to the questioning of Being, leading, finally, to Being as the questioned.

Because of this "questioning-power" (potential) of There-being as a way of its "to-be," Heidegger comes to the conclusion that There-being is the ontic-ontological condition of possibility of all ontology.[5] There-being has a threefold primacy before all beings. Its ontical primacy consists in the fact that this being (There-being) is determined in its own Being through existence; it is "defined" by the comprehension of Being and it can decide its own relation to existence. The ontological primacy means that this special being (There-being) is in itself "ontological" (the comprehension of Being is its own way of "to-be"). Because of this prerogative, There-being comprehends (*Verstehen*) the Being of all other beings or entities that are not like There-being. Therefore, There-being has a third primacy; it is the ontic-ontological condition (*Bedingung*) of all ontology. This is the primacy of There-being as the to-be-questioned (*Befragende*) before all other beings. Hence There-being is indeed the condition of all ontology.

Perhaps, one should ask at this moment these questions: Is this understanding of man as There-being a mere conceptualization? Do the existentials (*Existenzialien*) represent anything more than an idealistic view of man stemming from an irrelevant and abstract ontology? The answer to these questions is very clear and crucial for Heidegger's way of thinking: "But the roots of the existential analytic, for their part, are ultimately existentiell, that is, *ontical.*"[6] This claim calls attention to the fact that understanding of human existence (discernment of the essential qualities of existence in SZ) is rooted in the existentiell dimension, in the comprehension of the real and factual human situation of the "concrete" man (*Faktizität, Jemeinigkeit, Befindlichkeit, In-der-Welt-sein,* and so on). Ontological questioning is more primordial than the mere ontical way of inquiring (for instance, in the sciences), because it is concerned with the problem of the meaning of Being. The validity and meaningfulness of an ontology cannot be measured by a system of categories, as perfect as it might be, but by the standard of fidelity to the fundamental task, that is, to the elucidation of the meaning of Being. The ontological structure (expressed in the existentials) is not the drawing board of the imagination, but the ground of "daily life." The existentiell (the ontic) is the bearer of the existential; the existential is discerned within (grounded in) the existentiell. This is the reason why the meaning of Being is discovered not through a theorizing or a keen speculation but by means of the existential analysis of There-being. The consideration of There-being as the condition of all ontology is the best illustration of the existentiell roots of the existential, of the ontological problematic. The emphasis on There-being in SZ is shifted to an emphasis on the larger and more direct problematic of Being itself in the later Heidegger. This second phase (dimension) of Heidegger's development calls attention to a "docility" in the language and to the manifestation of Being as something coming from Being itself. The notion of Being-as-history and the idea of foundational, essential thinking (*wesentliches Denken*), in a way, can be regarded as the new and a more profound understanding of the existentiell "incarnation" of the existentials according to SZ. Thus, it can be recognized as rather evident that there is at least a minimum of continuity in Heidegger's way of thinking. This minimum is enough to allow us to see the "grounds" of the ontological problematic and to reject a mere "conceptual" interpretation of the Being-question. Even though the approach and the language are changed in the later Heidegger, nevertheless, the basic question—the meaning of Being—remains fundamentally the same.

The problem of Being is elaborated in SZ primarily from the perspective of man's relation to Being and according to the significance of the Being-question for man. The problem of Being includes man's relation to Being as well as Being's relation to man. The very way of man's Being (as There-being), the mode of "to-be" of man, is determined by the comprehension of Being. The structure of the human being may be described as follows: "The Being of the human being is to be comprehension of Being."[7] The works of the later Heidegger can be understood as a consequence of this comprehension of Being and as a progressive clarification of the relationship between man and Being. The notions of truth, history, and thinking shall lead to the primacy of Being; all this becomes possible through the foundational research of SZ, through the hermeneutics of There-being.

This primary concern with the question of Being in Heidegger's philosophy is the main reason for his views and attitudes regarding the problem of God. The *absence* of God in his way of questioning is the consequence of his way of thinking and analyzing the problem of Being. He clearly describes the place of man in his philosophy, and he can develop his thought without a theistic or an atheistic orientation. In his view the God-question (as a consequence of the Greek ontology) is irrelevant, because it represents a "mythological" explanation (a "telling a story" about the origin of beings) of the question about Being. However, this absence (of God) does not mean the absence of the *problem* of God as a meaningful philosophical question. His attitude toward theology reveals a preoccupation in this regard in spite of the apparent harsh judgment passed on the historical forms of theological thought. Theology tries to find a more primordial interpretation (*Auslegung*) of "man's Being toward God" (*des Seins des Menschen zu Gott*), of human existence in its relation to God; it is an interpretation that is based on and remains within the meaning of faith.[8] According to Heidegger, theology slowly begins to understand the insight of Luther, who claimed that dogmatic theology as a system was not based on the development of a genuine questioning (thinking) guided by the light of faith (*nicht einem primär glaubenden Fragen entwachsen*). Theological conceptualization (*Begrifflichkeit*), as Heidegger speculates, not only does not reach the theological problematic but even covers it up and distorts it. This remark is a serious "attack" against speculative theology. However, it ought to be kept in mind that the "attack" is directed against the pretended philosophical foundation of the theological system and not against theological thinking as such. This remark claims only that the so-called ontological foundation of theology is a misleading foundation, because it is based on an interpretation of Being that comes from Greek ontology.[9] Theology, as Heidegger says, has its own way of questioning that is grounded on faith. The *distance* between philosophy and theology is a definitive one in Heidegger's thought. He says, later on, that the believer cannot be a philosopher because through the acceptance of faith he has already answered "the" philosophical question (Why are there beings rather than nothing?) and therefore he cannot be regarded as true questioner.[10] All the writings of Heidegger insist that genuine, truthful questioning constitutes the very nature of philosophy.

It can be seen here how Heidegger himself experiences the question about God *as* a question that is present already in the beginning of the new ontology. He insists on the ontological primacy of the Being-question and shows how the basic concepts of the sciences presuppose an interpretation of beings according to the comprehension of their Being. Ontology, therefore, precedes the sciences.[11] From his point of view (from the perspective of the ontological foundation of the sciences) theology is not an exception, and this is the reason why the absence of God is *a meaningful absence*. Descartes and Kant, for instance, spoke of God in a more thematic way; Plato thought about the source of all beings. The mystery about Being always remained, and it was "situated" in the domain of the ultimate questions (death, immortality, meaning of life, guilt); it was connected, in the final analysis, with the problem of God (like the ultimate questions themselves). Heidegger "breaks away" from this historical tradition, and he "shifts," at least to a significant extent, the meaning of the mystery to the problem of Being. This is a considerable transformation of the philosophical meaning of the ultimate questions in the light of the Being-question defined as the "radicalization" of the preontological comprehension of Being.[12] This understanding of the meaning of the ultimate questions indicates that Heidegger reexamines the Aristotelian, scholastic definition of philosophy as the exploration (science) of things (beings) according to their last (ultimate) causes.

The main differentiating characteristic of Heidegger's phenomenology (and its difficulty at the same time) is the development of a new "notion" of Being. In his thought Being is "defined" in such a way that the traditional God-question can be eliminated from its comprehension. Temporality is considered as the meaning of Being itself. Time was viewed as the "designer" of the regions of beings (temporal and atemporal). In the new ontology (in the central thrust of Heidegger's way of thinking as a whole) time becomes a key issue in considering the temporality of Being and in "situating" the meaning of There-being in temporality.[13] Being, therefore, is the central problem of philosophy; it is beyond all beings: "Being and the structure of Being lie beyond every being and every possible determination of a being that is. Being is *transcendens simply (das transcendens schlecthin)*."[14] There-being is considered as *transcendens,* that is, as a being that passes beyond things (beings) to Being, because it comprehends the Being of beings. The comprehension of the Being of beings is the very structure of There-being. The human capacity to transcend to other beings, to the World, and ultimately to Being is not some external attribute but an essential quality of the inner Being of There-being, of what There-being is as an individual. "The transcendence of the Being of There-being is an outstanding one in as much as in it lies the potentiality and the necessity of the most radical *individuation.*"[15] There-being as *transcendens* (as transcending, passing over from beings to Being in virtue of its ontological structure) is the happening *(Geschehen),* the process, of the ontological comprehending. There-being is not the origin, not the source of its own Being. It is dependent on beings and finds itself as "thrown" and "fallen" ontologically. There-being is aware of its own finitude through the comprehension of Being.

There is no need to "dissect" any further the elements of the new ontology in order to understand the absence of God in it. The view of God as *maxime transcendens* (as the most transcendent) among beings is neither rejected (at least not in principle) nor explored further from the philosophical (phenomenological) perspective; it may be found, in the final analysis, as inadequate for a worthy notion of God, and thus it is neither examined nor interpreted by Heidegger. God is not considered (in the ontological context) as the *maxime transcendens* among beings. In *this* sense it may seem that man (There-being) replaces God, that the human being (as distinguished by the special relationship to Being, by the awareness or presence of Being) is the key to the comprehension of Being; God, therefore, is not regarded (or at least does not function) as the paradigm of (as the guide to) Being. However, neither the notion of There-being nor the concept of Being in Heidegger's thinking takes the "place" of God of classical (Western) metaphysics.

The traditional philosophical idea of God cannot be identified with the Heideggerian understanding of Being. Nor can God be reduced to There-being. Therefore, the classical notion of God as transcendent (as well as immanent in some special sense) seems to be "out of place" in the new ontology, in the hermeneutical phenomenology (in Heidegger's understanding of phenomenology). There is no "place" here for a "return of creatures to God." What is at stake here is the understanding of the meaning of Being as such, the understanding of the Being of beings through man as There-being who "lets beings be." The final aspiration of this philosophy is not a metaphysical perspective leading to the discovery of a highest being (God) as the source of all beings, but the comprehension of the hidden meaning of Being as it can be reached through the existential analysis of There-being in SZ. The one and only thought of Heidegger is the unifying principle of the different phases of his philosophy: it is clear already that this one thought is the thinking of Being.

8

Christian
Anthropology
and Greek
Ontology

The new ontology has a demythologizing dimension from the point of view of the problem of God. After the elucidation of the central place of There-being in the new ontology, SZ emphasizes the basic distinction between the characteristics of the existential analytic (as ontological, concerned with Being) and the nature of the sciences (as ontic, concerned with types of particular beings, entities); it analyzes the basic differences between the philosophical perspective and the anthropological (scientific) perspective. The sciences often contributed to the obfuscation of the Being-question in the course of history. They already presuppose a certain way of understanding the meaning of Being and assimilate the classical ontological interpretation of beings; they need the work of philosophy as their foundation.[1] Philosophy examines the foundations and the presuppositions of the scientific interpretation of beings. This connection between philosophy and scientific inquiry, however, leads to the following difficulty: The sciences (for example, anthropology) cannot wait for the "results" of the ontological work of philosophy; they "adopt" a certain (ready-made) interpretation of Being or at least the ontological perspective of an ideology. Thus the sciences may (often) imply, or even presuppose, a naive or "taken-for-granted" view of Being. Two remarks made by Heidegger in this context must be regarded as quite significant for the problem of God.

The first remark refers to the philosophy of subjectivity in Descartes. According to Heidegger, Descartes investigates only the *cogitare* (knowing, thinking activity) of the *ego* (the knowing subject, the thinker as subjectivity) and fails to deal with the *sum* (the ontological, the Being-dimension of the *ego*), thereby not reaching the ontological problematic (interpretation), the Being (*sum*) of the subject.[2] This is the reason why Heidegger criticizes the Cartesian notion and interpretation of subjectivity. There is no reference to God in this occasion. Later on, Heidegger shall explain that the concept of God as the ultimate (highest, absolute) subject comes from this philosophy of subjectivity. The criticism of the ontological shortcoming of the Cartesian notion of subjectivity also enters into Heidegger's examination of the problem of God in past philosophical systems. This observation does not imply a rejection of the philosophical idea of God as such, but rather it is to be regarded as an analysis of the ontology implied in those philosophical systems. This same criticism is applied by Heidegger to Dilthey, to Scheler, and to Husserl with regard to their philosophy of the person.

The second remark by Heidegger pertains to ancient Christian anthropology as another example of the misinterpretation of the problem of Being.[3] The definition of man as a "rational animal" (ζῷον λόγον ἔχον considers only the mere entity (thinglike) aspect (*Vorhandensein*) of "animal" and leaves in obscurity the meaning of "rational." This definition "passes by" and leaves unasked the question about the Being of man. The theological definition of the Being of man as created in the image of God (Gen. 1:26) is an assimilation of the ancient Greek anthropology (man as an entity; it leaves unexplained the human being's Being). The Being of God is (ontologically) interpreted in Christian theology in the same way as the Being of man, that is, according to the inadequate Greek ontology (*Vorhandensein*). Later on, in the course of history and especially in modern times, the Christian definition of man is detheologized (*enttheologisiert*), but this does not change the situation of the ontological perspective because the idea of "transcendence" is rooted again in Christian dogma. This idea of "transcendence" means that man is more than a simple being (thing) gifted with intelligence (*Verstandeswesen*); he somehow "transcends" even unto God and to eternal bliss (as a quotation from Zwingli illustrates it for Heidegger). This idea of "transcendence" has taken different forms; nevertheless, it remains basically dependent on Christian dogma (creation) that does not consider the Being of man as an ontological problematic, but rather takes it for granted according to Greek ontology.

These two remarks show forth the reason why Heidegger, in a sense, rejects this understanding of the Being of God (and of man) by means of Greek ontology. It can be said, therefore, that Heidegger distances himself *methodologically* and *thematically* from theology and from the "classical" philosophical approach to the question of God. He cannot accept the theological anthropology (the notion of man) and the anthropological theology (the interpretation of the Being of God) and, therefore, abandons this approach to the problem of God in philosophy (thematical distantiation). The main reason for the nonacceptance is found in the shortcoming of Greek ontology (the unaskedness of the Being-question), a shortcoming that is carried over into anthropology and theology alike because of the "taken-for-granted" characteristic of Greek philosophy as a foundation of the definition of man and God (methodological distantiation). In Greek ontology the Being of God and the Being of man remain unexamined because Being as such is not perceived as a real problem for the philosophical tradition of the West.

It seems that Heidegger had to say this (and to say it through a distantiation) in order to bring into the open the original significance of the ontological problematic. He refers in *this* context to the problem of God. He is not saying that there is no place for God in his philosophy or that the question about man's existence somehow takes the place of and the function of God. To draw this conclusion would mean a complete misunderstanding of his thought. The problem of God becomes a problem, a question for him, because he cannot accept the "classical" interpretation of the Being of God. The most that can be said at this time is this: The metaphysical idea of God is abandoned and its ontological relevance is assumed by the whole phenomenological problematic of There-being in SZ. It must be recognized, however, that this is a somewhat clumsy expression of the present state of affairs. But it should be remembered also that sometimes an awkward expression can "speak" better than a more "exact" formulation.

This examination of the first steps of SZ makes it clear that the problem of God is present in Heidegger's thought; it takes the form of demythologization and even indicates a renewed notion of theology itself (as based on the experience of faith).

9

A New Understanding of the World

T he Christian view of the world as the universe of all beings, as the work and the trace of the creator God, was regarded until modern times not merely as a religious contemplation of reality but also as a philosophical and scientific interpretation of things and of man alike. The pathway leading to the arguments for the existence of God was shaped through this worldview. The contemplation and the experience of the world, though in varying modes, were ways to find God in or through the world. This understanding of the world becomes the focal point for criticism and a favorite theme for atheistic meditation. In a sense, the world is demythologized because (modern) man determines the degrees (the ways) of distancing himself from the world (experience) and because, in this way, it becomes possible for him to translate it into different forms of language (thought); he can express (and interpret) the world on the scientific (ontic) level as well as on the ontological level of understanding. But the real world of our experience cannot be (completely) identified with the scientific description and experience. The world of our experience (in its spontaneity) is not destroyed, but rather it is enlarged and disclosed more profoundly through the process of explicitation (by the sciences and by philosophy), by progressing thematizations. This idea is emphasized by the mainstream of contemporary phenomenology.[1]

Phenomenology as a universal science, in Husserl's view, analyzes the foundational issues of philosophy; it calls (traditional) metaphysics into question (without rejecting metaphysics as such) by asserting that metaphysical questions, as far as they are meaningful questions, are to be resolved through phenomenology.[2] This substantial, Promethean claim is discernible also in Heidegger's overcoming of metaphysics and in his rethinking of the foundational concepts of philosophy. Heidegger's way of thinking, however, seems to bypass several metaphysical issues (such as the possibility and the value of the knowledge of God through the knowledge or interpretation of the world, the nature and the ultimate significance of the religious experience, the cultural relativity of philosophy, the question of immortality, the relationship between the metaphysical understanding and the phenomenological interpretation of the principle of causality) *as* metaphysical issues that are, nevertheless, quite significant for the appropriation of the tradition of philosophy (metaphysics). To some extent, then, the phenomenological perspective seems to respond to these (and to other) metaphysical questions. It should be kept in mind, however, that these (often indirect) responses may not (necessarily) be regarded as satisfactory solutions of these philosophical problems.[3] How far the metaphysical notion of the world and its relevance for the question of God can be accepted or rejected through phenomenology remains to be seen. Heidegger himself calls attention to the fact that the existential analysis of There-being as being-in-the-World claims no exclusiveness; it does not decide the theological-metaphysical meaning (dimension) of There-being as a worldly being.[4] This remark rejects the atheistic interpretation as well as a necessarily theistic understanding of the new concept of the World according to Heidegger's phenomenology.[5] The existential, phenomenological understanding of the World is quite significant for the philosophical problem of God; it includes a demythologizing dimension that is readily acceptable for philosophical thinking. The new (phenomenological) view of the World is not based on but rather removed from the "storytelling" ("mythological") explanation of the origin and nature of beings and things. Demythologization is an "accidental" aspect of the new interpretation of the World; its meaning for the question of God, however, is not accidental at all.

What aspects of Heidegger's existential, phenomenological

analysis of the World are the ones most relevant to the problem of God? Is the question of God related to the philosophical understanding of the World? What is Heidegger's description of There-being as being-in-the-World (that is, as to-be-in-the-World)? What is Heidegger's notion of the World? The following reflections respond to these questions and analyze the first phase of the question of God in Heidegger's thinking.

SZ identifies and describes an essential quality (ontological structure) of There-being with the basic term "to-be-in-the-World" (*In-der-Welt-Sein*).[6] This term designates the innermost nature of There-being as the comprehension of Being, as the coming to pass of transcendence. This is a way or a mode of "to-be" of There-being and not a mere external, spatial attribute of being in a place (like a bird in the classroom or the water in the glass). This "in" means to live in, to sojourn in, to be familiar and at home with the World. The "to-be-in" (*In-sein*) is an existential of There-being, an expression of the constitution of There-being as to-be-in-the-World. This constitution of There-being (the existential called "to-be-in-the-World") makes possible the spatial being-in (*Sein in*); it makes possible the everyday commerce of There-being with beings, with things that are inside the World (*das innerweltliche Seiende*). Heidegger develops a phenomenological analysis of everydayness (*Alltäglichkeit*) in order to show the coming to pass of transcendence; he describes the ways There-being transcends the things of the World. There-being is the condition of discoverability (*Entdeckbarkeit*) of the beings of the World; it lets beings be what they are and lets the World become World. Through There-being the worldliness (*Weltlichkeit*) of the World comes about. All knowledge that man (There-being) has of the World is made possible through this to-be-in-the-World. There-being in virtue of its own structure is with beings (things) of the World just discovered. The explanation of knowledge (cognition of the World and man) through the subject-object relationship is regarded in this context as a distorted view of the whole question of knowledge. For Heidegger's phenomenology, the idea of a "going-out" to discover the World (a going out into the World) is meaningless. There-being as characterized by the to-be-in-the-World is "out" (outside, *draussen*) already precisely because it *is* to-be-in-the-World at all times. This constitution of There-being is the foundation of knowledge as a way (a mode) of "to-be" (*Seinsart*). When we forget something, we lose a contact, we lose a relationship; we lose a "to-be-relationship" (*Seinszusammenhang:* connection of Being) to the always-known; we lose ontological contact. The same is true of deception and error. To know the World *is* a way of "to-be" of There-being. By knowing, There-being itself gains a new "to-be-status" (*Seinsstand:* status of Being), a new ontological state, with regard to the World.[7] There-being as (*als*) There-being is already outside in (*bei*) and with the World under the "guise" of different kinds of engagements that bring about the forgottenness and the obscuring of transcendence.

It already becomes possible to see not only the correlation (affirmed even by the subject-object view) but also the simultaneity of There-being and the World. The World is an existential of There-being: a structure, an essential characteristic of There-being itself.[8] The World is the "playroom" (*Spielraum*), the open space and the field of possibilities for man as There-being. Here it becomes clear that this analysis is concerned with the worldliness (essence, Being) of the World and that it is focused on human reality (There-being) as a being in the World. The term "worldliness" (*Weltlichkeit*) is an existential; it indicates that the World is where There-being lives and that the World is a constitutive element of There-being's to-be-in-the-World. The ontic as well as the ontological aspects of this notion of the World render it more human. This humanization, at the same time, indirectly implies a World become less "divine." This is the impression given by SZ. The examination of the later works of Heidegger, however, reveals a more comprehensive meaning and function of the humanization of the World. There-being inhabits (dwells in) the World "poetically" and thus opens up a human space in it. There-being lives in a human World that is more than just a place for procuring the means of physical survival; There-being explores all the dimensions of this World (the human and the divine; the earthly and the heavenly dimensions), prepares for the future coming of the "divine" and for living in "communication" with the "Holy" (Heidegger's description of Being and World with the term "Quadrate" (*Geviert*) is quite significant for the meaning of humanization). The humanized World "gives away" the presence of the human being as There-being.

The hermeneutical analysis of the meaning of the Being-structure of instrument (*Zeug*) as something functioning or failing, surprising or hindering, reveals the unique correlation between There-being and the World. The World is a World "wherein" (*worin*) There-being is and already was, and where There-being encounters purposeful beings during its preoccupation with the environment (*Umwelt*).[9] The World has already emerged with the accessibility

(*Zugänglichkeit*) of beings (entities); it has emerged and opened already for the circumspective preoccupation (*Besorgen*) with it. The preoccupation with the environment (the World-about) is founded on the familiarity with the World (*Weltvertrautheit*), on There-being's "to-be-at-home" in the World (nearness to beings in the World). In the life of this familiarity There-being can lose itself and thus be drawn to things. In the state of fallenness (*Verfallenheit*), when There-being is lost among things, the transcendence of the World is "lost." The analysis of reference (*Verweisung*) and sign (*Zeichen*) leads to the understanding of the Being of the World (*die Weltlichkiet der Welt*, the worldness or the worldliness of the World) as "meaningfulness" (*Bedeutsamkeit*).[10] The insertion of the instrument into a pattern of purposefulness leads to the understanding of There-being as the "whereunto" (the "for-the-sake-of-which") (*Worumwillen*) of all references. The unity of this complexity of relationships is There-being. This unity constitutes the purposefulness of the instrument, and, in this way, There-being is considered as the source of meaningfulness of the instrument. There-being is familiar with meaningfulness on the ontic level because it is familiar with "meaningfulness" on the ontological level. Comprehending itself, There-being comprehends the World because of its familiarity with the World. Total "meaningfulness" (the structure of the World) as already familiar to There-being renders possible the ontic encounter with the "concretizations" (purposefulness as particularity of an instrument) of discoverability. This basic conclusion of the phenomenological analysis of the World is quite significant for understanding the status of the question of God in the early Heidegger. There-being is related to an *ontic* World (familiarity with *Zuhandenes*, with beings as instruments, with beings that are ready-at-hand as useful for There-being's preoccupation with the environment) and transcends to an *ontological* World that renders possible the encounter with things as they are (There-being lets beings be).

The point of concern in the preceding analysis from the point of view of the God-question lies in the new ontology of the World and man. The traditional notion of transcendence as going beyond the World now is changed; transcendence becomes the meaning of the World itself. There-being is related to the World that is ontological (the totality of references and structures); the World is an existential (*Existenzial*), an essential characteristic, a final (ontological) structure of There-being. The World, therefore, is not considered as the work (gift) of a supreme being. The World is a World for man and any meaning is a meaning for man. There is no World without man and there is no man (There-being) without the World. This is a basic principle of phenomenology. The World is a "result" of meaningfulness for man; it is a network of meanings. The human being as There-being is structurally related to the World; human reality is to-be-in-the-World. The World is not a thing. It is a phenomenon of encounter between There-being and beings; There-being is World-building (*weltbildend*). The classical problems of realism, objectivity, and causality appear now as problems that pertain to the subject-object theory of the World. The notion of There-being as to-be-in-the-World overcomes the subject-object dichotomy of dualistic metaphysics. The dilemma of realism and idealism is surpassed (resolved) by the phenomenological principle of man-World relatedness (no World without There-being; no There-being without the World).

In *this* context, therefore, the World is not a "pathway" leading to the discovery of the Creator. The World, as it is understood phenomenologically in SZ, is demythologized precisely through its humanization. The finitude of There-being (finite transcendence) and the worldness of the World, in a sense, constitute an "atheistic" quality of this philosophy. The phenomenological view of the World and of There-being may be perceived as being in contrast (or as being in opposition) to the metaphysical understanding of the World as created by the supreme being.

The "mythological" ("storytelling" and causal) approach to the problem of God is overcome through the new interpretation of the World. The World is not interpreted (philosophically) as the handiwork and the sign of God. The World as the trace (*vestigium*) of God and man as the image (*imago*) of God are left "outside" the existential analytic. The analysis of reference and sign leads to an ontological problematic of the World (that is, the worldness or Being of the World); it is not concerned with the metaphysical background and causal origin of things but rather with the meanings of beings in the World. The act of indicating or pointing to something is a "concretization" of the instrumental structure; indication is made possible by the totality of instruments in the context of total meaningfulness (the World). The sign functions on the ontic level as the showing forth of the ontological structure of to-be-ready-at-hand (*Zuhandensein*), of the "totality of references," and of the worldness (worldliness) of the World.[11] The hermeneutics of sign discloses for us what the World as World is: the worldness (Being) of the World. The sign shows forth the meaning of the World because it (the sign) is discovered and constituted in a "house" of references; this reference discloses the ontological meaning of the World.

The World is a network (matrix) of relations (*Bezugszusammenhang*) of purposefulness, an existential of There-being as to-be-in-the-World. There-being is the ontic condition of possibility of the discoverability of beings encountered as "being-destined" (*Bewandtnis*) in the World. Through this encounter the "in-themselves" (*An-sich*) of beings can be disclosed. There-being *is* already referred to an ontic World to be encountered. Here appears the basic referential dependence (*Angewiesenheit*) of There-being on other beings (instruments). The World is a horizon, a "wherein" (*Worin*), within which the instrument is encountered by There-being. The World is the network of relations that renders possible the purposefulness (the Being) of an instrument. There-being is the unity of this interconnection of relations: the ultimate "whereunto" (*Worumwillen*) of all references. Therefore, There-being, by comprehending its own Being, comprehends the ultimate term of references (of instruments), and this disclosure of the "whereunto" is ontologically prior to the ontic encounter (with an instrument).[12]

There-being's familiarity with meaningfulness (*Bedeutsamkeit*)[13] is the ontological condition for the disclosure of meanings (as described before) and the foundation of the possible Being of word and language. A word, therefore, is the word of meaningfulness as the ontological structure of the World. There-being can disclose meanings by virtue of the familiarity with meaningfulness, with the World. This disclosure means that There-being lets beings be what they are.

There are several phenomenological principles and insights at stake in the preceding analysis of the World and There-being. The same principles play decisive roles in rethinking basic philosophical problems, such as the nature of knowledge, the essence of truth, the meaning of Being, the dilemma of realism and idealism, and the philosophical affirmation of God. The examination of the status of the problem of God in SZ requires the basic understanding of the guiding principles and main themes of the existential analytic. The preceding reflections already show that SZ says very little about God directly; they indicate that for the most part SZ speaks about the problem of God indirectly, by way of implication and additional (secondary) conclusions. The basic theme and task (the analysis of There-being for the sake of interpreting Being) of this seminal work, nevertheless, do have a significant relationship to the philosophical problem of God. What is the primary focus of the references to the problem of God in SZ? There cannot be a reliable answer to this question without analyzing the references to the question of God in the light of the basic phenomenological principles and notions that lead Heidegger to speak about this issue at least indirectly. The new notion of the World plays a key role in the development of the phase of demythologization of the problem of God in the early Heidegger according to SZ. The new approach to the philosophical question of God that may be discerned in the later Heidegger may not be grasped properly without its background in the early phase of Heidegger's thought. The task of the following reflections consists in analyzing the main characteristics of the demythologization of the traditional (Western) problem of God in connection with the notion (and interpretation) of the World in SZ.

Heidegger himself calls attention to the significance of the changed understanding of the World. He explains and emphasizes this change by evaluating the Cartesian interpretation of the "World" as *res extensa* and by examining the ontological assumptions of the Cartesian perspective.[14] These Cartesian meditations by Heidegger include some indications regarding the demythologization of the problem of God and even show the tendency to eliminate the problem of God from philosophy.

In Cartesian philosophy the "World" is viewed as a *res extensa,* as an extended thing. The ontological characteristic of this *res extensa* is described as substantiality (a notion and interpretation of Being). Substantiality and substance are called by the same word: *substantia.* The term *substantia* means the Being of a being that is a substance (this is the notion of substantiality, an ontological term), and at the same time it also means the being itself (a substance, an ontic term). The ambiguity (*Doppeldeutigkeit*) of the term *substantia* and the ensuing confusion come from the ambiguity of the original Greek concept of οὐσία . In the final analysis, this confusion indicates the obscurity about the ontological issues involved, the lack of clear distinction between Being and beings; it shows the confusion about the ontological difference. The *extensio* (extension in length, breadth, and depth) is the source of all the qualities of a bodily substance (*Körperding, res corporea*); it constitutes their Being, their substantiality. The real (genuine) Being (*Sein*) of a bodily substance (extended thing) is what remains the same in spite of all the changes. This permanent "element," according to Descartes, is the *extensio*; this is the Being of an extended thing and characterizes it substantially. The whole "World," therefore, is a *res extensa.* In the Cartesian view, Being is understood as substantiality. What is the Being (the substantiality) of a substance (thing, being) for Descartes? According to Heidegger's interpretation, substance means to Descartes a being (*Seiende*) that is self-sufficient, that has no need of other beings in order to exist (to be). Substantiality means the quality of nonindigence (*Unbedürftigkeit*), the quality of being in such a way that it needs no other being in order to be. This nonindigence constitutes the Being of a being, of a substance. The being (substance), therefore, whose Being has no need at all for any other being in order to be, fulfills (measures up to) the idea of substance in the true sense. The being that is a substance in this true sense is the *ens perfectissimum* (the most perfect being), and there is only one being (substance) that can be understood as needing nothing in order to be (to exist), namely God.[15] Heidegger shows that God, in this Cartesian context, is an ontological title, understood as the most perfect being. The notion of God functions as an ontological term in the philosophy of Descartes; God, as the most perfect being, is the reality of the ideal of (true) substantiality because God needs no other being in order to be. This notion of God, therefore, makes possible the ontological interpretation of the constitutive moment ("element") of substantiality (that is, of nonindigence) as something self-evident (*selbstverständlich*), because nonindigence is already contained in the notion of God. Nonindigence, then, is the main characteristic of substantiality. From this notion of substantiality it follows that every being (substance) that is not God is in need of others; it is in need of being caused and maintained in existence. Every being that is not God is, therefore, a created being (*ens creatum*).

Descartes distinguishes two kinds of beings: the most perfect being and the created beings. As Heidegger insists, there is an infinite difference between these two kinds of beings, yet they are still called by the same name: *being* (*Seiende*). In spite of the infinite difference between them insofar as their Being (*Sein*) is concerned, they are described and spoken of as beings. Though all the created beings are referred to God (through causality and conservation), nevertheless, they may be called substances because they have a relative nonindigence; that is, they are self-sufficient in certain domains (*res cogitans* and *res extensa*). The important point, however, is the fact that substantiality as such (the Being of a being) is interpreted from the perspective of the nonindigence of being-caused (produced) (*Herstellungsunbedürftigkeit*).[16] This means that Being itself is understood in this way; it is interpreted according to a definite perspective.

The word *Being* is used in a wide sense; it refers to all the three substances (God, *res cogitans, res extensa*) as constituting their substantiality. What is, then, the "common" meaning of Being? When we say "God is" and "The world is," continues Heidegger, we are making a statement (*Aussage*) about Being. The word *is*, however, does not have the same meaning when it refers to the created being(s) and when it refers to the uncreated being; its meaning is not univocal when applied to the "world" (created beings) and when applied to "God" (uncreated being). Descartes says that the meaning of Being is a "common" (*gemeinsam*) meaning. The scholastics said that the meaning (notion) of Being is analogous. Descartes, however, sidesteps the problem of the analogy of Being (of the "is"), and, therefore, his ontological work remains far behind the scholastic interpretation of Being; he leaves unasked the question about the meaning that is included in the notion of substantiality as nonindigence. According to Heidegger's interpretation, Descartes does not examine the problem of the "universality" (*Allgemeinheit*) and of the meaning of Being when it is referred to the different kinds of substances. Both medieval and ancient ontologies suffer the same deficiency because they leave undiscussed (*unerörtert*) the meaning of Being.[17]

The possibility for discussing the problematic of Being is renounced explicitly in Cartesian philosophy. "Being" itself, substance as such (substantiality), says Descartes, does not "affect" (*affiziert*) us through its existence, and, therefore, we cannot perceive it. Kant's statement that "Being is not a real predicate" is a reflection of the Cartesian idea that "Being" does not "affect" us. When Descartes speaks of substantiality as such, he speaks of Being. "Being," in fact, as Heidegger insists, is not accessible (cannot be known) as a being (*als Seiendes*). For this reason Being is expressed and described through the determinations (*Bestimmtheiten*) and the attributes of the (particular) beings in question. This means that Being is accessible *as* a quality (determination, attribute) *of a* being (and of beings in general) even though Being (itself) is not accessible as (a) being. In Descartes, those determinations and attributes of the particular being(s) are taken as the expression of Being that satisfies the unexpressedly (*unausdrücklich*) presupposed meaning of Being and that of substantiality. This is the ontological foundation of the Cartesian interpretation of the "World." The notion of substance functions ontologically (substantiality) and ontically (substance) at the same time, and this is the reason for the ambiguity of this philosophy. Descartes speaks of substantiality and understands it as (and through) a quality of the individual substance. Indeed, he understands Being itself as a quality of being. All this, in Heidegger's view, is the result of the Cartesian inability to deal with the ontological problematic.[18]

These meditations on Descartes clearly indicate the foundational significance of the question of Being for Heidegger. His claim that the Cartesian notion of God is an ontological title establishes the need as well as the main reasons for the demythologization (destruction, overcoming) of this philosophical (ontological) function of the concept of God. For Heidegger the question to be asked is the question of the meaning of Being as Being and not as a quality of a particular being. The reference to Descartes is a good example in this regard. Heidegger does not yet draw the final (radical) conclusion regarding the problem of God. He delays it to a later occasion when he seems to eliminate God from the domain of philosophical thinking. This idea becomes more prominent and developed especially in EM and in ID in connection with his reflections on the "place" of God in the history of philosophy. According to SZ, the ontological function of the idea of God brings Descartes's thinking about Being to a halt; there is an "ontological blackout," a certain blindness toward Being in the philosophy of Descartes. This is the main issue for Heidegger. Cartesian ontology considers Being as a being; it reduces Being to a being and leaves unasked the question regarding the "beingness" (*Seiendheit*) of a being (and of beings in general). This ontology is the source for interpreting God as the most perfect being. The ontological problematic is projected into the notion (and problem) of God. The Cartesian idea of the "World" results from conceiving Being as something static, self-sufficient, and permanent (eternal). Descartes consolidates the following opinion of traditional ontology: The ontical knowledge (*Erkennen*) of a (particular) being constitutes at the same time the access to the (more primary) Being (the "to-be") of this same being discovered in the ontical knowledge.[19] This means that, in his view, Being is described through the attributes of the particular being(s) (things, mere objects). This ontological presupposition indicates that Descartes is unable to grasp beings like There-being; he is concerned with the qualities of things (of nature). The problematic of the Being of things cannot be asked in the Cartesian view; Cartesian philosophy reaches that which really is by means of the certitude aspect of (mathematical) knowing based on the separation of the knower (subject) from the "World" (object) (dualism). The problem of the Being of things and the ontological foundation of values may be clarified, however, through the existential analytic. Existential (phenomenological) analysis considers the World in relation to man (There-being) and regards There-being as the point of departure of (the vehicle for) philosophizing (*initium philosophandi*), whereas Cartesian philosophy begins with (takes its departure from) mere things or with beings as things (entities) (*res cogitans, res extensa*). This is a difference of great importance for Heidegger.

According to SZ, the problem of God needs to be demythologized (not to be regarded as the answer to the question of Being) as a requirement for the elaboration of the Being-question. The idea of God in philosophy cannot function as an ontological title. The philosophical concept of God includes an interpretation of the meaning of Being, and this interpretation consists precisely in the unquestioned view of Being as a quality of a particular being exemplified through the notion of God as the highest being. Therefore, the *way* the notion of God had functioned in philosophy now is radically questioned in the light of the new approach to the ontological problematic. The philosophical notion of God cannot be considered as an answer to, or as a substitute for, the question about the meaning of Being. The idea that the notion of God is the answer to the most difficult philosophical question (What is Being? What is the meaning of the word *Being*?) has to be abandoned as it becomes inadequate; the problem of Being ought to be reexamined and asked *as* a question (unhampered by the concept of God).

The ontological enterprise, however, does not mean a rejection of the notion of God. An atheistic interpretation of the existential analysis would be a serious misunderstanding of SZ. The demythologization of the problem of God is not atheism; it implies mainly the criticism of the traditional concept of God. The possibility of a new approach to the problem of God is not destroyed but rather called for in the light of existential analysis. The question of God is not resolved by SZ. The need for a new approach to the problem of God is merely implied (indirectly) as a possibility that shall become more significant at a later stage of the process of questioning. The consequence (of demythologization) for theology, however, is already spelled out by Heidegger: Theology needs to find (rediscover) its (new) foundation and to persevere in fidelity to the experience of faith. From the philosophical point of view, the problem of God is a question about the "place" of God in philosophy as such and not so much a matter of his existence. Heidegger's intention is to explain (and to rethink) how God had entered into philosophy. The final thrust of his question is the following: Should (the question of) God enter into philosophy at all? This question remains a question even at the end of Heidegger's pathway of thought. The best "corrective correlate" to the demythologization of the problem of God in SZ is Heidegger's view of the relationship between philosophy and theology as developed in his lecture "Phenomenology and Theology" (March 9, 1927, Tübingen).[20] This lecture gives evidence of the Heideggerian appreciation of and respect for authentic theology; it emphasizes the fact that theology is grounded in the experience of (Christian) faith and on the notion of the "wholly otherness" (complete transcendence) of God.

The preceding reflections on the new understanding of the World in SZ show the basic nature and the significance of the first phase of the God-question in Heidegger's way of thinking. It is important to recognize the early presence of this problem in Heidegger's pathway of thought. In a sense, this is a somewhat negative phase; it brings forward the "how it is not" aspect of the philosophical problem of God. Some of the relevant references to this problem appear in the context of those passages and themes that do not examine the question of God directly. This makes the task at hand more difficult but also more rewarding. Here it is possible to see at work the Heideggerian idea of "keeping silence about God in the realm of thought."[21] The phase of demythologization of the problem of God, as it is present in SZ, should be understood ultimately as forming part of this silence.

The "Other"
as an
Existential

The phenomenological ontological interpretation of the World prepares the ground for a new understanding of other philosophical issues. The description of There-being as to-be-in-the-World, the concept of instrument, and the notion of fixed things (entities) belong to the main themes of the existential analysis. The new motion of the World as the totality of meaningfulness (network of relations) introduces the understanding of There-being as the special being that lets beings be what they are and "builds" (*bildet*) the worldness (worldliness, Being) of the World. The problem of God appeared in this context as an ontological title, and as such it is submitted to the demythologization process in order to ask the question about the meaning of Being. The absence of God indicates the new orientation of philosophy as well as the initial exigency of a new way to think the problem and the idea of God. These insights and conclusions, however, do not represent yet the comprehensive view of the experience of the human World. What is the status of interpersonal relationships (intersubjectivity) according to SZ? The existential analysis examines There-being's openness to the "other" (person), the notion of the self, basic human values, and other dimensions of human experience. Sometimes the preceding reflections used the term *man* according to its general meaning (human existence, human reality, human being) and thus also in reference to There-being. It should be kept in mind, however, that "man" (*das Man*) as a technical term in SZ stands for the everyday, inauthentic mode of existence (life of anonymity; man as member of the crowd, of mass society; people in general). Is there a place for a philosophy of love in the existential analysis of There-being? What is the "nature" of the human person? What is personal existence? What are the basic values of the human person? What is the fundamental structure of human relationships? Is human existence coexistence? Does to be mean to be with "others"? Is there a structural conflict between being an individual being and being with "others"? SZ does not give a comprehensive answer to all these questions; it examines them mainly from the ontological perspective. These themes of the existential analysis of There-being as a being that is (lives) with "others" in the World, however, also include descriptions of the psychological, anthropological, and axiological elements of human existence. The primary task of these considerations, nevertheless, is not the development of an existential psychology but rather the pursuit of the understanding of Being through the description of the "is-ness" of togetherness (coexistence) in human existence, through the examination of the Being-dimension of human existence, as existence with "others" in the World. According to Heidegger, the more one understands There-being the more one begins to comprehend and think (about) Being, the phenomenon of "to-be." The understanding of the ways There-being is with other There-beings in the World opens up the possibility for the comprehension of the "is-ness" of this "is," of the phenomenon of "to-be."

Who is There-being? Who lives in the situation (mode) of everydayness? How does There-being relate to other There-beings in the World? In what ways do other There-beings in the World relate to the "mineness" of There-being? What can be said about the personal and interpersonal life of There-being? What is the ontological aspect (foundation) of what is often called "human togetherness," of being with "others"? SZ responds to these questions by means of discerning the essential characteristics, the different modes of "to-be" of There-being as related to others and to the World. The essential ontological characteristics (qualities), the Being-structures (*Seinsstrukturen*), of There-being constitute There-being's ways (modes) of "to-be" (*Weisen seines Seins*), such as the phenomenon of "with-being" (the "to-be-with," the "being-with") (*Mitsein*) and the phenomenon of "There-being-with-others" (*Mitdasein*).[1] This means that to the very Being of

There-being belong the "to-be-with" ("with-being") and the "to-be-with-others." The phenomenon of "with-being" and the phenomenon of "There-being-with-others" reveal a fundamental (ontological) structure of There-being, and they show this structure as being equally original (*gleichursprünglich*) with the to-be-in-the-World. This structure is the existential called "with-being" ("to-be-with"). The "with-being" structure of There-being is the foundation of human community and of interpersonal relationships; it is not the product of social or cultural integration. In SZ, therefore, human existence is not solipsistic but open to the "other" and to the World at the same time. The description of There-being as a being that is "mine" (*Jemeinigkeit*) indicates an ontological constitution; it contains, at the same time, an ontical declaration (*Angabe*) by showing that the "I" of this being is me and not the "other." The analysis of the everydayness of the "who" (*Wer*) shows this "I" as a "subject," as a "self" (*Selbst*) that is unchanging and identical in spite of the variety of its experiences and attitudes. This view of the "who" as "subject," as the same "self," however, leads to an interpretation of the "who" that is based on the ontology of the subject as a mere entity (thing) (*Vorhandenes*). Such an interpretation, then, would reduce the "who" of There-being and thus There-being itself to the status of things. In the existential analysis the "not-I" is not a mere entity (a thing) that lacks "Iness" (Ihood) (*Ichheit*); it considers the "not-I" (*Nicht-Ich*) rather as a definite way of "to-be" (*Seinsart*) of the "I," such as the "I" losing itself in the mode of everydayness, in the situation of inauthenticity. "Mineness" and "Iness," however, ontologically always belong to There-being. The "I" reveals itself always in an ontological context; it is more than just something ontic. The description of There-being as to-be-in-the-World has shown already that there is no subject without the World. In the same way, Heidegger concludes, there is no isolated "I" without the "other."[2] This is an important principle according to Heidegger's phenomenology. The "other" is ontologically given with the "World"; the "other" is an existential.

What is the relationship between There-being and the "other"? How does There-being encounter the "other" in the World, in everyday living? The response to these questions is quite significant for Heidegger. He shows that There-being frees beings (*freigebendes Dasein*) and lets them be (*Seinlassen*). There-being encounters and lets be not only instruments and mere things—as this has been clarified by the new understanding of the World—but other beings too that not only are different from these (instruments, things) but have the way (mode) of "to-be" of There-being. There-being encounters (*begegnet*) them; they too can be described as to-be-in-the-World, as being-in-the-World. These beings are like There-being; they are characterized by the "to-be" (*sein*), by the "there" (*da*), and by the "with" (*mit*). These considerations indicate the ontological significance of and the new approach to the problem of the "other" in SZ.

The "other" is neither a mere thing nor an instrument for There-being. The "other" is different from mere things that simply are (*vorhanden*) as well as from instruments that are ready for use (*zuhanden*); the way the "other" is in the World differs from the ways these beings (mere things, instruments) are in the World. The "other" *is* like There-being; it is distinguished by the "with" and by the "there" as forming part of the World of There-being (*es ist auch und mit da*).[3] The "other" is another There-being that belongs to the World of my There-being. This means that There-being is essentially a There-being-with-others (*Mitdasein*); the way of "to-be" of There-being is "to-be-with" ("with-being"). The "other" reveals the World of There-being as a with-world (*Mitwelt*), that is, as a World where There-being is with "others" (with other There-beings). The "other," then, means not the rest of the human World outside myself but the World where I am and where I live. The "other" is found not by the process of distinction (as separation) but through the experience of the to-be-in-the-World. The "with" of There-being-with-others is an expression of an ontological characteristic and not a spatial (exterior) quality; it is an *existential*. The "other" "too" (*auch*) is a There-being; that is, there is an equality of Being (*Gleichheit des Seins*) between them; this equality is their Being as to-be-in-the-World in the mode of a circum-spective preoccupation (*umsichtig-besorgendes In-der-Welt-sein*). The World is a common world (*Mitwelt*, "with-World"), a World always shared with "others." The "to-be-in" is a "to-be-with" (*In-sien ist Mit-sein*): a "to-be-with-others."[4] The "to-be-with" or "with-being" is an exist-intial of There-being—this is the conclusion of the analysis. The "other" is an existential of There-being.

SZ describes There-being's basic relations to the "other" as various modes of solicitude (*Fürsorge*). The different modes of solicitude show forth the ways of "to-be-with" the "other." The authentic solic-itude for the "other" is not taking the place of the "other" (*für ihn einspringen*) by taking away his concern (*Sorge*) but rather the opening up of space for the "other," that is, forging ahead of him (*ihm vor-ausspringt*) in his existentiell dynamism to be and to become (*Seinkön-nen*). Authentic solicitude, then, does not take away the concern from the "other," but rather gives it back to him authentically. This positive and genuine solicitude, therefore, is not an imposition on the "other" but an unfolding of the "other"; it is a liberation, a becoming free (*frei*) of the "other" for and in his true concern. This kind of solicitude is indeed an authentic concern because it relates to the "other" in his existence and not to some "what" (*Was*) or quality of him. This is the foundation of authentic community (*Verbundenheit*) because this makes free the "other" for himself in his own freedom (*Freiheit*).[5] It may be concluded, then, that "to-be-with-others" (*Mitsein mit Anderen*) belongs to the Being of There-being, that There-being *is* "to-be-with-others"; it is essentially for the sake of (*umwillen*) "others." This is an essential existential statement.[6] The way of "to-be" of There-being *is* "to-be-with-others." The "other" is already disclosed (*erschlossen*) in its There-being and constitutes the meaningfulness, the worldness (the Being) of the World as World. The World, then, is not an aggregate of isolated subjects but the encounter with "others" through the different modes of solicitude. This is the philosophical foundation of community. Moreover, one should add, the existential called "to-be-with," the notion of solicitude, and the concept of encounter also represent some important components of the ontological foundation and nature of love. Thus the basic elements of a theory of love can be found in SZ; they remain, however, incomplete and undeveloped. These insights ought to be kept in mind in connection with the examination of human relationships and of the nature (and function) of human love in Heidegger's phenomenology.

How can we know the "other"? What is the foundation of knowing oneself? How can we know ourselves? Heidegger's thesis regarding these issues is expressed in the following statements: "because There-being's Being is to-be-with, in its comprehension of Being lies already the comprehension of others. . . . Knowing oneself is grounded in the originally comprehending to-be-with."[7] The "other" is disclosed through the various modes of solicitude. We know the "other" through our common preoccupation with the World and through our solicitude for and with the "other." We know other There-beings through our concrete, practical, and concerned relationships with them. Preoccupied, concerned solicitude (*besorgende Füsorge*), according to SZ, is the most obvious and frequent way human beings are disclosed to each other. SZ includes an insightful examination of basic human interpersonal relationships. The main issue at stake in this phenomenological analysis, however, is not the topology of human relationships but rather the existential, ontological structure and foundation of the various modes of human relationships in knowing and being. According to the previously quoted passage of SZ, knowing of oneself and knowing of "others" have an ontological structure and foundation; comprehension of Being, knowing of oneself, and knowing of "others" are structurally (existentially) unified, interrelated. The Being of There-being is "with-being" ("to-be-with"), and, because of this, There-being's comprehension of Being already implies the comprehension of "others." To "with-being" as an existential of There-being belongs the disclosedness (*Erschlossenheit*) of There-being-with-others (*Mitdasein*). This comprehending ("others"), in Heidegger's view, is not a theoretical, conceptual knowledge but an original existential mode of "to-be" (*Seinsart*) that makes such knowledge possible. Knowing oneself is grounded in "with-being" that involves the primordial comprehension of "others." Knowing oneself, therefore, is a way of "to-be" (a mode of existence) of There-being that may be authentic or inauthentic; it tells the way There-being lives (is) in the World.

What are the main characteristics of the everyday life of There-being with "others" in the World? SZ develops a concise analysis of the life of everydayness.[8] The true potentialities of There-being are not realized in daily living; one's relations to oneself and to "others" are ruled by the attitudes of indifference, neutrality, and impersonality (anonymity). The true self is "lost" in this mode of existence characterized by domination and submission, by the dictatorship of anonymity. The "who" of everyday There-being is nobody and everybody. This "nobody" is the neutral "man" (*das Man*) of mass society, the impersonal self, the average self that lacks true awareness of itself and of "others." There-being is dispersed and "lost" in this mode of existence, in this way of living; human relationships become confused because, to a significant extent and for the most part, nobody is (lives as) truly himself and everybody is (like) someone else. Where is There-being in this mode of "to-be"? According to SZ, the "loss" of the true self in the situation of everydayness is not accidental; the phenomenon of the impersonal "man" is an existential of There-being; it belongs to the constitution of There-being.[9] The life of impersonal "man" takes many forms according to the concrete possibilities of everydayness in human history. However, even in this situation, the real, authentic self remains the true source of existence in spite of the fact that its authentic understanding is twisted because of the twisted existence. There-being can and must "find" its true self that is not destroyed but only fallen away from the authentic mode of "to-be." There-being can become inauthentic only because it does have the potentiality to be authentic. There is a circular relationship between comprehension and existence. Since knowing is a way of "to-be," an authentic comprehension (and thus knowing oneself and others) cannot be achieved independently from an authentic mode of existence ("to-be").

The ideal of authentic existence in SZ is quite "ideal" and hardly achievable at the same time. There-being's authentic mode of "to-be" seems unobtainable because of the swaying power of every-dayness. This practical incompatibility of authenticity and everydayness can hardly be supported by a more comprehensive and realistic view of experience. According to A. De Waelhens, Heidegger ignores the (many) "real" forms of and opportunities for There-being's authentic way of "to-be" in the midst and in spite of the reality of everydayness.[10] The life of responsibility, the life and commitment of faith, the creative fidelity to one's tasks, for example, show that authentic existence *is* possible and that, indeed, it *is* lived in the situation of everydayness. This means, therefore, that the authenticity of existence (and the comprehension of it) is more "concretized" than it is supposed and acknowledged by the existential analysis. Existential authenticity is existentielly grounded; daily living and the concrete situations of existence do have a profound existential significance. Human authenticity takes many forms according to the many concrete opportunities offered by life to every individual person for the realization of meanings and values.

The preceding descriptions and reflections do not refer directly to the problem of God. However, this interpretation of the human person (the "self" and the authentic "who" of There-being) and of the relationship to the "other" (the existential significance of basic human relationships) may be viewed as part of the demythologization of the problem of God. According to Heidegger, the nature of the "other" and the discovery (recognition, knowledge) of the "other" are founded (ontologically as well as epistemologically) in the existential called "to-be-with" in a common World. The philosophical analysis of the "other" includes an interpretation of the nature of human subjectivity (personhood, for instance, the "acting person" for M. Scheler) and an examination of the basic structure of human relationships (intersubjectivity). Can God be considered as an "other," as the ultimately most significant "Other"? The answer to this question in the affirmative would mean a new approach to the question of God. The answer in the negative, however, would reinforce the demythologization of the problem of God. SZ says nothing regarding the possibility of a new approach to the question of God through the existential analysis of the "other." The analysis of the "who" of There-being and the description of foundational human relationships in SZ do not even raise the question regarding a possible relationship of these issues to the problem of God on any level at all. God is not attainable phenomenologically (at least not through the phenomenological method of SZ); he is not an equal of There-being. There-being's relation to God is not the same as its relation to the "other." The unfolding of the existential analysis in SZ, therefore, is progressing toward a unifying and this-worldly understanding of the Being, of the way of "to-be" of There-being. This understanding does not include a commitment either to a theistic or to an atheistic interpretation of the transcendence of There-being; it remains neutral regarding the question of God. The concept of the "other" as person, as subject, according to SZ, belongs to the metaphysical perspective. Heidegger is analyzing the existential (ontological) and not the metaphysical (ontic) dimension of the I-Thou (*Ich-Du*) relationship; he is examining neither the scientific nor the theological aspects of this relationship as he clearly indicates in ML (Marburg Lecture Course, Summer Semester, 1928).[11] These ideas reinforce the perspective of SZ regarding the demythologization of the question of God and allow for the conclusion that Heidegger does not speak of God as a Thou (for example, as the Ultimate or Eternal Thou, as the wholly Other) because this concept of God would be still metaphysical.

What does it mean, from a philosophical perspective, to understand God as a Thou? Is there any connection at all between the basic relation to the "other" and the relation to God? Is it possible to find the way toward (to discern and encounter) God through the depth of the authentic relationship with the "other," with the human Thou? If the analysis of the realm of things and the principle of causality do not lead the way to the affirmation of God, can the nature of human relationships and the principle of freedom open a new approach to the question of God? Heidegger's analysis of There-being does not include an exploration of these issues in connection with the existential analysis of human relationships. For Sartre, the definition of human existence and the principle of freedom discard the idea of God. Other philosophers, however, interpret the nature of the human person and the relation to the "other" in ways that are quite divergent from the perspectives of Heidegger and Sartre. The philosophy of the I-Thou relationship in M. Buber, the concrete philosophy of human existence (and the notion of the "other") in G. Marcel, and the understanding of the "other" as a person and as a revelation according to E. Levinas certainly open a new approach to the problem of God.[12] The mainstreams of depth psychology, the theory of logotherapy, and phenomenological psychology lead to a more comprehensive philosophy of the "other" as well as to the interpretation of the nature of religious transcendence.[13] These developments are quite significant for the contemporary analysis of the entire problem of God.

These considerations suggest that the comprehensive phenomenology of the "other" is able to go beyond the intended (metaphysical and theological) neutrality of the existential analysis according to SZ. It should be kept in mind that at least some elements of the phenomenological method of analysis may be used and practiced in a variety of fields of learning. As Heidegger practices the phenomenological method in reexamining the understanding and the question of Being, R. Otto (professor of Theology at the University of Marburg from 1917 to 1937) uses some elements of the same methodology in elaborating a phenomenology of the Holy (das Heilige).[14] There are many similarities between the existential analysis of There-being and some aspects of the phenomenology of religion in the writings of R. Otto. It is worthwhile to ask the following question: Is there a significant relationship between the Being-question in Heidegger and the problem of the Holy in R. Otto? This comparison may raise many questions regarding the phenomenon of religion (and of religiosity) and the interpretation of the ultimate meaning of There-being's transcendence. These issues are significant for exploring the possibility of a new approach to the problem of God (after the neutrality of SZ) as well as for clarifying the relationship of Heidegger's thought to Christian theology. The following two important questions ought to be distinguished from each other in this regard: What is the meaning, the significance, of Heidegger's thought for systematic theology? Does Heidegger's philosophy as such include any theological dimension or relation to theology? These are two separate questions; the answer to the first does not include the answer to the second. The usefulness and the theological "appropriation" of Heidegger's phenomenology may be possible irrespective of Heidegger's own intentions and interpretations.[15] Any claim, however, regarding the relationship (of origin, of meaning) of Heidegger's philosophy to theology (and religious metaphysics) ought to be justified by the laws of validity of contextual hermeneutics; they must be based on the interpretation, understanding, and balanced evaluation of Heidegger's thought in his published works. Therefore, the second question ought to be considered separately from the first. The publication of all the writings of Heidegger in the *Gesamtausgabe* now in progress shall make it possible to find the comprehensive and definitive response to the second question. The answer to this concern cannot be found by simply keeping silent about it. The suggestion, however, that Heidegger's philosophy is a "disguised theology" can hardly represent more than a simple and hasty answer to a complex problem.[16] This comment on Heidegger's philosophy disregards his understanding of the nature of philosophical thinking as well as his foundational concern with the question of Being.

These reflections on the meaning of the "other" in the existential analysis of There-being contribute to the clarification of the first phase (demythologization) of the development of the question of God in Heidegger. This phase shows the importance of the fact that the "traditional" approach to the problem of God is indeed eclipsed (devaluated) by SZ. Heidegger, in SZ, remains silent and neutral about the possible new approaches to this problem. This silence is a consequence of the fidelity to the pursuit of the question of Being and a sign of perseverance in patience in order to experience the event of thinking and thinking as an event. The process of demythologization, therefore, is not a rejection of the problem of God but rather the first phase of its development. This phase ought to be regarded as the prerequisite for a new way of asking the appropriate questions regarding the truly divine God. SZ represents only the beginning and not the end of Heidegger's thought on the problem of God.

11

A Principle of
Demythologization

The study of the problem of God in Heidegger's phenomenology cannot be based exclusively on the analysis of some relevant passages of his works; it cannot be satisfied by a simple description of the destruction of the traditional approach to this problem. It is not enough to study the various references to the problem of God; even a chronological systematization of such texts remains only a limited mode of understanding. The development of the experience of thinking (leading to thinking as an event)—in this instance, the discovery of the "where" of the unfolding of the God-question—is not identical simply with the exegetical probings of a variety of passages. The unfolding of the experience of thinking is disclosed through "entering into" the hermeneutical circle of understanding.[1] The interpretation of the references to the problem of God requires the understanding of several themes of Heidegger's philosophy. The main task of this study, however, does not consist in the elaboration of these themes but in the analysis of their relationship to the problem of God. Many areas of Heidegger's thought have been examined by several scholarly works. This fact eliminates the necessity to review the general tenets of Heidegger's philosophy and, at the same time, allows for concentrating on the pursuit of the special task of this study. This approach lends itself to meditative thinking (*besinnliches Denken*) on the problem of God insofar as it *is* present, though in varying modes, in Heidegger's experience of thinking.

The first phase of the problem of God in Heidegger shows that the thematic references to the problem of God, to the question of Being, and to the ontological understanding of There-being belong together: they are related. The God-question is present in the form of objections and through a meaningful absence. These references, however, represent neither digressions nor distractions from the main theme of Heidegger's thought; they belong to the unity of the problem of Being. The analysis of There-being is not psychological but ontological; it represents a basic step toward the discernment and the interpretation of the meaning of Being. This unity, nevertheless, may appear as an intentional unity, as the intended purpose and the final direction of the analysis. This concern leads to the asking of the following questions regarding the unified structure of the references to the problem of God and their connection with the problem of Being. What is the origin of the unified structure and the connection? Why is there a unity (unified structure) of the reasons for the objections to the traditional notion of God? Why are the reasons for these objections the same as the reasons for the absence of references to the question of God in other contexts? Why is there a unity of reasons for rejecting the traditional concept of Being? Why is there a convergence of the reasons for criticizing the concept of God and the reasons for criticizing the concept of Being? Why is it that all these questions, in the final analysis, relate to and are unified around the question of Being? Why do the question of God and the question of Being belong together, and why are they related to each other in SZ? Why is it that the existential analytic, throughout the unfolding of all the various themes, repeatedly discovers the same basic deficient understandings and even the failures to ask the Being-question? Where is, therefore, the source of this unity? This last question resumes the thrust of the preceding ones.

The following reflections respond to these questions by calling attention to and by analyzing a principle of demythologization of the problem of God. These considerations belong to the explanation of the origin (source and principle) of the demythologization of the problem of God in SZ. The ideas discussed in this context include what Heidegger calls the phenomenon of the equal-originality of the constitutive moments (*Gleichursprünglichkeit der konstitutiven Momente*) of the "There" ("*Da*") of There-being (*Dasein*).[2] After the analysis of to-be-in-the-World as "to-be-with," Heidegger develops the thematical analysis of "to-be-in" (*In-Sein*) as the basic structure of There-being as to-be-in-the-World according to sections twenty-eight to thirty-eight of SZ. These sections elaborate the existential constitution (the ontological structure) and the everydayness (fallenness) of the "There" of There-being. The "to-be-in," the "There" of There-being, is constituted by the moments (elements) of disposition (*Befindlichkeit*), comprehension (*Verstehen*), and logos (*Rede*).[3] This means that There-being is disposition, comprehension, and logos; these are the Being-characteristics of There-being,[4] the ways of "to-be" of There-being as "There." These elements must be understood in the ontological sense; they are ontological structures and not merely ontic qualities. According to Heidegger the intention of this investigation is "*a fundamental-ontological one.*"[5] To consider as ontic affirmations the ontological statements of SZ would mean precisely a basic misunderstanding leading to a false interpretation of the problem of God in this context. The equal-originality of the constitutive moments, interpreted according to the intention and the point of view of Heidegger, provides a key to the right meaning of the "negative" attitude of SZ toward the philosophical God-question. This is the reason why the phenomenon of equal-originality may be called, and regarded as, a principle of demythologization, the source of unity referred to in the preceding questions. For the sake of clarity about the issue at hand, it should be mentioned, however, that Heidegger himself does not reflect on the problem of God in connection with the equal-originality. It seems, nevertheless, that an occasion presents itself here for comprehending the source of the "indifference" and of the general "destructive" attitude of SZ in regard to the problem of God. In order to clarify the meaning of this principle[6] of equal-originality and its implications for the problem of God, it is necessary to examine (though very briefly) Heidegger's understanding of disposition, comprehension, and logos.

Disposition (*Befindlichkeit*) means that There-being somehow is aware of its situation, of its ways of being, in the World. There-being finds itself in the World as already-having-been, as already thrown into its "There"; there is a primordial disclosure of There-being to itself in its thrownness (*Geworfenheit*), in the fact that its facticity (*Faktizität*) is delivered over to There-being (the elements of existence that are given and not chosen do not represent a brute fact but rather something to be done with). Disposition includes not only the disclosure of There-being in its thrownness to itself but also the disclosure of the World as a whole that renders possible for There-being to direct (to turn) itself to things. There-being is (the fact, the given aspect of its Being) and has to be (the task, the chosen aspect of its Being). There-being (as it already is in the World) is not the author of its facticity but the recipient of it. There-being has its "to-be" as a task; it is given to it "to-be" (*zu sein*) as an assignment, as something to be chosen and "lived," as something to be concerned with (openness to Being, to its own "to-be"). The existence of There-being (its mode of being, of "to-be") is not a mere fact but a task still to be accomplished. This task-character of its existence comes from (becomes clear in the light of) its thrownness; the phenomenon of thrownness, then, represents the unity of the factness (givenness) and of the taskness (chosen, still to be accomplished) of There-being. Disposition, that is, There-being as already having found itself as "There" in the World (thus the exact terminology corresponding to *Befindlichkeit*, as suggested by Richardson: the already-having-found-itself-there-ness of There-being), does not only disclose the existence of There-being (There-being's Being as existence); it also discloses simultaneously the World because There-being is to-be-in-the-World. Finally, this disclosedness shows the basic dependence (*Angewiesenheit*) of There-being on the World and on the ontological structure of this referred-ness (dependence) as rendering possible the ontic encounter with beings. This kind of disclosure in the ontological disposition is not identical with the usually understood notion of knowledge (*Erkennen*); it is rather a process of "finding," a certain type of "awareness" of the "affective order" that somehow lets There-being "know" experientially (lets There-being be "aware of") the "how" of its "to-be" and leads There-being to its own Being precisely as "There."[7] The terms "mood" (*Stimmung*) and "being attuned" (*Gestimmtsein*) are used here by Heidegger as expressions of the thrownness of There-being (as having an essential existential significance) and not as merely psychological descriptions of feelings and affections (ontic qualities).[8] It is crucial, therefore, to distinguish between the ontological disposition and the many ontic phenomena, between the ontological and the ontic levels of analysis. The main thing here is that disposition as the primordial disclosure of There-being is an ontological disposition; it refers to the ontological constitution (to the Being-structure) of the "There."

The second constitutive element of the "There" of There-being is comprehension (*Verstehen*). This is the distinguishing characteristic of There-being, because by comprehending the Being of beings and the Being of its own being, There-being gains access to beings. This comprehension is an ontological comprehension and not an ontic understanding. Because There-being has an antecedent comprehension of the Being-structure (ontological knowledge), it is able to encounter beings (ontical knowledge). There-being precisely as "There" is disclosedness, luminosity, and seeing ("sight") (*Sicht*) on the ontological level before the ontic relation takes place. Comprehension is a potentiality (*Möglichkeit*), a "dynamism," a "tension," a "task" in the existential sense. This existential potentiality to comprehend renders possible the existentiell capacity (the many concrete potentialities) of knowing. There-being is a "power-to-be" (*Seinkönnen*), a dynamism to be and to become; the potentiality of comprehension is given to There-being as its own Being, as the existential Being of its own "power-to-be," as an existential. There-being is a project (*Entwurf*), a power to discern Being-structures and to progress in the "dialogue" or encounter with beings. There-being as project has a pre-comprehension of its structures, and as projected it "builds" these structures through the life of encounter; There-being projects the Being-structures. Comprehension as a project includes a comprehension of the World[9] both because There-being projects itself and because it is to-be-in-the-World. Therefore, there is a simultaneous comprehending of the World and of the "to-be-in." Comprehension means, then, the disclosedness of There-being as to-be-in-the-World.[10] The main conclusion, then, is that comprehension is an element of the disclosedness, of the luminosity of the "There." It is a project.

The third constitutive element of the "There" of There-being, of the disclosedness of the "There," is Logos (*Rede*). Logos expresses what There-being comprehends; it is an existential quality (element) of There-being as such. Logos is the existential-ontological foundation of language (*Sprache*) considered as the expression of There-being because There-being as to-be-in-the-World is already "outside" (*draussen*).[11] Language, therefore, is neither a process of "exteriorization" of an encapsulated (solipsistic, worldless) interiority nor merely an instrument of communication but rather a phenomenon of manifestation. Logos is a power of There-being; this power enables it to articulate (to express concretely) total meaningfulness (the World). Logos is a power of rendering or making "visible" meanings; it is "a power-to-let-be-seen what comprehension projects."[12] Logos is an ontological communication (*Mittelung*).[13] Through logos the total meaning of comprehensibility comes into words.[14] The life or the exercise of this power of manifestation might imply silence (*Schweigen*) or attending (*Hören*). Logos, then, is the ontological foundation of language and of expression.

These three elements or constitutive moments of the "There"

form a *unity*, and they are *equally original (gleichursprünglich)*. Heidegger insists on this existential unity and primordiality; he emphasizes the ontological significance of the phenomenon of equal-originality.[15] The essential unity of the three constitutive moments, however, is not explained by Heidegger. He insists on the *fact* of this unity, but he does not elaborate on how to understand it. W. J. Richardson, in view of this lack of clarification, proposes a hypothesis by saying that comprehension discloses There-being as transcendence, disposition as finite; and logos lets the process of disclosure be seen.[16] There-being as "There" is the "essential disclosedness" (*wesenhafte Erschlossenheit*) as the "There" of Being and has this disclosedness as a Being-structure.[17] There-being is disclosedness of the World and as the "There" it is comprehension, ontological disposition, and logos.

So far, one can understand to some extent the existential constitution of the "There" and the fact of unity of the components of this "There." This unity of the components of the "There" is a way of "to-be" and, at the same time, a principle of understanding according to Heidegger. From this point of view, then, he explains the everyday way of "to-be" of the "There" and the fallenness of There-being.

What is the import of these considerations for the examination of the problem of God according to SZ? What is the significance of the phenomenon of the equal-originality of the constitutive moments of the "There" of There-being for the question of God? Are there any implications of this equal-originality for the clarification of the origin of the question of God in Heidegger's phenomenology? Heidegger does not reflect directly on the issues raised by these questions. Nevertheless, his insights on the ontological significance of the equal-originality of the constitutive moments do respond indirectly, at least to some extent, to their main concern. In the same sentence where he insists on the equal-originality of the constitutive moments, he says that this equal originality was often forgotten in ontology and that this forgetting is a consequence of the unbridled tendency to demonstrate the *origin* (provenance) (*Herkunft*) of all things and to consider all beings as coming from a simple "original ground" (*Urgrund*).[18] The preoccupation with the "original ground" of things leads to the forgetfulness of the ontological problematic, of the phenomenon of equal-originality. This interpretation of the tendency to demonstrate the "original ground" represents a basic insight, a principle for Heidegger's way of understanding the problem of God. The question of God, according to the persistent claim by Heidegger's writings, was asked in the context of the search for the "original ground" of things. This approach to the problem of God is demy-thologized by Heidegger because it simply derives beings from one other being (the grounding being); it simply tells a "story" ("myth") about them; it forgets the ontological dimension of the search for the "ground." The search for the "original ground," then, becomes a search for God, and thus the ontological issue is forgotten. Therefore, his interpretation of the tendency to find and demonstrate the "orig-inal ground" of things functions in his writings as a basic insight, as a principle of understanding the traditional question of God; it emphasizes the ontological function and background of the question of God. The insight of equal-originality in SZ leads to an insight about the demythologization of the problem of God. Heidegger's preoccu-pation with the ontological problematic does not lead to the forget-fulness of the problem of God; it prepares the ground and calls for the rethinking of the question of God. Heidegger's principle regard-ing the search for the "original ground" of things is a source of objec-tions by him against the Cause-God (as this will be shown in Part III of this study).[19] The causal approach to the problem of God indicates the falling away from the exigencies of the ontological problematic. According to SZ the existential components of the "There" are the expressions of the modes of "to-be" of There-being. Knowledge, interpretation, and language are analyzed according to their ontolog-ical structures and not according to a scientific view of their ontical concretizations. Knowledge is an existential; it is the openness, the disclosedness, and the light of There-being as to-be-in-the-World (as being-in-the-World). The interpretation of knowing as seeing (ϑεωρία) includes a view of beings as mere entities (Vorhandenes) and ignores the existential meaning of knowing.[20] The richness of the World is lost in this view because it reduces all beings to the status of mere things. Thus, the World becomes an object viewed by the know-ing subject. There-being's view (Sicht) is something quite different from the Platonic vision; it is the disclosedness of There-being as a consequence of its thrownness (Geworfenheit); it is the transparency (Durchsichtigkeit) of There-being; it is the disclosedness of being-in-the-World.[21] The existential view of comprehension and that of There-being constitute the primal origin of the various kinds of think-ing and intuition.[22] The interpretation of logos by Plato and Aristotle as presented in this context by SZ foreshadows the reflections of ID and PW on the ontotheological structure of metaphysics.[23]

Finally, one can see a distantiation from theological problems in Heidegger's analysis of the fallenness (Verfallenheit) of There-being.

Fallenness is a way of "to-be" of There-being; it is an inauthentic mode of "to-be." The fallenness comes from finitude, from the everyday preoccupation with the ontical World. Fallenness is not just an accident: it is a positive potentiality (*Möglichkeit*) of There-being; it is the "not-to-be" of its own authentic self. This happens in the daily and usual commerce with things. There-being is lost in the World and fallen because of its factual (concrete) being in the World. There-being's fallenness cannot be interpreted as a "falling out" (*Fall auss*) from a higher status of being. We have neither an ontic experience of the "fall of There-being" from a higher "original state" nor the possible clues to its ontological interpretation.[24] Fallenness, in SZ, is an existential-ontological quality of There-being; it says nothing regarding the ontic, the metaphysical, and the cultural-historical aspects of the phenomenon of fallenness. The question of the ontic origin of fallenness is not considered in the existential analysis. Fallenness is not considered in relation to other beings encountered in the World. Therefore, the existential fallenness of There-being is not an ontic (and consequently, neither an anthropological nor a theological) judgment about the "corruption of human nature";[25] it is an ontological notion.

When faith and a worldview (*Weltanschauung*) speak of fallenness as a quality of There-being, they should take into account the existential structures of There-being and, hence, its existential fallenness.[26] This is an example of distantiation from theology and from anthropology. The reason for this distantiation is always the same: the fidelity to the ontological dimension.

The references of SZ to the problem of God express the ontological problematic; they do not represent an atheistic understanding of There-being. However, as indicated earlier, they imply, at least to some extent, a demythologization of some aspects of the traditional approach to the problem of God. This means that several classical ways of asking this question (such as the causal origin of all beings, the World as the trace of God) are eclipsed through the emphasis on the existential structures of There-being. This emphasis does not eliminate the problem of God as such; it suggests the exigency to inquire about the possibility of a new approach to this question. Heidegger also indicates, in this context, the need for rediscovering the authentic nature and the "originality" of theology as such. The "neutrality" of SZ does not preclude an openness toward other dimensions of There-being that are not considered in the existential analysis. The "There" of There-being is (ontological) disposition, comprehension, and logos. These constitutive elements of the "There" are unified ontologically. It should not be forgotten at the same time that the ontological structures (the constitutive elements) are ontically (existentielly) rooted and concretized; their ontic ramifications account for the diversity of understanding human existence as well as for the development of worldviews and ideological perspectives. The ontological, existential task, however, remains at a well-justified distance from these ontic concerns; it keeps philosophy immune from "alien" (pragmatic) and ideological interests. The "translation" (explicitation) of experience (awareness) into language through understanding, then, may take many forms (on the ontic level), even though this diversity is an "expression" of the same basic unified ontological structures. (The same ontological disposition, then, may be related to several ontic reactions and feelings; the same comprehension may allow for several ontic understandings; the same logos may be at work in various ontic languages.)

The description of the ontological structures does not suppress the problematics of the ontic level. The problem of God so far as it belongs to the ontic level, therefore, is still there, and it is not resolved by the existential analysis of There-being, that is, by the clarification of the ontological structures of There-being. The equal-originality of the constitutive moments is limited to the "There" as finite transcendence. This is the characteristic of the this-worldliness of the existential analysis. According to Heidegger's perspective, the question of "origin" calls to a halt the thinking of the ontological problematic. It may be suggested as an alternative, however, that the question of the "origin" (ground) of beings can be asked in such a way that it may represent a "going forward" (taking the right step) to the discernment of the equal-originality of disposition, comprehension, and logos. The knowledge of equal-originality is not given in the beginning of the search; it is discovered rather slowly in the process of questioning. The question regarding the "origin" of beings, according to the context of SZ under discussion, is situated within the perspective of ontic understanding; it is not unrelated, however, to ontological comprehension. Might not this kind of understanding lead to the discovery of unified ontological structures precisely through the awareness of the diversification of the ontological structures in their ontical concretizations? This is a reasonable question. The issue at stake here is the contribution of the ontic (scientific, anthropological) understanding to the ontological comprehension. If the existential is indeed rooted within the existentiell (the ontic), then ontic (experiential) knowledge ought to be quite significant for ontological knowledge (comprehension, disposition, logos). If this would be the answer to the preceding question, then the equal-originality principle (as discussed previously) may not remain as a mere principle of demythologization of the question of God; it would, much rather, require a simultaneous rethinking of the question of the "origin" of beings and of the entire traditional problem of God. Heidegger's thought after SZ includes the questioning and the rethinking of the question of God but only as an element of the development of his "new step" toward Being beyond SZ. Therefore, the response to the preceding question is contained in the development of Heidegger's thought. The existentials, according to Heidegger's emphasis, are rooted in the existentiell situations assuring their "reality"; they are not abstract concepts without foundation in "reality"; they are, ultimately, existentielly grounded. Is there an existentiell ground (root) to the equal-originality of the existential components of the "There" of Therebeing? Why are the existential components of the "There" equally original? The connection between the ontic aspects and the ontological dimensions of human reality, and the relationship between ontic understanding and ontological comprehension, ought not to be ignored in dealing with these concerns. Heidegger seems simply to presuppose and adopt the idea of equal-originality without explaining the why and the existentiell root of it. Here, therefore, can be seen the strengths as well as the weaknesses of the principle of equal-originality of the constitutive moments of the "There" that functions as a source (or at least as a background) for the demythologization of the problem of God in philosophy. The principle of equal-originality leads to some significant insights and conclusions regarding the problem of God; it views the question (understanding) of the "origin" of beings as an ontic issue. These considerations prepare the background for the examination of the foundational differences between the question of God and the question of Being.

According to SZ meaning (*Sinn*) is an existential of Therebeing; the question about meaning is asked in relation to There-being as to-be-in-the-World.[27] This context of the question of meaning tells something about the limits and the limitations of the existential analysis. The nature of the religious experience and the philosophical significance of a possible transcendence toward God remain unexamined by SZ in spite of the fact that Heidegger allows for this (religious, faith, divine) dimension of the total experience of There-being. Is there a hermeneutical "as" (*als*) proper to religious experience? The concretization, the "incarnation" of meaning as it is found in religious experience may be significant for the inquiry regarding a new approach to the problem of God. A more comprehensive phenomenology of There-being, therefore, ought to analyze the religious dimension of being-in-the-World. This way of questioning (the examination of the religious transcendence) is not pursued by SZ; the probing, then, needs to go on.

The demythologization of the problem of God, therefore, is not an indication of an atheistic answer to the unresolved problems of SZ. The demythologization is the result of the philosophical questioning about meaning and Being itself insofar as this can be elaborated through the existential analysis of There-being.

The Structural Unity of There-being

The more the existential analysis unfolds, the more it becomes possible to observe in it a distancing from those topics that are connected with the problem of God. Despite the fact that these topics appear in the more descriptive parts of the analysis, where their ontological dimension is discovered, they are easily dismissed because they belong to the ontic characteristics of beings (mainly of There-being); they often become an obstacle to the understanding of the problem of Being. Christian theology and anthropology as such are not rejected; they are regarded as the historical adaptations of the Aristotelian ontology and, consequently, as incapable of adequately analyzing the question of Being. Anxiety, faith, love, contrition, the notion of truth and that of reality—all these receive a place in the understanding of the Being of There-being as concern (*Sorge*); their possible relation to the notion of God, however, remains practically ignored by SZ. This situation obliges Heidegger to discern the limits of his philosophy and to point out some immediate conclusions, conclusions that can be easily misunderstood (such as the claim that there are no "eternal truths"). Here, again, the final perspective of SZ does not represent atheism but rather a process of demythologization. This means the metamorphosis of the philosophical problem of God, because the traditional approach is eclipsed by some basic insights and principles of the existential analysis. The problem of God, then, still remains, and it really becomes a problem precisely because of the process of demythologization. Therefore, it is more appropriate to speak of a phenomenological problem of God in Heidegger than of a phenomenological atheism or simply of a philosophy of the "death of God." The transformation of the philosophical God-question and the distancing from theological (and anthropological) problems can be understood properly only in the context of the interpretation of There-being as finite transcendence. The more deeply one enters into the analysis of There-being, the more one is confronted with the this-worldliness of Heidegger's philosophy. The attention of the following reflections is focused on these aspects and connotations of the structural unity of There-being.

The structural unity of There-being is found by Heidegger in the phenomenon of *concern* (*Sorge*) that contributes to the preparation of the question about the meaning of Being as such.[1] The whole analysis of There-being is geared toward this final purpose (the Being-question). After the "dissection" of There-being into its structural elements, the question of *unity* arises. What is the unity of all the structural elements? How can we understand the Being of There-being as the source of this unity? The answer to these questions lies in There-being's structural unity as concern. The interpretation of There-being as concern is based on the phenomenon of anxiety (*Angst*). There-being is defined by facticity and existentiality; it always finds itself as being in a situation of thrownness and as having a task to be accomplished (There-being is project). Facticity and existentiality are "lived" for the most part in fallenness because There-being is dispersed in the World and is dominated by ontical preoccupation with beings. The constant dependence on beings and fallenness reveal the flight from authenticity and give evidence of finitude. The everyday mode of "to-be" of There-being, however, covers up the meaning of There-being's Being and consequently makes it difficult to understand itself as a structural unity. The true meaning of There-being's Being is disclosed only when it is confronted with its own Being, when it is brought before its own Being. This situation or confrontation is brought about in the relatively rare phenomenon of *anxiety*.[2] The phenomenon of anxiety is understood here as an ontological disposition (*Grundbefindlichkeit*). This anxiety discloses the true Being of There-being and renders possible the interpretation of the structural unity of There-being.[3] Existential anxiety is not to be identified with fear (*Furcht*) because fear always refers only to a particular being or thing according to its concrete aspect(s) "here and now."[4] Anxiety has an ontological-existential meaning for Heidegger; it refers not to a particular being but rather to the World as World, to the World as such.[5] In anxiety There-being is confronted with the World (Being) as such and with itself. It is not a particular being that seems to slip away, but the whole World; it is not a fear of being "hurt" but a "fear" of (and for) itself; it is not a local or temporal event that is disclosed but the profound possibility of authenticity and inauthenticity. This most profound possibility is disclosed because in the phenomenon of anxiety the daily familiarity with beings is lost and thus There-being discovers that the World of its daily preoccupations is not its true "home" (*Unheimlichkeit*). In anxiety There-being is concerned about itself and for itself as to-be-in-the-World. Therefore, anxiety discloses in a special way the Being of There-being as concern.[6] Anxiety shows that in the phenomenon of concern the structural elements of There-being are unified as the Being of There-being. Concern is the Being of There-being, the meaning of There-being. Anxiety discloses all the three elements or ontological characteristics (facticity, existentiality, fallenness) of There-being as to-be-in-the-World. The unity of these three elements in the Being of There-being is concern. This means that There-being is concerned about its own Being (existentiality), that is, with being free for the potentialities of authenticity and inauthenticity, all of which bring There-being to an awareness of its thrownness into the World (facticity), and that in the World it is to be concerned with beings in the World (fallenness). Concern, then, is the structural unity of There-being. This formulation of concern expresses a basic conclusion of the existential analysis.

Heidegger insists that concern is to be understood as the expression of the structural unity of There-being and not as a psychological (ontic) characteristic. Concern is to be understood as a whole, as the Being of There-being. The misunderstanding of concern may be brought about by the differing interpretations of the phenomenon of anxiety. Heidegger presents an ontological and not an ontic interpretation of anxiety. Christian theology and anthropology often considered the phenomena of fear and anxiety, but generally they interpreted them on the ontic level, though in some instances they reached an ontological understanding of them.[7] Theological or anthropological considerations of these phenomena were concerned with metaphysical and ontical questions, such as man's relationship to God, faith, love, sin, and contrition. In all these theological interpretations of anxiety, the ontological dimension of this phenomenon is lost. They do not elaborate an existential analysis of There-being at all, and, in particular, they fail to understand the ontological disposition as such (*Befindlichkeit*).

Here one should add to Heidegger's remarks that even these unsuccessful efforts to reach an ontological interpretation (together with the metaphysical aspects of anxiety) concur with the following insight developed by the existential analysis: the phenomenon of anxiety discloses somehow the very "nature" of man as finite transcendence; it discloses There-being and renders possible a primordial comprehension of the structure of There-being. These efforts are indeed a sign of the special function and place of anxiety in the search for the "definition" of the Being of There-being. Anxiety constitutes a truly fundamental structure of the human being as such and reveals the innermost possibilities of human existence.[8] The metaphysical and the anthropological dimensions of anxiety are ultimately rooted in the ontological (disposition) nature of anxiety.

There-being is concern and concern as such cannot be reduced to an ontic quality of a being. Concern is, indeed, the Being of There-being. The reason for this irreducibility is simply that "Being cannot be 'explained' through being."[9] Here lies the difficulty in dealing with the Being-question. However, it is quite clear that the problem of the ontological difference is already present in this context. Being cannot be reduced to a mere quality of a being; the structural unity of There-being cannot be reduced to (or considered as) a more original element in the ontic sense. The ontological question cannot be resolved through a metaphysical reduction of Being to a being.

Here SZ finds the ground for an objection to the idea of God as the highest being. God as the highest being was functioning in the history of philosophy as a refuge from and a solution to the more radical question about the meaning of Being. The metaphysical, anthropological, and theological interpretations of concern as well as those of anxiety and Being have lost the clear awareness of the depth of the question of Being as such; they do not speak, therefore, of the Being of There-being (they do not have to focus on it). Heidegger does not intend to reject these ontical interpretations in themselves; he says only that he cannot accept them as the answer to the questions about the meaning of Being and about the Being of There-being. This assessment is part of the process of demythologization. Heidegger is interested in unearthing the ontological root and foundation of the anthropological interpretations of the phenomenon of concern.

He says that he came to this (existential) "idea" of concern (or rather the "idea" came to him—according to his aphorism on the experience of thinking) when he was studying Augustinian anthropology; there he discovered the pre-ontological interpretation of There-being as concern.[10] The ontological understanding of concern, therefore, is not a rejection but rather a further development of the traditional problem about the "essence" of man. The existential analysis, in a way, definitely limits the "greatness" of man; it considers the human being as finite transcendence and as finding meaning to existence in temporality. This "limiting," however, is not an exclusion but, much rather, a "bracketing" of (a suspension of judgment about) the theological interpretation of the "essence" and destiny of the human being, of the human condition.

The structural unity of There-being as concern has important implications for the problems of truth and reality. The following examination of these issues aims to clarify a seemingly "atheistic" statement of SZ. These ideas indicate a significant aspect of the process of demythologization.

Heidegger shows the ontological problem implied in idealism and in realism. These options represent inadequate perspectives on reality because they reduce beings to consciousness (subject) or make consciousness into a thing (object); they introduce into the World the dichotomy of subjectivity and objectivity. This means ontologically that they try to explain Being through beings; they identify a mode of Being (the real) with Being itself (reality ultimately). Through the existential analysis the whole question of reality and ideality, of realism and idealism, is changed. The comprehension of Being, the disclosure of the World, There-being as to-be-in-the-World, There-being's luminosity constitute the new "elements" of the whole problem. Reality ultimately depends on concern as Being depends on the comprehension of Being.[11] The whole problem of reality is "replaced" by the question about Being and by the comprehension of Being through There-being as to-be-in-the-World. The understanding of reality is founded on the phenomenon of the World and not on an a priori epistemological presupposition. There is no sense to speak of the World without man, and there is no sense to speak of man without the World in the context of the existential analysis. Man (There-being) *is* already in the World; there is no need for him to "go out" in order to reach the World. For Heidegger the true "scandal" of philosophy is not that philosophers were unable (unsuccessful) to find an irreproachable argument for the existence of the World (reality), as Kant had said, but rather the very fact that they were trying to find such an argument and that they even raised this question. According to SZ the ontological grounding of reality is related to the Being of There-being as to-be-in-the-World; the awareness (knowledge) of reality is a mode of to-be-in-the-World. The understanding of reality is related to the understanding of There-being. The notion of There-being, then, plays a central role in the existential-phenomenological approach to the entire question of reality. The understanding of *truth* in SZ undergoes a change; the understanding of reality changes in a similar way. The close relationship between truth and Being, the "identification" of truth and Being, is already attested to in Greek philosophy, as Heidegger points out. The theory of judgment as the "place" of truth, and the notion of truth as conformity between the intellect (*intellectus*) and the thing (*res*), are now reexamined by Heidegger.

SZ develops a new, existential orientation toward and a deeper understanding of the notion of truth. The study of There-being prepares the ground for the rediscovery of the question of Being; the phenomenon of truth is interpreted by SZ in this context. The structural unity of There-being is concern. Since concern constitutes the Being of There-being as to-be-in-the-World, it follows that There-being receives an important function in the new understanding of truth. Truth is an existential of There-being. The truth of an expression (*Aussage*), of a judgment (*Urteil*), is not the result of an assimilation of the object by the intellect but the consequence of the discoverability of beings and of the discovering attitude of There-being.[12] The expression (assertion) that is true shows forth being as it is; it is a letting be seen of being(s) in its (their) discoveredness (*Entdecktheit*).[13] Truth, then, depends on discovering. The truth of the expression (judging truly), of knowing, therefore, means having (exercising) a discovering attitude toward (*entdeckendes Sein zum*) the real being itself.[14] This discovering attitude is made possible through the structure of There-being as to-be-in-the-World.[15] The structure of to-be-in-the-World is the foundation of the phenomenon of truth. To discover is a way of "to-be" of There-being and, therefore, There-being is the "foundation" of truth.[16] Why is this "privilege" given to There-being? Because There-being as concern is already in the World preoccupied with beings; it is indeed discovering beings in the World. A being as encountered in the World is "there" because it is discovered; There-being is "there" in a more original sense because it is discovering.[17] There-being *is* a *discovering* being. The disclosedness

(*Erscholossenheit*) of There-being leads us to the original phenomenon of truth. The process of founding truth may be resumed as follows: beings can be discovered because of the disclosedness of the World *and* because of the disclosedness of the "There" of There-being, the luminosity of the "There" as disclosing the World, as a way of "to-be" of There-being. Beings are true because they are discovered, but There-being is true because it *is* disclosedness. Therefore, "There-being is 'in the truth.' "[18] This is an ontological-existential statement, and it means that disclosedness belongs to the very Being of There-being. Truth, then, is not merely the conformity between the judgment and the judged but disclosedness, a letting be seen of beings, a bringing them out of the "chaos."[19] Ontologically, then, truth is the "place" of the judgment (and expression); it is the ontological condition of possibility of true (or false) judgment (and expression). For the classical perspective, in contrast, judgment and expression are the "place" of truth; they are more primordial and foundational than truth. For Heidegger, then, truth is more primordial and foundational than the judgment.[20]

"There-being is 'in the truth.' " This affirmation has important consequences. Because disclosedness belongs to the very Being of a being called "There-being," and because the structure of There-being includes a preoccupation with beings (concern) and not merely to-be-in-the-World, then, together with the disclosedness of There-being is given "equally originally" (*gleichursprünglich*) the discoveredness of beings in the World. There-being is thrown; therefore, the disclosedness is factual; that is, it is situated in a "concrete" world (that is mine, having its special qualities in space and time). There-being is a project (*Entwurf*); it can choose its own mode of "to-be." Disclosedness as a mode "to-be," consequently, is the truth of existence (what There-being truly is). Truth is a mode of authenticity.[21] However, because There-being is fallen (*Verfallenheit*) and can choose inauthenticity—that is, it can be lost in the daily commerce with things—it is also in the "untruth."[22] To be in the untruth means to cover up beings and to close off There-being itself. Truth belongs to the comprehension of Being. In the same way that Being can be misinterpreted, so truth can be distorted. The historical destiny of truth depends on the degree of the authenticity and on the degree of the inauthenticity of There-being's existence.

The notion of There-being, then, plays a focal role in the existential-phenomenological interpretation of truth. Being is insofar as comprehension of Being (that is, There-being) is; truth is insofar as disclosedness (of There-being) is. The way of living of There-being in the World is at the same time a "life" of Being, of truth, and of beings. Heidegger formulates quite clearly the presuppositions of as well as the consequences that follow from his conception of truth. He claims that all truth is relative to, related to, the Being of There-being.[23] We must presuppose (*voraussetzen*) that truth is given (that truth is) because we exist in the mode of "to-be" (*Seinsart*) of There-being and, thus, we *are* "in the truth."[24] It is indeed truth itself that makes possible any presupposition. There-being is a presupposing being already, both because it is determined by disclosedness and discovery and because it *is* concern, its very life being in the World (to-be-in-the-World).[25] Here, again, it is easy to see the focal role of There-being in this philosophy. The notion of truth, the concept of Being, and the comprehension of Being cannot be spoken of without There-being. The awareness of this central function of There-being is something essential for the right understanding of the "atheistic" aspects and connotations of the existential analysis. A simple comparison of the phenomenological notions of truth, Being, and reality and the meaning of these same notions according to other philosophical systems would contribute very little toward the understanding of the questions of theism and atheism in SZ.

All this may appear as a form of complete relativism. In a certain sense, it does represent an epistemological (and even ontological) relativism. Truth is disclosedness, discoveredness; it is the coming forth (of beings) from the dark into the light, a breaking-out from the enclosure and a breaking-into the disclosure. Truth is essentially historical and relational. It is a progressing disclosure, a process of enlightening, and not an object of possession once and for all. In SZ the finitude and the function of There-being are emphasized in connection with all the main themes of the existential analysis. This attention focused on There-being, however, does not mean a detour from the examination of the question of Being; the task of SZ is ontological and not anthropological. The other (later) works of Heidegger speak more (differently) of Being; their attention is focused more (differently, directly) on Being. The renewed, refocused attention to Being, in spite of the change in language, is the unfolding of the discovery of the question of Being in SZ. The unity and the continuity of Heidegger's thought (the question of Being) are manifested in all his writings; the purpose of the existential analysis is the comprehension of Being so far as it is made possible through the comprehension of the Being of There-being. The notion of (and the emphasis on)

There-being as a discovering, disclosing being, its central role in interpreting the notion of truth and the meaning of Being, then, do not
distract from the way toward Being.

In the context of the existential-phenomenological notion of
truth, one should not be surprised (at least not too much) by Heidegger's statement on "eternal truths." Since truth is only insofar as
there is There-being (discoveredness and disclosedness are only as
long as there is There-being),[26] the existence of "eternal truths" could
be justified only by proving that There-being was always existing and
that it will be always existing eternally. Without this argument, which
is impossible in the existential analysis, the affirmation of "eternal
truths" is nothing other than a "fantastic contention" (*phantastische
Behauptung*) that cannot gain validity by the claim that most philosophers believed in them, that is, in "eternal truths."[27] The (philosophical) affirmation of the existence of "eternal truths," according to SZ,
is nothing but a remnant of Christian theology in a set of philosophical problems, a remnant that has not as yet been radically expelled
from the realm of philosophy (the same is true of the philosophy of
the "absolute subject").[28] The notion of There-being as finite (finite
transcendence) and the existential interpretation of truth preclude
the affirmation of "eternal truths." There-being is being-unto-death
(*Sein zum Tode*), marked by death in its innermost structure. Truth is
truth for and of There-being. Truth is a structure (a function) of
There-being as "There" (luminosity and disclosure). And because
There-being is finite, truth is temporal; there is no sense of speaking
of "eternal truths."

The universality of truth is not the mark of eternity but a consequence of the existential notion of truth (discovery) as the way of
"to-be" of There-being.[29] We all are There-beings and this is the constitutive element of the "universal validity" of truth. Finitude and
temporality are evidenced through the World and through transcendence. There-being achieves an authentic mode of existence precisely
by accepting freely its innermost potentiality: its immanent ending
(death), its "Being-toward-the-end."[30] Man's existence is finite and this
finitude is the hallmark of human life. Facticity (*Faktizität*) limits man's
possibilities and he has to be himself in his World as thrown-already
and as still-to-be-achieved. This philosophy is based on man's concrete
situation and not on some speculative "insights." Heidegger's phenomenology is a hermeneutical phenomenology; it is a hermeneutics
of facticity.[31] The existential analysis (SZ) is structured by the finitude
of human existence as such. This affirmation of finitude cannot be

taken as a denial of the possibility of other dimensions of There-being. Heidegger can speak even of a renewed theology[32] and of a philosophical reflection on the eternity of God,[33] although he remains silent about the "how" of this sort of reflection.

These seemingly marginal aspects of the existential analysis show that an atheistic interpretation of the reference to the existence of "eternal truths" would be a misunderstanding of SZ. The openness of human existence toward the idea of a divine God appears as the accompanying "shadow" of the rethinking of the notion of Being in several works of Heidegger. Heidegger, in SZ, simply rejects the philosophical argument and the philosophical notion of truth implied in the classical affirmation of the existence of "eternal truths." His understanding of truth is an ontological interpretation of truth as such; he analyzes the notion (essence) of truth in relation to There-being. Heidegger's writings describe the original connection of Being itself with the phenomenon of truth, and, thus, they establish a new way of thinking the problem of God.

This consideration of the structural unity of There-being as concern constitutes the completion of the demythologizing process. The understanding of There-being as concern limits the field of There-being's "view" to "this" World and defines the notion of truth as a function of There-being. There is no direct reference to the problem of God here; yet this phase of the existential analysis remains important for the examination of this problem. The "nature" of the human being and the World is defined in such a way that there is no need in this context to ask the traditional question of God in connection with the notion of the World and human existence. The existential analysis points to the unacceptable dimensions of the God-question and shows that the philosophical idea of God entered into the traditional concepts of truth and knowledge. Clarification begins with this kind of demythologization—a demythologization proposing not an atheistic philosophy but preparing the ground for the question about the meaning of Being. The process of demythologization by itself, therefore, is not atheistic in the sense that as an aspect of her-meneutical phenomenology it would require the denial of God; demythologization is merely a byproduct, an indirect consequence of the ontological (existential) interpretation of There-being. The process of demythologization is completed in this phase of the existential analysis because the structural unity of There-being, i.e., concern, implies both the "new" notion of truth and the radical incapacity of escaping from the immanent ending of There-being as finite transcendence.

The next step of the existential analysis gives only the final conclusions of the present analysis by situating the meaning of There-being (and that of Being) in temporality (the ecstatic notion of timeliness).[34]

13

The Totality
of There-being
and the
Ultimate Questions

The process of demythologization has already been clarified in the preceding reflections. Concern as the structural unity of There-being represents the culmination of the demythologization aspects of SZ; it leads to the final step in the examination of the existential analysis. The main task of this study consists in following the development of Heidegger's phenomenology insofar as it has something to say about the problem of God. The pursuit of this perspective on SZ disclosed the demythologization of the problem of God as an indirect consequence of the existential analysis. The examination of the structural unity of There-being as concern contributed significantly to the understanding of the nature of demythologization. The following analysis of the totality of There-being includes several issues that are related to the problem of God. The reflection on these issues represents the final stage of the process of demythologization in SZ. The existential interpretations of death, time, history, conscience, and the meaning of existence by SZ, belong to the understanding of the totality of There-being; they raise the ultimate questions regarding There-being. What is death? What is the meaning of death? What is history? What is the nature of time? What is conscience? What is the meaning, the ultimate structure and significance, of human existence? What is the final significance of death for the conduct of life? Traditionally, these questions were elaborated in relationship with the problem of God and also formed part of the philosophy of religion. In the existential analysis, however, these questions receive another meaning because their ontological significance transcends the atheistic as well as the theistic interpretations of human reality.

The totality of There-being is disclosed in the phenomenon of death. The structural unity of There-being as concern has manifested this finitude already, but this finitude was considered only in the context of the life of There-being. Now, the consideration of the totality of There-being embraces the entire dimension of existence and asks the question about the meaning of existence. The examination of death and the question of "afterlife" belong to this part of the existential analysis. Death reveals the totality of There-being, and, thus, it manifests the meaning of the ultimate questions regarding human existence.

The phenomenon of *death* is the seal of finitude. Death is an existential, a way of "to-be" of There-being. This means that death is not merely an end but, rather, a basic characteristic of the whole life of There-being. It is indeed the most personal and the greatest, the most certain and the most indeterminate, the final and the most authentic potentiality (*Seinkönnen, Seinsmöglichkeit*) of There-being.[1] Death as the greatest potentiality of There-being is understood by Heidegger as "the potentiality (possibility, *Möglichkeit*) of the impotence (impossibility, *Unmöglichkeit*) of existence altogether."[2] There-being is destined to death; it is a being characterized by finitude, by "to-be-unto-death" (*Sein zum Tode*).[3] Death belongs to the very core of There-being, to what There-being truly is. There-being *is* "to-be-unto-death." This "to-be-unto-death" is the most original concretization (real life expression) of concern as the Being of There-being;[4] "to-be-unto-death" is the definition of There-being in its totality. Existence (project), facticity, and fallenness are ontologically unified in the phenomenon of death; they are understood as concern, as the totality of There-being. Concern, then, belongs to the ontological grounding of death and dying. Death, therefore, is not something extrinsic to the human being but, rather, something intrinsic to it; it is a continual internal threat, the nontransferable phenomenon of the process of ending, the way of "to-be" of human reality. Death as the continual ending (according to the verbal sense of "end-ing") of There-being (*Tod als Enden des Daseins; Sein zum Ende*) is the greatest limitation of There-being that permeates its entire existence all the time. Death is a fundamental structure, the very essence, the way of life of There-being; it is the phenomenon of the wholeness of There-being. This is an existential-ontological interpretation of death; it is neither a metaphysical nor an anthropological (psychological) description. The existential-ontological analysis of death as the end(ing) of There-being as being-in-the-World does not include the ontic decision regarding the possibility of survival or immortality of There-being beyond death.[5]

Since death is the greatest and the most personal (inner) potentiality of There-being, authenticity consists in the acceptance of this innermost finitude and in the readiness for the actualization of this potentiality. This exceptional potentiality of There-being is realized (lived, actualized) through continually choosing authenticity, through re-solve (*Entschlossenheit*).[6] Resolve, therefore, is an exceptional way of disclosedness (*Erschlossenheit*) of There-being, and, because of this, the original truth of There-being is achieved in it (in resolve).[7] Death contains a revelation. The understanding of resolve as disclosedness is obvious, since in resolve there is a recollection and an awareness of the true nature of one's existence. Resolve, then, is the manifestation of the acceptance of the true existence of the "self" and an overcoming of the daily flight from a genuine confrontation with one's real situation. An important act of resolve, a decision that involves the whole of a personality, always manifests (discloses) the true nature of personal existence. This existential understanding of resolve as disclosedness, therefore, is confirmed by daily experience and by depth psychology as well. Heidegger claims that There-being is all too often lost, dispersed, in the daily commerce with things (beings) and lives in the state of inauthenticity. There-being lives in the state of fallenness. The constitutive moments of There-being (disposition, comprehension, and logos) now (in the phenomenon of death, in anxiety) reveal the totality of There-being as finite transcendence. Existential authenticity consists in comprehending, in being-aware of this immanent finitude, and in having a comprehending acceptance of "to-be-unto-death," in being free and ready for death (*Freiheit zum Tode, Sein zum Tode*).[8] The ontic condition of existential authenticity (in "freedom-toward-death") is the free choice of this authenticity through resolve and by means of listening to the voice of conscience (*Gewissen*).[9] The analysis of conscience and guilt (*Schuld*) clarifies this relationship between the existential (comprehension of death, being free toward death) and the existentiell (choice or acceptance of death) meanings of authenticity. In this context, one can see a distancing from theological issues because all the traditional connotations of guilt and conscience remain outside the existential analysis. *Conscience,* for Heidegger, is a call of concern (*Ruf der Sorge*).[10] Conscience calls There-being in the situation of uncanniness (expatriation, *Unheimlichkeit*); it calls There-being back to authenticity; it invites There-being to leave the emptiness and the "taken-for-granted" qualities of everyday existence. Conscience, then, is for There-being a form of logos because it lets the situation be seen and understood. Conscience reveals the true nature of There-being; it allows understanding of the existential guilt (finitude, nothingness) of There-being and calls There-being back to an authentic way of existence (death as resolve). Conscience is neither an alien power nor a divine power (or consciousness);[11] it is a "fact"; it is the way of "to-be" of There-being.[12] It is There-being who is the caller (the voice of conscience, There-being as authentic existence, the ontological disposition) and the called on (There-being in the situation of fallenness, in the state of homelessness). Conscience is, then, like a nostalgia for a better home or a remembering of the true potentialities of existence. The easy association of conscience with remembering is another indication of the existentiell roots of the existential interpretation of conscience.

The phenomenon of anxiety (death, uncanniness) wakes up There-being and discloses the existential *guilt* as a structure of There-being's existence. There-being is, in its most profound Being, guilty; There-being is a ground of negativity.[13] The guiltiness and the ground of negativity mean that There-being is thrown and that it always remains behind its potentialities; it is living in changing modes of inauthenticity. The thrownness and the limitation of There-being belong to the very existence of There-being as a project. The potentialities of There-being are not potentialities that are chosen by There-being. Rather There-being is thrown into its potentialities. There-being never can be a ground of its potentialities; it can only accept them. It has no power over the ground, and this lack of power belongs to the facticity of There-being's existence. It is clear, therefore, that the guiltiness of There-being cannot be identified with the notion of inauthenticity. There-being can listen to the voice of conscience and achieve authenticity (in resolve) through freedom (disponibility to and readiness for the voice of conscience),[14] but it cannot escape from its immanent finitude.[15] Responsibility, then, leads to the discovery disclosure) of guiltiness, because it discloses the lack of power to master the potentialities according to the demand of conscience. There-being as such is already guilty, and because of *this* guiltiness one can speak of the guiltiness of an act or of conscience as remorse.

The existential notions of guilt and conscience as such belong to the Being of There-being; they are phenomena of There-being and represent ontological potentialities; they precede (are more primordial than) any anthropological, psychological, and theological notions of guilt and conscience.[16] The choice of authentic existence consists in the free acceptance of death, in the liberating openness toward the always present ending of There-being. Death is not the terminus but, rather, the focus of the life of There-being. The acceptance of death is the meaning of "being-free-for-death" as a consequence of resolve. This attitude of freedom consists in the acceptance of existence as project, as thrown, and as fallen. The meaning of existence, of living, is not the liberation from but the being free for death. This is the foundational answer to the ultimate questions in the context of the existential analysis. The distancing from the theological and from the anthropological dimensions of finitude and death is clear enough in order to confine the existential interpretation to its own limits and thus to separate it from any other kind of interpretation. Death and nothingness represent the final response to the ultimate questions from the point of view of the existential analysis. Heidegger himself raises this question: *"Does-the-to-be-in-the-World have a higher instance (authority) for its power-to-be (Seinkönnen) than its own death?"*[17] Death as the final answer to the question regarding the meaning of human existence is nothing else but the comprehension of the Being of There-being and not a prefabricated idea of existence. There-being is existence; its innermost nature is existence. It "has" its life (its existence) as something to be achieved (*um zu sein*), as a task, and not as something given and defined definitively. Existence is not an external quality but the innermost structure of There-being. Heidegger is interested in the comprehension of this ontological (Being-) structure as such. He is not rejecting the metaphysical and the anthropological interpretations of death. He only elaborates the meaning of death as a phenomenon of the comprehension of the Being of There-being as existence. Through this choice (of existence) Heidegger limits his points of view and consequently cancels out beforehand any other dimension of human existence. He is remaining faithful to his task of preparing the question about the meaning of Being through the comprehension of the Being of There-being. This is the purpose of his research.

In spite of the basically areligious characteristic of the Heideggerian notion of existence as "to-be-unto-death," it is possible to recognize in it a profound similarity or closeness to the idea of human
existence in Christian thought. What is closer to the Christian understanding of human existence than the meditation on death as the
destiny and the final judge of human living? The Heideggerian
notion of authenticity (choosing one's way of "to-be") may be viewed
and interpreted as something quite analogous to the idea of Christian
commitment (in faith). The awareness of death and the phenomenon
of concern are emphasized by the existential analysis as well as by
Christian thought. The understanding of conscience and of guiltiness
as involving the entire Being (nature) of man together with the concrete (existentiell) situation in the World, the nostalgia for an "ideal"
mode of existence, the daily life of perdition, the thrownness and
helplessness of man as being-in-the-World: all these indicate the existentiell ground of the existential analysis, and, at the same time, they
manifest some relationship to the Christian hermeneutics of human
existence. When reading Heidegger's writings, one experiences this
"strange" phenomenon: When he refers to traditionally "religious"
matters the tone of his "voice" sounds profane; when he speaks of
"profane" topics his "voice" becomes as a "sacred" utterance of a
prophet. This "change" in the way of speaking is a sign of thinking
(an event) and the experiencing of thinking as questioning. However,
the great distance between Heidegger's phenomenology and Christian thought remains. In the final analysis, this is the primal distance
and the basic difference between the certainty of death and the hope
in resurrection, the distance between the inescapable finitude of
human existence and the expectation of salvation that "breaks into"
the human condition. There is no need to harmonize these two views
of human existence; they have their own functions, merits, and intentions in the experience of thought.

The phenomenological notions of finitude and death have
their ultimate source in the new interpretation of time as the sense
of concern and of the World. Time *is* the meaning of concern (There-
being) and of the World (Being). History itself is the consequence of
the historicity (*Geschichtlichkeit*) of There-being, that is, of the continually ending nature (death) of There-being.[18] The new philosophy of
time in SZ does have a significance for the understanding of the
question of God. The following reflections, then, examine those
aspects of the new interpretation of time that include a relationship
to the ultimate questions and to the problem of God.

Temporality (*Zeitlichkeit*) is interpreted by SZ in relationship to

There-being; it represents the sense (the meaning) of There-being and, in some way, of beings in general. The meaning of the Being of There-being is not something other than and outside There-being; it is "the self-comprehending There-being itself."[19] To comprehend a being in its Being (as the meaning of a being) consists in situating it as a project (*Entwurf*), in locating a being in the project of Being, and in understanding the ultimate "whereunto" (*Worumwillen*), the meaning, of the projection of a being. The comprehension of Being (of beings) by a being is the key to the question regarding meaning, since it is Being that gives meaning. The comprehension of Being underlies the comprehension of (a) being. This is the reason why Heidegger tries to clarify (to bring into the light) There-being's Being-comprehension, its ontological understanding. There-being is a structural unity (concern), a unified totality ("to-be-unto-death"), a finite transcendence. The ultimate source of the structural elements of concern is time, and this is the reason why the notion of time, here, refers to a time proper to There-being. SZ does not speak of time as the continuity of "nows" (the popular notion of time) but as the "unified phenomenon of temporality," as the unity of the three (future, past, present) directions (ecstases) of temporality (the existential notion of time).[20] The authentic life of There-being in time, then, is not like the mere duration of a thing (entity) but the coming to pass of temporality; existential time is the meaning of authentic concern. There-being is always coming to itself and, therefore, it is always having to achieve itself (existentiality). There-being becomes more the "There" of Being; it comes closer to Being and Being comes closer to it. The future is precisely this coming. But There-being finds itself as already thrown into a concrete situation, as already having-been (facticity); therefore, the coming to itself (the future) is a coming to itself as already having-been (past). According to its existential structure, There-being is preoccupied with beings in the World; it is lost (dispersed) in the daily commerce with beings (fallenness) and lets beings be manifest for what they are (according to their Being). This letting be seen, this rendering manifest, is the present. The temporality of There-being (the structure of future-past-present) is the foundation of all the elements of concern and, therefore, the ultimate meaning of There-being and of the World.[21]

This notion of temporality represents a new, radical interpretation of There-being and of the World. There-being is abandoned to the negative ground of its own self, and this abandonment is the result of the ecstatic character of its existence. This facticity includes the undisclosedness of the ontic "whereunto" and of the ontic "how" of thrownness. The ontological "whereunto" of There-being is Being; There-being is projected toward Being; it is the comprehension of Being. For There-being "to-be" is always the main concern; the essence of There-being lies in its existence, in its "to-be." The World is transcendent; its transcendence is grounded on the ecstatic nature of temporality, on the tridirectional process of temporalization. There-being encounters beings in the World and discovers them. This discovery is not the work of a capricious will; it is grounded on (made possible by) freedom within the limits (limitations) of thrownness. The relations of meaningfulness (a network of meanings) constituting (determining) the structure of the World with which There-being is already familiar are not a "network of forms laid over some sort of material by a worldless subject."[22] When the "There" of There-being is disclosed, the World is disclosed with it because There-being is to-be-in-the-World. There-being comprehends its own ecstatic self (a unity of past-future-present) *and* the World *in* the unity of the "There" *by* comprehending the unity of this "There." "If no There-being exists, no World is 'there' either."[23] There-being is in and open to (orientated toward) the World according to the three directions (ecstases) of the process of temporalization; it is "out" in the World by its nature, and, therefore, it encounters beings there. Temporality, therefore, renders possible the many ways of encountering beings. This is the existential meaning of the fact that There-being encounters beings. There-being is not a thing but a subject; that is, There-being in its Being is founded on temporality. The World as transcendent is not the totality of objects; it is founded on temporality. The World is open and ecstatically accessible (according to the three ecstases of temporality), and this accessibility renders possible the encounter with beings. The discovery of beings presupposes the World as being there already, since discovery is possible only as a way of to-be-in-the-World. In this sense, then, the World is a "subjective" World (a timely and a transcendent one), but this "subjective" World is more objective than any other "object."

It may be seen now that the traditional question regarding the ultimate purposefulness or sense of the World (as well as of human existence) is not considered in this context of SZ. The explanation of the metaphysical cause ("why") and the elucidation of the final metaphysical purpose ("whereunto") of the World constitute essential elements of the traditional (especially of the scholastic) elaboration of the problem of God; these issues are not resolved by the existential analysis. The meaning of Being is conceived in SZ as temporality (There-being and the World are finite), and temporality as the meaning of concern is disclosed in There-being's encounter with beings in the World, in its preoccupation with the environment (*Umwelt*), and in the phenomenon of anxiety. The existential understanding of the World and time explains human existence (There-being) without advocating an Absolute (God). The concern with a possible ultimate religious (divine) meaning and goal of human reality remains outside the existential analysis; SZ does not examine all the issues connected with the traditional approach to the problem of God. This is a main reason why the comprehensive problem of God is not answered in SZ.

What is, then, the life of There-being in the World? It is *history*. The very life of There-being is constituted by "being stretched out" between birth and death; this "between" (*das "Zwischen"*) is indeed the Being of There-being[24] and not something extrinsic to it. There-being is history (*Geschichte*) because it is temporal (*zeitlich*) and historical (*geschichtlich*). "*Authentic to-be-unto-death, that is, the finitude of temporality, is the hidden ground of the historicity (Geschichtlichkeit) of There-being.*"[25] The original historicity of There-being is a destiny (*Geschick*); it is the authentic history of existence that springs from the future of There-being. There-being can re-collect (gather together) its history. There-being is this re-collection or re-petition (*Wiederholung*) of the past possibilities (potentialities) of existence. History is the way (mode) of "to-be" of There-being and has its root in the future (a continual coming to the true self). Death as the innermost potentiality of There-being brings (draws) back There-being (as dominated by the anticipatory drive or tension toward the future) to its factual thrownness and gives precedence (preponderance) in historicity to the past. The authentic history of existence (the authentic life of There-being), however, has its source in the future. History, therefore, originates from the historicity of There-being and not from a "supratemporal design."[26] History is a potentiality of There-being and not an external mark of existence. In Heidegger's view, history is of ontological significance; it is, in the final analysis, the history of Being (metaphysics is the historical destiny of Being). Heidegger's philosophy and his notion of history represent a hermeneutics of facticity. Here, once more, it is possible to observe the this-worldliness of the existential analysis.

The inauthentic existence of There-being, the inauthentic history of There-being, as the life of everydayness, gives origin to the usual (vulgar) interpretation of time as a continuity of "nows." This

view of time is the product of the ontology of entities (ontology of
Vorhandenheit), and this ontology considers Being as the quality of
stability (permanence) of things. Time, consequently, is interpreted
as the indefinite continuance of (past, future, and present) "nows."
This popular notion of time represents inauthentic temporality; it is
based on the understanding of things and not on the comprehension
of There-being as different from mere things. The "now" as the present of authentic temporality is based on the ontology of There-being;
it is an ecstasis, a moment or instant (*Augenblick*) of re-solve.[27] This
authentic present is at the same time the disclosure of the past and
of the future. The authentic present unifies the self (There-being).
The inauthentic "now" (present) is an absorption into the immediate
preoccupations and possibilities of everydayness; it is an escape from
the past and from the future. The authentic present (*Augenblick*) as a
moment of resolve unifies and discloses the total situation of There-
being. The static and "viewing" ontology (Being as stability and permanence of things) interprets the *eternity of God* as a never ending
continuity, as a series of comings and passings of "nows." Time, as
Plato says, is the image of eternity. In Heidegger's view, all this is the
result of inauthentic temporality[28] preoccupied with the continuity of
time and forgetting the "tension" (tenseness, *Gespanntheit*) of time as
the "outstretchedness" (*Erstrecktheit*) of the ecstatical unity of temporality. For Hegel the true present is eternity.[29] He explains time as the
"now" of contemplation. These ideas, Heidegger suggests, reflect the
popular, inadequate conception of time. The problem of the eternity
of God, however, is not elaborated by Heidegger. He prescinds from
the religious, theological meaning of eternity and of time (as well as
of resolve). SZ elaborates the nature of the temporality of There-
being; it does not consider, in this context, the notion of eternity as
atemporality (timelessness). The existential analysis, however, leaves
open the possibility of a philosophical reflection regarding the eternity of God. Heidegger says that the philosophical "construction" of
the eternity of God could be understood as a more original and "endless" temporality. The feasibility of understanding the eternity of God
as a more primordial, "endless" temporality through the traditional
approach of the *via negationis et eminentiae*, however, Heidegger suggests, remains to be seen.[30] SZ leaves its readers without giving the
answer to these concerns.

The preceding examination of Heidegger's insights regarding
the ultimate questions shows that he remains faithful to the primordial task of SZ: to prepare the way toward the elaboration of the

question of the meaning of Being through the clarification of the existential-ontological structure of There-being.[31] SZ does not intend to resolve the problem of God even though the demythologization of the traditional (Western, metaphysical) approach to this problem is a significant result of the existential analysis.

According to the phenomenological perspective, the World exists for the sake (in view) of There-being; There-being is the meaning, the ultimate "whereunto" (*Worumwillen*) of the World. There-being, however, is its own end as advancing continually toward its own potentialities; it exists for its own sake (in view of itself) and not for the sake of something else (some other reality); the meaning of There-being is There-being. There-being is essential freedom; it transcends beings and passes beyond them to the World and to Being. This passing-beyond (transcending) is the realization of its own potentialities (self-creation) as well as the structuring (creation) of the World. There-being becomes (is what it is) by projecting (throwing) itself into and by assuming its own potentialities and thus by constructing (forming, building) the World at the same time. Every action of There-being is a realization of its own potentialities. There-being as transcending is freedom. The radical capacity to transcend, then, makes possible the formation of the World as well as the process of self-realization (self-creation).[32] The meaning of the World and the meaning of human reality are interpreted according to this foundational significance of transcendence and freedom. These insights constitute the basis and the background of the existential-phenomenological answers to the ultimate questions (meaning of human existence, the final end of the World) in SZ. The existential-phenomenological interpretations of There-being, of the World, of death, of transcendence, and of time (the main issues at stake in deciding the ultimate questions), however, do not imply (at least not necessarily) a denial of the theistic view(s) of human existence; their identification with atheistist worldview or ideology (or with any worldview or ideology) would be a misunderstanding of the nature and task of existential analysis. The usual (popular, traditional) approach to the God-question is demythologized through the this-worldly temporality of There-being. This change (demythologization) does not resolve the philosophical problem of God; it questions, however, the ontological background of the traditional approach to it.

Conclusion

The preceding examination of SZ disclosed the "where" and the meaning of the *first phase* of the problem of God in Heidegger's thinking. This phase may be called a demythologization because it is neither an affirmation nor a negation of God, but a transformation of the traditional philosophical approach to this problem. This transformation is a consequence of the existential analysis (the "how" of the transformation) and includes an abandoning of some of the historically important "ways" leading to the affirmation of God (the "what" of the transformation). The import of SZ in this regard does not consist in a categorical answer to the God-question, but rather in the "how" of this problem as a problem in hermeneutical phenomenology. The meaning of this "how" shall be clarified through the "recollection" of the main characteristics of the first phase of the problem of God in Heidegger's thought:

a) The examination of the question of Being by means of the analysis of There-being does not include the denial of God; it cannot be interpreted as representing an atheistic intellectual and existential attitude toward the question of God. Though SZ may be described as "atheistic" in the sense that it is a philosophy without God (it does not lead to the philosophical knowledge of God), nevertheless it is not a philosophy opposed to the affirmation of God's existence; it neither excludes nor precludes, but rather leaves open the possibility of the relationship of human existence to God. There is no final resolution of the question of God within the perspective of SZ. Despite his strong remark in SZ about expelling all remnants of theology from the realm of philosophy, despite his criticism of theological anthropology, Heidegger is not proposing a solution to theological and anthropological problems. He is always conscious of the task and the boundaries as well as the limitations of the existential analysis. Its very methodology confines the analysis to the phenomenon of existence (existentiality) as it is disclosed in the comprehension of There-being (facticity). SZ explores the meaning (structure) of existence, the understanding of the Being of There-being, and it prepares the ground for the re-awakening (*Wiederholung*) of the question of Being; it represents neither a (traditional) metaphysical nor a theological but, much rather, a this-worldly existential-phenomenological interpretation of human existence. What Heidegger says (mostly indirectly) about the problem of God is very little indeed, and it refers basically to the ontological presuppositions implied in the metaphysical notion as well as in the affirmation of the existence of a supreme being.

b) SZ does not develop a treatise on the problem of God; there is no explicit (completely thematized) elaboration, no comprehensive (direct) analysis of the philosophical God-question as a whole that could be found in it.[1] The phenomenological understanding and the existential-ontological interpretation of There-being as finite transcendence give a comprehensive account of this "no."[2] The nature of transcendence, the idea of Being, the concept of the World, the nature of contingence, the definition of truth, the nature of time, the notion of meaning, and other issues are analyzed by Heidegger in relation to and as meanings for There-being. The methodological and the thematic perspectives of SZ, then, indicate that it neither can nor intends to give a final, comprehensive answer to the problem of God, even though it implies the demythologization (rethinking) of several aspects of the traditional approaches to the philosophical notion and affirmation of God. At the same time, SZ leaves open the possibility of a new philosophical approach to the problem of God. The existential analysis, nevertheless, "leaves aside" the exploration of There-being's possible relationship to God; it does not examine the possible religious meanings of transcendence and freedom. The life based on faith, the religious (Christian) way of being-in-the-World, can be a mode of authentic existence; this dimension of the life of There-being, however, is not considered in SZ.

c) The problem of God as such remains a problem for the author of SZ. The references to the notion of God give sufficient evidence of this fact. Certainly, there is a clear distancing with regard to theological and anthropological issues and perspectives. Nevertheless, Heidegger speaks in SZ of a renewed theology that is based on the insights of faith and on the awareness of the "wholly otherness" of God. He mentions even the possibility of a philosophical understanding of the eternity of God. The main question for Heidegger's phenomenology, in the final analysis, is not how the human mind reaches out to God but, much rather, how the voice of the transcendent God breaks into and becomes discernible in the human condition.[3]

d) The problem of God appears on several levels of understanding. As a philosophical question it is demythologized through the existential analysis. The analysis of the truly theological and primordial nature of the problem of God in SZ is clearly isolated and distinguished from (and transcends) the strict domain of merely philosophical reflection; its investigation, however, is "left aside" by the existential-ontological interpretation of There-being. Heidegger distinguishes, furthermore, the metaphysical, the anthropological, the psychological, and the epistemological aspects of the entire God-question.

e) All that can be found in SZ about the problem of God is the result of the ontological inquiry, of the question about the meaning of Being. The examination of this question implies the rethinking of the God-question; this is the reason why one can (and even ought to) speak of the presence of a phenomenological problem of God in SZ.

The phase of demythologization of the problem of God prepares the ground for a *new* approach to this same problem. The new approach will only come about through and after the discovery of a new kind of *questioning* (thinking) about (the notion and the meaning of) God. The basic elements of this new way of questioning are already present in SZ, and they shall be developed (in the rest of Heidegger's writings) together with the new dimensions of the Being-question. The problem of God in SZ, then, remains undeveloped. This limitation of unfoldedness, the unthought element of a great thought, however, is a sign of hope and of readiness for the coming of thought(fulness), because, as Heidegger says of Nietzsche's thought of the "eternal recurrence," "at the first dawning of a great thought all the essential is there, but it remains undeveloped."[4]

PART   3

THE
GOD-QUESTION
AS A QUESTION

As it is called to mind by Heidegger, a genuine philosophy is necessarily misunderstood by its contemporaries; even the philosopher himself must cease to
be his own contemporary. A fundamental and an
epoch-making philosophical doctrine requires the
education of individuals and of generations if it is to
be understood by them.[1] The basic experience (and
knowledge) of a thinker comes not from a predisposition or from an education but, ultimately, from the
truth of Being.[2] The primordial task of the thinker is
to share (endure and participate) in as well as to try
to understand the history of Being. Philosophy,
therefore, is neither the production of a doctrine nor
merely an exercise of the power of reflection but a
"pathway" of thinking that allows for "forging ahead"
as well as for "turning" in order to find somewhere
the "hidden"; it is indeed, as Heidegger describes his
own philosophy, the "nameless pathway of thought."[3]
This continual disponibility (readiness) and attentiveness of the thinker are the key to the understanding

of his developing thought. The changing of opinion
(reversal), a characteristic of great philosophers, is to
be situated in the context of a development that is
marked by the fidelity to the happening (*Geschehen*)
of the history (*Geschichte*) of Being (*Sein*). The "story,"
the unfolding of the events, of this history constitutes
the living background of Heidegger's attitude toward
the problem of God.

The existential analysis of There-being contained
a demythologization of the philosophical problem of
God (the first phase of the God-question in Heidegger's phenomenology.) What is the "story" of the
God-question after the first period (SZ) of Heidegger's pathway of thought? Is there any change in the
Heideggerian question about God during and after
the "reversal"? The epoch of SZ and of what is often
referred to as the earlier ("first") Heidegger is followed by the epoch of the later ("second") Heidegger.[4] The problem of the ontological difference and
the emphasis on the primacy of Being become more
and more pronounced with the unfolding of Heidegger's way of thinking, especially in the later works.
This change of emphasis, whatever its intensity may
be, brings with it a new attitude toward the understanding of the problem of God. The thinking of
Being has its "almost insurmountable difficulty in
making oneself understood"[5] as part of the entire
question of Being. This difficulty (that comes from
the "inside" of the thinking process) of expression
and of understanding is a necessary burden for the
study of the God-question in Heidegger's writings.
However, despite all the obstacles, it is possible as well
as rewarding to follow up the "story" of the question
of God in Heidegger and thus to distinguish the
phases of its development. Part 3 of this study, then,
examines the situation of the question of God in the
works that followed SZ. These writings lead to the
discovery of the main insights of the later Heidegger
regarding the notion of God and the nature of philosophical thinking.

These reflections discern the *second phase* of the
question of God in Heidegger and indicate even a

third phase of its development. The second phase can
be described as the phase of *questioning,* since the
God-question is present in Heidegger's thought precisely as a question. This phase should be considered
as a going-forward in the direction given by the existential analysis of SZ. The philosophical problem of
God, therefore, is not merely demythologized and
thus made more difficult; it becomes (during this second phase) even *questionable* (*fraglich*) as a philosophical question altogether. Is the God-question a
genuine philosophical question? Is it not an obstacle
to an authentic way of questioning? May the philosopher as a genuine questioner remain a believer? Can
the believer still be a genuine questioner, a philosopher in the Heideggerian sense of this term? Is not
phenomenological atheism a condition of philosophizing? These are some important questions about
this phase of Heidegger's developing thought from
the point of view of the philosophical problem of
God.

This second phase seems to lead to the discovery
of the basic irrelevance of the problem of God from
the point of view of the Heideggerian meditation on
the question of Being. This irrelevance, however, can
be qualified neither as indifferentism nor as an
implicit atheism, even if it is going beyond the original
neutrality of the existential analysis. The changes and
the new elements of this phase of the God-question
should be regarded as the outcome of the change of
emphasis from "There" to Being, as the consequence
of the meditative experiencing of the coming about
of the ontological difference and of the deepening of
the question of Being. The slow transformation
(growth) and the refocusing of Heidegger's meditations include a reexamination as well as a new interpretation of the relationships between Christian
metaphysics and mathematical metaphysics, between
"faith-knowledge" and "philosophical rationality,"
between the claims of reflection based on the knowledge of the causal origin of beings (principle of causality, science, ontotheological metaphysics) and the
thinking of the grounding-process of beings through

Being (mystery of Being, phenomenology, thinking). This new way of questioning-thinking, in turn, leads to some new horizon, to a deeper dimension of thought; it brings some new light into the struggle between the traditional approach to and the new perspective on the problem of God in philosophy. Therefore, it becomes possible to speak of a third (final) phase of the question of God in Heidegger's thinking.

The study of the second phase of the God-question in Heidegger's thought ought to be based upon a comprehensive evaluation of his most significant works in this regard. Thus the following reflections are the result of a close examinaation of KM, *Kants These über das Sein*,[6] *Die Frage nach dem Ding*,[7] EM, WW, *Platons Lehre von der Wahrheit*,[8] WG, WM, and HD. This study of the God-question by its nature requires an ordered approach in dealing with such a variety of works. This order, however, should be imposed by a thematical unity of Heidegger's thought rather than a mere chronological continuity of the writings in question. This is the reason for taking into account KS (though it was written in 1962) and reflecting on EM (written as a lecture course in 1935 and reworked later for the first edition in 1953) together with "Überwindung der Metaphysik"[9] (written between 1936 and 1946). The discernment of the third (final) phase of the question of God in Heidegger includes the analysis of and reflection on basic insights in several of his works (TK, HB, WP, VA, ID). This examination of the development of the question of God in Heidegger's way of thinking after SZ relies on a comprehensive analysis of his writings as a whole; its focus on the selected group of writings, however, is due to the limitations of space.

In these works there are more thematic references to the problem of God as there were in SZ. The name of God occurs quite often[10] in some of these writings. Though this occurrence cannot be considered a decisive factor in evaluating the meaning of these phases of the Heideggerian God-question, nevertheless it represents a growing and a more intensive "preoccupation" in this regard. Heidegger seems to become more and more aware of the problematic relationship

between the ontological difference and the philosophical problem of God. Both the thematic and the
indirect references (together with some "accidental"
remarks) definitely reveal a new phase of the God-
question. This new phase is distinguished by the questioning attitude toward the (classical) philosophical
understanding of God and by the "overcoming"
(*Überwindung*) of the theism-atheism dilemma
through a rightly understood irrelevance of the traditional approach to the problem of God. This second
phase of the Heideggerian God-question should be
understood, therefore, in the light of the meditation
on the coming about of the ontological difference.
The first phase of the Heideggerian God-question
appeared as an "outcome" of the problematic about
Being in the context of the existential analysis of
There-being. The second phase represents a progress
in the same direction because it is a consequence of
a more profound comprehension of Being through
the manifestation of the ontological difference. This
phase, even more than the first one, shows the existence of an intrinsic relationship between the discernment of the ontological difference and the
understanding of the problem of God. This relationship (of implication) is a constant characteristic of the
whole development of the Heideggerian question
(and questioning) about the problem of God. The
third phase (the final phase) of Heidegger's thinking
on God opens up a new perspective on (even a new
way of asking) the entire question of God.

The preceding "preview" of the development of
the God-question leads to an experiencing of questioning (regarding the problem of God) through a
thoughtful "review" of Heidegger's writings. The
order of this meditative "review" is as follows: (1) the
questioning in the Kant studies; (2) the problematic
of genuine questioning and believing according to
EM; (3) ontological difference and theological indifference (WW, PW, WG, WM); (4) a new dimension
of the questioning in HD; (5) the final phase of the
questioning (TK, HB, WP, VA, ID), that is, the third
phase of the God-question.

14

The Metaphysical Questioning

The purpose of the following reflections is the understanding of the problem of God insofar as this problem is present in the Heideggerian interpretation of Kant. In the Kant studies Heidegger speaks not merely of metaphysical problems (questions), but he is asking the problem *of* (questioning) metaphysics as such. These (Heideggerian) meditations on Kant (together with the Nietzsche lectures) constitute an easily understandable expression of the interpretation of metaphysics and, thus, clarify the devaluation of the metaphysical notion of God. Metaphysics as such becomes questionable. The nature of metaphysical questioning is examined through a "re-petition" (*Wiederholung*)[1] of the Kantian problematic that consists in the effort to lay the foundation of metaphysics (*Grundlegung der Metaphysik*).[2] The laying the foundation (*Grundlegung*), the grounding (*Begründung*), of metaphysics, entails a question about man (anthropology),[3] because it refers to a basic potentiality (*Grundvermögen*) in man enabling him to practice metaphysics, to metaphysicize. Kant's final aim is to ground special metaphysics (*metaphysica specialis*), which includes the disciplines of cosmology, psychology, and (natural) theology.[4] This grounding consists in the Kantian critique of pure reason (*Vernunft*, the most intimate essence of human reason).[5] The essence of human reason becomes manifest in the following three questions representing the legitimate interests (*Interessen*), concerns, of human reason: What can I know? What should I do? What may I hope for? These three questions belong to the domain of special metaphysics (knowledge of things: to cosmology; human action and freedom: to psychology; the hope of immortality as union with God: to theology); they determine the nature of man and constitute the field of philosophy. The three questions can be reduced to (summarized in) a fourth, single question: What is man? Therefore, as Kant says, only a philosophical anthropology can lay the foundation of special metaphysics.[6] The central problem of philosophy, then, is man himself.

The three questions manifest the innermost nature of man; they determine (bestimmen) him not as merely a being of nature (Naturwesen), but as a "citizen of the world" (Weltbürger). No other epoch of history has possessed the vast knowledge about man that ours does and, still, no other history has known so little of what man really is (was der Mensch sei) as the present one. This is the reason why Max Scheler spoke of philosophical anthropology (of the "place" of man in the totality of Being, of his relationship to the cosmos and to God); he called attention to the difficulty of defining the nature of man, since man became questionable (fragwürdig) in our time more than ever before.[7]

According to Heidegger, the three questions are reducible to the fourth question (What is man?), because all three are basically asking the same question: the question of finitude. Human reason asks the three questions precisely because human reason is finite. Heidegger shows how the three questions reveal this finitude.[8]

The first question (What can I know?) is a question about the power (Können) of knowing. This question manifests that the questioner is already conditioned by (situated in) some negativity, by the lack of power (capacity), and by a nonpower (Nicht-Können); an all-powerful being cannot (and needs not) ask the question about its own potentialities. This question, therefore, reveals the innermost finitude of the questioning being.

The second question (What should I do?) refers to man's obligations, to the concern with the duties of the human being. When an "ought to" (Sollen), an obligation, is brought into question, the questioning being is in the state of "suspension" (tension), of hesitation between a "yes" and a "no." This hesitation about what this being ought to do shows, ultimately, the questionable (fraglich) character of the "ought to" altogether. This questionability is the sign of a being who understands himself through a "not-yet-having-fulfilled" (Noch-

nicht-erfüllt-haben); this being hesitates about the "ought to" as such, and thus he is compelled to ask himself what he should do. This "not-yet" (the lack) of the fulfillment reveals (proclaims) the essential finitude of the questioning being, that is, of the being that questions the "ought to." An omnipotent being does not need to ask what he is able (and ought) to do.

The third question (What may I hope for?) is a question about man's hope. The questionability of this "may" (*Dürfen*), of this "being allowed to" hope, is an indication of something to be gained or lost for the questioning being. Man's hope is at stake in this question. All expectation (*Erwartung*) reveals privation, a want (*Entbehrung*), an indigence that comes from the innermost interest (concern) of human reason and manifests the essential finitude of human reason as such.

The metaphysical questioning, therefore, reveals the essential finitude of the human knower. The finitude of There-being is not a mere thinglike attribute (*Eigenschaft*) but a constant, and for the most part hidden, structure (Heidegger speaks of "shivering"—*Erzittern*) of all that exist.[9] The three questions are reducible to the fourth one (What is man?), because they reveal the innermost nature, the finitude of man; they all ask the question of finitude.

The problem of finitude is a central problem in KM. The understanding of finite transcendence gives a new occasion for Heidegger to reflect on the traditional notion of metaphysics. This issue, at the same time, also relates to the problem of God and, thus, indicates the development of Heidegger's thought in this regard. The traditional notion of metaphysics was dominated by the Christian interpretation of the World.[10] According to this interpretation, every nondivine being is a creature. The universe is viewed as the totality of created beings. Man has a privileged position in this universe because of the salvation of his soul and because of his eternal existence. Therefore, in the Christian view, there are three regions of beings: God, World (nature), and man. These three regions of beings constitute the objects of special metaphysics (theology, cosmology, psychology). The object of general metaphysics (ontology) is being in general (*im allgemeinen*), the *ens commune*. Metaphysics is considered as the science of the highest dignity because its object is the *ens commune* and the *highest being (das höchste Seiende)*.

Metaphysical knowing is a very rigorous (and therefore binding) way of knowing. Indeed, it corresponds to the ideal way of knowing (mathematical knowing); it is a science of pure reason independent of experience. This traditional structure (and understanding) of metaphysics is analyzed by Heidegger on several occasions, though, in the end, he always returns to the same basic insight. He likes to emphasize that the ontotheological questioning is a consequence of the metaphysical interpretation of Being.[11] When analyzing the notion of Being in Kant's philosophy (KS), Heidegger shows the relationship between the Being-question and the metaphysical God-question. This mere external circumstance is a revealing one: Kant's thesis about Being is found in that section of the *Critique of Pure Reason* that speaks of the impossibility of an ontological argument for the existence of God. What is the reason for this strange coincidence (togetherness) of the two questions? The answer is quite clear for Heidegger.[12] The question of Being according to the metaphysical understanding is being asked as a question about (a) being, as a question regarding the Being of particular beings as such; it is not a question concerned with Being as such. The question of the Being of beings, continues Heidegger, is a twofold question: (1) What is being in general? (2) Which one of the particular beings is the highest being (the supreme being among them), and how is it the highest? The twofoldness (*das Zwiefältige*) of the meaning of the question of the Being of being (*Sein des Seienden*), that is, of the question "What is being?" (*Was ist das Seiende?*), accounts for the nature of ontotheological questioning. The described Being-question is a question of ontology (being in general) and of theology (the highest being). The metaphysical Being-question, therefore, is an onto-theological question.

The reason for this twofoldness (and ambiguity) of the Being-question, according to Heidegger, lies in the fact that the Being of beings shows itself (for our reflection) as having the characteristic of ground *as* foundation (ontology) *and*, at the same time, as a ground (*Grund*) that lets originate (*entspringen lässt*) beings; it lets beings come into Being, and, therefore, it "explains" the origin of beings (theology: the study of the highest being). The first (the ontological) meaning of ground is that of a "common foothold" (*Boden*) of all beings as a common "playground" for any further consideration of being(s). The second (the theological) meaning of ground is that of the highest being (the supreme being) as the originating ground that lets beings come into Being, into existence.

Heidegger calls attention to the fact that, as it appears in the preceding metaphysical Being-question, Being is defined as ground (*Grund*). This meaning of Being, Heidegger insists, is taken for granted. However, this "most-taken-for-granted" (*Selbstverständlichste*) meaning (understanding) is precisely the most questionable (*das Frag-würdigste*) aspect of the whole metaphysical interpretation of Being.[13] When Kant defines Being as "position" (*Sein als Position*) he remains in close relationship with the definition (*Bestimmung*) of Being as ground, since "position" and *ponere* mean to put (*setzen*), to lay (*legen*), to lie (*liegen*), to lie before (*vorliegen*), be lying as ground (*zum Grunde liegen*).[14]

The history of the ontotheological questioning is a history of the problem of the highest being; it is a preoccupation that is trying to show *what* is this highest being, and, before everything else, to prove that this highest being *is* (that God exists). The history of this theological philosophy is nourished by the ambiguity of the metaphysical interpretation of Being. Heidegger presents a new notion of Being by indicating that which remains still "unthought," "unsaid," and "unasked" in all metaphysics.[15] For him, the relationship between thinking and Being is the thoughtworthy element of all genuine thinking. The most thoughtworthy task of thinking and speaking (logos) consists in bringing somehow Being into language, in letting Being come into words.[16] In the phenomenon of "is" hides itself all that is worthy of thought about Being; Being, however, is not in the same way as a being is; it is not a being. Being as such becomes manifest to the thinker in and through the coming about of the ontological difference; it makes this difference. It can be said, then, that Being cannot be like a thing (a particular being) is: "otherwise it would not be Being but just a being."[17] The main task of thinking consists in discerning the thought-provoking fact that "there is Being," in meditating on the truth of the ontological mystery, on the meaning of the primordial wonder that "Being is granted" (*es gibt Sein*).[18] Being is the offering of and the coming into presence (*Sein—eigentlich: das Anwesenheit Gewährende*).[19] The task of the genuine thinker, then, is to think the meaning of Being according to its primordial giveness and to discover that it is truth (ἀλήϑεια) that speaks in "to-be" (εἶναι), since revealing (truth) is the process of letting come into presence ("to-be") (*Anwesenlassen*).[20]

This new understanding of Being is something quite different from the ambiguity of that meaning of Being (ground) that is taken for granted by traditional (ontotheological) metaphysics. The problem of metaphysics as such, then, reveals the reason for the intrinsic relationship between the Being-question and the God-question.

A second occasion for explaining the structure of metaphysical questioning is given, for Heidegger, when he speaks of the historical change (transition) from Christian to (modern) mathematical meta-physics.[21] This change means a changeover from the metaphysical notion of God as the creator-ground of all beings to the concept of the "I think" not merely as the form (nature) but even as the content of questioning. The "old" way of questioning and answering was determined by the metaphysical notion of God. In the "new" way of questioning ("I think") man has a central place in the questioning about (and of) beings. Metaphysical questioning is always a question-ing about beings (God, World, man). It contains a decision about the essence and about the possibility of these beings. This decision is to be made by pure reason (according to the change from Christian to mathematical metaphysics as Heidegger insists in FD), that is, ration-ally, by means of the concepts acquired in pure thinking. A precon-cept (*Vorbegriff*), an anticipatory seizure (comprehension) of being (*Seiende*) on the whole, has to lead any inquiry about beings, because only after elaborating a concept of being in general does it become possible to define a particular being as God, or as World, or as man. When thinking becomes "mathematical" (rational), the project (*Entwurf*) of being on the whole (*überhaupt*) as such becomes the ground of all beings. Therefore, modern metaphysics has the same structure as classical (Christian) metaphysics; in it, too, general meta-physics (the idea of being in general) precedes special metaphysics (the understanding of the types of particular beings). However, the new ("mathematical") general metaphysics is based upon a set of axioms (*Schema des Setzens und Denkens*). The axiomatic definition of being(s) is the reason for speaking of divine, of worldly, and of human beings.

Therefore, the beingness of a being or the thingness of a thing is determined by certain axioms. This means that the beingness of a being is decided (defined) not by the Christian understanding of the World (creation) but by the law (the principle) of pure reason. This is the nature of the important changeover from Christian to modern ("mathematical") metaphysics.

The ontology of modern times (the general metaphysics of "mathematical" metaphysics) is characterized by the self-affirmation of pure reason. This ontology is a system of the basic axioms of pure reason, the project (the organization) of the general determination (definition) of the Being of beings. Special metaphysics, then, is a consequence of this axiomatic ontology.

Heidegger resumes his description of modern metaphysics by saying that in modern metaphysics the law of reason is above the

Being of beings; the superiority of reason and the inferiority of the Being of beings are ensured by the laws and principles of reason.[22] This is an important conclusion for Heidegger because it represents his interpretation of the last phase of metaphysics as the history of Being, and also because it explains his view of modern technical science (a science that "does not think at all," but serves as an instrument in the hands of "rational man" in order to secure the dominion over beings).

Another aspect of the emergence of "mathematical" metaphysics consists in the "dechristianization" of knowledge and, according to Heidegger's own expression, in the development of natural knowledge.[23] Knowledge is no longer regarded as something based on the Christian revelation (Bible and tradition); it is understood as worldly, natural knowledge based on the ground of pure reason. Experience and reason have become authentic and self-reliant. Heidegger claims that before the emergence of the mathematical, scientific mentality the truths of the Church and those of the faith were considered the ideal of truth, the standard truth. True knowledge of beings was to be gained through the interpretation of the sources of Christian revelation (Scripture and tradition). All knowledge was situated in the Christian framework of thought. The natural, nonrevealed knowledge had no appropriate foundation; basically, there was no worldly knowledge at all.

The negative consequence of the new mentality consists precisely in the distancing from Christian revelation as the primary source of knowledge and in the refusal (rejection) of tradition as the authoritative mediator of knowledge.

The scientific, mathematical project of thought, however, brings about more than a liberation (*Befreiung*) from Christian revelation. It indicates a new experience and a new configuration (*Gestaltung*) of freedom itself. This new freedom, according to Heidegger's emphasis, represents (*dar-stellt*) a new foundation of knowledge. This new foundation of knowledge is an important event of our time. Mathematical knowledge lays its own foundation, a foundation that is nothing else than the very essence of the mathematical as such. Mathematics lays the foundation for all knowledge; it is the law of reason. Metaphysics, continues Heidegger, comes from the same root as mathematics. However, the root of metaphysics is situated in a more profound ground than that of mathematics, because metaphysics is a knowledge of beings as a whole. Mathematics, nevertheless, becomes the measure (*Massstab*) of all thinking (*mathesis universalis*).[24] All this leads to the dominion (*Herrschaft*) of the mathematical (scientific) mentality and, thus, to a transformation of the understanding of There-being, to a falling away from the lighting-process (*Lichtung*) of the Being of beings.[25]

This Heideggerian review of Christian metaphysics cannot be regarded as a rejection of the truth of Christianity. Heidegger's critical examination of what he frequently calls "Christian metaphysics" does establish the important distinction between the theological truth (and essence) of Christianity and the philosophical (metaphysical) elements in the history of Christian thought. His repudiation of the metaphysical system (the philosophical influence and expression) of Christianity does not mean the rejection of the true essence of Christian revelation. The analysis of Christian metaphysics constitutes a philosophical theme and concern; it is not a judgment on the validity of the truth of the Christian message. The awareness of the distinction between the theological (religious) and the philosophical (secular) dimensions of Christian thought is essential for the right understanding of Heidegger's final assessment of Western, Christian metaphysics as well as for his views regarding the question of God. When analyzing Leibniz's theory about the Being of beings, Heidegger emphasizes the fact that his criticism of Leibniz is not a rejection of the truth of Christianity. For Leibniz, the Being of a thing (the thingness of a thing, the beingness of a being) is its quality of being-created by God. Every thing, every being, is something unique and irreplaceable according to Leibniz's principle of identity of undiscernibles. Every thing is a unique and irreplaceable thing because it is created by God and because this quality of being-created constitutes the very essence of a thing, of all beings outside the creator. The uniqueness and the irreplaceableness of beings are a consequence of their essence, of their creature-status. If two things were to be similar to such an extent that they became undiscernible, this would mean a repetition of the (exact same) divine creative act: a repetition that would be incompatible with the perfection of the creator God (who always lets be something new and unique). Therefore, concludes Leibniz, there cannot be two identical (entirely similar, undiscernible) things because of the very essence of beings (being-created by God). Heidegger questions the viability of the theological foundation of Leibniz's principle. He claims at the same time, however, that the impossibility (the nonviability) of the theological foundation can be shown in such a way that is prescinding completely from the judgment regarding the truth of Christianity as such.[26] This critical evaluation, then, is not the rejection of but a distantiation from Christianity and theology.

If the meaning of Being (the definition of the Being of beings) does not consist in being-created by God, then the entire speculation by Leibniz remains groundless. This reflection by Heidegger, once again, calls attention to the structure of metaphysical questioning (and thinking) and to the preestablished idea of Being, an idea that is implied by the way (by the endemic structure) of the process of questioning, by the assumptions underlying the inquiry. It is clear, therefore, that Heidegger's thought is focused on the thingness of a thing, on the Being of the thing, on the thisness of the thing. He insists that the understanding of the thingness of things (the Being of things) should be grounded on the very Being of the things themselves and not merely on their reference to the space-time situation. In the final analysis, one should add, he is looking for an explanation *ab intra* and not for an explanation *ab extra*.

Heidegger begins with an examination of the common and scientific way of questioning the thingness of things and then slowly discovers that the scientific understanding of things is based upon and includes a certain interpretation (an often implicit understanding) of Being itself. Man, therefore, as There-being (as concerned with Being), does have a basic role to play in defining things; the meaning of things (and their Being) cannot be defined without a reference to the question about man. This appears quite clearly in FD, as the preceding reflections suggest.

The ambiguity of the metaphysical questioning acounts for the connection between the Being-question and the God-question. The notion of creation, as Heidegger claims, predetermines the course of Western philosophy and defines the meaning of Being. However, in Heidegger's view, it is "impossible to show that man is an *ens creatum*."[27] And even if this impossibility could become a possibility, even if one could prove rationally that man is a created being, even then, the argument could show only the mere fact (*Faktum*) of man's finitude and not the essence of this finitude as the ground-constitution or basic condition (*Grundverfassung*) of man's Being. The problem of finitude is a central problem for both Heidegger and Kant because this is the problem of metaphysics.[28]

The problem of knowing, the distinction between infinite (divine) and finite knowing, shows again the finitude-centered problematic in Heidegger's and in Kant's philosophy as well.[29] In traditional metaphysics both the *ens creatum* and the *ens increatum* (God) were the "primary facts." This dualism of finitude and infinitude is changed into the central problematic of finitude as such. This is one of the basic characteristics of Heidegger's philosophy. Heidegger's meditations on Kant, therefore, lead back to the basic questions of SZ.

Is there a difference between SZ and the Kant studies from the point of view of the problem of God? Yes, there is some difference between them: they adopt subtly diverging attitudes toward the problem of God. The negative, demythologizing, and on occasion impatiently critical orientation of SZ, which called for the expulsion of Christian ideas from the realm of philosophy, is gradually overcome and replaced by the attitude of questioning; it is transformed into the problem of the questionability of the metaphysical questioning. Questioning becomes a characteristic of the content as well as of the method of Heidegger's way of thinking.[30]

The entire Heideggerian problem of God ought to be situated in this attitude of questioning. The problem of God in Heidegger's thought is a question; it should be regarded, therefore, as such. A critical evaluation, then, becomes meaningful when its attention is focused on the questioning-process, when it is prepared to "read the signs" of authentic questioning. The explicitation of the ontological difference should further clarify this questioning attitude toward the philosophical notion of God and, therefore, prepare the ground for the right understanding of the God-question as an "irrelevant" question from the point of view of Heidegger's thought.

The Kant studies offered just a few references to the problem of God. However, it was necessary to reflect on them in order to gain a right understanding of them. This study of the nature of the (Western) metaphysical questioning (in Heidegger's view) has provided an introduction to the analysis of the Heideggerian distancing (emphasis on the otherness) of genuine questioning (thinking) from Christian faith (believing).

15

A Condition
of Genuine
Questioning

here are some expressions of Heidegger that "transmit" his thought in a concise manner (for example, the Being of There-being is situated in its existence, thinking is the thinking of Being, language is the house of Being, through language Being comes into words, Being is granted, an epoch of history is a mittence of Being, science does not think, why are there beings rather than nothing?), yet, to the listener, do not adequately answer the very questions they ask. The reason for this "strange" lot of many Heideggerian statements is simply the fact that they introduce the listener into a new way of questioning. Among these expressions, there is one ("Why are there beings at all and not rather nothing?") that has a close relationship to the problem of God. The meaning and the original context of this expression, of this substantial question, are quite significant for the understanding of the entire Heideggerian God-question because they seem to imply a phenomenological "atheism." Heidegger claims that the person who truly (questioningly) asks the question "Why are there beings at all and not rather nothing?" ceases to be a believer. The genuine questioner (the true thinker) cannot remain a believer, and the believer, then, cannot be a true questioner (thinker): this is Heidegger's contention. This statement opposes true

questioning (thinking, philosophy) and Christian believing (the Biblical doctrine of creation, faith, theology). What is to be thought of
this presumed opposition? What is the meaning of the otherness of
philosophy in comparison to theology and that of theology in comparison to philosophy? Are they characterized by a hermetic enclosure? What is the right meaning of Heidegger's statement? What is
the final intent of his claim? Is phenomenological "atheism" a condition of genuine questioning? The issue at stake here is not the denial
of God through philosophy but, much rather, the elimination of genuine thinking (philosophizing) from the Biblical understanding of
God. Heidegger's reflections on the relationship between philosophy
and faith seem to call for eliminating philosophy (as genuine questioning-thinking) from the problem of God.

All the preceding considerations indicate that the unfolding of
Heidegger's thinking creates a new kind, a new level, of questioning.
This new kind of questioning leads to one of the most questionable
aspects of the Heideggerian questioning-process itself, to the (presumed) fundamental opposition between questioning (thinking) and
believing (the act of faith); it establishes phenomenological "atheism"
as a condition of true questioning. This is a crucial issue in the development of the Heideggerian God-question as a question.

After the analysis of the nature of the (Western) metaphysical
questioning, therefore, one should enter into the new kind of questioning and, thus, gain some new insight into the question of God in
Heidegger's thinking. This is the reason for the next phase of this
study, for the reflections on EM as the solid example of the new way
of thinking, of the meditation on the meaning of Being in the later
(the "second") Heidegger. This thematic continuity of thought (the
focusing on the types of thinking and questioning) bridges the chronological distances between the writings selected for closer analysis. EM
(the text of Heidegger's lecture course at Freiburg during the summer
semester of 1935, first published in 1953 and most recently in 1983
as volume 40 of the *Gesamtausgabe*) will be examined first, and then
some other works written before as well as after its composition. EM
includes the description of the genuine questioner; it clarifies some
important aspects of the question of God in Heidegger. It should be
emphasized that this work represents a "new" phase in the development of Heidegger's way of thinking (the ideas of the later Heidegger); it examines the nature of thinking as an essential element of the
question of Being and even indicates some possible new dimensions
of the problem of God. The relationship between the Being-question

and the God-question, therefore, remains an important dimension of Heidegger's thought as a whole. EM shows the "newness" of the later Heidegger as well as the continuity of his thought; it is committed to the primordial project of rethinking the foundation of metaphysics by means of thinking the question of Being.

The claim regarding the opposition of questioning to believing, according to EM, should be considered as something more than an accidental remark. This antinomy, indeed, is an expression of the situation of the problem of God in the later Heidegger. The antinomy of questioning and believing leads to a definitive separation (distan-tiation) of the metaphysical notion of God from the concept of Being.[1] This separation leads, ultimately, even to the irrelevance of the meta-physical problem of God, an irrelevance understandable (and perhaps valid) only in the context of Heidegger's thought.

Heidegger's reflections on the nature of metaphysics as the core of philosophy (the thinking of Being) distinguish the leading-question (*Leitfrage*) and the ground-question (*Grundfrage*) of meta-physics.[2] The leading question, the question that guides traditional metaphysics, is essentially the following: What is being as such? This question is concerned with "what" (a) being is, with the "whatness" of beings in general (thus reducing metaphysics to physics); it does not thematize Being as such, even though its formulations in the history of philosophy represent an inquiry into the Being of beings. The history of traditional metaphysics is dominated by the leading-ques-tion, by the study of beings as such without going beyond (particular) beings to Being as such. The ground-question of (genuine) meta-physics is focused not on the "whatness" but on the "why" of being(s), on the fact (rather: event, process) "that" there are beings (on the "thatness" of beings, on Being as such). The ground-question of meta-physics in the final analysis is the following: Why are there beings at all? This question is an inquiry into the wonder "that" there are beings and not rather nothing; it thematizes Being; it tries to think and say that "Being is." The ground-question is a truly ontological question; it is a concern with Being. To ask the ground-question of metaphysics, to ground (the "new") metaphysics (according to Heidegger), means to raise and confront the most radical form of the why-question: "Why are there beings at all and not rather nothing?"[3] This ground-question has its own history; its unfolding is part of the history of the problem of Being. The history of the ground-question manifests the problem of Being as the destiny (*Schicksal*) of the Western world, as the lot of Western culture. What is the meaning of Being? How does it stand with Being? This is the preliminary question (*Vorfrage*) of the ground-question, a question that precedes and is included in the ground-question; it is, at the same time, the dynamic element, the heart of the ground-question and that of all essential, authentic questioning.[4] The question regarding the meaning of Being (What is Being? How does it stand with Being?), the preliminary question contained in the ground-question of metaphysics, constitutes a fundamentally historical inquiry (*geschichtliches Fragen*), because the meaning of Being (the way Being is comprehended and interpreted) determines the entire history of the West. We need to retrieve (*wiederholen*), to find again, the beginning (*Anfang*) of our historical There-being and thus to transform it into another beginning.[5] This retrieval (recapturing) shall allow us to ask the question about the meaning of Being and, thus, to grasp this question as a question about our situation with regard to Being itself (about our attitude toward "what" and "how" Being is). We need to reconstruct, we need to commence again more originally (*ursprünglicher wiederanfangen*), our history, because our relationship to Being has been disturbed (it became ambiguous), because we have fallen out (*herausgefallen*) of the true "place" (situation) of our existence (strayed away from the authentic way of being) where we could understand and listen to the language that speaks in the word *Being*.[6] Indeed, according to Heidegger's analysis, we have fallen out of Being itself and, therefore, we cannot find the meaning and the weight of the word *Being* in the light of this historical situation. The reconstitution, the new (another) beginning (retrieval) of our existence (of our relationship to Being) is a historical task; it is a fundamental event (*Grundgeschehnis*) of our history.

This means, then, that the Being-question is a completely historical question[7] and that the task of rethinking (retrieving) the history of this question (in Heidegger) is to find a new relationship to Being. It is precisely this relationship that characterizes our life and destiny. Metaphysics as a historical destiny of Being shall be overcome (*Überwindung*) through an original thinking of the history of Being (as it becomes manifest in the history of the Being-question) and through the understanding of Being as history. This new, essential thinking, however, is not granted without a transformation of our classical, limited idea about thinking. The new way of thinking is not easy. The task of philosophy, as Heidegger explains it, consists precisely in "making things more difficult" (*Erschwerung*), in giving back to things (beings) their weight (*Gewicht*), in giving them back Being.[8] This is the Heideggerian notion of philosophy. Making things more difficult, therefore, means giving them back their true meaning, giving them back Being and thus overcoming their "emptiness" through this recovery of meaning. Such a recovery is the ground-condition of true history. To think Being, to "get back" or to "find again" the meaningfulness of the word *Being*: such is the purpose of the Heideggerian reawakening (repetition, retrieving) of the "past" (tradition) of philosophy. This is the reason for unearthing and reflecting on even the unthought elements in the thoughts of the great thinkers.

The essence of philosophy, therefore, consists in questioning, in the meditative (essential) thinking of Being. Philosophy, for Heidegger, is ontology. However, Heidegger refuses to use this term because of the traditional meaning attached to it.[9] Heidegger's philosophy (a phenomenological ontology) is an "ontology" in a special way since it is an effort to bring Being into word(s) (*das Sein zum Wort zu bringen*) through a questioning-thinking through of the question of Being (What about Being?). Traditional (that is, scholastic) ontology, in Heidegger's view, remains on the level of the question of beings; it leaves unasked the question of Being. The Heideggerian ground-question of metaphysics (Why are there beings at all and not rather nothing?) already contains the preliminary question of metaphysics (What about Being?). Therefore, the ground-question of metaphysics (in Heidegger) cannot be reduced to the question that is concerned merely with beings (as the leading question of traditional metaphysics: What is being? What are beings?) and ignores the question of Being.

These considerations on the nature of philosophy and on the discernment of the foundational question of Being constitute an indispensable background for the following examination of Heidegger's claims regarding the relationship between philosophical thinking and faith-knowledge.

"Why are there beings at all and not rather nothing?" EM's meditations on the nature of metaphysics and on the concept of Being elaborate the primordial and historical significance of this question. This is the broadest (it comprises all beings), the most profound (it refers to the ground of all beings), and the most original (it deals with beings-in-their totality and it involves the questioner, the human being, in the question) philosophical question according to Heidegger's phenomenological analysis of the human concern with the meaning of Being, with the comprehension of Being.[10] Heidegger insists that there is no question here of grounding beings through a particular being, because this question simply refers to all beings and

thus also to the grounding being itself. The "why" of this philosophical question does not refer to a grounding being (*Seiendes als gründendes*) of all beings. A grounding-minded interpretation of the "why"
of this question would be a misunderstanding of the entire question
at stake in this question. Heidegger acknowledges the fact that many
philosophical systems presuppose precisely a grounding-minded
interpretation of this question by calling the grounding being Matter,
Spirit, Creator, or God. However, Heidegger regards these ground-
ings of all beings as the result of an incomplete understanding of the
fundamental philosophical issue at stake. According to Heidegger's
phenomenological analysis, philosophy begins with the most radical
meaning of the "why," with the thinking of the "why of the why" of
all beings. The asking of the philosophical "why" is an important
event (*Geschehnis*) that leads the questioner to the very source of philosophizing. The philosophical why-question is something so profound that it is necessarily being asked with (*mitgefragt*) and in every
truthful (*wahrhafte*) question.[11] All authentic questioning includes the
asking of the philosophical "why" as the source (*Ursprung*) of all
human questions.

Philosophy is a radical questioning about beings and Being as
such; it is a fundamental and foundational way of knowing that ought
to go deeper than a mere talking about the "why" or the unexamined
acceptance of a ready-made answer that is already contained in the
asking of the question itself. The differing interpretations of the question of Being (Being as Matter, Being as Spirit, Being as God), according to Heidegger's reflections on the history of philosophy, remain
inadequate because they identify (they let coincide) Being (as such)
with a particular being; they ignore the ontological difference and
leave unexamined (unquestioned) the meaning of Being. The
grounding-minded interpretation of the question "Why are there
beings at all and not rather nothing?" ultimately refers all beings to
a particular being (as their cause and ground), and thus it ignores the
fact that the "why" of this question relates to all beings, even to the
grounding being itself because the grounding being is still one of the
particular beings. The radical nature of the "why" as a true ontological
question is obscured and forgotten by accepting "the-taken-for-
granted" meaning of the "why" that is in the last analysis based on
the unexamined identification of the meaning of Being with a particular being. According to Heidegger's phenomenological ontology,
there cannot be a genuine understanding of the "why" contained in
the original question without discovering the ontological difference,

and thus, without thinking the question of Being. Philosophical knowledge becomes foundational knowledge by rethinking the foundations and assumptions of all knowing, by searching for the "why" of all human "whys." The Aristotelian distinction between philosophy as the concern with the ultimate causes (whys, explanations) of things and science as the concern with the immediate causes (whys, explanations) of things is based on the radicalization of the "why" and thus on the understanding of the differing dimensions of questioning and interpreting things and beings. For both Aristotle and Heidegger, the scientific questioning as such, that is, the scientific "why," does not constitute the more radical philosophical (ontological) "why" but ultimately is possible only on the ground of the genuine philosophical why-question.

Heidgger's ontological analysis of the question "Why are there beings at all and not rather nothing?" leads him to the claim that the acceptance of the Biblical doctrine of creation as the answer to the philosophical question about the "why" of beings takes away the radicalness of the "why," and, thus, it is not compatible with genuine philosophical questioning-thinking. If the Biblical doctrine is interpreted as the answer to the "why," that is, if it is understood as saying that there are beings at all and not rather nothing because beings have been created by God, then, there is no "place" here for a true "why" of beings at all because one of them (the highest being, God) that is still "just" a particular being functions as the "why" or the explanation of all the other particular beings. Therefore, the Biblical doctrine should not be interpreted as revealing the answer (as constituting the response) to the ontological dimension of the "why." It seems, consequently, that phenomenological "atheism" (or at least "atheologism") ought to be a condition of, a prerequisite for, genuine philosophical questioning. However, the problem is not so simple. Heidegger's claim should be understood in its right context. The relationship between philosophy (phenomenology) and faith (theology) is examined here by Heidegger mainly from the perspective of the clarification of the ontological question of Being. The following four considerations present and analyze his claims.

a) According to the expression of EM, the acceptance of the Biblical doctrine of creation as divine revelation and divine truth means "having the answer" to the philosophical question about the "why" of beings at all even before this question is being asked.[12] Biblical faith teaches that everything is created by God and that God is the uncreated being. Consequently, the "why," the explanation of why there are beings at all and not rather nothing, is God. If someone stays on the ground of such a faith, he can, in a way, take part in the asking of the philosophical "why" (*das Fragen unserer Frage in gewisser Weise nach- und mitvollziehen*), "but he cannot really question without ceasing to be a believer (*er kann nicht eigentlich fragen ohne sich selbst als einen Gläubigen aufzugeben*) and taking all the consequences of such a step."[13] For Heidegger, therefore, the man of faith (the believer) is not a genuine questioner but merely an "actor" of a disguised (pretended) questioning; that is, the believer can only act "as if" (*als ob*). The question "Why are there beings at all and not rather nothing?" is not a true question for the man of faith, for the believer. When the man of faith asks this question, he already knows the answer. Where philosophy creates a question mark, faith replaces it by an exclamation mark. The antinomy between philosophy (thinking) and faith (believing) is emphasized here quite strongly.

b) Heidegger's examination of the relationship between philosophy and faith acknowledges the dynamic nature and the complexity of the faith attitude, of the act of religious faith. The attitude of faith is continually challenged and tested by its opposite, by the temptations of other intellectual alternatives, by the real possibility of unfaith. The attitude of faith and the attitude of unfaith call out each other and are engaged in a continuous struggle with each other; the danger of unfaith or unbelief (phenomenological "atheism" or "atheologism" as a prerequisite for genuine philosophical questioning) is regarded in Heidegger's interpretation as a contextual element of the faith attitude or belief. He says, "On the other hand, a faith that does not perpetually expose itself to the possibility of unfaith (*Möglichkeit des Unglaubens*) is no faith (*kein Glauben*)," but sheer convenience (*Bequemlichkeit*) and an agreement with oneself to hold on to the traditional teaching.[14] This attitude of indolence is neither faith nor genuine questioning, "but the indifference (*Gleichgültigkeit*) of those who can busy themselves with everything, some times even displaying a keen interest in faith as well as in questioning."[15]

c) Heidegger acknowledges here a theological epistemology of the faith attitude. The strength and the security of the faith attitude (*Geborgenheit im Glauben*), according to his own expression, are special ways of staying in the truth (*in der Wahrheit zu stehen*). However, he also calls attention to the fact that this recognition of the security in faith (or of faith) does not yield a philosophical epistemology of the content of religious faith because the quotation of the teaching of the Bible (God created heaven and earth) does not contain the answer to the philosophical "why." The Biblical statement, regardless of its truth status from the perspective of faith, cannot represent an answer (*keine Antwort darstellen*) to the genuine philosophical ("why"-) question, because the Biblical statement has no relation to such a question (*weil es auf diese Frage keinen Bezug hat*). Indeed, continues Heidegger, the Biblical statement cannot be brought into relation to the philosophical question precisely because what is being asked in the genuine philosophical question (Why are there beings at all and not rather nothing?) is regarded as foolishness from the perspective of the faith attitude.[16]

d) This last remark indicates the antinomy between philosophical knowledge and faith knowledge, between questioning-thinking and theological reflection. Heidegger regards faith knowledge (theology) with an attitude of respect. Theology, he says, is a thinking-questioning (*denkend fragende*) elaboration of the Christian experience of the world (*christlich erfahrene Welt*): it is a thoughtful reflection on the content and meaning of religious faith. The epochs that do not believe in the true greatness (*wahrhafte Grösse*) of the task of theology, however, come to the fatal opinion (*verderbliche Meinung*) that "with the help of philosophy, theology can be renewed or even substituted, and then it can be adapted to the taste and needs of the time."[17] However, for the genuine and original Christian faith, according to Heidegger's conclusion, philosophy is foolishness and the idea of a "Christian philosophy" is a square circle (*ein hölzernes Eisen*, literally "a wooden iron") and a misunderstanding. The thinking-questioning (reflection) elaboration of the Christian experience (faith) cannot be called philosophy; it is theology. Philosophy is foolishness for true theology. To philosophize, Heidegger insists, means to ask, "Why are there beings at all and not rather nothing?" To ask this fundamental question authentically in a philosophical manner, with an entirely open mind, means "to dare to exhaust this inexhaustible question by unveiling what it calls us to ask; to pursue our questioning all the way through (*durchzufragen*)."[18] Where such a questioning occurs (*geschieht*), there, concludes the author, is philosophy.

For Heidegger, therefore, the philosophical why-question is not exhausted by finding the ultimate cause of all beings, by explaining all beings through a particular being as the source of all beings. The philosophical "why," according to the preceding four considerations, ought to be pursued to its outmost limit by regarding all beings (even the highest being) in virtue of Being, by asking, "How does it stand with Being?" The most essential task of philosophy, then, is to ask this question, to practice the art of thinking in such a way that the disclosure of Being and thus a more profound understanding of beings may come about. The early Greek philosophers' meditations on "nature," their way of grasping beings in the light of "nature," represent a "fundamental poetizing-thinking experience of Being," a way of asking the question "How does it stand with Being?"[19] To philosophize is to listen to the "voice" of Being. True philosophy does not need to worry about being "modern" or fashionable. Philosophy often remains "untimely" (*unzeitgemäss*) and unpopular. The so-called popularity of a philosophical system is not the sign of its authenticity. Philosophy is not the concern with ordinary, popular "modern" ideas; it is an attempt to investigate the extraordinary, to examine that which is beyond the routine and fashionable content of thought. To philosophize means to inquire into the extraoridnary (*Fragen nach dem Ausser-ordentlichen*). This notion of philosophy illuminates the "atheistic" connotations of the passage of EM just analyzed. This passage is a clear expression of the second phase (the phase of questioning) of the Heideggerian God-question. It appears now that the traditional problem of God is marginalized by and even pushed "outside" of this philosophy; it is an irrelevant question in this new (phenomenological) way of thinking. But it is precisely this irrelevance that becomes the relevant dimension of the problem of God in Heidegger's thought. This irrelevance comes from the distancing of philosophy from theology, from the opposition (in Heidegger's view) between the nature of thinking (philosophizing) and the act of faith (and theology as the reflection on the given content of faith).

The antinomy of philosophy and faith ought to be understood in the context of the Heideggerian notion of philosophizing as radically different from all the other ways of knowing and thinking. There is a distantiation (a source of autonomy) of philosophical knowing from faith knowing that is the result of the "distance" that separates the philosophical "why" from the why of theological questioning "predetermined" by the Biblical answer of creation. The true questioner ceases being a believer (a man of faith) in order to be (or to become) a genuine questioner: a questioner who is "freed" from the answer given by the security of Biblical faith. This antinomy between philosophical knowledge and faith knowledge is not a judgment on the truth value of faith; it is merely a prerequisite for pushing the questioning process to its very end. Surely, this view is built on the assumption that the man of faith, the believer, cannot be a genuine questioner-thinker. Heidegger, at the same time, rejects the atheistic interpretation of the antinomy between philosophy and faith by claiming that he is not questioning (rejecting) here the teachings of faith, of the "dogmas of the Catholic Church."[20] Thus the atheological dimension of philosophical thinking (the "atheistic" condition of philosophical questioning) emphasizes the ontological interpretation of the meaning of Being (the main task of philosophy) and not the original Christian doctrine of creation. Philosophical questioning-thinking goes beyond the doctrine of creation—it is different from and it tries to overcome the Christian understanding of the Being of beings as being created (*Geschaffenheit*) by God[21]—because philosophy is a concern with the question of Being, with the "why" of all beings at all. The question about the ontic origin of beings is another question and a metaphysical one that is not resolved by these considerations. Heidegger's reflections in the final analysis are focused on the ontological assumptions of the doctrine of creation (on the Christian interpretation of Being) and not on the religious, theological idea and message of creation.

However, it is difficult to accept the Heideggerian interpretation of the believer, of the man of faith, insofar as this one cannot be a true questioner. That the believer cannot be a true questioner remains questionable. Obviously, there can be a way of understanding the doctrine of creation (and of other faith claims) that creates an obstacle to a true questioning attitude. But, even in this case, the particular interpretation of creation could be understod as being a "reduction" (and thereby a transformation) of the original content of faith to an intellectual attitude that is not necessarily a consequence (nor a condition) of the acceptance of the content of faith as such. Therefore, the Heideggerian claim that the true questioner (thinker) ceases being a believer is hardly acceptable without the further clarification of this problem.

The following three remarks indicate some important dimensions of the problem involved in Heidegger's claim.

a) The acceptance of the Biblical teaching on creation should not be regarded as an *eo ipso* obstacle to genuine questioning and thinking. Indeed, it should be recognized that the acceptance of the Biblical teaching on creation is no less an obstacle to genuine questioning than its a priori rejection as a possible answer to the "why." The believer, the theologian, is a questioner; he asks the question of the "why" of creation and thinks over the freedom of God in creating. Therefore, the acceptance of the Biblical answer to the question does not mean an exemption from further questioning and searching for understanding.

Nevertheless, it seems to Heidegger that the believer answers his questions even before asking them. It is possible to understand this claim of Heidegger by situating it "inside" the entire ontological context of his philosophy. He is concerned with the meaning of Being and tries to understand beings in themselves together with their relationship to Being as such. A clear distinction between the ontological interpretation of beings and the theological understanding of the world is always maintained in Heidegger's phenomenology. This distinction, however, should not be regarded as the elimination of any concern with the question of God from the horizon of the phenomenological understanding of the truth of Being. EM speaks of (Christian) faith as a way of "staying in the truth" and understands theology as a thinking-questioning elaboration and examination of the Christian experience of the world.[22] These remarks may be regarded as some indication of an openness of the phenomenological reflection toward a possible new approach to the question of God. Finally, it should be kept in mind that Heidegger never claimed that his ideas contain all the answers to the questions of our time. The fundamental historicity of truth, the epochal mittence of Being, the notion of philosophy as questioning, and many other elements of Heidegger's thought ought to be taken into consideration by anyone who listens to the "atheistic" overtones of the thinking of Being.

b) As Heidegger says, "a faith that does not perpetually expose itself to the possibility (*Möglichkeit*) of unfaith, is no faith."[23] This important remark becomes significant in the light of the theological reflection on the question of contemporary atheism. Today's theological understanding of human existence speaks of the unbelief of the believer, of the fragility and complexity of the act of faith; it recognizes the danger (the temptation element, the negativity) or possibility of unfaith (unbelief) in the experience of faith (belief). J. B. Metz, for instance, calls attention to the question of unbelief as a theological problem: "The experience of free faith remains *before and for itself* essentially ambivalent; it is ultimately and inevitably endangered by the possibility of unbelief."[24] This ambivalence of the experience of faith may well correspond to the Heideggerian idea on the exposure of true faith to the possibility (danger) of unfaith. K. Rahner, when analyzing the structure (*Gestalt*) of faith today, speaks of the "character of questionability" or doubtfulness (*Bezweifelbarkeit*) as a permanent quality of the "faith of the pilgrim."[25] This danger of unbelief is "part" of the experience of Christian faith precisely because even the believer remains a questioner according to the theological understanding of the act of faith.

Faith cannot be reduced (at least not entirely) to an act of the intellect. Faith is a commitment of one's whole existence (*Dasein*) to God. As R. Bultmann insists: true Christian faith is a resolution (*Entschluss*), a decision (*Entscheidung*), "an answer to the word of God," "a gift of God."[26] The act of faith as a response to the word of God means that that word is a word to be understood by man as a response to man's questions, and, as Bultmann continues, this understanding of the word of God and of man's response is impossible without thinking (questioning), an understanding that sometimes becomes impossible without a "philosophical thinking" (*philosophisches Denken*).[27] However, this kind of thinking, from Heidegger's point of view, is already theology. This is the reason why Heidegger insists that the true questioner, the philosophical questioner, ceases to be a believer when genuinely asking the ground-question of metaphyhsics: "Why are there beings at all and not rather nothing?" Heidegger claims at the same time that his view on the antinomy between philosophy and faith does not include a decision about the truth value of the Biblical response. Therefore, as T. Langan says, "Heidegger tries to found a phenomenology of finite truth that can guard a sense of mystery."[28]

c) In spite of the fact that Heidegger insists on the distinction (and "distance") between philosophy and faith (theology), he himself seems to situate the Biblical teaching on the same level as the ontological concern of his phenomenology. Thus he is not following his own advice. This "one-dimensionality" (*Eindimensionalität*) and "indistinctiveness" (*Ununterschiedenheit*) of the above-analyzed passage in Heidegger's EM are clearly pointed out by M. Müller,[29] who calls attention to the difference that separates the level of religious questioning (faith-thinking) that is concerned with historical facticity from the level of ontological-metaphysical questioning that is concerned with ontological structures and meanings (*Sinn-Ursprung, Seinszusammenhänge*). Heidegger himself is aware, very much indeed, of the differences (the "otherness") between religious (faith) questioning and philosophical questioning. These differences come from the original nature of the experience of Christian faith. He says "the Christian experience is something so entirely different (from philosophy) that it has no need to enter into competition with philosophy."[30] It seems, therefore, that M. Müller rightly speaks of an inconsistency in the above-analyzed passage of Heidegger dealing with the relationship between philosophical thinking and faith-understanding.

However, it seems (especially here) that the problem of the

Heideggerian antinomy between questioning (philosophy) and believing (faith) *remains,* because Heidegger's claim is that the genuine questioner *as such* (the philosophical, the ontological questioner) ceases to be a believer (a man of faith). The ontological answer (concerned with meaning and ontological structures) does not include a solution (answer) either to the ontical or to the religious questioning and interpretation of beings and vice versa.[31] In fact, Heidegger himself says in the text analyzed earlier in this study that the Biblical answer to the "why" of all beings at all cannot be an answer to the philosophical question precisely because it has no relation at all (*keinen Bezug hat*) to the philosophical question. The above-mentioned inconsistency of Heidegger, therefore, does not resolve the problem of the antinomy between philosophy and faith. The question *remains* even in and with Heidegger.

An analysis of the nature and the meaning of the act of faith ought to be considered as of vital importance for the entire question about the relationship between philosophical knowledge and faith-understanding. Questioning as such is not an alien element to the faith attitude. When the Christian "accepts the faith" (a gift offered to the human being) through a personal and free "decision" he does not shy away from questioning; rather he "takes a step forward" with all the risks of such a "venture," a venture and an adventure that is the quality of genuine questioning according to Heidegger's expression.[32] The believer, the man of faith, remains *and* becomes, again and again, a true questioner, because he cannot grasp God in the act of faith. He can only experience, as R. Otto says, the mystery of the "wholly other," of "that which is no-thing."[33] The genuine Christian, the man of faith, precisely as a believer, *is,* in the expression of Paul Ricoeur, "an adversary to absurdness and a prophet of meaningfulness."[34]

Therefore, it may be concluded that the true questioner, the questioner of the meaning of Being included, does not have to cease being a believer, a man of faith, just because he is intent on the radicality of questioning-thinking. The man of faith, the Christian included, is not being "taken out of" but rather "drawn into" the "circle of understanding" (*Zirkel des Verstehens*), because even his faith has to be an understandable faith (at least to some extent) and, therefore, characterized by "the unity of meaning."[35]

16

The Indifference of the Questioning

I t seems that the nature and the final goal (direction) of the process of questioning (philosophical thinking) in Heidegger leave "aside" and remain indifferent toward the entire metaphysical problem of God. The reason for this indifference is the theological indifference of the ontological difference.

The ontological difference comes about through the "overcoming" of metaphysics. When this difference of Being and being(s) occurs (*ereignet*), then Being can lighten (*lichten*) in its truth.[1] The forgottenness of Being comes from the fact that the difference is being wrapped up in darkness (*verhüllt*), because the "primacy" (*Vorrang*) of being(s) over Being characterizes metaphysics. The culmination (*Vollendung*) of metaphysics, that is, the coming to an end of its history, is a preparatory phase (*Vorbereitung*) of the appearance (*Erscheinen*) of the "ambivalence" (*Zwiefalt*) of twofold character of Being and being(s). Metaphysics constitutes the lot of the Western world; it assures man's domination over beings. Metaphysics is history; it is the history of Being in its forgottenness (*Seinsvergessenheit*). Hence the "overcoming" of metaphysics is a sign of the beginning disappearance of the forgottenness of Being. This "overcoming" should be thought according to Being-as-history (*seinsgeschichtlich*); it

should be situated entirely in the history of Being. This means, therefore, that the "overcoming" of metaphysics is a disappearance (*Ver-
windung*) of metaphysics and an event (*Ereignis*), a lighting-up, of the
truth of Being. The "overcoming" of metaphysics is a "handing over"
(*Überlieferung*) of metaphysics to its own truth, to the truth of Being,
because "the truth of Being is the ground of all metaphysics."[2] The
lot of metaphysics is the lot of Being; it is the manifestation of Being
in its history and a hidden coming forth of Being as history.

The retrieval (rethinking) of the history of philosophy is understood as an effort to overcome the metaphysical forgottenness of
Being; thus it prepares the ground for the coming forth of the ontological difference as the manifestation of the truth of Being. Philosophical questioning means a "revival" of history; it is a "waking-up-
from" the undisturbed security of the rational (law of "reason") and
technical (Will-to-Power) tyranny of being(s) over Being and a "wak-
ing-up-to" the "daylight" that comes from the lighting-process (*Lichtung*) of Being in its truth through the event of the ontological
difference.

How does this event of the ontological difference come about?
The forgottenness of Being is not the result of some negligence of
man; it is, ultimately, rooted in the nature ("quality"), in the mystery
of Being itself.[3] The human being, therefore, can only wait for this
historical event because the ontological difference comes about
through authentic thinking. However, authentic (essential, meditative) thinking (*wesentliches Denken, Gelassenheit*) is something very difficult for man. It is not the result of a philosophical "brainwashing,"
and it cannot be considered as something to be stirred up within man
(*nicht von uns aus bei uns*). Man can only wait and remain open for the
hidden manifestation of truth and in this way learn the art of authentic thinking as an act of "remembrance" (*Andenken*) and as a "changing
of our relationship to Being."[4]

The ultimate reason for the forgottenness of Being is the finitude of Being, the finitude of the mittence of Being. This finitude
constitutes the cornerstone of Heidegger's philosophy.

For Heidegger the essence of philosophy is questioning and
thinking. It is the questioning-thinking of Being, of the ontological
difference. Philosophy is thinking as the thinking of Being. The main
thrust of Heidegger's thought is the unfolding of the full dynamics
of questioning; it is the search for and not the possession of answers.

The questioning-thinking of the ontological difference constitutes the basic perspective of the works of the later ("second") Hei-

degger. There is no place here for the description of the history of this development. It is not the task of these reflections to retrace the period of "transition" to the later Heidegger; their established objective consists in situating and understanding the meaning and the function of the question of God in Heidegger's developing thought. Thus, after this preview of the main thrust of Heidegger's questioning, it becomes possible to grasp the indifference of this same questioning toward the philosophical (metaphysical) problem of God. This indifference comes from the questioning-process, and thus it should be understood as the indifference of questioning and not as the indifference of a philosophical agnosticism. The issue at hand consists precisely in grasping the theological indifference implied *in* the ontological difference, in seeing the possibility of a theological difference *after* the comprehension of the ontological difference. The theological indifference of Heidegger's meditation on the ontological difference can be shown clearly enough because Heidegger himself is quite explicit about it. The question of the theological difference goes beyond Heidegger's immediate task of thinking the ontological difference even though there are some indications in his works about the difficult question of the theological difference from the point of view of the question of Being.

The thinking of Being is described by Heidegger as an experiencing of the "nothing" of beings (*das nichtende Nicht des Nichts*) and as the thinking of the ontological difference (*das nichtende Nicht der Differenz*). The first description is the theme of WM (written in 1929, with an epilogue in 1943 and an introduction in 1949); the second is that of WG (written in 1929). This advancing in the thinking of Being is revealed also in the meditation on the essence of truth (WW, written in 1930, some change of the text in 1949). The interpretation of Plato's doctrine on truth (PW, written in 1940) shows clearly that the Heideggerian meditation on the truth of Being is a reflection on the history of the Being-question. Metaphysics as the errance (*Irre*) of the Being-question begins with Plato's metaphysics and reaches its final phase (*Vollendung*) in Nietzsche's metaphysics of Will. EM gives a clear analysis of the change that takes place in Plato's understanding of Being.[5] The lectures and essays on Nietzsche (N, 1 and N, 2; 1936–1946) contain extensive meditations on the history of metaphysics and show the meaning of the end of philosophy as metaphysics; they interpret the history of metaphysics as the destiny of Being.

The writings just mentioned introduce the reader into the thinking of the ontological difference, the only thing that "makes the difference" in Heidegger's thought. This difference appears as indifference toward the philosophical problem of God. This indifference as a distinct characteristic of the ontological questioning results from the fidelity to the process of "overcoming" (traditional as well as modern) metaphysics. However, the God-question remains a question; even more, it appears as a question that should be asked and rethought continually during the entire process of "overcoming" metaphysics. Heidegger rejects the metaphysical understanding of God insofar as it is a metaphysical understanding. The Heideggerian indifference toward a philosophical notion of God cannot be taken for an elimination of the philosophical problem of God but rather as a "pointing to" the crisis of the God-question as part of the entire problem of metaphysics as such. When metaphysics rediscovers its original ground, when it is "handed-over" (*Überlieferung*) and "driven back" (*Schritt zurück*) to the truth of Being, then, and only then, could the God-question be asked *again*, that is, it could be asked in a new way. The "destruction" of metaphysics, therefore, cannot be regarded as a decision about a possible affirmation or negation of God. The God-question as a question remains without a solution.

The thinking of the ontological difference claims to be indifferent towards the possibility of There-being's relationship to God. Consequently, the ontological difference should be understood as theologically indifferent, as characterized by theological indifference. It is important to understand the meaning of this dimension of indifference of the ontological difference. What is the reason for this indifference? To what extent does the God-question still remain a question? To what extent is the way it was asked in metaphysics doubtful or questionable? What is the difference, then, between the traditional (metaphysical) approach to and Heidegger's new perspective on the problem of God? What is the nature of this new question of God? What is the reason for the "irrelevance" of the problem of God in the context of the Being-question? There is no other answer to these questions, according to Heidegger, than the questioning of the ontological difference. This questioning as such is indifferent toward the affirmation as well as toward the negation of God. The nature of this indifference is shown through the following reflections on WG (a), WM (b), WW, and on PW (c).

a) The meaning of There-being as being-in-the-World was explained in SZ. This meditation is continued in WG with the themes of grounding, transcendence, and truth. The notions of freedom and ground acquire an ontological (phenomenological) meaning. Heidegger meditates, ultimately, on the meaning of Being, on the nature of the ontological difference. The following considerations analyze those remarks and insights in WG that have a special significance for the problem of God.

The ontological interpretation of There-being as to-be-in-the-World remains basically indifferent with regards to the possibility of There-being's relationship to (Being-towards) God (*Sein zu Gott*); it decides neither positively nor negatively about this question. However, continues Heidegger, the clarification of transcendence enables us to understand There-being as a being that transcends beyond beings to Being; this concept of There-being (*Begriff des Daseins*) makes it possible to ask what There-being's relationship to God is from the ontological point of view.[6] Heidegger's notion of transcendence, at the same time, remains indifferent with regard to "dialectical theology and medieval scholasticism."[7] There-being transcends (*Dasein transzendiert*), There-being "builds" the World; it is (according to the very essence of its Being) "World-builder" (*weltbildend*) and thus renders it possible for beings to manifest themselves.[8] The World is an existential; it belongs to the very essence (*Wesen*) of There-being. The new (existential, phenomenological) understanding of the World in Heidegger's way of thinking differs quite significantly from the many (anthropological, Biblical, theological, and metaphysical) interpretations of the World and of human existence according to the history of Western thought.[9]

Another indication of the theological indifference of the ontological questioning is the meaning of the finitude of things. The finitude of things is defined from the point of view of finite knowing and, therefore, as given already. As this new meaning of the finitude of things in Kant (as interpreted by Heidegger) is defined, the "argument" (*Nachweisung*) is not based on the consideration of things as being created by God (*Geschaffenheit durch Gott*). This later understanding of finitude represents a mere ontical view of things and does not reach the ontological problematic: such is Heidegger's conclusion.[10] The World, in Heidegger's ontological understanding, is the "original project (*Entwurf*) of There-being's possibilities."[11] The why-question (*Warumfrage*), referring to the ontical origin of the World, is made possible by the ontological understanding of "grounding," by the comprehension of Being, by the ontological truth that renders possible ontical truth.[12] For Heidegger, "ground" is the essential (transcendental) characteristic of Being as such; thus, this ground-character of Being allows one to speak of a ground of beings, and this is the reason for the validity of the "principle of ground" with regard to beings.[13]

The essence of the finitude of There-being is explained through the Being-structure (*Seinsverfassung*) of There-being itself. This ontological understanding of finitude should precede all description of the qualities of finitude and, especially, the clarification of the ontic origin of man's finitude.[14]

Finally, it should be mentioned that for Heidegger "*Freedom is the origin (Ursprund) of the principle of ground.*"[15] This is a result of the Heideggerian view of transcendence and of the understanding of There-being as to-be-in-the-World. The question of grounding and the entire problem of ground, from Heidegger's perspective, belong to the question about the Being of truth.[16] It is not feasible to develop the analysis of the just-mentioned meaning of freedom (contained in the third part of WG) because it would require a more comprehensive elaboration, which, in spite of its importance in Heidegger's philosophy, would go beyond the objective of these reflections.

Heidegger remains indifferent toward the affirmation as well as toward the negation of There-being's relationship to God. This indifference appears clearly in the ontological interpretation of finitude and that of the question of origin (the why-question). He rejects the atheistic as well as the anthropological interpretation of his ontological meditations. He says explicitly that the ontological interpretation of Being by means of the transcendence of There-being does not mean an "ontical derivation of being(s) other than There-being from (out of) the being called There-being" (*nicht ontische Ableitung des Alls des nicht-daseinsmässigen Seienden aus dem Seienden qua Dasein*).[17] The right understanding of There-being, however, can prepare the ground for asking the question of There-being's possible relationship to God. The possibility for asking the question of God, therefore, remains. This question, nevertheless, is not thought through (at least not fully) by Heidegger's phenomenology; it is not the primal focus of his way of thinking. The God-question seems to become irrelevant (to an extent) for the ontological interpretation of There-being and of the World. This irrelevance indicates that in Heidegger's philosophy there is a definite separation (distantiation) of the entire Being-question from the philosophical problem of God. The God-question as a question (as a philosophical question), however, can be asked again after the elucidation of the meaning of Being.

b) WM explains the nature and the ontotheological structure of metaphysics; it calls attention to the ambivalence (*Zwiegestal*) of the metaphysical understanding of Being.[18] The "new" and main theme of WM, however, is the development of the problem of Being as one with and in terms of the problem of "nothing" or Non-being (*Nichts*).[19] Non-being is revealed in anxiety "together with beings-in-the-ensemble" (*in eins mit dem Seienden im Ganzen*).[20] Anxiety discloses the "original openness (*ursprüngliche Offenheit*) of beings as such: that (*dass*) they are beings and not Non-being."[21] This means that there is an important relationship between the manifestation of Non-being and the manifestation of beings as such to There-being. Thus Heidegger explains: "Non-being is that which renders possible the manifestation of beings as such for the human There-being."[22] Non-being, therefore, is not an undetermined "opposite" (*Gegenüber*) for being, but it belongs to (*zugehörig zum*) the Being of being.[23] Man as There-being is the "placeholder" (*Platzhalter*) of Non-being.[24] This later expression means that There-being is characterized by its thrust into Non-being (*Hineingehaltenheit des Daseins in das Nichts*) and that it is so profoundly permeated by its way-of-being-finite (*Verendlichung*) that it cannot, by its own will and resolution, bring itself face to face with Non-being.

Non-being is revealed to There-being in and through the phenomenon of anxiety. It is this revelation of Non-being to There-being that renders possible the manifestation of beings as such to There-being. This manifestation (*Offenbarkeit*) of Non-being (ontological truth), therefore, makes it possible that beings can appear to There-being as beings. In the phenomenon of anxiety, when beings sink into Non-being, There-being perceives that beings-in-the-ensemble are other than Non-being; There-being discovers the marvelous fact *that* beings "are." This astonishment (*Verwunderung*) as the result of the manifestation of Non-being is the source of the "why?" of all questioning.[25] "Why are there beings at all and not rather Non-being?"[26] This ontological "why" is the ultimate source of all (for example, scientific) and every "why," of all questioning and grounding.

The experiencing of Non-being through the ontological disposition of strangeness (*Befremdlichkeit*), therefore, enables There-being to understand beings and thus to enter into comportment with them (*sich verhalten*).

However, understanding and discovering beings *as* beings, experiencing beings-in-their-totality, are made possible through the comprehension of Being; discovering beings as beings is the function of Being itself. Heidegger concludes, therefore, "In the Being of beings comes-to-pass (*geschieht*) Non-being in its very essence."[27] He resumes the main insights by saying that "Non-being . . . reveals itself (*enthüllt sich*) as belonging to the Being of beings."[28] He writes in the "Epilogue" of WM: "Non-being as the other than being is the veil of Being" (*Schleier des Seins*).[29]

Non-being and Being, therefore, belong together; they are one and the same. As Hegel says, "Pure Being and pure Non-being are thus one and the same."[30] Heidegger interprets this statement in the preceding context. For him, Being and Non-being belong together "because Being itself is finite in essence and is only revealed in the transcendence of There-being as thrusted into Non-being."[31] This indicates clearly that both transcendence (*Transcendenz*) and thrust into Non-being (*Hineingehaltenheit in das Nichts*) are taken to be equivalent; this equivalence (both mean There-being, *Da-sein*) is the reason for the "togetherness" of Non-being and Being.[32]

This is an important conclusion. It may be resumed as follows: There-being, therefore, can pass beyond beings, and it can comport itself toward beings by reason of the original manifestation of Non-being to the human There-being. The phenomenon of "going beyond" belongs to the essence of There-being; the human being (There-being), therefore, is metaphysical (it has a concern with transcendence, with Being).[33]

The entire question of Non-being, like the question of Being, pervades the whole of metaphysics, because it obliges us to face the origin of negation (*Verneinung*); it leads to the clarification of the legitimate place of "logic" in metaphysics."[34] The Heideggerian notion of Non-being is not the same as the traditional understanding of nothing (Non-being). The notion of Non-being in Heidegger cannot be grasped without at the same time understanding There-being, because There-being itself is essentially involved in the entire question of Non-being, in the encounter with nothing. The question of Non-being is a metaphysical question; it is a "going beyond" beings as beings-in-the-ensemble (*Hinausgehen über das Seiende als Seiendes im Ganzen*).[35] Non-being is more original than the "not" (*das Nicht*) and the negation (*Verneinung*). If Non-being is defined (according to the vulgar understanding) as "the negation of the totality of beings" (*Verneinung der Allheit des Seienden*), then this shows (toward the right direction) that to encounter this Non-being we must encounter somehow not so much this totality as its negation.[36] Non-being, therefore, is more original than the "not" and the negation; it belongs to the understanding of beings-in-their-totality, to the notion of Being.

Traditional metaphysics speaks of Non-being "in the quite ambiguous (*freilich mehrdeutig*) proposition: *ex nihilo nihil fit*, Non-being comes from Non-being."[37] This proposition interprets Non-being from the point of view of the metaphysical conception (*Grundauffassung*) of beings, and thus it leaves unasked the whole question of Non-beings and Being as such. Therefore, Heidegger insists, the metaphysical notion of Non-being (though important for metaphysics) speaks to us more about the metaphysical conception of being(s) than about the question of Non-being.

Ancient metaphysics defines Non-being (*Nichts*) as *not-being* (*Nichtseiendes*), as unformed matter that cannot form (*gestalten*) itself into being (*Seiendes*) and, therefore, cannot present an appearance (*Aussehen*, visage, (εἶδος). In this view, a being is "self-forming" (*sich bildende Gebilde*) and presents itself in an image (*im Bilde sich darstellt*); it "offers a view" (*Anblick*).

Christian dogma denies the truth of the proposition *ex nihilo nihil fit* and changes it into *ex nihilo fit—ens creatum*. Non-being means, then, the complete absence (*Abwesenheit*) of all beings apart from God. "Non-being now becomes the counterconcept to being in the true sense (*zum eigentlich Seienden*), the *summum ens*, God as *ens increatum*."[38] However, adds Heidegger, if God is God, he cannot know Non-being (*das Nichts*) as long as the "Absolute" excludes from itself all negativity (*Nichtigkeit*).

These two historical reminders (ancient metaphysics and Christian dogma as metaphysical) show, for Heidegger, that traditional metaphysics considers Non-being the counterconcept to what truly is (beings), as not-being, as the negation of beings. Finally, this "raw" (*roh*) historical review proves, in Heidegger's view, that traditional metaphysics leaves unasked the problem of Being and, with it, the problem of Non-being. However, when Non-being is discovered as something that creates a problem, then Non-being ceases to remain a mere negation; it reveals itself as belonging to the Being of beings.

Therefore, Heidegger can interpret the old proposition of *ex nihilo nihil fit* in a new way: in a way that is appropriate to the problem of Being. Thus he can say, *ex nihilo omne ens qua ens fit*.[39] This means that every being as (a) being is made out of (comes from) Non-being. The phenomenon of beings-in-their-totality comes to itself in the Non-being of There-being. In anxiety Non-being is disclosed together with beings-in-their-totality. The manifestation of Non-being renders possible the disclosure of beings as such. It can be seen, then, that the Heideggerian formulation of the old proposition is the expression of what was explained earlier with regard to Non-being. Beings as beings are "born" out of the experiencing of Non-being, out of the manifestation of Non-being to There-being. Man as There-being discovers beings as beings and understands them as being other than Non-being when he is brought face to face with Non-being. At the same time he experiences that beings are by reason of Being and that Being is by reason of beings. Non-being, then, is the "veil of Being." The problem of Non-being cannot be separated from the problem of Being. Non-being is the ground or possibility of all negation (and of all "not"); Being is the source, the ultimate ground, of all "why." It becomes quite clear that Heidegger is meditating on the problem of Being, on the problem of the coming about of the ontological difference.

The question about the meaning of Being remains indifferent to the problem of God because the metaphysical notion of God remains a metaphysical interpretation of beings (as being-created by God out of nothing, out of Non-being), and, therefore, it leaves unasked the entire question of Being as such. In the context of the Being-question, therefore, it is the metaphysical notion of God that is "overcome" by the meditation on the Being-question. The God-question as a question, however, *remains,* and it becomes a *new* question; it becomes a true question that should be asked in the context of the new understanding of Being. Heidegger shows clearly the need for this new kind of questioning, but he shall give just some general indications with regard to the "prerequisites" of this new questioning, of the new way of asking the God-question.

c) WW and PW contain Heidegger's deep insight into the entire problematic of truth. This original understanding of the meaning of truth develops the phenomenological notion of truth (SZ);[40] it foreshadows the coming phases of the author's developing thought. The four brief references[41] to the metaphysical notion of God give some evidence of the indifference of the Heideggerian questioning to the philosophical problem of God; they indicate the definitive separation (distancing) of theological questions from the philosophical problematic as such. Heidegger calls attention to a "theological explanation" (*theologische Erklärung*) contained in the traditional understanding of truth and intends to keep the philosophical definition of truth completely free of the "interference of theology" (*Einmischung der Theologie*).[42] WW is a meditation on the nature and meaning of truth as such. PW shows the historical dimension of the Heideggerian meditation on the problem of truth. The following reflections on these two essays are concerned with those aspects of the thinking of truth that have a more immediate relationship to the problem of God.

WW examines the traditional concept of truth and its ontolog-ical foundation.[43] Truth in the traditional sense is defined as *adae-quatio rei et intellectus* (truth is the correspondence, the conformity, between the intellect and the thing). This definition may mean that truth is *adaequation rei ad intellectum* (the conformity, the approxima-tion of the thing to the intellect); it also can mean, however, that truth is *adaequatio intellectus ad rem* (the conformity of the intellect to the thing). According to the later interpretation, truth means the confor-mity (*Angleichung*) of knowledge (of the intellect's act of judgment) to the thing (to the judged, to beings). In this case, then, truth means propositional, logical truth (*Satzwahrheit*). According to the former interpretation (*adaequatio rei ad intellectum*), however, truth means the conformity of things to knowledge. In this second case, then, truth means ontological truth (*Sachwahrheit*). In both cases truth itself is defined as the rightness (*Richtigkeit*), as the correctness of the confor-mity. The place of truth is the judgment, the act of the intellect.

This notion of truth as rightness, continues Heidegger, has its origin (*Ursprung*) in the medieval Christian faith that understands things to be true insofar as they (as creatures) conform to the idea of things in the divine intellect. Human knowledge, therefore, is true insofar as it conforms to the divine order of creation, that is, to the order of things (beings) insofar as this conforms to the divine idea. This means, then, that the conformity of things (creatures) to the *divine* intellect is the guarantee of the conformity (of the rightness of this conformity) of the *human* intellect to things. Human judgment and things (human knowledge in the intellect's act and beings) are true because they both conform to the divine order. The truth of human knowledge is rendered possible through the fact that all beings are creatures (the human intellect included) and that they all (things and the human intellect as true) conform to the divine idea. Human knowledge, therefore, is grounded upon the divine plan of creation as the "norm" for both human knowledge (the intellect's judgment) and created things. Finally, the notion of truth as rightness (of the conformity) is nothing else than the concordance, the harmony, with the order of creation (*ein "Stimmen" nach der Bestimmung der Schöpfungsordnung*).

This order, adds Heidegger, can be understood as a World-order (*Weltordnug*) without the idea of divine creation. The order of things can be regarded as an order according to reason (*Weltvernunft*), as the origin of the laws and of the intelligibility (*Verständlichkeit*) of things (objects). In this case, then, the logical truth needs no further foundation, because truth as such is understood as rightness. Onto-logical truth, at the same time, means the conformity of things to their "rational" concepts (*die Einstimmigkeit des vorhandenen Dinges mit seinem "vernünftigen" Wesensbegriff*). A final consequence of this under-standing of truth is the consideration of untruth (*Unwahrheit*) as non-concordance, as a simple nonconformity.

Heidegger, after having analyzed the traditional notion of truth as the rightness of the conformity, explains the inner possibility of conformity and the ground for the rightness of this conformity. A judgment is true because There-being (the being that judges) encoun-ters beings (the to-be-judged things) in their truth. The conformity is made possible through the relationship (of encounter) between the judgment and the judged (things). This means that There-being is characterized by the overtness of its comportment (*Offenständigkeit des Verhaltens*) with beings, by "standing open" toward that which is open (objects, beings).[44] This openness of There-being's comportment ren-ders possible the encounter with beings. Hence, beings can stand in the Open (*das Offene*), being what they are and in the way they are, and, thus, they come to be "sayable" (*sagbar*) in the judgment, in the expression. The Open, that is, the World as the project of There-being's possibilities and as the ground for all disclosure, renders it possible to encounter that which is open (*das Offenbare*).

The open character of There-being's comportment (*Verhalten*) as the possibility of the correctness of the judgment (truth) is grounded upon freedom (*Freiheit*) as the openness of There-being toward the Open and toward that which is open: "the essence of truth is freedom."[45] This freedom lets beings be what they are (*Freiheit als Seinlassen von Seiendem*); by letting them be manifest There-being "lets-itself-in-on the Open and its openness, within which all beings abide and comport themselves."[46] Truth, then, is freedom; it is lib-eration from concealment. For Heidegger, then, the problem of truth is the problem of the revealedness (*Entborgenheit*) and of the revealing (*Entbergung*) of beings-in-their-totality. This is the reason for the Hei-deggerian understanding of truth as nonconcealment (ἀλήθεια, *Unverborgenheit*).[47] "Truth is that unveiling of beings (*Entbergung des Seienden*) through which an openness comes to presence."[48] The unveiling of beings becomes possible because There-being is freedom; it is open toward and exposed to (*Aussetzung*) the Open. There-being is exposed to the revealment of beings as such. Thus, There-being is ek-sistence (*Ek-sistenz*), freedom; it is the unveiling of beings in their "what" and in their "how" (the way they are).

This new understanding of truth as nonconcealment is the source of the Heideggerian understanding of untruth (*Unwahrheit*) as something intrinsic to truth, as the concealment (as the hiddenness) of beings-in-their-totality (*die Verborgenheit des Seinden im Ganzen*) prior to the manifestation of this or that particular being. This means that the letting-be (the manifestation-process) of beings is, at the same time, a concealing of beings, and that the manifestation of beings in-their-totality does not coincide with the total of particular beings known.[49] The concealment of the concealed in its totality, that is, of beings as such, is what Heidegger calls the mystery (*Geheimnis*) as the authentic nonessence (*Un-wesen*) of truth that permeates the entire nature of There-being.[50] There-being forgets this mystery by the adherence to beings, by the daily ontic commerce with them. This possibility of "ontic perdition" is the result of the fact that There-being is not only ek-sistent freedom but also in-sistent freedom; it can be tied down to beings. Briefly: "There-being not only ek-sists but at the same time *insists*."[51] This means that the mystery remains forgotten. A second form of untruth (the first: mystery) is "errance" (*Irre*).[52] Heidegger explains it as something that belongs to the very nature of There-being, as the counteressence (*Gegenwesen*) of the original essence of truth. "Errance" is the insisting turning-to the (ontically) accessible beings and the ek-sisting turning away from the mystery. This is the inner structure of There-being's situation as a playground (*Spielraum*) for the change from ek-sistence to in-sistence. "Errance" opens itself as the Open for the counterplay (*Widerspiel*) to essential truth; it is the "open place" and the ground of error (*Irrtum*).

Truth, then, is founded upon the ek-sistent in-sistent freedom of There-being. This understanding of truth remains indifferent to the philosophical notion of God. This indifference, it ought to be emphasized, relates to the concept of God in the context of the traditional definition of truth as conformity guaranteed by the theological idea of creation. This way of asking the question of God, then, remains irrelevant as well as inadequate from the perspective of the Heideggerian meditation on the essence of truth. The nature of this irrelevance can be seen in PW, where Heidegger speaks of the divine intellect and of the philosophical notion of God as the highest (supreme) being and as the origin (*Ursprung*) of all beings.[53]

Heidegger claims that the original meaning of truth as non-concealment, a notion that characterized the beginning of Western thought, has been lost in Plato's philosophy. This loss, then, characterizes the history of Western metaphysics. This important change in the notion of truth means that truth as nonconcealment (ἀλήθεια) becomes rightness (ὀρθότης) of perception (*Vernehmen*) and of assertion (*Aussage*); truth is subjugated to the "idea." Nonconcealment, explains Heidegger, is still a characteristic of beings. However, nonconcealment as the rightness of "viewing " (*Richtigkeit des "Blickens"*) comes to be a quality of human comportment with beings.[54]

With Plato begins the thinking of the Being of beings as metaphysics. Being is interpreted as "what-being" (*Was-sein*) because it is the "idea" that defines and makes a thing (a being) be what it is: beings shine forth and they are what they are by reason of the "ideas."[55] Philosophy consists, then, in the viewing of the "ideas"; it is the viewing, the intuition of the "idea" (the Being) of beings since the "ideas" make things (beings) be what they are. The "ideas" are discovered through a nonsensuous (*nichtsinnlich*) view, hence they are suprasensuous (*übersinnlich*); they transcend the (material) realm of the senses. The "idea" of the "ideas," the highest "idea," is the origin-cause (*Ursache*) of the existence and of the appearing of beings (appearing as coming into presence). This highest and first cause is called by Plato and Aristotle "the divine" (τὸ θεῖον). Metaphysics, therefore, interprets the cause of beings as God, as the origin of the being of beings, because this cause as the highest being (the supreme being) is the most authentic being of beings (*das Seiendste des Seienden*); it is the being that *is* the most. This means that the interpretation of Being as "idea" leads to the interpretation of the cause of beings as the highest being, as God. Such an interpretation of Being is clearly a metaphysical one; it understands Being as a particular being. Metaphysics is theological in nature; it views Being as God, as the highest among all the particular beings. This is the reason for the phenomenological rejection of the Cause-God. From Heidegger's point of view, the Cause-God is nothing else than the result of the metaphysical explanation of Being (as "idea") and, thus, an evasion of the Being-question, of the examination of the ontological difference. Metaphysics, therefore, identifies being(s) with Being; it identifies that which comes to presence (*das Anwesende*) with the presence (*Anwesenheit*). It should be called to mind that Heidegger's understanding of the Cause-God as an evasion of the Being-question, of the difference between Being and being, cannot be regarded as atheism; he clearly rejects such an interpretation of his thought.[56]

PW emphasizes the metaphysical interpretation of Being as the main characteristic of Western thought. This metaphysics represents the "story," the destiny, of the question of Being and of philosophy as such according to Heidegger's brief references to Aquinas, to Descartes, and to Nietzsche.[57] The problem of the truth of beings, according to Heidegger's claim, should lead to the thinking of the truth of Being—such is the basic task of philosophy. However, the thinking of the truth of Being shall become possible only through the overcoming of metaphysics[58] and through the discovery of the "positive" element in the "privative" essence of nonconcealment (ἀλήθεια).[59]

These reflections on the theological indifference of the ontological questioning in Heidegger indicate the right meaning of the "atheistic" aspects of the thinking of the ontological difference. This way of thinking leads to a relevant irrelevance of the traditional approach to the philosophical problem of God. At the same time, this irrelevance can be regarded as a sign of the questionability of the philosophical God-question. However, the God-question *remains* a question even for Heidegger's way of thinking. Is there some new kind of questioning about God or some new way of understanding the "critical aspects" of the philosophical God-question as it is shown by Heidegger's ontological phenomenology? This question leads to a new dimension of these reflections on the Heideggerian God-question as a question. This is the task of the following analysis of HD.

A New Dimension
of the
Questioning

HD represents a new dimension of Heidegger's way of thinking;
it shows the relationship between poetizing and thinking. This
"poetical" dimension of Heidegger's philosophy is a thoughtful experiencing of the profound meaning of language and a listening
to the voice of Being. Heidegger's Hölderlin commentaries try somehow to say the unsayable and, thus, to think the whole domain of
Being; they awaken the meditative thinking of the ontological
difference.

Through a thoughtful dialogue (*Gespräch*) with Hölderlin, Heidegger "goes back" to the source of words, to original language. The
true thinker is characterized by his closeness to the essence of language. This is the reason for the Heideggerian meditation on the
relationship between the poet and the thinker. Both the poet and the
thinker are the guardians (*Wächter*) of language as the "house of
Being."[1] The Heideggerian meditation on the nature of language is
a way of thinking the meaning of Being.

The Hölderlin interpretations speak abundantly of the experience of the absence of God as the main characteristic of the present
age. Heidegger interprets Hölderlin's experience of the absence of

the gods and of the Holy as the phenomenon of distress that reveals the forgottenness of Being.[2] History, for Heidegger, is the history of Being in its finite mittence. The Hölderlin meditations try to put into words the essence of the Holy as mediated by the poet and the gods to mortal man.[3] This is a dangerous undertaking because by the activity of saying (through the process of expression) the very essence of the Holy can be distorted. There is a need for sobriety as a basic disposition of preparedness for the coming presence of the Holy.

The new dimension of the Heideggerian meditations is indicated by the richness of the new vocabulary.[4] Thus Heidegger uses the following: God, gods, the Holy (*das Heilige*), half-gods (*Halbgötter*), half-god (*Halbgott*), divine (*göttlich*), the divine (*das Göttliche*), holiness (*Heiligkeit*), divinity (*Gottheit*), divines and mortals, earth and heaven, time and nature, poet (*Dichter*), thinker (*Denker*), Being, Non-being, history, danger, and godlessness.

The new vocabulary and the new problematic (language, poetry, history, the Holy) suggest a new aspect of the Heideggerian attitude toward the philosophical problem of God. Thus, a new understanding of the thinking (poetizing) experience should lead to the discovery of the relevant irrelevance of the God-question in Heidegger's thought. The Hölderlin meditations constitute a new dimension of questioning; they examine the phenomenon of the Holy and interpret the meaning of the absence of the divine.

What is the significance of this new dimension of Heidegger's thought for his views regarding the problem of God? These dialogues with Hölderlin's poetry, perhaps, may have something to say, or may give something to think, about the notion and the meaning of God. The main concerns from the perspective of the problem of God may be expressed in the following question: What is the meaning of the new vocabulary of HD (and of HW)? The new terminology can be regarded as the language of a phenomenology of the Holy as well as a poetical (mystical) description of the religious experience; it may be interpreted as an expression of romantic immanence or as a sign of religious transcendence. This is the reason for asking the following questions: Is HD merely a meditation on the Being-question (on the ontological difference) through a new understanding of language and of thinking? Is the experiencing of the Holy by the poet nothing more than an experiencing of Being as thinking-poetizing (a thoughtful and poetic contemplation) of the ontological difference? What is meant in these texts by the terms *God* and *gods*? There are no final, definitive answers to these questions, because, as Heidegger likes to remind us again and again, we do not even know how to ask (*fragen*) these kind of questions.

HD speaks of the experiencing of the Holy by the poet. What is the meaning of this experiencing of the Holy? Is there any relationship between the poetic interpretation of the Holy and the God-question? The following reflections should suggest some answers to these questions; their attention is focused on the essay "Wie wenn am Feiertage . . ."[5] This commentary on a poem of Hölderlin was written in 1939. Other sections of HD are examined whenever they contribute some new insight and further clarification to the issue at hand.

This analysis is concerned (a) with the poet, (b) with the Holy, (c) with the gods, and (d) with the notion of God.

a) The poet is situated between the gods (immortals) and the mortal beings (*die Sterblichen*). He can reach the depths and the heights; he is like an angel, a messenger and mediator, because he brings to man the "immediateness" of "nature" as the Holy.[6] The poet listens to the call (*Ruf*) of the Holy; he cannot experience the Holy as he can experience an object. The poet is close to the Holy; therefore, he can put into words of song his experiencing of the Holy as always coming (*als Kommendes*).[7]

The distinguishing qualities (attitudes) of the poet include soberness (*Nüchternheit*) and readiness (*Bereitschaft*) toward the self-disclosure of the Holy. The word of the poet is the event of the Holy (*das Ereignis des Heiligen*) because in the poetizing word (*das dichtende Wort*) the Holy itself is coming into (this) word.[8]

b) The attention of Heidegger's interpretation is focused on the phenomenon of the Holy. Another name of the Holy in Hölderlin is "nature" as the expression of the all-embracing characteristic of the Holy.[9] The Holy is far and almost inaccessible for the mortals; its home is in the brightness of light, in holiness.[10] The coming of the Holy into the words of language (song of the poet), the mediation (*Vermittlung*) of the Holy by the poet and the God, represents a danger for the Holy; it brings about the danger of its deessentialization (misrepresentation, distortion). This is the danger of dangers because the Holy seems to lose its character of "immediateness" and thus appears as something mediate and easily accessible for all.[11] This danger of becoming deessentialized is a fundamental event for both the language of the poet and our knowledge of the Holy. Indeed, this danger is an important event for the history of man because history is founded upon the Holy.[12]

The Holy is the "first," the "once," the "future," the "always." It is the "most ancient time"; it is "the time" that renders possible the "times."[13] The coming presence of the Holy is a decisive aspect of history since the coming of the Holy is the coming of an original beginning. Even the word is an event of the Holy when it is the word of a poetical saying.[14] The Holy is above the gods and above man; it is more ancient than the "times": it is the continual "once." Hölderlin's poetic words speak of (express) the Holy; they are foundational words because, according to Heidegger's interpretation, they designate (name) a unique time-space, a historical opportunity, where an initial decision that will affect the essential structure of the future history of the gods and of humanity can be made.[15]

What do we know about the nature of the Holy? The poetic vocabulary and thought contain the following description of the Holy: the Holy is the essence of "nature"; the Holy is the unapproachable (*das Un-nahbare*); it is the original well-being (*das ursprünglich Heile*) that gives the well-being of dwelling to all things.[16] The Holy is characterized also as being dreadful (*das Entsetzliche*) because it is frightening (*entsetzend*) for the world of everyday experience; it places the routine world in dread.[17] The coming of the Holy cannot be forced; the Holy discloses itself to the poet who stays in the dimension of the Holy and remembers, or tells us about, the self-opening (self-disclosure) of the Holy. The function of the poet consists in being a mediator between the Holy and those under the Holy (gods and men). He lives in the "between" (*Zwischen*) as a sign for the gods and for man. He is under the gods and above men, yet he is unlike gods and unlike men. The poet, as a sign, is able to portray the Holy and to think the different, that is, that which is different from both man and gods; thus, he can think that which "makes holy" (*heiligt*) both gods and man. Finally, the poet can invite the gods as guests, as helpers of man's "poetical dwelling upon earth." This notion of the poet as a mediator is resumed by the expression, the poet is a "demigod" (*Halbgott*).[18]

c) The term *gods* appears quite often in this essay; the gods cannot be identified either with the Holy or with the (singular) God. The Holy is above the gods. The absence (or the flight) of the gods is a characteristic phenomenon of the present age considered from the perspective of the history of Being.[19] Hölderlin says that the God of the Christian is not the only (*nicht der Einzige*) God.[20] What is the meaning of this claim? What is the difference between the gods (in the plural) and the God (in the singular)? What are these gods of Hölderlin's experience? The following description of the gods should suggest some answer to these questions.

Heidegger points out that the Holy is the word of the poet for "nature," and that the expressions "all-creating" (*allerschaffende*), "omnipresent" (*allgegenwertige*), "all-living" (*allebendige*) "nature" refer to the powers of the gods (*Kräfte der Götter*).[21] The gods are what they are in virtue of these powers (forces). However, the powers of the gods do not originate from (in) the gods; rather the gods are the concretizations of the powers of "nature" (the Holy). For this reason the poet speaks of the divine beauty of "nature" (*göttlichschöne Natur*). This "nature" is misunderstood by man when he considers it merely from the perspectives of practical utility (*Nutzen*) and function (*Dienst*). The utilitarian and instrumentalizing attitudes toward "nature" lead to (become the cause for) the misunderstanding of the Holy by man. Indeed, the Holy itself is forced into enslavement (*Knechtgestalt*); it is objectified and manipulated.[22] This description suggests an ontological interpretation of the misunderstanding of the Holy. It may be said that this description of the Holy and of the gods is a poetic expression of the ontological difference (for example, the Holy as "nature," as Power; the gods as the concretizations of the powers of "nature," of the Holy) and of the forgetfulness of Being (the poet's understanding of the Holy; the misunderstanding of the Holy by the utilitarian, objectifying perspective).

A second description of the gods can be found in connection with the mediative function of the poet who "sings" and re-calls the self-disclosure of the Holy.[23] Neither the gods nor men by themselves can approach the immediacy of the Holy. Gods and men need each other in order to find the relation to the Holy. When gods are gods and men are only men, they cannot be without each other; there is love between them. This love, then, makes them not belong to themselves but to the Holy. Gods and men, therefore, find the Holy through the mediatorship (*Mittlerschaft*) of love.[24] The poet can recall (remember) the self-opening (*das Sich-öffnen*) of the Holy because he is surrounded by the Holy.[25] The poet, indeed, stays in the "Open" and belongs to the Holy.[26]

A third description of the gods is given by the historical dimension of the Holy. The destiny of the gods and of men is decided by the Holy as the ground of history.[27]

d) The notion of God. Hölderlin and Heidegger often speak of God as the God (*der Gott*).[28] This "the" calls attention to the fact that this notion of God cannot be identified with the Christian concept of God. What is the notion of God in Heidegger's interpretations of Hölderlin's poetry? What are the main contributions of these philosophical and artistic meditations to the analysis of the question of

God? These questions call attention to some essential elements of Heidegger's studies of Hölderlin.

According to Hölderlin, God is closer to man on a day of rest when the world is peaceful.[29] The powerfulness of "nature," for Hölderlin, is due to its divine beauty (*göttlichschöne Natur*). The omnipresence of "nature" is a revelation and, at the same time, a concealment of its fascinating beauty. A God can reveal or conceal this fascinating aspect of "nature." God is the "highest" appearance or manifestation of beauty and, as such, comes close to the pure appearing of the omnipresence as the fascinating aspect of "nature."[30] The poet lives in the milieu of divine beauty.[31] "Nature" is also called the "most ancient time" because it gives the lighting-process (*Lichtung*) to all beings; it renders it possible for them to come into the "Open" and to appear.[32] Obviously, this idea of "nature" as the "most ancient time" cannot be interpreted in the metaphysical sense of "supratemporality." It has no relation to the Christian notion of "eternity." It means simply the omnipresence of "nature" as the "place" of "light" where things may come to presence. According to Hölderlin, the essence of "nature" is the Holy. The Holy is not holy because it is divine, but the divine is divine because of being holy in its own way.[33] The Holy is unapproachable even for the God; it is above the God. The poet can name the Holy because a God gathers together the Holy into a unique "beam of light" and, thus, irradiates it into the soul of the poet and communicates it to men. This is the reason for the "community" of gods and men. The God and the poet can mediate (transmit, communicate the unapproachable) the Holy to men.[34] God, therefore, is a mediator of the Holy because he is close to the Holy. This view of God as mediator (like the poet) allows this poetic (imaginative) language and thought to speak of several kinds of gods and not only of one God. In this sense, then, it may be said that the Christian God is not the only God, that there are many mediators of the Holy.[35]

All this does not clarify the notion of God sufficiently. However, it does become clear through these considerations (the Holy, the poet, the God, gods, "nature," men) that Heidegger is trying to unwrap the nature of the ontological difference. Perhaps it can be said that the Hölderlin interpretation is a "poetic phenomenology," a poetic meditation on the ontological difference.

What is the meaning of Heidegger's interpretations of Hölderlin's poetry? The description of the Holy indicates that these meditations are concerned with the problem of Being. The word *Holy*, then, is another name for Being. The absence of God and of the gods is an experiencing of the history of Being. The phenomenon of godlessness (*Gottlosigkeit*) is interpreted by Heidegger as an event of the history of Being (*ereignete Geschichte des Seins*).[36] Heidegger's interpretations of Hölderlin's poetry indicate that the final focus of his meditations is the coming about of the truth of Being that shows itself as the Holy. The Holy manifests itself through the poet and through the gods. This is the reason why Heidegger can speak of the gods and of God in connection with the history of the truth of Being.[37]

The Holy never shows itself to mortal men without the intervention of a mediator; it shows itself in the form (*Gestalt*) of a god. This is the historical destiny of the Holy. Men encounter the Holy through the mediative "intervention" of the gods and through the poet who can somehow portray and experience the Holy. This inaccessibility or immediateness of the Holy is a description of Being as the immediate, of Being as nonmediated. Being renders present beings; beings are mediated (they are "mediate"). Being itself is the source of this mediation, and, thus, it cannot be mediated (*Unmittelbarkeit*). This quality of Being as the "immediate" is pointed out by Heidegger's reflections on the nature of the Holy.[38] The idea of the self-opening (*Sich-öffnen*) of the Holy manifests this same understanding of Being.[39] M. Müller sees in this immediacy (*Unmittelbarkeit*) and in this unutterable, unsayable (*Unsagbare*) characteristic of Being (in the final unutterableness of Being as such) the main reason for Heidegger's dialogues with Hölderlin.[40] This understanding of Being accounts also for the difficulty in thematizing the experience of Being as M. Müller points out.

The Hölderlin studies show clearly that Heidegger creates his own language; his words and expressions are the results of the thinking of Being. A word (an original Greek term or a poetic expression of Hölderlin) is a source of understanding (of thinking) for him, because its primordial meaning cannot be grasped fully without uncovering in (and through) it some comprehension (some way of thinking) of the meaning of Being. It is possible, therefore, for Heidegger, to think about the question of Being with the help of the poetizing word, to meditate on the meaning of the word *Being* with the help of the word *Holy*. In the final analysis, then, the discovery of the Holy is part of the discernment of Being, of the unfolding of the essential nature of the ontological difference. The connection between the task of the thinker and the task of the poet (according to HD and HW) accounts for the closeness of Heidegger's language to that of Hölderlin. However, as B. Allemann remarks, it is difficult to describe this relationship of closeness, which appears more clearly in the works of the later Heidegger.[41]

Heidegger reflects on Hölderlin's writings because Hölderlin is a poet who thinks and who stays in the "Place" (*Ortschaft*) assigned for him by the lighting (clearing) of Being. Therefore, Hölderlin's thinking comes from the openness of Being, and, thus, it belongs to the destiny (*Geschick*) of Being.[42]

Is there a new dimension of questioning in HD? It seems that the experience of the absence of the divine and the Heideggerian interpretation of the Holy can be regarded as a new dimension of the questioning-process, as a main characteristic of the hermeneutic phenomenology.

The Holy and the phenomenon of godlessness (*Gottlosigkeit*) open up a new opportunity (they constitute a new "place") for meditating on the ontological difference. The new vocabulary (the foundational language of the poet) has, first of all, phenomenological significance; it is a new way of "saying" (*Sagen*) the ontological difference and the meaning of Being. In this sense, then, the term *Holy* may stand (and "speak") also for the word *Being*. It may be, in some sense, a poetic term in thinking the question of Being; it is the closest to Being without, at least formally, being identified with Being. The poet stands for There-being. The God and the gods are beings insofar as they are what they are by virtue of the Holy, by virture of Being; their destiny and their coming-to-presence (*Anwesen*) are decided and grounded by the Holy that "shines forth" through them. This is why There-being and the gods (and the God), the mortals as well as the divines, belong to the history of the Holy as part of the history of Being; they and the foundational poetic language are the event (*Ereignis*) of the Holy,[43] in the final analysis, the event of Being. Being, language, and the Holy, though in different ways, "decide" the destiny of human beings.

The experiencing of the Holy is part of the historical experiencing of Being. What is the difference between these two experiences? What is the difference between Being and the Holy? What is the relationship between the Holy and the God (and the gods)? What is the relationship between Being and the God (and the gods)? Is there some specific reason for using these poetic (and to some extent mythological) words when meditating on the ontological difference? Certainly, they have a descriptive function and an ontological meaning in Heidegger's phenomenology. However, it remains possible to ask the following questions: Have they also some "metaphysical" ("theological," religious, and even ontic) meaning? Why speak of the God and of the gods? Is there a reliable, final meaning to this language? Is there a solid ground for this way of speaking? The possibility of a "metaphysical" meaning remains even though Heidegger himself does not enter into this aspect of the experiencing of the Holy. According to Heidegger, the absence of the gods is the "result" of the forgottenness of the Holy. He says that even the trace of the Holy remains unknown;[44] he suggests that we cannot even find some "trace of the trace" (*Spur zur Spur*) of the Holy. These insights constitute the description of the "needy time" (*dürftige Zeit*); they describe, in the final analysis, the forgottenness of Being itself. Man cannot understand the meaning of the divine and of the God (and of the gods) without having understood first the meaning of the Holy. When we know what we mean by the Holy and when we understand Being, only then shall we be able to ask the question regarding the meaning of the word *God* and about the gods. The "project" of understanding, therefore, is a progressive understanding (from Being and the Holy to God) that ought not to be reversed because such a reversal (from God to the Holy to Being) would mean a misunderstanding. The absence of and our undecidedness about (the) God, the flight of the gods, the loss of the sense of the sacred, divine dimension of dwelling in the World, Heidegger insists, are the "results" of such a reversal (of the order of understanding, of the way of thinking) as the sign of the forgottenness of the Holy, of the forgottenness of Being.[45] The thinking of Being, therefore, is a prerequisite of the thinking of the God-question.

The God-question, then, remains a question and, indeed, becomes a question as such. The God-question *is* present in Heidegger's way of thinking precisely as a question. ID, HB, and some passages of TK and VA (2), indicate clearly that, in the preceding sense, the God-question is a question for Heidegger's way of thinking; the God-question can be asked when we are able to understand the meaning of Being and the meaning of the Holy (and, therefore, we will be ready to grasp the meaning of the divine, the meaning of the gods, and the meaning of God).[46] However, according to Heidegger's emphasis, we, as yet, do not understand even the meaning of Being. This is the reason why he prefers "philosophical silence" with regard to God. Even the suggestion of a possibility of thinking the problem of God in Heidegger cannot be separated from the entire problem of the ontological difference and, above all, cannot be understood without situating both the Being-question and the God-question in the context of the Heideggerian interpretation of language.[47] These considerations indicate the potentialities of the way of thinking in the works of the later ("second") Heidegger.

HD, then, shows the historical situation of the question of God and prepares the ground for a new way of thinking about God.

The Final Phase
of the
Questioning

The analysis of the question of God as a question (the second
phase of the question of God) in the works of Heidegger that
followed SZ shows that Heidegger separates the question of
Being from the question of God; it also indicates that the questioning
attitude (the recognition of the question of God as a question) overcomes the metaphysical concept of God. This overcoming (not a
destruction but a different mode of understanding) opens the possibility of a new approach to the problem of God in the light of the
new understanding of Being and that of language. There are some
ideas, some tentative though "prophetic" insights and remarks in Heidegger's writings, especially in the works manifesting his later and
latest development, that represent at least some recognition of as well
as a definite openness toward a new way of asking the question of
God. Therefore, it is possible to distinguish a third and, thus, final
phase of the question of God in Heidegger's phenomenology. The
following reflections examine the main characteristics and the final
significance of this third phase. However, it ought to be kept in mind
that Heidegger does not elaborate very much on the nature and on
the methodology of this possible new perspective on the question of
God; his remarks contain some guidelines and hints without the inten-

tion of a systematic and comprehensive development. He speaks little, and his words remain tentative; what he is able to say, nevertheless, is quite significant and thoughtworthy. Even this final "answer" to the question of God, then, includes and demands questioning. The response ("answer") to a question, according to Heidegger, is only the very last step of questioning, of the way of thinking; a response that dismisses questioning and rethinking destroys itself; it cannot found true knowledge, but it rigidifies mere opinion.[1] This openness of the final perspective of the question of God in Heidegger shows that his way of thinking, like that of Nietzsche, remains faithful to his task; that it does not abandon the goal, the place of destination (*Bestimmungsort*), of its attention (*Grundstellung*);[2] genuine thinking does not remain a slave to its past, but is nourished by an openness toward the future, toward always new possibilities. The thoughts of a great thinker, Heidegger suggests, are the "echo of the not yet recognized history of Being" in the words of human language.[3] The nature of thinking and the essence of philosophy cannot be understood without discovering the essence of language. Philosophy is a listening to the voice, to the language of Being;[4] language, in the final analysis, is inhabited by Being; it is "the house of Being,"[5] and man is the "neighbor" and the "shepherd" (guardian) of Being.[6] The final phase of the question of God, then, is situated in this ontological-phenomenological way of language, of saying; it is defined not merely by what is said (the content of language) but, even more, by the way (the context, the nature of language) it is said. Heidegger's dialogues with Hölderlin, Nietzsche, and the tradition (metaphysics) as a whole do not distract him from his original pathway of thought; they, rather, focus his mind on the history of Being and allow him to "bring Being to language,"[7] to think that which lies hidden and unthought in the history of thought.

The study of the first two phases of the problem of God in Heidegger indicates that his thought in the final analysis does not destroy the meaningfulness and thus the thoughtworthiness of the concept of God; the thought of Heidegger as a whole, including its later and latest development, remains open toward a new way of speaking and thinking of God after the overcoming of the metaphysical conceptualizations of the world and of human reality. The third phase of the question of God sheds a new light on the first two phases because it represents an aspect of his philosophy as a whole. Indeed, the first two phases can be understood as constituting a process of preparation (and as a liberation) for the third phase, for the

new approach to the question of God. The demythologization and
the questioning, that is, the first phase and the second phase, respectively, therefore, may represent only one side (the first part) of the
entire problem of God in Heidegger's way of thinking, at least according to its final horizon, though not necessarily according to its (immediate) actual elaboration. The third phase should be understood as
the second side, as the second part, of the question of God as a whole
according to its final possibility. Consequently, this third phase,
though it is not fully developed, ought to be examined in its full
dimension and profound implications. This study, however, can be
neither complete nor final at this time because of the limitations that
condition the research even without taking into account the difficulties of alternative interpretations. The identification of these limitations constitutes an integral part of the following reflections on the
suggested third and, thus, final phase (status) of the question of God
in Heidegger.

a) What is the main characteristic of this third phase, and how
does it come about? The meditation on the ontological difference
represents a "going beyond" the metaphysical concept of God (in the
light of the critical examination of the ontological presuppositions of
the notion of the highest being as part of the demythologization, the
first phase, of the problem of God in Heidegger); it leads, according
to the analysis of the second phase of the God-question in Heidegger
(connected with the thinking of Being itself as well as with the notion
of language), to the affirmation of the significant irrelevance and
"uselessness" of the traditional interpretation of the entire question
of God. This separation of the question of God from the question of
Being (a main aspect of the second phase of the question of God in
Heidegger) seems to make questionable the philosophical nature of
the entire question of God. Is the question of God a truly philosophical question if philosophy is a listening to the voice of Being, if philosophy becomes the language of Being? Is there a "place" for God
in the thinking of Being and in the language of Being (that is concerned with Being itself) after the "destruction" of the metaphysical
identification (and thus "short-circuiting") of the concept of Being
with the idea of God? Can the thinking of Being say anything about
God? Is there a new way of asking the question of God after the
overcoming of the forgottenness of Being and after the departure of
the Holy, after the disappearance of the sense of the sacred? Can the
question of God become once again a genuine, meaningful question
even in the context and from the perspective of the ontological reflec-

tions in Heidegger's final development, which concentrates on Being and on trying to think everything from the "side" of Being itself, from the sense of wonder that "Being is granted"? The answers to these questions can be given in the affirmative; the development of Heidegger's thought indicates the need for as well as the conditions of a new way of thinking the meaning and the "place" of God in the history of Being. This means, then, that the second phase of the question of God (the phase of questioning), in the final analysis, prepares the way for yet a third (final) phase that gives some hints regarding the postmetaphysical meaning of God. The metaphysical exigency (positing) of God as ultimate foundation and as highest value, according to Heidegger, does not know (of) the true essence of God; the way to God in the true sense becomes accessible only after surmounting traditional metaphysics. Only by abandoning the metaphysical God does thinking become free for (can ask the question of) the divine God, for God in the true sense. Heidegger's way of thinking, therefore, can ask the question of God in a new way.

What is the main characteristic of this suggested new approach to the question of God especially in comparison to the metaphysical approach? The new approach, the new way of thinking the idea of God, may well be described as a movement of descendence (descending) in opposition to the movement of metaphysical transcendence (transcending). Metaphysical thinking transcends from the notion of finite, contingent beings to the idea of the infinite, necessary, highest being, to God as the "subsistent Being itself" (*ipsum esse subsistens*); the movement of metaphysical transcendence, then, leads to the identification and thus to the confusion of the concept of God with the concept of Being as such. The new approach to the question of God, however, becomes possible as a movement of descendence from the idea of Being to the concept of God and that of beings. This descendence, the rooting of transcendence, consists in this: first we ought to understand the meaning of Being, and then we will be able to understand the meaning of the Holy (of the sacred); consequently, we will be able to think the essence of the divinity and, thus, in the end, and only in the end, in the light of the essence of the divinity, we will be able to understand and to express the meaning of the word *God*. The phenomenological movement of descendence, therefore, leads from Being to God; it does not confuse the concept of Being with that of God because its source is in Being beyond the metaphysical concept of God. The (phenomenological) idea of God, according to Heidegger's "final words," is contingent neither on the religiosity of the human person nor on the theological ambitions of philosophy and of the sciences; the meaning and the presence of God in the true sense come about inside and as part of the destiny of Being. This movement of descendence, then, leads to the idea of the truly divine God according to Heidegger's suggestion. This positive attitude toward the question of God represents the most significant aspect of the final phase of questioning; its meaning, however, ought to be analyzed carefully according to its "place" in the free horizon of thinking beyond the limitations of traditional metaphysics and without the objectifications of language.

b) The final (third) phase of the question of God, then, is more than the criticism of the metaphysical, of the ontotheological way of thinking about the World, the human being, and God; it is, rather, an element of the task of thinking at the "end of philosophy," at the culmination of the metaphysical destiny of Being. This new way of thinking is not retrospective but prospective; its main quality is not the search for the (past) causes of being but the openness to the coming lighting-process of Being.[8] Where is the "place" of the question of God in the lighting-process of Being? Where are the "sparks" (if any) in the light of Being that may suggest at least the possibility of a nonmetaphysical way of thinking about God? Why does the thinking of Being, even in its final stages, speak about God at all? How is it that the word *God* does not disappear from the language of thinking that comes from listening to the voice of Being?[9] There are only fragmentary responses to these questions in Heidegger's writings; they include some suggestions regarding the new way of thinking about God.

The conference, *Die Kehre* (TK), given by Heidegger in 1949, includes a clear description of the ontological destiny of Being as well as a historical indication of the function of the human being in bringing Being into language. The famous theme of the "reversal" (*die Kehre*) consists in the turning away from the forgetfulness of the essence of Being and in the turning to the truth of the essence of Being. This process of turning is a historical event; it involves the cooperation of the human being[10] because Being needs the human being in order to guard its truth in the midst of beings. The essence of Being comes into language through authentic thinking when the human being, the thinker, corresponds to the demands of Being itself. The "reversal" is situated in the destiny (*Geschick*) of Being; it is connected with the insight into the essence of the technological attitude as a way of dominion over the earth.[11] Being itself, according to Hei-

degger's emphasis on the primacy of Being that even seems to hypos-
tatize Being, is undergoing a historical destiny in technology, in the
essence of technology as "enframing" (*Gestell*): as "the self-gathering
in which Being as Being refuses itself."[12] The essence of "technology"
(*Technik*) is Being itself as the danger (*Gefahr*) in the form of "enframing," and, therefore, this danger in Being can never be overcome by
human activity because man is not the master of Being.[13] However,
the essence of "technology," the "technological" destiny of Being, cannot be changed without the cooperation (*Mithilfe*) of the human being;
Being as Being needs the human being in order to be safeguarded
in its essence in the midst of beings, because the essence of man
belongs to the essence of Being, and because "technology" is a destiny
of Being, a form or historical epoch of the mittence of Being. Being,
then, needs the human being. Man can open himself to the true
essence of "technology," to Being; he can safeguard the essence of
Being in its truth by corresponding (*Entsprechung*) to the demands of
Being. Being emits, sends itself, and emerges as a destiny; the transformation of a destiny (of an epoch) itself is a mittence of a destiny
of Being itself.[14] The realization of the danger in "technology" as the
forgottenness of the essence of Being becomes the rescuing of the
essence of Being itself.[15] This change, the rescuing of Being, happens
all of a sudden; it is not the result of some causality, of some activity.
The "reversal" is the lighting-up of the lighting-process of the essence
of Being; abruptly out of the essence of concealedness occurs (*ereignet*)
Being in its epoch, in its historical destiny.[16] The "turning" is "unme-
diated" (*unvermittelt*).[17] The epochal mittence of Being comes out of
its essence of concealedness;[18] its destiny is neither preceded nor followed by a Cause as Being or by an Effect as Being.

   This means, then, that Being and the alteration of the destiny
of Being cannot be thought of as operational causal connections. The
primordial originality (the primacy) of Being is beyond the cause-
minded thinking; ontological phenomenology goes beyond the metaphysical level of thinking. The cause-approach to God, therefore, is
not considered in phenomenology; the dilemma of theism and atheism, then, does not seem to be relevant to these considerations about
Being. The epochal mittence of Being is not a theory of causality of
Being but a phenomenology (a descriptive meditation) of the (historical) destiny of Being. In the "reversal," in the historical epochs of
the destiny of Being (in the ontological history of the truth of Being),
the lighting-process of the essence of Being lights itself; the glimpse
into this light (clarity) sees what is the meaning of Being itself and

thus grasps that in the "is" dwells and emerges Being, that what the "is" names occurs (*ereignet sich*) in and as out of Being, that which properly is Being.[19] The insight, the glimpse (*Einsicht*) into the lightning (*Blitz*) of the truth of Being in the contemporary situation, where the prevalence of the technological attitude obstructs the essential ontological disposition, is, at the same time, according to the emphasis of the later Heidegger, a rediscovery of man and of the World. The glimpse into that-which-is (the truth of Being), the event of the glimpse into Being, is also, at the same time, a glimpse into man, because the human beings through the event of the glimpse are touched (encountered) by the lightning of Being; in the glimpse, then, the human beings are rediscovered; they are thought of from the perspective of Being. Man, therefore, overcomes the attitude of stubbornness and that of self-centeredness; he projects himself into the glimpse, and, thus, by adapting to it becomes capable of seeing the World for what the World is. Man, therefore, as mortal can glance at the divine as the safeguarded element of the World (the World is the "foursome," the interplay between the mortals and the divines, between earthly and heavenly beings). By standing in the light of the truth of Being, then, man is able to see the many dimensions of the World, of the interplay between the beings in the World; there cannot be any other way for the coming about of this view because even (the) God, if he is, is a being and as a being stays (*steht*) in Being, in the essence of Being.[20] This remark on God explains that beings, in the final analysis, stand in, are what they are (have their root) in Being. This statement refers to divine and to human beings, to all beings, even to (the) God if (when) he is. But why does Heidegger speak of God at all in this context, at this height (depth) of his ontological meditation? He mentions God as an example of how beings (including even God as a being) are rooted in Being. A new emphasis on Being (a deeper grasp of the primordiality of the "is") always opens up new ways of thinking about beings and, thus, also about God as a (particular) being. The question of Being, the question of God, and the question of Nothing are interrelated in Heidegger's phenomenology as well as in the history of thought.

What is the meaning of Heidegger's preceding remark about God? This reference simply claims that when God is, he is a being. As a being, God is (stays) in the essence of Being; the comprehension of Being is the source of the final understanding of all beings, even that of God. Heidegger is not taking a position regarding the existence of God in this remark; he is meditating on the primacy (primordiality) of the Being-event, on the possibility of looking at the World as World (ontologically). The idea of God as being in Being, however, should not be interpreted as the subordination of God to Being as Cause; the primacy of Being in relation to beings is not identical with the idea of a causal connection.

There is another question that may be asked about God's relation to Being. Is God (does he stay, dwell) in Being in the same way as the other beings are in Being? Heidegger responds to this question in the negative. All beings dwell in Being but not all of them in the same way. The divine beings (thus God) and the human being somehow bring (help) the light of Being.[21] Being needs these (divine and human) beings in order to safeguard its truth in the midst of beings, in the World, in nature, in history. Being speaks to us in its constellations,[22] in its historical destiny, that is, in the dimension of dangers (for example, in technology), in the "reversal."[23] The refusal (*Verweigerung*) of Being is the "highest mystery of Being" in the dominion of the "framing,"[24] of the attitude of manipulation; this attitude leads to the withdrawal (refusal) of the realm of beings. Heidegger emphasizes the fact that "Whether God is God comes to pass (*ereignet sich*, takes place) out of the constellation of Being and within it."[25] The manifestation of the true nature of God occurs (takes place) on the ground of the historical destiny (manifestation) of Being. "Whether the God lives or remains dead is decided not by the religiosity of men and even less by the theological ambitions of philosophy and of natural science."[26] Even the life or the death, the presence or the absence, the coming or the departure of God are determined by, come to pass, according to the constellation of Being; the God-event, then, is taking place within and is contingent on the Being-event, on the destiny of Being. The true understanding of beings and even their relationship to God, then, are a coming to pass of (and made possible by) the truth of Being; the openness of human existence, of the human being, toward God is coming about not by using human initiative but by being open toward Being, towards the truth of Being, towards transcendence. In the final analysis, the human being can only respond (adapt) to the gift of Being, to the presence of God. All openness to beings, including the relation to God, is an event of the destiny of Being, of the coming to pass of the openness and attentiveness to Being.

These ideas clearly indicate a new and thus final phase of thinking about God. This thoughtworthy and phenomenologically reliable approach to the question of God, according to the suggestions in TK, is bound up with and conditioned by the coming to pass of the truth of Being; the discernment of God becomes possible by the glimpse into that-which-is (Being). It ought to be kept in mind that these indications in the conference *Die Kehre* representing a new way of raising the question of God do not constitute an affirmation of the existence of God; they clearly refer to God in the hypothetical sense ("if God is," "if God lives or remains dead"). These remarks should be regarded neither as frivolous nor as bordering on making the reflection on God practically impossible. It is surely quite significant that at the culmination of the meditation on Being itself there is a new way of thinking (and speaking about) the meaning of the word *God*. The question of God, therefore, remains open.

This final phase of Heidegger's way of looking at the notion of God from the perspective of the thinking of Being is expressed without any ambiguity in HB (written as a letter to J. Beaufret in 1946, first published in 1947). This work may be viewed as a background that confirms and clarifies the preceding reflections on *Die Kehre*. It is basically a response by Heidegger to some misunderstandings of his philosophy, and as such it represents his own interpretation and clarification of his development (the later Heidegger) with a good synthesis of his main and initial insights (the earlier Heidegger). The fact that the term *God* appears twenty-nine times in this text[27] is not a decisive element of these considerations; it calls attention, never-theless, to the precision and to the clarification of Heidegger's position regarding the problem of God. This reflection on humanism rejects the mere ontic (psychological, anthropological, Sartrean-existentialist) interpretations of the existential analysis of SZ as well as the meta-physical reductions (objectifications) of the concept of Being to an ultimate cause, ultimate ground, and to the highest value, that is, to God; it develops a more rigorous, more essential and attentive way of thinking the relationship between man (human existence) and Being. The new way of thinking is attuned not only to man's relation to Being but also, and in a radical way, to Being's relation to man and to the connection between these two relations. The human being's relation to Being, in the final analysis, is (founded on) the relation of Being to the human being. Thinking is not causing or bringing about this relation; it is concerned with the relation of Being to the human being; it "accomplishes (*vollbringt*; brings full) the relation of Being to the essence of man"[28] as "something handed over to it from Being."[29] The essential relationship of the human being to Being is situated within (founded on) "the relation of Being to the essence of the human being."[30] The human being is concerned with grounding the truth of Being, with the shining forth of being in the light of Being (with the shining forth of beings for what they are) because he "is 'thrown' from Being itself into the truth of Being" in order to exist (ek-sist) in this way;[31] man is not the ruler but the guardian of Being; his way of being is bound up with the destiny of Being. There-being is the "There" (presence) of Being; human existence is, in the final analysis, the openness to Being, "the standing in the lighting-process of Being" (*das Stehen in der Lichtung des Seins*).[32] The human being dwells in the light of Being; the lighting-process (Being) "grants the nearness to Being."[33]

The new way of thinking of Being, as shown in HB, leads to a new (more essential, existential, and ontologically rooted) way of looking at beings, at the human being, and at God. HB is an exercise in learning to think Being as Being itself. "Being is farther than all beings and is, nevertheless, nearer to the human being than every being, be it a rock, an animal, an artwork, a machine, be it an angel or God."[34] Heidegger asks the question "What is Being?" His main response is that "It is It itself" and that it is "not God and not a cosmic ground."[35] The human being lives (ek-sists) in the World as the lighting-process of Being, in the openness of Being.[36] This worldly nature (being-in-the-World) of the human being and the clear rejection of the identification of God with Being, however, according to Heidegger's warnings and explanations, remain in a state of "indifference" regarding the question of God; they do not decide (philosophically) for or against the existence of God.[37] This essential thinking of the ontological difference from the perspective of Being, as the lighting-process of Being (as the thinking of Being as further than all beings and yet closer to the human being than any being), remains in a state of theological indifference; it does not exclude, then, the possibility of a theological difference, that is, the possibility for a relation of There-being (man) to God (the religious meaning of transcendence). The issue at stake for Heidegger is not the immediate resolution of the question of God but, much rather, the experience of Being in its truth and the readiness for the light of Being as the overcoming of homelessness as the destiny of man and of the World; the presence and the withdrawal of God (as well as of the Holy and of the gods) are a part of the manifestation of the forgottenness of Being, of the lack of thinking the truth of Being.[38] This lack of essential thinking can be reversed (retrieved) by returning to the source of all rigorous thinking, to the thinking of the truth of Being beyond metaphysics.

The presence and the withdrawal of God in the contemporary situation, consequently, can be grasped only by a new way of thinking that is willing (ready) to return to the Open, to the lighting-process of Being as the true "place" and "home" of the human being. The "indifference" of this new way of thinking to the affirmation of God goes beyond the dilemma of theism and atheism in the classical sense; it may be described as the expectation of the overcoming of homelessness, as the preparation for the experience of Being and thus for the new way of looking at beings, and even at God as a being.

How does it become possible to think (about) God at all beyond the metaphysical attitude? Is it possible to think and to speak of God from the (phenomenological) ontological perspective? The ontological way of thinking the notion of God is possible, according to Heidegger's incisive statement in HB, as a process of descending from Being to God (in contrast to the metaphysical transcending from beings to God). From the thinking of the truth of Being (a more radical questioning-thinking than metaphysical thinking) it becomes possible to move to the thinking of the essence of the Holy; from the essence of the Holy the essence of the divinity can be thought, and then, in the light of the essence of the divinity, it becomes possible to think and to say what the word *God* is to name.[39] This reference to a possible way of thinking the notion of God from the perspective of Being (the descending thinking), however, was not meant to suggest that the new kind of thinking, the thinking that shows (points to) the truth of Being, "decided in favor of theism. It can be theistic as little as atheistic."[40] This "undecidedness," according to Heidegger's explanation of his view, comes about not on the ground of a "position of indifference" toward theism and atheism but "out of respect for the boundaries that have been set for thinking as thinking . . . by what gives itself to thinking as what is to be thought, by the truth of Being."[41] This new way of thinking is committed to what is more essential than all values and all types of beings: to the truth of Being. The new essential, ontological thinking, therefore, overcomes metaphysics not "by climbing still higher" than metaphysics (by somehow transcending, surmounting metaphysics) "but by climbing back down (descending) into the nearness of the nearest."[42] There is nothing closer to the human being than Being; to be consists in being in the nearness of Being. This refinement of Heidegger's position regarding the connection between the meaning of Being and the meaning of God opens up the possibility of thinking the question of God; it does recognize the thinkability of the concept of God. However, it also establishes the boundaries of this thinking from the perspective of the thinking of Being; ontological thinking, the meditation on the truth of Being, remains "undecided" regarding the affirmation of God because of the boundaries of thinking set by the greater depth of the truth of Being. God, in the final analysis, can be thought, but this thinking is without the actual commitment of limited thought to the existence or the nonexistence of God.

Heidegger's reflection on his (final) position regarding the question of God from the perspective of the truth of Being and from that of the experience of Being does not examine any further the "boundaries of thinking" regarding the term *God*. The new essential, deeper than metaphysical thinking opens up new possibilities; it also establishes, however, new boundaries for itself. Where are these boundaries? Are they the dangers of falling back into metaphysical thinking? Are they the boundaries of the language of Being? Would this suggest that the thinking of Being becomes detached from beings? Is there a conflict, if not even a contradiction perhaps, between opening up a new possibility and then taking it practically away at the same time, that is, between the claim that the truth of Being as the essence of thinking leads to the possibility of thinking the notion (and the meaning) of God (and even to the preparation for a possible experience of man's relation to God) and its explanation that the boundaries of this possibility preempt (or that at least they cannot justify) a decision regarding the dilemma of theism and atheism? Even if the answers to the last two questions may be given in the negative, even then, the responses to the first two questions may not be clear. There are dangers (obstacles) that ontological thinking ought to struggle with; Being is not hypostatized; it is always the Being of beings. The experience of the truth of Being is not enough to liberate thought for thinking the concept and the meaning of God, even though essential (deeper than the metaphysical) thinking is closer to God than metaphysical speculation about the highest being, about the highest value, and about a cosmic ground. Essential thinking as listening to the voice of Being sees all beings in the light of Being (thus it sees being better). Why is it that it cannot see (or experience) God in the light of Being if God is a (particular) being? May it be because God is a special being who does not fit inside the boundaries of all thoughts? Heidegger does not respond to these questions because he is not asking them. It may not be unreasonable to suggest that man can speak of God only "after" and on the basis of God's speaking to man; to think of God means to listen to the voice (presence, withdrawal) of God (this listening is not without analogy to the nature of thinking in general as listening to the voice of Being). This suggestion, however, is clearly not made by Heidegger; even the final phase of his question of God remains a process of questioning (and a part of the questioning about Being). Thus, HB shows new possibilities as well as unforeseen difficulties.

It may be tempting to suggest (and conclude) that Heidegger makes the requirements for reflecting on God so high that they are unrealizable, that practically the idea of God is left for the outside of philosophical thought, that he prefers the ambiguity of his thought, even though the openness toward the question of God remains a main result of his phenomenology.[43] The idea, however, that the emphasis on the limitations of thought about God would be a disguised agnosticism, or at least the admission of the practical impossibility of thinking the meaning and the concept of God, seems to be a hasty, forced conclusion. It may well be more reasonable to maintain that Heidegger, in the final analysis, transfers the mystery of God to the mystery of Being, that he "transforms" (deepens) the mystery of God in the light of the mystery of Being. However, even this suggestion has many limitations because the idea of the "boundaries of thinking" in Heidegger, at least regarding the question of God, remains unclarifed and thus not really settled.

The understanding of the boundaries and of the nature of thinking in Heidegger is connected with his notion of philosophy as such. His lecture, *"Was ist das—die Philosophie?"* (WP), given in 1955, makes it quite clear that the Being-question is not merely a main theme in Heidegger, but the very essence of his conception of philosophy. Philosophy consists in listening to the voice of Being, in the attentive disposition toward the intimations of Being in and through the many beings, in a correspondence (dialogue) with the Being of beings.[44] Philosophy today is dominated by doubt and by blind attachment to untested principles, by the calculating and dominating mentality; these attitudes lead thinking away from the way of Being. The task of philosophy is very demanding; its realization often seems practically impossible. The Being-question is never fully explored; the ideal of philosophy is not achieved, not even by Heidegger. This notion of philosophy becomes almost "mystical" in nature; its lighting-process is not only poetic but also "mystical," suggesting the depth and the unique nature of philosophy. The intimation (voice, appeal) of Being is not without comparison to the idea of the intimation of God in the depth of the soul according to the language of the great mystics (such as M. Eckhart). The Being-question itself, in the final analysis, comes to the situation where it seems to be no less thinkable than the religious (mystical, Christian) notion of God. WP does not reflect on the notion of God (and even the remark on medieval philosophy and on the idea of ultimate cause or ground remains without an indication of their relationship to the question of God);[45] nevertheless, its conception of philosophy is quite enlightening regarding Heidegger's attitude toward the tradition as well as about his final position on the question of God. The refusal to decide neither for nor against the affirmation of God is not (in and of itself) a shield against intellectual commitment but a sign of the boundaries and of the limitations of Heidegger's definition of philosophy. However, the notion of philosophy as the open correspondence with Being also opens up the possibility of restructuring the question of God, of reflecting on it after the retrieval of the history of the Being-question. The retracing of the history of philosophy, the dialogue with the tradition, is a way of actualizing the original philosophical intention. The historical way of philosophizing is a main element in Heidegger's rethinking the question of Being. It should be remembered that the mediation on the question of Being already includes, at least indirectly, a reexamination of the question of God; the thinking of Being "calls" Heidegger to think also of the idea of God. Being always remains the focus of his thought, but, even so, he is "forced" and feels himself obliged to pay attention to the other issues in the constellation, especially to the problem of God. The rejection of the metaphysical concept of God (of the entire ontotheological structure of metaphysics) already represents at least a limited retrieval of the idea of God in the history of philosophy as a part of the retrieval (rethinking) of the concept of Being in the tradition. Even this indirect and limited retrieval of the idea of God in the history of Western philosophy leads Heidegger to a new way of asking the question of God (to the "search" for a more "divine" God, to the mystery of the God of religious experience in prayer and faith) that is comparable, at least in some ways, to the transition from the traditional to the phenomenological concept of Being. It seems, then, that, even according to Heidegger's way of thinking, there is something "more" in the traditional God-question than a detour from the comprehension of Being, than a mere absorption of the concept of Being into the concept of God, than the historical-ontological foundation of the idea of God. Thus, at least indirectly, in the final (later) phase of his development, Heidegger can speak and think more positively (even in the context of critical reflection on the tradition) regarding the idea of God. The rethinking of the question of God (the restructuring of the methodology as well as of the "place" of God in philosophy), therefore, does not lead to the destruction of the notion of God but rather to the unearthing of a more authentic and "divine" conception of God, to the recognition of the originality of the mystery of the meaning of the word *God*. His attitude of reserve, his silence, then, is not a mask for disguised and culturally refined atheism but the disposition of openness toward and the sign of "waiting" for the coming about of a greater sensitivity toward the "divine" at the boundaries of thinking that may be enlarged not by human initiative but by the presence of the "unthinkable" mystery of religious faith-experience. The absence (*fehlen, Wegbleiben*) of God in the contemporary situation, an element and manifestation of the destiny of Being, is "not nothing" but the "hidden plenitude" of the "having been" (*Gewesene*) of the divine.[46]

The openness toward and the recognition of the possibility of asking the question of God (as the final phase of the Heideggerian God-question) in a new (more authentic) way are discernible also in the lecture *"Dichterisch wohnet der Mensch"* (VA, 2), given by Heidegger in 1951. This description of human existence as a "poetical dwelling" upon earth includes the openness toward the "divinity," toward God as the unknown and as still the "measure" for the fullness of living; it recognizes that the manifestation of God is full of mystery, that he is present and yet unknown.[47] This dialogue with Hölderlin and the meditation on the divine, on the larger dimension of human existence, emphasize the manifestation of God and not just God himself as mysterious (*geheimnisvoll*). These ideas, then, regard God as a liberating dimension of human living as suggested by the poetic insight into the "place" of human living "between" heaven and earth. These references to God, however, may not necessarily correspond to the religious, Christian notion of God. They suggest, nevertheless, that Heidegger can think about the possibility of the "coming" (presence) of God and about the preparation (openness) of the human being for the "appearing" (presence, coming) of God.[48] God is not to be compared with entities,[49] though he is part of the original unity of the "Foursome" (of the World), of "earth" and "heaven," of the "divines" and of the "mortals."[50] The measure (*Mass*) of poetizing is the concealing-revealing of the "divinity," of "God," in the final analysis, of Being. But, Heidegger asks, "Who is the God?" and he suggests, "Perhaps this question is too difficult and too hasty for the human being."[51] He concludes in the same passage that we should ask, therefore, what is to be said about God, "What is God?" What is the meaning of these references to God? These remarks indicate that in the dialogues with Hölderlin Heidegger is meditating on the idea of Being; the terms *divinity, God, gods*, then, in some way are helpful in thinking about Being and being(s). We are not yet ready for the comprehension of the question of Being, and, therefore, we are not yet really prepared for asking the question of God. Heidegger's reflection thus also suggests that there may be a new way of thinking about God in the light of the openness toward Being as such. It may be claimed that the meditations on Hölderlin also represent a quest for the meaning of God. This conclusion is not without some difficulty. However, it does allow one to think that Heidegger's final attitude toward the idea of God is neither atheism nor agnosticism but rather openness; it recognizes at least the possibility of the meaningfulness of the idea of God even in the light of the notion of Being beyond the metaphysical way of thinking. It seems, then, that Heidegger is always concerned single-mindedly with the thinking of Being even when his language speaks also about God.

The position of the later Heidegger about God is clearly synthesized in his seminar lecture, *Die onto-theo-logische Verfassung der Metaphysik*, given in 1957 (ID).[52] The rejection of the traditional metaphysical concept of God (as the *causa sui*, as the highest being, as the ground of all beings) by Heidegger is based on the fact that the ontotheological character of metaphysics (the identification of Being with a being, with God; the forgetting of the ontological difference as became "questionable" (*fragwürdig*) not on the ground of some atheism but in the light of a new way of thinking the yet unthought unity of the essence of metaphysics.[53] This is the reason for his "silence" about God in the realm of thinking,[54] in philosophy. To the metaphysical cause-God, Heidegger claims, man can neither pray nor offer sacrifice; he cannot fall on his knees; he cannot dance and play music before this (philosophical) God.[55] The metaphysical idea of God objectifies, diminishes, "dedivinizes" the truly divine God; the metaphysical God is not worthy of the truly divine God. Therefore, Heidegger concludes, the "godless" (*gott-lose*) thinking (the nonmetaphysical thinking), the nonobjectifying way of reflecting, the letting go of the philosophical Cause-God, "perhaps is closer to the divine God": it is "freer" for God than the ontotheological (metaphysical) thinking.[56] This remark represents more than just an awareness of the difference between the God of philosophical conceptualization and the God of religious faith-experience; it indicates that the final phase of Heidegger's thinking remains open and free toward the truly divine idea of God, toward a "postmetaphysical" (nonobjectifying) way of asking the question of God from the perspective of the awareness of the ontological difference, that is, in the light of the destiny of Being. The criticism of the metaphysical concept of God cannot be regarded as the rejection of God; it is neither a disguised form of atheism nor a practical agnosticism. Heidegger's "silence" about God is not the sign of indecision but, rather, an attitude of openness and that of expectation, a form of listening to the yet unheard language of the final mystery of the World, of Being, and of God. The final phase of his meditation on Being does not lead to an end but to a new beginning, to the discernment of a new horizon; his final position regarding the idea of God cannot be captured in a new concept but, rather, in a new sense of wonder regarding the authentic meaning of the mystery called "God."

c) What is the final significance of the third phase of the question of God in Heidegger's way of thinking? What conclusion can be drawn from his suggestions regarding the notion of God from the perspective of his new understanding of the concept of Being? The most significant conclusion that can be drawn from the third and final phase of the question of God in Heidegger's way of thinking is that we ought to think further (in greater depth and breadth) the question of God; the final dimension of the meditation on Being is free for God; it is open toward a new and yet indescribable way of speaking and thinking the meaning of the word *God*. The process of questioning about the truth of Being leaves open the possibility for a true, divine idea of God; it recognizes, at the same time, the boundaries of the human conceptualizations not only of the truth of Being but also of the mystery of God. Heidegger's reflections on the question of God, even in their final phase, relate basically to the obstacles on the way toward a new method of thinking about God; they prepare the preconditions for a greater sensitivity to the more essential dimensions of human living; they indicate the need to overcome nihilism and to rediscover the primordial function of language as the "letting to shine forth," as the "lighting-concealing setting-free" of the World,[57] of the interplay between heaven and earth, between the divines and the mortals. The new way of thinking and speaking about God, therefore, is a task that lies ahead of the thinker; it is bound up with the destiny of Being. In the final analysis, then, the rethinking of the meaning of Being does not take away but rather reawakens the mystery of God.

The assessment of the "place" of the question of God in Heidegger, it should be kept in mind, is limited by the fact that his works are still in the process of publication. There are neither final nor "last" words of Heidegger on Being, on the ontological difference. He spoke about the "end of philosophy and the task of thinking,"[58] but this "task of thinking" has yet to be adequately worked out. The full and final understanding of the third phase of the God-question is conditioned by the entire and final Heideggerian interpretation of Being. The meaning of the word *God* in Heidegger's thought can be found by following (by participating in) his experience of thinking in all his works as they become available and not by hypothesizing "anticipation" of his mind.

Conclusion

The *second phase* of the problem of God in Heidegger's way of thinking should be understood as a questioning-thinking of the most difficult aspects of the philosophical problem of God. For Heidegger, the process of questioning-thinking constitutes the very essence of philosophizing. The meditation on the ontological difference goes beyond the metaphysical problem of God and points toward a relevant irrelevance of the traditional interpretation of the God-question. The overcoming of metaphysics includes an overcoming of the metaphysical notion of God; the God-question, then, becomes questionable. Is the question of God a philosophical question at all? The second phase of the Heideggerian God-question seems to lead to a philosophical indifference toward the problem of God. Is there, perhaps, a new way of asking the question of God? Heidegger's developing thought suggests, first of all, the need for a questioning-process, and *then* through this questioning-process (which tries to overcome the state of forgottenness of Being and of the misunderstanding of the Holy) prepares the ground for the *third* and thus final *phase* of the question of God, for a new way of thinking the meaning of the word *God.* The second phase of the Heideggerian problem of God, then, may be called the phase of questioning; it examines the God-question *as* a question. The first four chapters of Part III analyzed the meaning and the main dimensions of this questioning in the light of a variety of Heidegger's writings; the fifth chapter showed and investigated the third (and thus final) phase of the question of God in Heidegger. These concluding reflections do not intend to repeat the unfolded thoughts; they indicate, however, the most relevant aspects of the last two phases of Heidegger's attitude toward the problem of God.

a) Heidegger's way of thinking the ontological difference remains basically *indifferent* toward a philosophical elaboration of the problem of God. This indifference should be understood as an indifference toward the traditional metaphysical notion of God and not as a rejection of the God of religious faith and experience. This attitude is the unfolding of the orientation already established in SZ. Heidegger himself insists again and again (for example, in WG and in HB) that the ontological notion of ek-sistence and that of transcendence cannot be interpreted either theistically or atheistically.[1] Even when analyzing the structure of ontological questioning (EM), he remarks that he does not intend to question the truth of Christian faith as such. The Heideggerian indifference (as one of the main characteristics of the second phase of the God-question), therefore, is nothing more and nothing less than the theological indifference of the ontological difference.

b) Heidegger's developing thought (after SZ) shows a definitive *separation* (and a distantiation) of the whole Being-question from the God-question. This is the outcome of his interpretation of the tension ("alterity") between believing and thinking (questioning). In his view, the metaphysical questioning is "dominated" by the Christian understanding of finitude (creation); therefore, it does not reach the real depth of the ontological problematic (EM, KM, FD, WW, WG). Heidegger considers not so much the mere fact as the way of understanding finitude and its structure.[2]

c) The entire metaphysical approach to the problem of God comes to be *irrelevant* in the context of ontological phenomenology. The traditional philosophical God-question is an irrelevant question from the point of view of ontological questioning as such. The metaphysical God-question is overcome, at least in some sense, by the ontological Being-question. The new ontological understanding (structure, meaning) goes beyond the metaphysical and ontic interpretations of beings. The metaphysical notion of God as the highest being (as the most perfect being, as the first cause) is the result of the traditional (metaphysical) interpretation of Being (PW, WM, KS, SF, ID, HW, SG, VA, HB, WP). This is the meaning of the relevant irrelevance of the metaphysical God-question from the point of view of Heidegger's thinking on the ontological difference, on the meaning of Being. The classical dilemma of theism and atheism, therefore, is overcome by the entire problematic of Being and by the thinking of the God-question as a question.

d) The questioning phase of the Heideggerian God-question indicates that the question of God *remains* a meaningful *question* for the Heideggerian meditation on Being. The "destruction," the overcoming of the metaphysical notion of God, is concerned only with the metaphysical character of the problem of God. The understanding of the meaning of Being, the overcoming of the forgottenness of Being as such, constitutes one of the prerequisites of a new way of asking the question about the meaning of God again. The present absence of the gods (a sign of the withdrawal of the Holy and of God) represents a mittence (a destiny) of Being, its concealment and forgottenness in the metaphysical history. The meaning of the Holy and of the divine shall be discovered again when human thinking comes closer to the original experiencing of Being (*ursprüngliche Seinserfahrung*). Thus, it is possible to speak of a new dimension of Heideggerian questioning that includes a concern with the meaning of God (HD, HW, TK, SG, F).

e) In the light of the thinking of the God-question as a question, then, it is possible to discern a *third* and thus final phase of the question of God in Heidegger (TK, HB, WP, ID, VA-2); the new understanding of Being (after the overcoming of the metaphysical way of thinking) opens up the possibility of a *new* approach to the question of God. The discussion of the nature, of the significance, and of the implications of this third phase of the question of God in Heidegger (in the fifth chapter of Part III) leads to the conclusion that the meditation on Being in the final analysis is free for the truly divine notion of God, that it is open toward a "postmetaphysical" way of asking the question of God in the light of the destiny of Being. The reexamination of the meaning of Being does not destroy but rather reawakens the mystery of God. The first two phases of the God-question have led to a definitive separation of the Being-question from the philosophical God-question; the third phase of the God-question is concerned mainly with the new meaning of God and with the obstacles on the way to the manifestation of the presence of God, of the essential and sacred dimension of being-in-the-World. The third phase, then, confirms the insights of the first two phases and goes beyond them by discovering a new way of thinking about the meaning of the word *God*. This new way of thinking, however, remains undeveloped; it leads to keeping "silence" about God. This "silence" is not a refusal of God; it is a way of listening to the yet unheard language of Being and that of God. The later development of Heidegger's thought is sometimes presented as having the characteristics of an ineffable (and even religious) manifestation and experience.[3] This aspect of Heidegger's meditation on Being, however, cannot be separated from his view of language as the "house of Being." The assessment of Heidegger's position regarding the question of God ought to keep in mind his distinction between the cultural (historical, political) form of Christianity and the Christianity of the New Testament[4] as well as his descriptions of the various kinds of atheism[5] and nihilism, especially in his lectures on Nietzsche. In the final analysis, his thought may be described not as the finding of but as the search for God in the true sense; it is a way of rethinking the "place" of God in philosophy.

The last two phases of the question of God in Heidegger do not lead to a definite, final answer to the question of God; they show that the God-question is a question that is to be asked again and again. The understanding of the meaning of God in the experience of thinking as well as in the light of religious faith cannot be regarded as a final possession (for once and for all) but, rather, as something to be gained, discerned, and accepted through "going through" the "dangers" of the questioning-thinking process. This thinking, according to Heidegger, is not ruled by the will-to-define (*Definierenwollen*);[6] it is an experience of Being, an attempt "to listen to the voice of Being" (*auf die Stimme des Seins zu hören*).[7]

PART   4

SOME
CLARIFICATIONS
OF THE
QUESTION
OF GOD

The publication of the complete edition (*Gesamtausgabe*) of all the works of Heidegger began in 1975 and is planned for completion by the year 2005. The fact that it is still in progress makes it difficult to search for final, definitive conclusions about Heidegger's thought as a whole as well as his position on the question of God. At the present,[1] more than one-third of the total body of his writings (thirty-five volumes of a total estimated one hundred volumes, mainly his lecture courses at Marburg and Freiburg) is available in the *Gesamtausgabe*. The editing and the publication follow the guidelines established by Heidegger before his death in 1976. These writings (as well as the works published during his lifetime) bear witness to the

lasting question-worthiness (*Fragwürdigkeit*) of the
question of Being; they are "ways—not works"
(*Wege—nicht Werke*); they represent the journey of
thinking and not a final opus according to Heidegger's remark a few days before his death. Philosophical thinking is always on its way toward that which is
worthy of thinking; philosophical works, then, show
the ways of thinking practiced by their author. They
should not be viewed as merely communications of
viewpoints and opinions of their creator. Heidegger's
way of thinking is present in all his works; it is basically the same in its depth and direction in the most
recent and first-time-published lectures and essays as
in the books published earlier during his lifetime. It
is reasonable to infer, then, that the current status of
the publication of all his writings should neither deter
nor detour the investigation of his thought. Each volume, be it a new edition of a text published earlier or
a hitherto unpublished university course or lecture,
brings some additional background and light to the
more comprehensive and genuine understanding of
his philosophy.

What are the main contributions of the writings
appearing in print for the first time (as part of the
Gesamtausgabe) to the examination of Heidegger's
thought as a whole and to the final assessment of his
views on the question of God? Do the new, complete
edition of all his writings published earlier and the
new volumes (first-time-published writings) alter in
any way the substance of his philosophy as embodied
in the works published in his lifetime, which became
the focus of scholarship and a source of influence?
Will the completion of the editing and publication of
the entire manuscripts of Heidegger bring about a
new meaning of and a new perspective on his
thought? The final response to these questions will
become possible only in the future when all the writings will be available for analysis and reflection; only
the passage of time will reveal the definite response.
However, some basic conclusions can be drawn from
the examination of the works available at this time

that constitute significant, even though at times provisional, responses to the preceding questions.

Perhaps the most significant and the first teaching
of the "new" works of Heidegger is the emphasis on
the continuity as well as on the unity of his thought.
The development of his philosophical task is always
governed by the attentiveness to the question of
Being. The seeds of the later ideas are already there,
at least implicitly, in the earlier works; the later writings "merely" unfold the task of the earlier works.
The emergence of the pathway of thinking that leads
to Being is not a wandering around in the vacuum of
abstract and detached conceptualization; it is, rather,
an attentive examination and reappropriation of the
tradition of philosophy. Heidegger's phenomenology
is deeply rooted in the history of philosophy; it can
be neither grasped nor evaluated without the recognition of its historical background. The lecture
courses at Marburg and at Freiburg are the best
examples of this second teaching of Heidegger's writings; they are unceasing meditations on the great
thinkers (for example, the Pre-Socratics, Plato, Aristotle, Kant, Hegel, Nietzsche, Hölderlin) and on the
most foundational issues of philosophy (such as truth,
time, Being, language, human existence, God, science, and philosophical knowledge). A third teaching
of the new volumes of Heidegger consists in showing
that Heidegger is a masterful teacher and commu-
nicator of philosophy. The pedagogical structure of
the lectures is quite substantial; clarity is achieved by
gradual explanation and analysis as well as by judi-
cious use of repetition (review). These works are readily readable; they also include additional background
and themes (the analysis of boredom, the examination of finitude, reflections on World, life, and the
human building of the World) that are quite helpful
for discerning the right meaning of Heidegger's
thought as a whole. Finally, a fourth teaching of these
writings is that, in the final analysis, he is engaged in
thinking only "one" thought like all the great thinkers; his attention is always focused on the "one" issue

worthy of all thought, on the truth of Being, on the phenomenon of the "is," on the meaning of Being that in many ways speaks in all beings. This unity and the persistency of his philosophical perspective suggest that the basic thrust of Heidegger's thought may be grasped clearly enough in the light of the works already published; it is possible to conclude, then, that the writings published in his lifetime represent the substance of his thought though the editing and publication of the rest of his works enrich significantly the final grasp and accomplishment of his task.

The analysis of the question of God in Heidegger's phenomenology, as developed in Parts 1 through 3 of this study, is based on comprehensive research of Heidegger's thought as a whole; it is aware of all the works of Heidegger, including those in the *Gesamtausgabe*, even though it selected for close examination the writings published during his life. The presentation of the detailed research of those writings (mainly university lecture courses) that gradually became available after his death would (at least) double the space of this study, and it would entail extensive repetition of ideas already discerned by the preceding parts. Because of the current status of the availability of Heidegger's writings and for reasons of methodology as well as for the sake of clarity, however, these writings ought to become the focus of distinct, special attention to the extent that they may represent some additional clarifications of the question of God. Many of these writings include some additional documentation for the development of the three phases of the question of God; they do not indicate, at least according to the available evidence, any substantial change for the thematic and systematic understanding of Heidegger's position on the question of God. They basically confirm and reinforce the ideas and perspectives of the works analyzed in the preceding parts of this study.

Are there any aspects at all of Heidegger's attitude toward the question of God in the group of his texts under discussion (that is, the writings published for

the first time in and after the beginning of the complete edition of his works) that are not discernible in
his other works (before the beginning of the complete
edition)? What are the most valuable insights of these
writings that represent some additional clarification
(more than a documentation and a restatement of the
earlier expressed ideas) of his views on the rethinking
of the philosophical notion of God? Can there be a
last word of wisdom on this issue according to his way
of thinking? How should the question of God be
thought after and even beyond Heidegger? The following reflections respond to these questions and
related concerns; they analyze those insights that clarify some aspects of the question of God in Heidegger
or at least confirm some basic attitude toward it. The
order of these considerations, therefore, is governed
by the thematic connections between the works at
hand and not so much by their chronological relationships. These discussions, accordingly, deal with
(1) the task of philosophy and atheism, (2) the meaning of transcendence, (3) the notion of the World and
creation, (4) the "other," (5) questioning beyond
Heidegger.

19

The Task
of Philosophy
and Atheism

Heidegger's attitude toward the question of God is intimately
connected with his understanding of the task of philosophizing as the this-worldly search for the truth of Being, with
his definition of the very nature of philosophy as the most unique
way of thinking that precedes and structurally underlies (or at least
makes possible) all other forms of the search for knowledge as de-
rived (and thus "secondary" though by no means insignificant or
negligible) modes of essential (truthful, philosophical) thinking.
Philosophy as the most radical, foundational thinking, according to
the many and often repeated explanations of Heidegger's university lecture courses, is a distinct mode of thinking; it never should
be confused with worldview (final, closed, and concrete wisdom for
living), ideology (totalitarian claim on truth in theory and praxis),
or science (knowledge of particular beings as particulars, for example, knowledge of the things of nature and of the spirit, study
of God as the highest being). Philosophical thinking is neither for
nor against the affirmation of God as such; it is "a-theistic" in the
sense of being "without" God because it is "with" or "for the sake
of" the coming of Being (of the mystery of the "is") into language.
Heidegger's definition of the very nature and task of philosophical

thinking may be described as a methodological atheism; it is neither "for" nor "against" but rather "without" God (as the last and first explanation of beings and thinking); it comes from and returns to Being (and not from and to God, who cannot be forced into the categories or concepts of philosophical reflection). This quality of being "godless" (that is, not being closed by a narrow philosophical, metaphysical notion of God as a principle of explanation), according to the "final word" of Heidegger on the question of God, can also be understood as a new and liberated, genuine (philosophical) thinking becoming free for God, for a larger (more transcendent) and more profound idea of God. Whatever the final status of this being "free for God" may be, it is quite puzzling though not incompatible with the "methodological atheism" suggested previously as a constant element of Heidegger's journey of thought.

Some aspects of this definition of the task of philosophy and its significance for the "place" (or "no place") of the question of God in phenomenology are well explained and even further clarified in the earlier as well as in the later university lecture courses of Heidegger. The following seven volumes (published for the first time) of the *Gesamtausgabe* contain some valuable insights in this regard: PA (early Freiburg Lecture Course, Winter Semester, 1921–22), PZ (Marburg Lecture Course, Summer Semester, 1925), GP (Marburg Lecture Course, Summer Semester, 1927), AM (Freiburg Lecture Course, Summer Semester, 1931), HH (Freiburg Lecture Course, Winter Semester, 1934–35), HA (Freiburg Lecture Course, Winter Semester, 1941–42), H (Freiburg Lecture Course, Summer Semester, 1943 and 1944).

a) The nature and the depth of Heidegger's methodological atheism become clearly manifest in his views on the relationship between philosophy and faith. His entire idea on the alterity of (on the tension between) philosophy and faith is explained tersely and unambiguously in the recently published (early) Freiburg Lecture Course, (Winter Semester, 1921–22) on the phenomenological interpretation of Aristotle (PA). This early formulation of his views on the nature of philosophy and on the question of faith shows that Heidegger realized very early in his philosophical development the significance of the "death of God," of the nature of pluralism in philosophy. Thus, the way the notion of God is thought or not thought (yes, no, one, many, Spirit, Matter, Will, Life) basically determines the philosophical activity, the freedom, the creative journey of the human mind. The confrontation with the question of God is crucial for Heidegger's phenomenology. This may well be the most central lesson he will learn from Nietzsche's Zarathustra. The early foundation of methodological atheism is not a simplistic affirmation of a secular worldview but, rather, the recognition of the possible plurality of the meaning of the phenomenon of the "death of God."

PA contains a unique statement by Heidegger on his notion of philosophy as a methodological atheism. Philosophy takes its authentic (*eigentliche*) stand in questioning, in the execution (practice) of questionability; philosophy is a process of questioning, doubting. Philosophical thinking is quite different from the absolutist attitude (dogmatic predisposition) of the skeptic[1] as well as from the attitude of commitment (openness and resoluteness) of the religious individual (faith). Questionability, according to Heidegger, is not religious, but it may prepare the ground (lead to the situation) of a religious decision as such.[2] This comment seems to suggest that questionability (the attitude of questioning) may precede or follow a religious (faith) discernment; questioning, the attitude of questionability (doubting), then, prepares the ground of possibility for religious discernment, for a decision regarding religious meaning(s). Philosophy as such, however, is a-religious; it is not a religious activity per se. Heidegger clarifies his views by the following statement in the first person singular (quite unusual in his writings): "I am not religious in philosophy, but as a philosopher I can be also a religious man."[3] The "trick" (skill), according to Heidegger, consists in philosophizing and in being genuinely religious at the same time; philosophy is an activity in the concrete, historical world and not an involvement in religious ideology. The task of philosophy is a this-worldly task; it does not belong to the realm of religious ideology. Heidegger's final conclusion is that philosophy is atheistic in the sense of being without God: "Philosophy, according to its radical questionability, must be atheistic in principle."[4] Philosophy, according to its fundamental tendency, must not be allowed to have and to determine (fix) God.[5] The more radical philosophy is, the more determinedly it (philosophy) is "away from him" (from God); the more radical the "way," the more difficult it becomes to pass "by" him. Philosophy does have its own task; it must not engage in idle speculation about God.[6] Philosophy is a clarification of the World in a radical way; it is not an empty theorizing but the grasping of facticity, of human existence. Therefore, Heidegger explains again, "philosophy *itself* as such is atheistic" (note his emphasis) when radically understood;[7] philosophical questioning is "atheism in principle" in the sense that it is a fundamental (in principle) confrontation that recognizes Being as "objective."[8] The basic sense of wonder (the radical question) about Being goes beyond the notion (and the question) of the highest being (God); it is not a theological contemplation of beings but a questioning about (and of) Being.

What is the significance of these remarks by Heidegger for the question of God? To what extent do they bring to light his views on philosophy and God? His claim that philosophy is atheism (or rather: atheistic) in principle does not really resolve the question regarding the philosophical affirmation of God even if it suggests that speculation about God belongs to the field of religion. This way of speaking does not really tell much about Heidegger's own mind on the question of God. What is the meaning of the word *atheism* in the context of his claim? It (the word *atheism*) means a-theism, that is, being without God. Philosophy as such is without God; it is neither for nor against God. But, it may be suggested, this attitude of mind merely places the notion of God outside philosophy; it merely "expels" a basic, existential question from the domain of philosophical reflection. This seems to be an a priori exclusion based on the nature of philosophical thinking according to Heidegger. It may well be unreasonable, though not absolutely impossible, to regard this "a priori" as an intellectual or ideological prejudice. What, then, is the meaning of the term *atheism* in Heidegger's claim? Philosophy is called "atheism" in the sense that the very nature of philosophizing consists in questioning (in being neither "for" nor "against") the accepted meanings (for example, God) and principles (for example, creation); philosophical thinking, then, is marked by the attitude of questioning (not by the eagerness for affirmation or negation) toward the notion of God; it questions everything, including the meaning and the reality of God. This restrictive meaning of Heidegger's claim, however, cannot exclude another dimension of questioning: the notion that the questioning of the accepted meanings and principles reopens the questions regarding the new (future, provisional, or even final) status of the questioned meanings and principles. This aspect of questioning, therefore, adds a new expansive meaning to Heidegger's claim. The questioning of the accepted (or "taken-for-granted") meanings and principles (Being, God, existence, World, man) opens up new questions at least regarding the status of the final thematization of the meanings and principles in question; the process of questioning (once its inner dynamic is allowed to run its course) becomes more and more radical without reaching a final, unalterable formulation. The question of Being never comes to an end; the question(ing) of the meaning of the word *God* never comes to a halt.

The "expulsion" of the question of God at least as a question from philosophical thinking, it must be concluded, is not consistent with Heidegger's notion of philosophy as radical (in principle) questioning; the exclusion of the question of God (at least a priori) from philosophy cannot be justified on philosophical grounds. The claim that philosophy is "atheism" in principle, therefore, indicates only that philosophy is a questioning of all, even of the idea of God, by the human mind; it begins without God and remains without God in the sense that it never substitutes (nor does it renounce) human reflection for divine (faith) wisdom. In the final analysis, the early idea of Heidegger (1921–22) may be grasped properly only if it is viewed in the light of the final phase of his views on philosophy and God, that is, as anticipating the idea that the questioning of the accepted (metaphysical) notion of God (and of philosophy) as a way of thinking without God is in fact freer (or becomes free) for God. Philosophical thinking makes the question of God more difficult, more weighty, and more thoughtworthy; it gives to the word *God* its proper weight. The philosopher can also be a religious person; his religious attitude, however, will be genuine only if his philosophizing remains authentic questioning. Independence and respect for autonomy are the signs of authenticity as well as the ground of possibility for the relationship between philosophical (secular) thinking and the attitude of (religious) faith.

b) The origin of Heidegger's methodological "atheism" is situated in his understanding of the notion of phenomenology and in his phenomenological reexamination of the nature of the particular (ontic) sciences. His criticism of the ideological uses (and thus abuses) of philosophy and of the sciences leads him to the affirmation of the absolute freedom and independence of philosophizing. He seems to be quite aware of the possibilities for misinterpreting his positions on phenomenology and on the question of God. His Marburg Lecture Course in 1925 (Summer Semester), now published as *Prolegomena zur Geschichte des Zeitbegriffs* (PZ), analyzes the status of philosophy and the sciences in the second half of the nineteenth century and shows the emergence of phenomenology as the new, definitive potentiality of philosophy; it represents an early conception of many themes of SZ (There-being, Being) as well as the rejection of the misconceptions of phenomenology. These clarifications of the nature and of the task of phenomenology anticipate his responses to the misinterpretations of the existential analytic of SZ and, at the same time, show the continuity of his meditations on the question of Being.

Sections eight and nine of PZ describe phenomenology as a method of investigation, as the analytical description of the a priori (of the ontological structure) of intentionality. These sections represent a valuable background for the right interpretation of the phenomenological method of investigation concisely developed in section seven of SZ. Phenomenology is not a doctrine, but an original method of research; it is not a science that precedes the traditional philosophical disciplines, but a radically philosophical task, a return to the phenomena, "to the things themselves." Phenomenology as the method of research of the structures of intentionality (the analytical description of the modes of being in the World) represents a new beginning in philosophizing; its task is neither prophetic nor pragmatic, but strictly philosophical. Its self-understanding is opposed to all tendency to dominate life; it is not a worldview, nor an ideology, nor a claim about having the answers to life's questions. "Philosophical research is and remains atheism, . . . as atheism it becomes 'joyful science' as a great thinker once said."9 This profession of "atheism" shows a forceful (almost abrupt) reaction (in the classroom) against the ideological misunderstandings (even misuses) of philosophy. This passage does not mention the word *God,* but it refers to the authentic philosophical nature of phenomenology as a whole; it may lead easily to some misunderstanding of Heidegger's position that philosophy (phenomenology) is "atheism." This profession of "atheism" is as easily misleading as M. Merleau-Ponty's (radical, comparative) descriptive statement that phenomenology is "the disavowal of science."10 The intended, real meaning of Heidegger's profession of "atheism," however, is the affirmation of the inner dynamics of philosophy, of the liberation of thinking from submission to worldview, ideology, or even theology; it is a clear emphasis on the "objectivity of philosophizing" (*Sachlichkeit des Philosophierens*),11 on the freedom of thinking. Phenomenology as a method of research is without God, without ideology; it is grounded on (going back to) the phenomena, on the many manifestations of Being in the many beings; it is not founded on, nor is it governed by, the task of defending a worldview, an ideology, a way of life, a hope, or a system of values. The use of the phenomenological method in the descriptive analysis of human existence (There-being) entails neither a "hidden theology" (*versteckte Theologie*) nor a concern with moral teaching, even though the existential structures may be recognized by and thus play a role in theological anthropology.[12] From the perspective of phenomenology, according to Heidegger, even the word *God* as designating the most perfect being as the realization of the very idea of Being (in Descartes as well as in other thinkers) is simply a purely ontological concept.[13] Phenomenological, existential anthropology, according to Heidegger, represents a secular, this-worldly definition of the human being; the existential analysis, the explanation of There-being (in PZ as well as in SZ) is founded on the remarkable, "distinguished" relationship of human reality to Being (*ausgezeichnetes Seinsverhältnis*).[14] The psychological and the spiritual composition of There-being is not considered in this context.[15] Heidegger regards Husserl's definition of man as being "profane," and he describes M. Scheler's philosophy of the human person as being oriented (governed) by the Christian concept of man as the image of God.[16]

This profession of "atheism," however, does not mean at all that Heidegger rejects the notion of God as such or the possibility of a meaningful concept of God. It is quite significant and enlightening for his views that his examination of the crisis of the sciences in PZ describes theology as a faith-relationship to reality, as a striving for the renewal of faith in order to gain an original explanation of man's Being-toward-God.[17] These remarks suggest that the rethinking of the nature and of the task of theological science (built on the experience of faith) is part of the analysis of the crisis of the sciences. The very crisis of the sciences indicates that the sciences need an original interpretation (explicitation, *Auslegung*) that they themselves are not able to provide.[18] Ultimately the sciences are nothing else than concrete potentialities of human existence (*Dasein*) that speak about (express) the World and about the human being.[19] Science, therefore, is an ontological potentiality (*Seinsmöglichkeit*) that is rooted in human existence; it is not an arbitrary understanding that rests on the tradition. Heidegger responds to the crisis of the sciences by rethinking the key concepts of science (beings, things, discovery, truth) and by rooting the scientific activity in the human being as a questioning being in the World; he tries to unearth (disclose) the constitution (state, structure) of Being

(*Seinsverfassung*), ontological knowledge, which underlies and determines the basic structure of the objects of the particular sciences. The task of phenomenology consists in making understandable the domain of things (particular beings) prior to the scientific elaboration and thus in making comprehensible the scientific elaboration itself.[20] The ontological assumptions of the (natural, cultural, humanistic, theological) sciences govern their ontic (concrete) descriptions of the particular beings; the rediscovery of the ontological concepts and assumptions, then, leads to a new and deeper grasp of the ontic notions and descriptions. The way of rethinking theology, like the need to reexamine the other sciences, originates with the explication of the special ("distinguished") relationship of the human being to Being; the description of the relation of human existence to God is influenced (and preceded) by the relation of There-being to Being. These ideas anticipate not only many insights of SZ but also those of WM and WW.

    c) Heidegger's methodological atheism and his critical reflections on the question of God do not come about (and thus should not be interpreted) as an antagonistic, polemical confrontation between two opposing, hostile philosophical perspectives (or systems). His "destruction" and his "reconstruction" of the question of God are essential elements of his way of thinking, of his dialogue with the tradition of philosophy. Phenomenology is not an ahistorical ("science") philosophy; what phenomenology is concerned with today was already "alive in the beginning of Western philosophy."[21] Heidegger's philosophical roots in the tradition as well as in Husserl's phenomenology are fully manifest in GP, in his lecture course at Marburg on the basic problems of phenomenology, given during the Summer Semester, 1927, the same year as the publication of SZ. This work shows well that the existential analysis of SZ represents a step-by-step appropriation of the Western philosophical tradition on the question of Being; it develops the intended but never accomplished third division of the "first part" of SZ (provisionally entitled "Time and Being") and a systematic elaboration of the ontological difference (in the second part of GP). The meditations on Being, time, There-being, essence, and existence and the gradual unfolding of Heidegger's philosophical perspective entail a prolonged dialogue with ancient, medieval, and modern philosophers as well as a rethinking (and thus a transformation) of basic concepts of Husserl's phenomenology. The works of Aquinas, Duns Scotus, Suarez, Descartes, and Kant and the basic principles of phenomenology constitute an indispensable source and background for the systematic analysis of the essential structure of the ontological difference. GP not only makes SZ more graspable but goes beyond it.

Heidegger's view (clearly defined in GP) that philosophy is not the science of being(s) but the foundational science of Being (ontology, using phenomenology as the method of inquiry) determines the nature and the boundary of his reflections on the question of God. The particular, positive sciences (biology, psychology, theology, and so on) explore the field of particular beings (life and the body, the psyche and the human person, God). Reflection on God, the domain of theology, then, is a part of the study of the particular beings. The question of Being transcends the question of God because the concept of Being as such ontologically transcends the notion of God as a particular (even though the highest) being according to traditional metaphysics. But the notion of God historically functioned also as an ontological concept, as the concept of Being; therefore, any reexamination of the comprehension of Being brings about a confrontation (dialogue) with the philosophical conceptualization of God. The scientific exploration of the domain of particular beings includes an a priori and "taken-for-granted" (nonreflective) ontological understanding (a concept of Being defined, for example, as Matter, as Spirit, as Will, as God, as Substance, as Cause, as Subject) that is operational (practiced or implied) in the thematizations of the field of beings as the objects of the particular (ontic, positive) sciences. Philosophy is not a worldview (with ontic claims, with established attitudes toward beings) but the foundational science of Being, a structural interpretation of the potentialities of Being (ontological claims); it unearths and examines the implicit and often unthought assumptions and (ontological) understandings that govern the nonphilosophical sciences (biology, physics, psychology, theology).[22] Theology is a positive (that is, bound to the "posited," to the particular being, to God) and not a transcendental (philosophical, going beyond beings to Being, focused on Being) science according to Heidegger.

Philosophy, therefore, is able to "tell" something to the sciences (and thus even to theology) by examining their foundational presuppositions and by analyzing their nature from the perspective of Being as such, from the ontological, transcendental horizon. Heidegger's philosophy of science unmasks the metaphysical assumptions of the sciences (including those of theology as the science of the highest being) and describes the phenomenological attitude in getting close to things (beings) for what they are by "letting them be"; it rediscovers beings as ways to Being and thus recognizes the ontological difference. The traditional metaphysical explanation of beings by way of "reducing" (relating) them to another and ultimately to the highest being (to God) is a scientific (ontic) and theological (divine) understanding, a science of being(s). However, this traditional metaphysical explanation is using the term *God* as being identical with Being as such; it is also, therefore, a definite way of grasping beings from the perspective of Being (an ontological thinking). The critical rethinking of the traditional theses about Being (for example, that Being is God), the "destruction" of the tradition of metaphysics (Aquinas, Suarez, Kant), "displaces" the ontological assumptions of the positive (ontic) sciences; it raises basic questions regarding the validity and the nature of theology because the phenomenological meditation on the traditional notion of Being and on the disclosure of the ontological difference (a key task of GP) inevitably includes the separation of the question of Being from the question of God. Even in examining Kant's evaluation of the ontological argument for God's existence, Heidegger is interested mainly not in the arguments themselves but in the question of Being, in Kant's interpretation of Being.[23]

These ideas represent more than just a clarification and a historical background of Heidegger's position on the question of God as developed in SZ; they go beyond the more negative perspective on the metaphysical (theological) idea of God according to SZ and suggest a more positive, comprehensive review of the ontological and theological functions of the philosophical concept of God. Heidegger's way of thinking the question of God, therefore, as GP suggests, has several phases. The "destruction" of the metaphysical identification of God (as the highest being) with Being (God as *ipsum esse subsistens,* as Being itself) is the consequence of the fact that God is still a particular being; the notion of God, therefore, does not reflect (cannot stand for) the concept of Being as such that is not a particular being. The elaboration of these issues constitutes the first (the more critical, "demythologizing") phase of the question of God. The phenomenological notion of Being as transcending all beings and the unfolding of the ontological difference (clearly formulated in GP and developed in the works after SZ) make possible (and even feasible) the asking of the question of God as a question (the second phase of the question of God in

Heidegger) in the light of the new grasp of Being and lead to an initial, new, more "divine" way of thinking the meaning of the word *God* (the third and final phase of the question of God in Heidegger). In the final analysis, GP may be viewed as the "bridge" between SZ and the later works of Heidegger. The texts of the complete edition of Heidegger's work make even more understandable the development and the unity of the three phases of his discussion of the question of God.

d) Heidegger's interpretation of Book IX of Aristotle's *Metaphysics* in his lecture course at Freiburg during the Summer Semester of 1931 (AM) maintains the radical separation of the question of God from the question of Being; it reinforces the phenomenological criticism of metaphysics and of the metaphysical concept of God. This work (AM) contains three passages dealing with some aspects of the notion of God.

The first passage refers to the shortcoming of medieval ontology. Heidegger claims that the medieval theory of the analogy of Being (*analogia entis*) represents neither the solution to nor a real elaboration of the question of Being; it functions essentially as a philosophical expression and formulation of Christian faith, of the conviction that God is the creator and preserver of the world.[24] The finite beings are infinitely different from God as the infinite being. How is it possible, then, to grasp the created beings and the highest being (God as the uncreated being) with the same concept called "Being"? The question remains for Heidegger, Is the meaning of Being univocal, equivocal, or analogical? Meister Eckhart, according to Heidegger, was, for a while at least, the only one seeking a solution to this question when he said that God "is" not at all because the term *Being* is a finite predicate and thus it cannot be said (predicated) of God.[25] These remarks clearly indicate that it is the question of Being that determines Heidegger's comments on the question of God, on faith, and on theology. The reference to M. Eckhart even suggests a transition toward a more questioning perspective on the question of God; it goes beyond the sometimes "hostile" attitude of SZ.

The second passage (in AM) includes a reference to God in connection with the description of the nature of language. Language is more than a means of expression and communication; it is the manifestness and the annunciation of the World. Language originally, then, is not as much utilitarian as poetic; it is poetry as the "proclamation of the World in the call of the God."[26] The nature of the World, the power of Being, and God speak through the poetic, ontological language. Utilitarian language is not capable of speaking of God. Heidegger's lectures on Hölderlin further develop the poetic nature of language. The later writings of Heidegger (such as HB) make the language about God conditioned not only by the poetic, original nature of language but (even more) by the language of Being.

The third passage (in AM) contains a criticism of the notion of God as almighty, of the idea that God is force.[27] The conclusion of Heidegger's interpretation of Book IX of Aristotle's *Metaphysics* claims that there is an essential finiteness of all force; force is potentiality, and thus it needs actualization, realization, determination. The application of the term *force* to God, then, is unthinkable; it is a notion unworthy of God. The conception of God as "almighty" is not a divine, genuine idea of God. God, the divine being, should not be regarded as a worldly being, as worldly power. It should be remembered that Aquinas' notion of God as "pure act" (*actus purus*) excluded all "potentiality" from God in order to explain the divine nature as being other than and different from the rest of things (beings). Heidegger, nevertheless, still rejects Aquinas' view because of its ontological presuppositions (the thinglike conception of beings and of presence included in the idea of the "pure act").

The commentary on Aristotle, then, just reinforces the phenomenological criticism of metaphysics and of the metaphysical concept of God (as the highest being, as the creator, as the almighty). This rejection is based not on the fact that the concept of God is determined by ontological theories (by ideas of and about Being) but rather on his judgment that these ontological theories (for example, that Being is identified with being) remain inadequate. At this phase he is not suggesting that the notion of God does not belong at all to the field of (genuine, real) ontological investigation.

e) The unceasing dialogue of Heidegger with Hölderlin represents a search for a more primordial language and thought about Being and about the sacred, divine dimension of human existence. His lecture course on Hölderlin at Freiburg during the Winter Semester, 1934–35 (HH), indicates that his analysis of the absence of the divine and his criticism of the culturally relativized notion of God constitute not a rejection of but rather the search for a more genuine (divine) grasp of God, of the divinity. The "flight of the gods" represents a historical experience (an essential experience), the withdrawal of the divinity; it teaches not the death of but the possibility of a new encounter with the gods, with the divine horizon of human reality.[28] There is no genuine human culture as long as the gods are gone.[29] Heidegger's interpretation of the "flight of the gods" is not atheistic; the phenomenon of the "death of God" is not synonymous with atheism. The eclipse of the divine (God, gods) does not mean that it is not at work; if it would be possible to step out of the domain of the divinity, there would be not even dead gods (absence is a mode of presence). "Whoever seriously says that 'God is dead' and bets an entire life on it like Nietzsche, is not an atheist."[30] Losing God is not at all comparable to losing an object; when a thing (an object) is lost, it is gone. The enduring of the renunciation of the old gods is the "preserving (*Bewahren*) of their divinity."[31] Many of those who remain quite comfortable in the "cage" of a traditional creed without questioning it (because of laziness or subtlety) "are more atheistic than the great doubters."[32] These remarks clearly show that the phenomenon of the "death of God" is experienced in Heidegger's thinking not as the final end (conclusion), but as a new beginning (departure) of the search for (as questioning) the meanings of the words *God, divine,* and *divinity.*

The doubt of the genuine (open-minded) doubter, according to Heidegger, is prompted by the will to know as well as by the true not-knowing. In true doubting occur (*ereignet sich*) the collision of knowing and not-knowing and the temporalization of original distress (*Not*) that transports There-being into basic dispositions. This doubting, then, does not consist in negation; it is not the running (away) from one opinion to another, nor is it identical with the skeptical attitude that claims that we know nothing. All these reflect intellectual laziness, a tiredness of questioning. In the final analysis, doubting is an original experience of the questionability (*Fragwürdigkeit*) of human existence (*Dasein*); it is an expression of not individualistic but existential distress, of the human condition.[33] This doubting, then, is a way of thinking; it shows that Heidegger is able to approach the question of God as a question, that he can experience the "flight of the gods" questioningly according to the basic structures of human existence. Man and God (cor)respond to Being; they have their own relationship to Being as destiny.[34]

Hölderlin speaks of the truly divine God who is faithful to the original divine source.[35] The Christian God, in Hölderlin's poetic language, is not the only God; his conversion to Germany and to

Christianity is not a turning away from Greek culture.[36] His experience of the crisis of his own time transcends the dilemma of Christianity and paganism.[37] Heidegger regards the preaching about Christ (in 1935!) as "the leader" (*Führer*) as being a "blasphemy against Christ," who, according to the first Council of Nicaea, is "true God from true God" (*deus verus ex deo vero*) and "consubstantial with the Father."[38] Hölderlin's poetic thinking helps Heidegger to overcome this thoughtlessness and confusion; it enhances his grasping of the significance of the absence of God. His statement about the divinity of Christ, however, should not be viewed as a profession of personal faith; it is a rejection of the "modernization" and "politicization" of Christian faith (similar to Kierkegaard's criticism of Christendom) with no judgment on the truth of authentic Christian teaching.

Heidegger's meditations on Hölderlin are an integral part of his lifelong search for the way to a new, more essential, primordial kind of thinking. His three lecture courses on Hölderlin (HH, Winter Semester, 1934–35; HA, Winter Semester, 1941–42; and *Hölderlins Hymne "Der Ister,"*[39] Summer Semester, 1942) at Freiburg definitively show that Hölderlin is inspiring and helping him in reexamining the traditional Western way of thinking, in finding a more thoughtful and "remembering" (*andenkende*) thinking; they indicate that his turning to poetry is not at the expense but rather for the benefit of philosophizing.

The poetizing word is more than an expression of feelings; it is the coming into words of that which "inspires" the poet as the listener of the origins, of new beginnings. The poetic word is filled with an inexhaustible richness of meanings; it is foundational and primordial.[40] The attitude of openness is the hallmark of the poetizing remembrance of the origins; the attitude of listening is the key to the new experience of thinking, to the rethinking of the tradition as listening to the true beginnings (origins) of thought. It is the exercise of recollection, of remembrance. Heidegger's dialogue with Hölderlin's poetry is an experience of thinking, a discovery of the "togetherness" (of the gathering) of language, thinking, and human destiny. Thinking, according to Heidegger as well as Socrates, takes place in dialogue (dialoguing); the dialogue, then, is essentially an activity (an event) of thinking, a recollecting and thoughtful way of thinking that is more than a representation of things.[41] The poetic word is philosophical; it ascends from beings (multiplicity) to Being (oneness, origin, unity).[42] The calculating and technological imperialism of scientific rationality (scientism) and intellectualistic metaphysics lack this openness and freedom toward the truth of Being and that of beings.[43] They cannot grasp the deeper dimensions of the human World and history. Poetizing and thinking, then, represent seeking (openness) and questioning.[44] Poetry, therefore, is part of the search for the truth about human "dwelling" and about the divine.[45]

Calculating, technological science and merely intellectualistic (idealistic) metaphysics cannot find the true foundation of man and being(s); their attention is focused (closed in) on the thingness of beings, on representing and on "positing" beings. The Holy and God are inaccessible by means of the theological and historical sciences; they are not simply identical with the "divine" of an established religion (such as Christian religion). For Heidegger, the theological method (theology as such) is not "poetic" but scientific (theology is a positive, historical science). The Holy, according to his remark, cannot be "located" (discerned, defined) theologically; the rise (work) of theology indicates not the finding but the "flight of the God."[46] Theology, according to Heidegger's conclusion, represents not a search for (openness, incertitude) but a certitude about (enclosure, mastery of) God; theology presupposes already (ultimately "posits") "the God" with certainty. These ideas, then, suggest that there is (or at least there may be) a possible posttheological (transtheological, metametaphysical, "poetizing," mystical) way of thinking about the nature of the Holy and about God. The three university lecture courses on Hölderlin by Heidegger contribute to the understanding of the nature of the openness (as well as of the limitations) of his thought on the idea of God, to the awareness of the third (and thus final) phase of the question of God in his phenomenology.

f) H contains two lecture courses by Heidegger at Freiburg (Summer Semester, 1943 and 1944) on Heraclitus. This work and the text of the seminar on Heraclitus conducted by Heidegger with E. Fink at Freiburg (Winter Semester, 1966–67) and published as a separate volume with the title *Heraklit* (HS),[47] contribute to a better understanding and to the realization of the significance of two texts of Heidegger on Heraclitus published in 1954 ("Logos," written in 1944; "Aletheia," written in 1943) in the third volume of VA. These meditations on the fragments of Heraclitus clearly show that Heidegger's dialogue with Heraclitus constitutes a substantial phase of the long journey to the unearthing of authentic, essential, thinking (*denkerische, denkende*) thinking that is the primordial though hidden nature of philosophy.[48] They intend to bring to light the unthought (that which remained hidden) in the entire history of thought and thus a deeper grasp of the nature of truth.[49] For Heraclitus, the essence of the human being is grounded on and consists in the relationship to Being;[50] he brings to light the ontological distinction between Being and beings and leads to the discovery of the thoughtworthiness of Being. Heraclitus, then, guides Heidegger in recapturing the primordial vigor of philosophical thinking that is different from both mythology and theology. The original word *Being* is conserved (safeguarded) in poetizing and in thinking,[51] in poetry and in philosophy.

For Heraclitus, according to Heidegger's meditations on his fragments and key words, the true essence of man originates in the relation to Being; man essentially belongs to Being.[52] The human being, then, has the potentiality to define (to gather together) itself based on this relationship and thus to be "the place of the truth of Being."[53] The fixation of man on beings, his dispersion in the midst of and attachment to beings (things), however, transform him (that is, human beings for the most part) into a source of confusion about Being and thus also about his true (human) nature. Heraclitus' teaching on "logos" is a meditation on Being and on man's relationship to Being; his thinking is not theological but ontological in nature. Thus Heidegger claims that we should not grasp the word *logos* by means of representations, that we ought to think this word in such a way that we do not include in it a "spiritual being," a "God," or some "providence."[54] Being and God are not the same; God rules over the human being but not over the "is" (Being).[55] Heidegger intends to keep theology out of philosophy because the theological interpretation of Greek philosophy (of Heraclitus on "logos," of Aristotle) empties the original (often ontological) meanings of the Greek words and of Greek philosophy.[56] Heidegger sees in the thought of Heraclitus even a premetaphysical experience of "Being," "truth," and "nature."[57] The meditation on the ontological difference, then, brings about a theological indifference and a detheologization of the concept of Being; God and Being are not identical. H, therefore, clearly indicates that Heidegger's remarks on theology, faith, and Christianity should not be viewed as the rejection of theology, God, religious faith, and Christianity; they should be understood, rather, as the separation of the question of Being (philosophy) from its theological contexts and interpretations. Heidegger's "atheism" in the final analysis is not doctrinal but strictly methodological (in the sense described at the beginning of this chapter).

20

The Meaning
of Transcendence

According to ML and GP, Heidegger's view of the nature of the phenomenon of transcendence is neither axiological nor theological but ontological. He explicitly rejects the atheistic interpretations of his fundamental ontology, of his analysis of human existence and of transcendence; he regards the charge of "extreme individualistic, radical atheism" (leveled against him) as an ideological interpretation, as a misunderstanding of his thought.[1] The human being is ontological and not simply ontic in its constitution; it is distinguished in the midst of beings by the (at least implicit) comprehension of Being. The hermeneutics of human existence, then, leads to the hermeneutics of Being, and the interpretation of Being, in turn, relates back again to the understanding of human existence. This "hermeneutic circle" is an integral element of human understanding; it is the indispensable background of the discernment of meanings, of meaningfulness. The comprehension of Being (at least some comprehension of it), like the concern with meanings, therefore, is not an abstract idea but a movement, a continuous going from existence to Being and from Being back to existence. The reality of this movement is not a fixture of the teleology of things (*Vorhandenes*); it is the foundational dynamism of the openness of existence (*Dasein*) to Being (*Sein*), the phenomenon of primordial transcendence (*Urtranszendenz, ursprüngliche Transzendenz*).[2] Heidegger's understanding of the nature of the phenomenon of transcendence accounts for his view of the notion of God as well as for his claims regarding the ultimate questions about human existence (death, ultimate meaning, immortality).

The phenomenon of primordial transcendence is described by Heidegger as ontological-existential, as identical with the very constitution of existence as being-in-the-World, with the nature of the thinking human being. ML, his last lecture course at Marburg (Summer Semester, 1928), explains his phenomenological interpretation of primordial transcendence in the following four steps.[3] The first step of the explanation claims that to exist is to go beyond; to be a subject means to transcend. Transcendence, then, is not the consequence but the ground of all comportment with beings in the World. Transcendence is an essential quality, a basic constitution of the very nature (Being) of the human being (There-being). The second step of the explanation identifies the transcending quality (movement) of existence as going beyond the very particular beings that belong to the facticity of being-in-the-World. This indicates that existence is freedom, that the transcendence of the human being is something alien to nature, to mere things. The human being belongs to the realm of beings and, at the same time, is also different from the other beings. The third step of the explanation describes the World as the "where-to" (*Wohin*) of the process of transcending; human existence goes over to the World (relates to the World) and not simply to this or to that particular being or thing. The fourth step of the explanation designates the ground-phenomenon of the transcendence of existence as "to-be-in-the-World." To transcend is to be in the World.[4] Transcendence, then, belongs primarily to the Being of the human being. It is important to keep in mind, however, that the transcendence of human existence is an ontological-existential, not an ontic-existentiell structure.[5] GP (Heidegger's lecture course at Marburg, Summer Semester, 1927) defines the ontological interpretation of transcendence as the very movement of transcending (as the process of going beyond); transcendence is the way of "to-be" of the human being that "is beyond itself" (*in seiner Sein über sich hinaus ist*) in the World and understands itself from the World.[6] The human being, therefore, is transcendent (transcending beyond itself) and not immanent; "the *selfhood* of existence *is grounded in* its *transcendence*" (*Die Selbstheit des Daseins gründet in seiner Transzendenz*).[7] Human existence is open toward other beings, toward the World, and toward Being; it can discover and interpret them for what they are according to their nature. LW (Heidegger's lecture course at Marburg, Winter Semester, 1925–26) views human existence as "world-open" (*welt-offen*) according to its inner nature; it is open for the World and the World is open for it.[8]

The movement toward Being is the most radical and foundational way of going beyond. Being is transcendent (transcending) simply in the sense of being beyond and being different from all beings, even from the human being, as well as from God as the highest being; Being, then, clearly transcends all beings. This is the reason why the seventh section of SZ regards Being as "*the transcendens simply*" and describes the transcendence of human existence as "an outstanding one."[9] The disclosure of Being in the philosophical experience of existence (in the relationship of existence to Being) is the disclosure of something transcendental, of something that is true beyond the realm of particular beings; phenomenology, then, leads to transcendental, ontological truth. According to ML, the inmost capacity of the human being to transcend is the most primordial phenomenon of existence. Thus human self-transcendence is much more than a psychological (or axiological or even theological) quality; it is grounded in the ontological potentiality to relate to the Being of all beings, to reach out to Being even beyond the realm of particular beings. The acts of intentionality of human consciousness (ontic-existentiell transcending), such as knowing, perceiving, valuing, loving, believing, giving and receiving meanings, are made possible by and grounded in the primordial (existential-ontological) transcending; they are rooted in relating to Being.

The distinction between ontological transcending (from beings to Being) and ontic transcending (from subject to object, from one particular being to another particular being; for instance, from man to God or to another human being) is quite significant for the understanding as well as the critical evaluation of Heidegger's interpretation of the phenomenon of transcendence and for the clarification of the difference between ultimate meaning (the ultimate "logos" and horizon of human living) and Being (ultimately). The ultimate questions regarding human existence (death, God, final goal, and significance) belong not only (and perhaps not even primarily) to the question of Being but also (and perhaps more basically and concretely) to the question of the nature and reality of ultimate meaning.[10] Transcendence as the basic ontological constitution of human existence (the primordial transcendence of There-being toward Being) is the source of the human capacity for ontic transcending, for all the specific, concrete acts of intentionality. The interpretation of the ontic (concrete axiological, religious, humanistic) aspects of human existence (especially of the relation to God, of immortality and human values) is contingent on and ought to be preceded by the analysis and interpretation of the primordial, ontological notion of transcendence.

Heidegger's consideration of primordial transcendence is an essential element of his meditations on the question of Being, on the ontological understanding of truth and freedom, and on temporality; it does not develop the analysis and the interpretation of ontic transcending, of the many ontic issues that may be grasped better in the light of the primordial transcendence. This restraint, however, not only allows him to keep his mind steadily on Being, but, at least by indirection, also makes his views vulnerable to some misapprehensions and misunderstandings. The existence of God and faith in God, for instance, are ontic issues according to Heidegger's final definition of transcendence; the ontological interpretation of the primordial transcendence of existence remains indifferent (undecided, uncommitted) to the affirmation as well as to the negation of God. The concept of God as the exemplary being (as the leading ideal of an authentic being), for instance, in Leibniz's notion of knowledge, "appears in the light of a definite conception of Being altogether."[11] It identifies Being with a particular being at the expense (or at least neglect) of the ontological difference. The concept of Being as such, according to ML, determines the light in which God appears. This significant claim is made by the "earlier" (ML, 1928) as well as by the "later" (HB, 1946) Heidegger. This claim, then, is a clear indication of the unity as well as the consistency of the question of God in Heidegger; it is also a significant expression of the connection of the question of God with the question of Being, of the right "place" of the question of God in his phenomenology.

Transcendence in the final analysis, according to Heidegger, is ontological and not theological (religious). Even the attempts to think about (to conceptualize) God as eternal (absolute) Thou and as the highest (absolute) Value represent objectifications of God as well as a forgetfulness of Being, of the essential nature of the ontological difference, of the transcendence of Being beyond all beings; they belong to the history of traditional metaphysics.[12] These ideas may be easily misinterpreted; they are not meant, however, by Heidegger to suggest the rejection of the existence of God. Transcendence as such, the transcendence of the human being, is interpreted by ML as the origin (source) of the comprehension of Being and not as ontic identification of the divine (of the religious, of faith). The term *transcendence* does not stand for that which is inaccessible by means of finite (one should add: ontic) knowledge. Primordial transcendence, as interpreted by Heidegger, is "essentially ontologically different" from the (metaphysical) idea of Being as "Superior Force," or as "Eternal," or as "Holiness."[13] The analysis of the possible transcendence of the human being toward God (the divine being) is intentionally left aside by the ontological-phenomenological view of transcendence. Even the ultimate meaning of human existence is examined by Heidegger as an ontological concern, as a part of the pursuit of the comprehension of Being. He recognizes, however, that there are ontic (axiological, religious, psychological) questions connected with the ontological interpretation. Many misunderstandings and misinterpretations regarding Heidegger's positions on human subjectivity, existence, God, faith, death, immortality, and other classical philosophical issues may be prevented by keeping in mind that his interpretation of the ontological meaning of transcendence does not claim to decide (but even leaves open) the anthropological, theological, and other (mainly ontic) questions that may be connected with it.

The Notion
of the
World and
Creation

The devaluation of the metaphysical perspective on the notion of God by Heidegger is deeply rooted in his phenomenological definition of the notion of the World and in his analysis of the interpretation of (particular) beings as the products of creation by God, as produced by the highest being. His lecture courses, for instance, PZ, GP, and ML, include a vast amount of documentation from the history of philosophy in this regard as well as a substantial confirmation and clarification of his claim that the unearthing of the essential nature of the ontological difference remains indifferent to, but definitely does not annul, the theological difference. What is the final significance of this indifference? It originates in the criticism ("destruction") of the metaphysical concept of God; it includes, at the same time, a rethinking of the basic philosophical concepts (transcendence, World, creation) connected with the ontotheological structure of metaphysics, and the openness toward the possibility of a new way of thinking the question of God. These three elements (criticism, rethinking, and openness) of the indifference correspond to the three phases of the question of God in Heidegger. The indifference and the undecidedness of his position on the affirmation of God, on the relation of human existence to God, on the nature of (religious) faith, therefore, are manifestations of the radicality as well as the complexity of his way of thinking; they should not be used as pretexts for an ideological (secular or religious) interpretation (distortion) of his thought.

A main accomplishment of the publication of Heidegger's university lecture courses may well be the unmistakable clarification of basic philosophical concepts and their phenomenological understanding; most of these concepts play a crucial role in grasping the question of God. Thus, the tendentious and "pre-textual" interpretations of his views can be preempted and unmasked more readily. Heidegger's lecture course at Freiburg (Winter Semester, 1929–30) on the basic concepts of metaphysics (GM),[1] for instance, includes a comprehensive and clear analysis of the notion of World, of the openness of human existence, of finitude, and of the basic dispositions of existence (a unique dissection and interpretation of boredom); these notions, though they can be distorted intentionally, confirm the basic thrust of SZ. His lecture course at Freiburg (Winter Semester, 1937–38) on the basic questions of philosophy (GL) reexamines the traditional concept of truth as conformity and indicates the connection between the essence of truth and the essence of man as the guardian of the essence of the truth of Being; it shows that the question of truth is a preliminary question for all future thinking.[2] In the light of this work, then, the connections between the notion of truth, the nature of philosophical thinking, and the lighting (and concealing) of Being become less elusive.

a) Heidegger's extensive reflections on the concept of World and his comprehensive analysis of basic human dispositions (such as boredom, anxiety, and indifference) do not lead to a natural theology; they try to reach and explore the "depth of There-being,"[3] of human existence. The phenomenological notion of the World does not deal with the relation to or the creation by God; it is concerned with the clarification (thematization) of the primal phenomenon of the World as World that was left aside by the traditional way of viewing the world as a thing of nature accessible by means of the physical-mathematical way of knowing (by taking for granted and measuring the World as space and environment).[4] Heidegger unmasks the ontological presuppositions of the traditional "leaping over" the phenomenon of the World (in Descartes, Leibniz, and Kant)[5] and leads to the phenomenological notion of the World in many of his university lecture courses

(PZ, GP, ML, and GM). These lectures reinforce and deepen the analysis and the description of the notion of the World presented in SZ. They also show, at the same time, that the concept of God and the idea of creation played an ontological role in philosophy, and that his criticism is directed at this ontological function. The evaluative, critical attitude is an indispensable element of the rediscovery of the question of Being and of the new understanding of the World from the perspective of human existence as being-in-the-World.

The human being is a worldly being; human existence is being-in-the-World. The term *World* designates an essential quality of human existence; it is an existential (ontological, ultimate, structurally fundamental) and not merely ontic (immediate, concrete, existentiell) concept. The expression "being-in-the-World" describes the way of "to-be" (the special mode of being) of the human being; man and the World are equally original (inseparable) from the phenomenological standpoint. The structure of being-in-the-World belongs to the definition of the Being of the human being. The World, then, is not a thing, not even a conglomeration of all things, but the basic way of human existence,[6] a network of meanings.

What is the significance of this concept of the World for the question of God and for the ultimate questions about the human being? What is the meaning of human existence in the World? What is the ultimate meaning of human living in the light of the phenomenological notion of the World? The phenomenological response to these questions, according to Heidegger, claims that the human being is destined to the World (man is a worldly being) and that meaning for (as well as the meaning of) human existence is always a worldly meaning. The human self and World belong to the unity of the existential, fundamental structure of being-in-the-World, to human existence.[7] The "for-the-sake-of-which" (*Umwillen*) of the human being (as existence), therefore, includes both existence and the World at the same time. The ultimate meaning (end, goal, destiny) of existence includes and is shaped by the World. The human being exists for its own sake (with a noninstrumentalized worth) in the World; it is for itself as worldly, as world-bound. The "for-the-sake-of-which" is a constitutive element of the worldness (*Weltlichkeit*) of the World, of the ontological World.[8] It is crucial to keep in mind that the term *World*, in the final analysis, is understood not as the manifestation of a divine creative presence (as, for instance, in Augustine) but as a "network of meanings," as a "system of total meaningfulness."[9] The human being is destined to the World and to itself; it transcends to the World as its ultimate meaning and not to God as the creator of its life and of the World. Human self-comprehension includes the comprehension of the World; their unity makes possible the understanding of things and of persons (of the "other") as well as their meanings in the World.

There are some vital questions regarding this phenomenological notion of the World that ought to be raised. Can the notion of God as the ultimate meaning and goal of all beings be reconciled with the concept of the World as the ultimate meaning, as the system of total meaningfulness? May there be a meaning, at least for the human being, that is higher and more comprehensive than the World as described in Heidegger's phenomenology? Should the affirmation of the this-worldly destiny of human existence be viewed as the final, definitive resolution and identification of the ultimate meaning and destiny of the human person? Does the phenomenological notion of the World as the network of meanings necessarily represent also the ultimate, exclusive meaning of all meanings? Heidegger's responses to many of these questions are neither complete nor decisive; he is not reflecting on all the ramifications of his central insight and notions. The this-worldliness of human existence, the finiteness of the human being, the worldness of the World (an ontological description), and the existentiality of existence are endemic to his phenomenological methodology. Heidegger also claims, however, and quite persistently, that his existential, phenomenological analysis does not decide the ultimate destiny and value of the human being; his definition of human existence, for instance, neither affirms nor denies the relationship of human reality to God.[10] The view on this relationship does have a bearing on the interpretation of human destiny as well as on the question of meaning. Heidegger's way of asking the question of ultimate meaning, therefore, is not truly comprehensive (at least regarding the content of ultimate meaning). There are some metaphysical, theological, and even psychological dimensions of the question of ultimate meaing. Heidegger's way of thinking neither resolves nor examines (at least not directly, not adequately) many of these elements of the nature and function of meaning in human living; his attention is focused primarily on unearthing the ontological and the ideological presuppositions of the concrete definitions and (ontic) interpretations of ultimate meaning.

b) Heidegger's way of looking at the World does not discern in it the handiwork of God; his reflections on the very idea of creation do not include the contemplation of the creator in and through the created beings. The phenomenological criticism of the traditional philosophical function of God as the creator (producer) of all other beings and of the notion of beings as created by the highest being (God), however, does not represent a judgment on the theological (anthropological, ontic) value of these teachings; its intention is nothing else but the questioning of their function in interpreting the Being of beings (ontological significance). Does the notion of creation, then, lead Heidegger's thought away from and not to the Creator? Is this radical departure from the basic human, philosophical experience of creatureliness (contingency) a mask(ing) of rejection of, a hidden resentment against, the very idea of God? Heidegger is not suggesting that the concept of God as the creator of all beings is entirely meaningless or contradictory (as Sartre likes to characterize it); he merely shows the limitations and questions the adequacy of the function of the idea of creation (of the productive attitude) in the ontological interpretation of beings. The right understanding of the hermeneutical (interpretative) function of the idea of production (creation), quite extensively examined in GP, is crucial for the assessment of Heidegger's views on God as well as on Being.

Heidegger shows that the idea of creation permeates the history of ontology and shapes the formation of fundamental ontological concepts. The unshakable conviction that being(s) must be understood as created by God represents a merely ontic explanation (it derives beings from one particular being), and thus it makes impossible the ontological questioning.[11] The notion of God as the producer (*Hersteller*) of things, as the giver of the reality and actuality of beings, accounts for the interpretation of the Being of beings (for the ontological constitution of things) as produced, as made (*als eines Hergestellten*).[12] Heidegger wonders whether this interpretation (defined by the horizon of production) constitutes an intolerable one-sidedness. Can we understand all beings as made, as the results of production? Can we obtain genuine ontological concepts, can we reach Being, if our search and endeavor are governed by the attitude of production, by the assumption that the way things (beings) are made tells us something about their Being? Heidegger's way of thinking remains skeptical about the ontological reliability of the horizon (divine or human) of production (creation).

How does the production-attitude come about? According to Heidegger, production is a way of relating to beings that need to be produced, made, brought forth, created. The origin of the idea of production is rooted in the production (producing, productive) comportment of human existence (*Dasein*). The productive activity of human existence indicates that production always makes use of a material that is already given and not the result of productive activity. Production is always the production of something out of something; it is not an accidental mode of relating; it is guided by the essence of production. Thus the ontological concepts "material" and "matter" come from here. These two concepts play a fundamental role in ancient philosophy, according to Heidegger, not because the Greeks were materialists, but because matter is a basic ontological concept that comes about necessarily when beings are interpreted according to the production-attitude in comprehending Being. Being as such is viewed in the light of this attitude of production that underlies (in viewing and in producing) the relationship of human existence to beings; all beings are viewed as produced (as made) or as in need of being produced. This way of thinking leads to the ontology of thinghood (*Vorhandenheit*).

However, not all beings are the products of the productive comportment of human existence; nature, cosmos, thus many beings, do not come about through human creativity. God is the only being that is uncreated; all that is not God is created by God. This assumption is the result of the merger between ancient ontology and Christian thought.[13] Creation is interpreted as production (*Herstellen*), as bringing forth, as realizing something. Even though creation out of nothing (by God) is not identical with production of something out of a preexisting material (human creativity), nevertheless the activity of (divine) creation does have the general ontological character of production (*Herstellen*). God is not produced by any other being; he is the *ens increatum* (uncreated being), the *causa prima* (first cause) of all beings. This mode of thinking (dominated by the idea of production) remains the main characteristic of ancient, medieval, and modern philosophy. The main objection of Heidegger to the production-based ontology is that it is guided by the thing-model of beings, that the thingness of things is inadequate for the examination of beings and for the elaboration of the ontological questions.[14] The horizon of thinghood (*Vorhandenheit*) in the final analysis identifies all beings with mere things (*Vorhandenes, Washeit*); it does not pay attention to the diversity and richness of beings that are not mere things. The existential analysis makes quite clear this limitation and inadequacy of classical ontology.[15]

What are, then, Heidegger's objections to the philosophical uses of the concept of God as creator? The notion of God as the creator implies, according to Heidegger, the ontology of production (*Herstellung*) because it divides beings into two categories: created (God) and uncreated (all beings outside God). Accordingly, God is viewed as the being not requiring production (*ens increatum: das herstellungsunbedürftige Seiende*) and as the first (ultimate) cause of all other beings; the idea of production, therefore, is the model or meaning that explains all beings in their Being.[16] In the final analysis, the notion of God as the uncreated creator functions in this view as the ontological explanation of reality as a whole. This explanation regards beings as made (created, produced) or as unmade (uncreated, not in need of being produced); it ultimately understands Being (the structure of "to-be") as Createdness (*Hergestelltsein*), as Production, and thus it grasps beings as the result of Production. This type of ontological understanding is rooted in human comportment, in the human mode of dealing with the realm of things as things, as objects of production and manipulation. Beings are regarded as products, as things to be used and mastered by the human subject or by God. Thus, the state of being-produced (*Hergestelltsein*) is the very structure of the Being of beings; the activity of production functions as an ontological explanation and structure. Heidegger calls this theory the "ontology of thingness" (of *Vorhandenheit*). The human relationships to things, the mastery and the experience of thinghood, lead to the ontology of thingness.

Heidegger's phenomenological analysis of the history and of the origins of fundamental philosophical concepts (essence, existence, Being, substance, person, finiteness, creation, infinity, uncreatedness) unearths the many inadequacies of the ontology of thingness (of the production-based ontological horizon) and discerns the reasons for as well as the shortsightedness of the imperialism of the concept of God as the creator of beings. The overcoming of the inadequacies of traditional ontology, however, requires both the rediscovery of the ontological perspective as separate from the question of God and the reopening of the notion of Being, of the essential nature of the ontological difference, of the ultimate source of all difference. This task entails a new way of thinking; it includes the reappropriation of the philosophical tradition. Phenomenological analysis tries to find the origin of the ontological concepts in the phenomena themselves; it is guided not by the production-perspective on things, but by the openness of the human being (of human existence), by the attitude of "letting-be" toward beings, by the intention to disclose the relationship of beings (especially that of the human being as *Dasein*) to Being in order to grasp beings in the light of Being shining forth through beings. Traditional ontology is rooted in the "whatness" of beings; phenomenology, at least according to Heidegger, is focused on the "thatness" of beings, on the thoughtworthy fact (phenomenon) "that" they are. Heidegger's main contention consists in claiming that the production-based (creation-oriented) ontological explanation distracts from the phenomenon of the "is," from the fact "that beings are and not nothing," by remaining attached to the causal derivation and connection of beings, by explaining them as owing their being in Being (their reality) to a first (highest) being.

What is the essence of the production-based ontological perspective? It is the conviction that in producing (creating, making) something (a being) lies the primary and basic relation to the Being of a being; the Being of a being, then, means nothing else than Createdness, the state of being-produced (*Hergestelltheit*).[17] The author (creator) of a being, as Kant claims, knows this being in its Being. Only the originator (*Urheber*) of being(s) is capable of knowing authentic Being, of perceiving a being in its Being, of genuine ontological knowledge. Finite beings are only in part creators and originators; they do not produce themselves (out of nothing); rather, they are produced (by the highest being, ultimately). Finiteness (*Endlichkeit*) is a relationship of dependency, of receptivity; it is the impossibility of being the origin and producer of another being[18] and of one's self. Thus, finite beings know only what they partially create and to the extent that they can create it; the Being of any being cannot be created (produced) by another finite being. The Being of finite beings (of things and persons), therefore, is grasped a priori under the horizon of producedness, of being-produced. The production-creation ontology, according to Heidegger, accounts for the notion of God as the ontological prototype (*Urbild*) in Kant and in Descartes, as well as in ancient and medieval philosophy. God as the uncreated, as the self-producing (creating, causing itself) being, is the authentic creator and knower, the authentic (ideal) being.[19] God is the original "sculptor" (*Urbildner*) of all things, of all beings; he is *actus purus* (pure act, pure spontaneity). The finiteness (receptivity, secondary maker) of all beings (things, persons) is grounded in and accounted for by their createdness; the finite being is finite (*ens finitum*) because it is a created being (*ens creatum*). This shows that the a priori idea of production (creation) underlies the interpretation of Being; Being (*esse*), being (*ens*), and being-a-being (*Seiend-sein*) are thought of as creation-production (*Hergestelltsein*).[20] God, then, as the uncreated creator of all beings, becomes the prototype and maker of all beings, the original "model" ("archetype," imager) and author (precomprehender and producer) of beings in their Being. The ontological comprehension (the view of Being), according to Heidegger's conclusion, is governed by the idea of production (creation) typified in (and by) the notion of God as the prototype of authentic being, of the very idea of Being.

The unmasking of this ontological usage of the idea of God, according to Heidegger's intention, excludes neither the ontic explanation of the origin of beings from the highest being (God) nor the theological notion of creation. How, then, should one think the notion of Being beyond the ontological reductionism of the production-attitude? Is it possible to think the idea of God without preempting the primordial transcendence of Being as going beyond the transcendence of God? Is it possible to think of God as not being a being, as not one of the particular beings (as not even the highest of beings)? What would it mean to consider God as not being a being (as being not a being)? How would this new way of contemplating God differ from the thinking of Being as not a being? Heidegger's way of thinking, even in its final phase, suggests no more than some limited guidelines for the unfolding of these questions; their comprehensive analysis and resolution may not become viable without the openness and the courage of thinking that are free to go further than Heidegger.

22

The "Other"

The preceding reflections show the nature as well as the background of Heidegger's position on the question of God. They
lead to the conclusion, in the light of his university lecture
courses, that the phenomenological criticism (revaluation) of the
metaphysical affirmation of God does not represent a merely (perhaps
not even mainly, but surely not exclusively) negative perspective on
the notion of God as such; it, rather, if well understood, opens up a
new horizon on the methodological dimensions as well as on the
entire nature of the problem of God. What are the new ways (if any)
of reflecting on God after the discovery of the questionability of the
metaphysical approach to the idea and the affirmation of God? Many
thinkers may share (at least some of) Heidegger's insights, and they
may recognize that God cannot be thought of (that he cannot be just)
like any other being (not even as the greatest among all beings)
encountered in the World. However, these thinkers also explore at
least some new ways to deal with the harvested questions. Some of
them try to "find" and thus "speak" of God as the ultimate, eternal
Thou; they take as the point of departure for "reaching out" toward
God the depth (height) of human relationships, the encounter from
being to being (the turning of human beings to each other from and
with their entire Being), the interhuman relationship (dialogue) with
the "other" (person, Thou). God as the "personal" (rather: "meta-
personal") being cannot be found in the world of things; he may be,
nevertheless, discerned and met in some way in the living depth of
dialogical relationship with the "other," with the human, temporal

Thou. At least some ideas of M. Buber, G. Marcel, E. Levinas, and V. E. Frankl, to suggest a few examples, deserve serious attention in connection with these issues; they do have "something" to say about the contemporary experience of and approach to the question of God. Heidegger, according to all his writings published so far, definitively does not take this way out of the crisis; his existential analysis of "being-with," of the "other," of the human self, and of its relations with the "other" does not examine the potentiality of even the most profound human encounter (of the truly dialogical relation to the "other") for an openness and attentiveness toward a divine "other," toward God as the "Other." Why? What are his reservations about this approach? Does the meditation on the question of Being take place at a distance from the "other" in a creative, attentive solitude, remote from all "Thou(s)" (divine and human)? Is there a philosophy of dialogue, of basic human relationships, of the "other" in Heidegger's way of thinking? These are crucial and interrelated questions; they may be considered here, however, only concisely and to the extent that they can help to grasp the final position of Heidegger on the question of God. Some of these issues may even shed a new light on Heidegger's thought and on its boundaries and limitations.

The nature and the extent of Heidegger's analysis of primordial human relationships (of the potential to relate to the "other") can be discerned quite clearly in PZ (1925), GP (1927), and ML (1928). These lecture courses preempt any misapprehension of the existential analysis of "being-with," of the dialogical elements of the relation to the "other" developed in SZ (1927). PZ includes some remarks on the nature of love and on friendship and defines the task of the existential analysis.[1] Love makes one see; it is an ontological mode, a mode of "to-be" of concern (*Seinsmodus der Sorge*). Friendship consists in a mutually open and liberating "settling-together" (*Miteinandersetzen*) in the World. The existential analysis, according to its basic task, explores the "remarkable" (*merkwürdige*) and "distinguished" (*ausgezeichnete*) relationship of existence (of the human being as a questioning being) to Being; it is neither psychology nor the examination of the goal and meaning of human living (anthropology). GP (lecture course given in the same year as the publication of SZ) indicates a basic "epistemology" of the self and leads to the conclusion that human self-knowledge is "just" self-disclosure in the World.[2] The self is included in all intentional activity; the disclosure of the self belongs to intentionality. Reflection is not a primary mode of self-disclosure; There-being understands itself from all that it pursues and from all that it concerns itself with. GP also reclaims the individuality and the this-worldliness of human relationships. Man (human existence) is not a means for the will of the "other" (not even for God); he is his own end even in relation to God.[3] Heidegger recognizes the ontological dignity of the human being in connection with his analysis of Kant's view of the human person. This does not mean, however, that the existential analysis follows from a psychological description of the human person; psychology presupposes an ontology, a notion of knowledge, a view of perception. Psychology cannot clarify philosophical concepts.[4] ML brings the reasons for Heidegger's reservations regarding the philosophical potential of the I-Thou relationship even more into the open. The I-Thou relation obscures the philosophical problem when it (the I-Thou relation) is regarded with sociological, theological, political, biological, and ethical interests; the I-Thou relation is grounded on the ontological "Egoity" of Therebeing, and the "ontological selfhood" precedes the "I-self" and the "Thou-self."[5] Thus, for Heidegger, God cannot be found as a Thou; this notion of God would be still metaphysical.[6] The "ultimate questions" (God, death, the ultimate meaning of existence) raised in SZ belong to the analysis of the phenomenon of transcendence[7] (as discussed in Chapter 20). The transcendence of There-being does not lead the existential analysis to the "absolute Thou" but to the comprehension of Being.[8] The divine meaning, the religious dimension of primordial transcendence, is neither excluded (at least not in principle) nor examined by ML.

Heidegger's phenomenology, therefore, one must conclude in light of the preceding considerations, does not explore the potential (for example, methodological) significance of the essential nature of the relation to the "other" for the contemporary question of God. His way of thinking takes on the question of God "only" in connection with the question of Being; it is a reflection on Being and not on interhuman relationships, not a philosophy (not even a philosophical anthropology) of dialogue in spite of the fact that the attitude of openness (an essential element of dialogue) plays a crucial role in his thought. Psychology (even existential psychology) presupposes and is grounded on ontology, on philosophy; it, then, cannot clarify (rather it may obscure) philosophical concepts. This view of psychology and of the description of the I-Thou relationship accounts for Heidegger's reservations about the possible contribution of the study of the relation to the "other" to the problem of God as well as to the meditation on Being. Heidegger does not investigate the potential of the most profound interhuman relationships for a new way of "experiencing" the problem of God and the question of Being. The notion of the ultimate Thou, he seems to think, remains the prisoner of the philosophy of subjectivity; the concept of absolute Value, the idea of personal being (for example, the acting person in M. Scheler, the view of personhood in Kant), and the ontic affirmation (based on faith or on philosophy) of God, in the final analysis, according to his assessment, reflect metaphysical, anthropological, objectifying thinking. These "humanizations" (anthropomorphic, metaphysical conceptualizations) of God, according to Heidegger's view, diminish the "divineness," the "wholly otherness" of God. Self-disclosure of existence is just that, the disclosure of the human self and not of a divine transcendent self; there is no knowledge of God by means of self-knowledge.

There are many elements of a possible philosophy of essential human relationships, of the basic structure of the relation to the "other" in Heidegger's existential analysis, in spite of the fact that his thought does not develop a systematic elaboration (ontological as well as anthropological) of the I-Thou relationship as emphasized by L. Feuerbach and M. Buber, and by other thinkers. Heidegger's philosophy does not explore all the basic human experiences; it surely does not examine all the depths of the relation to the "other." Life as really lived, the whole of life, cannot be fully disclosed in the categories of thought; not even the existentials (the essential qualities of existence, of *Dasein*) can represent the complete, definitive grasp of the existentiality of existence. Indeed, Heidegger may have neglected and underestimated the philosophical weight of interhuman relationships, of the relation to and with the "other." However (as a concise view of SZ and PZ, GP, and ML indicates), it would be an overstatement (to say the least) to claim with M. Buber that he "knows nothing of any essential relation with others or any real *I-Thou* with them which could breach the barriers of the self."[9]

It may be suggested in this context, irrespective of any phenomenological thematization, that the word *openness* stands for a basic human phenomenon, for the essential relation of existence to the "other," to the Thou, for human existence as the event (*Ereignis*) of "dialogue." Can there be an openness of existence (of thinking) to Being without the openness to the "other"? Can the human being (the thinker) be open to Being without being open to human beings, to "others," to the Thou? Can this openness to the "other" open up a way (and perhaps even essentially condition it) to the "experience" of Being? Can it be that the openness (the attitude of I-Thou, of dialogue) to human beings is even more radically significant for becoming open to Being than the openness to things (beings) and to one's self? The basic response to these questions ought to be given in the affirmative. If this is the appropriate response, then it may be said that the openness to the "other," to the Thou, is significant not only for being open to Being, but also for being open to God. The "neglect" of the further exploration of the openness to the Thou, then, represents not only a boundary (incompleteness) but perhaps also a substantial limitation (a "flaw" that may be even tragic) of the focus of Heidegger's thinking of Being. M. Buber remarked (in 1938, in the midst of his sometimes hasty critique) that Heidegger "has undoubtedly had a profound experience of the mystery of being . . . but he has not experienced it as one which . . . challenges us . . . to breach the barriers of the self and to come out of ourselves to meet with essential otherness."[10] Even if this assessment may not be necessarily accurate (mainly in its second half) on all counts, it may well be considered today, especially in the light of the preceding reflections, quite prophetic. The word *openness* is a key to and consistent with Heidegger's way of thinking.

23

Questioning
beyond Heidegger

The examination of the question of God in Heidegger in the light of the preceding four steps (the task of philosophy and atheism, transcendence, the notion of the World and creation, the "other") includes a dialogue with his thought, the questioning of his way of thinking, and even a questioning that goes beyond Heidegger. This "going beyond" is an essential element of the genuine dialogue with the thought as well as with the unthought dimensions of the thought of a thinker; it is grounded on the discovery of the depth of the key insights and on the awareness of their boundaries and limitations. In the process of entering into the "matter" (*Sache*) of thinking, the "text" (the writing) of a thinker is a means and not the goal;[1] it is a help in grasping the authentic, true thought of a thinker (the goal), in going always further on the pathway of thought. This means, then, that the suggestions (the insights) of "going beyond" Heidegger belong to the clarification of the question of God altogether. Why is it vital to pursue the questioning regarding the question of God even beyond Heidegger? Why is this "going beyond" a natural outcome of grasping Heidegger's way of thinking about Being and God? The following considerations deal with these questions; they show further horizons of the reflection of God.

Heidegger's claim that the concept of God appears in the light of a definite interpretation of Being essentially means that the idea of God played an ontological role in the history of philosophy. The concept of Being as such determines the light in which God appears;[2] the notion of God as the exemplary (highest) being reflects a concept of Being as such. This claim is of substantial significance for grasping Heidegger's reflections on God and Being (and thus for his entire philosophy) as well as for seeing the need for a questioning of Heidegger that goes beyond Heidegger. The liberation of the concept of Being from the notion of God is the result of Heidegger's meditations on the great philosophers; it is a part of the recognition of the "danger of the ontological difference," of the metaphysical representation of Being as a being.[3] The ontological difference in Heidegger is neutral (indifferent) to the theological difference; the separation of the concept of Being from the idea of God means that Being as such is not God, that the concept of Being is without God. This separation, however, is not tantamount to a denial of God. Heidegger suggests only that the concept of Being is more transcendent than the notion of God, that Being as such is more transcendent than God, that Being is *transcendens* simply (entirely). It may be better to say, then, that the transcendence of Being is "other than," that it is "different (in its nature) from," the transcendence of God. The issue at stake here can be developed further by that way of thinking that is willing to go further than Heidegger's. The differentiation of the danger(s) and of the nature of the theological difference may become possible only by means of that questioning that is open to go beyond (further, deeper than) Heidegger's. For instance, the theological difference entails the difference between beings and God as well as the difference between God and Being. In the same way, the ontological difference may be thought of as including the difference between beings and Being as well as the difference between Being and God. This "going beyond" (Heidegger), the "thinking over" of the relationship between the ontological difference and the theological difference (as well as of the dangers inherent in them and in their relationship), then, is called for by the inner dynamics of thought.

The claiming of the ontological function of the notion of God in the history of philosophy, however, does not suggest that this was (and is) the only function (and meaning) of God. The phenomenological meditation on the question of Being and on the question of God goes beyond the separation of the notion of Being from the notion of God; it examines the consequences that follow from this separation. What is the value of the metaphysical notion of God? Is the God of metaphysical speculation the true, divine God? Is it possible to think about God without comprehending Being as such? What is the relationship between the notion of God in philosophy and the idea of God in theology and religion? What are the main relationships (if any) between philosophical thinking and theological reflection? These are some questions that arise in the course of the phenomenological meditation on the meaning of Being beyond the discovery of the ontological difference. The unfolding of the question of God in Heidegger is inseparable from the development of his thinking on the meaning of Being. Thus, the analysis of the main phases of the question of God in Heidegger's works can make a substantial contribution to the grasping of his thought as a whole. The discernment of the ontological difference represents the rethinking (a "destruction") of the traditional ways of interpreting Being and God; it indicates a new beginning of the search for understanding Being and a new way of thinking about the meaning of the word *God.* In the final analysis, the question of God, it seems even in Heidegger, cannot be isolated completely from the question of Being in spite of the fact that Being as such and God are not the same. This situation makes language and thought about God more difficult, more problematic. It may be suggested that, perhaps, even Heidegger's writings (at least sometimes) speak too much and too soon about God.

The ontological function of the idea of God is a matter of record in the history of philosophy, according to Heidegger. Is this fact (the ontological function) simply an "accident" of history or is there something more to it? Is there also a thematic and not merely a historical relationship between the concept of Being and the notion of God? Is it possible, in the final analysis, to exclude the theological difference as such completely from the ontological difference? Is it possible to separate entirely the question of Being from the question of God? Is it possible to discern the (final) meaning of Being without relating it to any (philosophical, theological, religious) notion of God at all (or at least without also necessarily reflecting on the idea of God in its light)? Does the question of Being as such have no relation to the question of God? What is the relationship (if any) of the notion of God, especially in the later Heidegger (of the remarks about the "divine," "nonmetaphysical" God) to the God of religious faith and experience? These questions arise within Heidegger's way of thinking; they indicate some basic issues that are intrinsically connected with the thought of the ontological difference, with meditation on Being beyond beings. These questions come about not only in the course of judging the successfulness of the philosophy of Being; they arise in the process of discerning the final horizon and meaning of the question of Being in Heidegger. Philosophical thinking is both historical and systematic at the same time. Philosophy is a free self-understanding and a historical reminiscence (*Erinnerung*); these two characteristics belong to the essence of philosophy. The historical character of philosophy is dead (irrelevant) when it is not also systematic; the systematic dimension is empty (fruitless) when it is not historical. Thus, the distinction between historical and systematic philosphy is an artificial one, according to Heidegger's own definition of philosophy.[4] The connection between the notion of Being and the notion of God is not an "accident" of history; it belongs to the very nature and to the systematic aspect of philosophy as such.

However, one should not leap from here to the conclusion that the historical identity between the idea of God and the notion of Being also represents a systematic (and thematic) identity between them. This false conclusion would identify Being with God at the expense (at least according to Heidegger) of the ontological difference. Heidegger consistently rejects this identification. The historical connection is surely not accidental, according to Heidegger's explanations (for example, in ID); it is an expression of the nature, of the very system, of the metaphysical tradition as onto-theology. The very nature of metaphysics is such that it identifies Being with God; it ignores the essential nature of the ontological difference. Thus Heidegger begins the rethinking of the system of metaphysics. But the rethinking of the system of metaphysics, then, is itself a historical event. This is precisely the conclusion Heidegger draws from interpreting the tradition of philosophy. Philosophical knowledge is finite; philosophical activity is always under way: it does not reach final perfection. Insights and knowledge, especially in the field of philosophy, are clarified and discovered again and again anew; the unfolding of thought is never complete; explicitation (*Auslegung*) does not come to a halt for the human mind. Philosophizing with Heidegger, for instance, calls forth the rethinking of his thought and the reexamination of his way of philosophizing. However, even in thinking with and within Heidegger's philosophy, the new relationship between Being and God goes beyond the "expulsion" of the idea of God from the notion of Being. The later Heidegger does speak in a new way about God because he is able to think (about) Being in a new way. This development in Heidegger's thought does not lead to a relationship of identity between Being and God, to the identification of the question of Being with the question of God. Nevertheless, in the light of this development, the questions raised earlier regarding the relationship between the notion of Being and the notion of God acquire greater weight and become even more worthy of thought.

What is the final significance of the historical connection between the question of Being and the question of God? Is it legitimate to conclude from this connection that ultimately the concept of Being as such cannot be clarified without the notion (and perhaps not even without the final resolution of the question) of God? Heidegger's response to this question is given in the negative. Is it legitimate to conclude from the historical connection between the question of God and the question of Being that ultimately the notion of God (and thus the relation of human existence of God) cannot be clarified without the concept of Being (without the comprehension of the ontological horizon) in the light of the ontological difference? The answer to this question is clearly given by Heidegger in the affirmative at least in relationship to the philosophical notion of God. Thus, Heidegger seems to suggest that it is possible to think (of) Being without the idea of God (the thought of Being is godless), but it is not meaningful (philosophically, after the discovery of the ontological difference and of Being as such) to think (of) the idea (and the very meaning) of God without interpreting the meaning of Being, without comprehending Being. At the same time, he also seems to claim that the language of theology does not need the thinking of Being. This last claim raises some additional questions regarding Heidegger's views (and their consistency) on the relationship between philosophy (phenomenology) and theology (faith-knowledge).

The historical connection between the question of Being and the question of God should not be taken and interpreted lightly; the phenomenon (fact) of this relationship as such is quite significant irrespective of the final conclusions and views that may follow from it. Heidegger's suggestion that the definition of the notion of God is conditioned by a certain conception of Being raises no insurmountable difficulties from the perspectives of philosophy and speculative (systematic) theology. His claim, however, that it is possible (and actually imperative) to think (of) and comprehend (the notion of) Being without the concept of God (at least without taking any position on the question of God at all) is often misunderstood and rejected by philosophers (for example, classical metaphysicians and several existentialists) and religious thinkers. This claim of Heidegger, it can be suggested, may well remain questionable (though it is not without serious merit) or at least "mysterious" even with the acceptance of the thesis that Being is not God, that Being and God are not the same. The foundational issue at stake (at least in Heidegger) is not the thesis of the nonidentity of Being and God but, much rather, the nature of the relationship between them (especially in the light of the third, that is, the final phase of the question of God in his philosophy). Heidegger's thought is quite powerful as well as clear on the non-identity of Being and God; it gives a thoughtful account of why and how Being is not God. His way of thinking about the relationship between Being and God, however, remains less convincing even if the "oracular" nature of some of his utterances is recognized and accepted as such. Is there something unthought in Heidegger's thought about this issue? Is this unthought (if indeed it is) element in (of) Heidegger's thought an indication of some incompleteness as well as of the inconclusiveness of his experience of (experiment with) thinking? It is quite fair and wise to respond with "yes" to these questions.

Conclusion

These reflections show that the valuable clarifications of some aspects of the question of God in the new texts of the complete edition of Heidegger's works do not alter but rather confirm the three phases of the question of God in Heidegger's thought as a whole as developed in the preceding parts of this study. The new publications bring additional background and historical perspective to Heidegger's position on the question of God and on the nature of philosophical thinking as focused on the question of Being. It is quite clear in the works examined in this part that the pursuit of the Being-question (*Seinsfrage*) "sparks" the new and inevitable light (or at least a twilight) on the God-question (*Gottesfrage*). The meditation on the question of Being cannot dispense with (it is not able to make less thoughtworthy) the question of God. It is not pretentious to conclude, then, that Heidegger's thought does remain open, though with a basically questioning attitude, toward the sense of wonder that includes the search for the ultimate being and the ultimate meaning, for the mystery called "God." Heidegger's way of thinking, in the final analysis, releases the restrictive (ontic) conceptualizations of God and, at the same time, allows thought to be free for a more worthy way of thinking about the notion and the meaning of God. This ambitious destiny and potentiality of thinking, however, ought to be free to go even beyond and without the measure of Heidegger's thought. This "going beyond" or "without" may be coming forth from the inner dynamics of Heidegger's pathway of thought. The resolution of the question of God as raised in Heidegger may not be found without pursuing the "matter" (*Sache*) of thinking even beyond (and perhaps to some extent also without) Heidegger. His thought on God should not be viewed as a final opus but, like his work as a whole, as a way of thinking that is always under way.

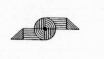

PART   5

CONCLUDING
REFLECTIONS

With the close of this study of the question of God, it is possible and worthwhile to call attention to some relevant basic aspects of the thinking experience involved in understanding Heidegger's developing thought. The main purpose of these reflections was to grasp the right meaning of the question of God insofar as this question can be asked from the perspective of the ontological problematic, in the light of the thinking of Being. This investigation of the problem of God, however, does not lead to some final conclusion containing a philosophical doctrine about God but, much rather, opens up a way[1] to a new approach to the thinking and questioning meditation on the problems entailed in the traditional method and in the new way of asking the question of God. There is no final result (doctrine) to such a meditation; there is no (at least not entirely) satisfactory answer to this questioning. It is precisely this seeming "no-result," this "not-having" the final answer, that is so characteristic of the unfolding of the question of God in Heidegger's thinking. This means, then, that the entire problem of God goes beyond (it is deeper than) the commonly understood discussion of the dilemma of theism and atheism. The seeming "no-result" is not the sign of a philosophical despair; rather, it suggests an existential hope that is born of the innermost structure of thinking as an expectation and an awaiting questioning that is strong enough to endure even a whole lifetime.[2] The radicalization of the questioning and the consideration of the question of God as a meaningful question (as a problem that somehow can be thought in the context of the meditation on the question of Being) constitute the most distinctive and decisive element of Heidegger's reflection on the problem of God. Such thinking includes a reexamination of the history of the traditional approach to the problem of God; it prepares the ground for (and thereby renders possible) a more profound, genuine understanding of what is meant by the word *God*. This new perspective on the question of God, then, is not isolated from (it is not at the expense of) the authentic "astonishment" (*Erstaunen*) and "respect" in facing (encountering) the mystery of Being (of the hidden meaning of the "is") as the primordial source of philosophical reflection.[3] This thinking can lead to a new beginning, to changing history, by overcoming opposition and thus by recovering the essence of creativity in the truth of Being.[4]

There is nothing significant to be gained by merely resuming the content of the preceding parts and by restating again their conclusions as set forth at the end of each. It may be valuable, however, to focus attention on the main aspects and accomplishments of Heidegger's thinking on the question of God. These closing reflections, then, include (1) a concise review of Heidegger's position on the question of God and (2) a positive evaluation as well as (3) a critical assessment of his approach to the notion of God in the light of the thinking of Being.

24

A Review

Heidegger's entire philosophy is a meditation on the meaning of Being, on the coming about of the true essence of the onto-logical difference. This way of philosophizing involves a profound rethinking of the essence of metaphysics as such; it does not pretend, however, to resolve the final mystery of Being that underlies the diversity and the conflict of metaphysical questions and perspectives. The question of Being and the question of God were interrelated during the entire history of Western philosophy. This connection is the hallmark of the tradition and of metaphysical reflection. Phenomenological analysis (as a new possibility of thought) sheds a new light on and brings about a new way of grasping the relationship between the Being-question and the God-question. The thinking of the ontological difference and the attention to Being as being beyond all beings imply (and establish) a new way of looking at the philosophical approach to the problem of God. Even though the question of God cannot be called the direct thematic "object" of Heidegger's thinking, nevertheless the ontological meditation includes some definite attitudes toward as well as some significant remarks about the philosophical question of God. In this sense, therefore, it is possible to speak of a problem of God in Heidegger's phenomenology. Heidegger is bound to "speak" of God as something endemic to the historical meditation on and to the unfolding of the question of Being. Thus there *is* a "place" for the question of God in Heidegger's thinking.

The emphasis on the radical difference between the Being-

question and the God-question remains the fundamental characteristic of Heidegger's pathway of thought. Is there any relationship
between these two questions within Heidegger's thinking? The assessment of their (often antagonistic and even antinomical) relationship
has its own "story" within and according to the history of the author's
developing thought. It is crucial to distinguish clearly and to describe
carefully the different phases of the question of God in Heidegger's
thinking. This study, therefore, identified a *first* phase of the question
of God, that is, a demythologization (a critique of the "storytelling,"
causal, metaphysical explanation) of the problem of God, by means
of a close examination of the existential analaytic of SZ. Through the
study of several works of Heidegger (after SZ), it became possible to
discern a *second* phase of the question of God. This second phase was
described as the phase of questioning, as the presence of the question
of God as a (genuine and meaningful) question in his way of thinking.
The problems raised by this second phase and the examination of the
rest of Heidegger's writings led to the unearthing of a *third* (the final)
phase of the question of God in his thought. This third phase was
described as a new way of asking the question of God, as a new perspective on the meaning of the word *God* in the light of the meaning
of Being. However, this third phase, precisely because of its profound
implications, defies final and fully comprehensive analysis as long as
the entire body of Heidegger's writings is not available for further
investigation according to the suggestions in Chapter 18. The new
volumes of the complete edition of Heidegger's works that are currently available (as indicated at the beginning of Part IV) reinforce
the preceding description of the three phases of the question of God
and clarify some of the notions (such as World, transcendence, and
creation) that are at stake in Heidegger's position on this issue. The
development of the suggested new approach (the way out of the crisis)
to the question of God and the resolution of the many questions
connected with it (Is it possible to think of God as not a being? Can
the ontological difference discard entirely the theological difference?),
however, may become feasible only by that way of thinking that is
free to question and to think even beyond (further than) Heidegger's
pathway of thought.

25

A Positive
Evaluation

The question of God in Heidegger's thinking reveals the distance that exists between the theological (ontic, anthropological) dimension of human existence and the originality of the onto- logical problematic as such. Heidegger's thinking is focused on the question of Being itself, on unearthing the true essence of meta- physics; its fundamentally ontological task (the thinking of the mean- ing of Being) prescinds from any theistic as well as from any atheistic interpretation of human existence and of the World. The most sig- nificant accomplishment of Heidegger's philosophy consists in the reawakening of the question of Being. The ontological comprehen- sion also recognizes and calls for the rediscovery of the proper orig- inality and "alterity" of the experience of faith as the ground of Christian existence. The antimony of thinking (philosophy) and believing (faith), according to the phenomenological perspective, should not be interpreted as the construct of some a priori philo- sophical (or even ideological) hostility toward the theological problem- atic; it ought to be understood, rather, as the manifestation of the radical difference between the primordial task of philosophical think- ing and the authentic goal (and nature) of theological reflection. The awareness of the distance between the thinking of Being and the science of the experience of faith, then, includes a recognition of their independence as well as mutual respect. Heidegger rightly claims that any contribution by philosophy to theology ought to be grounded on the autonomy of philosophical thinking.

The metaphysical concept of God as the highest being (and as an ultimate, self-causing cause) is not worthy enough of a truly divine being, of God as envisaged by the religious experience. The phenomenological critique of the ontotheological structure of metaphysics shows the need for a new way of thinking about Being as well as about God. The "dedivinization" of God by metaphysical thinking and the absence of the divine from the horizon of modern consciousness are described quite impressively by Heidegger. His response to the philosophical and religious (theological) inadequacy of the metaphysical approach to God, however, does not consist in prophetic proclamations of atheism but, rather wisely, in the choice to keep "silence" about God in the realm of philosophical thinking. His thought is open to (prepares and waits for) a new way of thinking (for a more primordial listening) that can bring about a new way of raising the question of God and a greater freedom and openness of thinking toward the mystery of a more "divine" God.[1] Heidegger's rethinking of the question of God mirrors quite sharply the contemporary skepticism about ultimate meaning and ultimate being. His insights into the phenomenon of the "death of God" (as announced by Nietzsche) do not extinguish but rather quite radically reawaken a more authentic thinking about God.

Heidegger calls attention to the special nature of an authentically philosophical way of knowing and questioning. He intends to keep the freedom and the limits (boundaries) of philosophical thinking; his thought claims to be rooted in the primordiality and originality of the philosophical experience. This emphasis on the uniqueness of philosophical thinking, however, should not be regarded as a philosophical imperialism (as an intellectual totalitarianism); Heidegger himself claims a healthy measure of self-relativization as a characteristic of the experience of thinking. His philosophy is "a" way and not "the" way, not the only way of thinking; his writings open up ways and do not coalesce into one magnum opus. They raise questions on the "matter" (Sache) of thinking.[2] He clearly distinguishes philosophical thinking from all the other ways of knowing and understanding (theology, anthropology, psychology: the sciences of beings). His philosophy allows and even prepares the thinker to "go beyond" (further than) his thought. Philosophical thinking consists primordially in listening to the "voice of Being"; its language is the "abode of Being," that is, a "place" where Being comes into words.

This understanding of the nature of philosophy is indispensable for distinguishing the three phases (dimensions) of the question of God.

The problem of God acquires a new sense of direction in Heidegger; it goes beyond (it represents a rethinking of) the traditional approach entailed in the dilemma of theism and atheism. The comprehension of Being as being beyond all beings (as more transcendent than any and all being) raises new questions about the transcendence of God as well as about the affirmation-negation perspective on the entire problem of God. It may become possible to think in a new, nonobjectifying (nonontic) way about the very notion as well as about the entire question of God in the light of a free, nonobjectifying, unprejudiced (nonontic) interpretation of the Being of beings. This would mean the liberation of the question of God from the ambiguities and from the dangers of the ideological and apologetical approach inspired by the fixation on the dilemma of theism and atheism. The main issue at stake, then, becomes the very idea of God, the inquiry into what is meant by God. This way of looking at the question of God is focused on the special nature of thinking about God and on the significance of the notion of God for the understanding of human existence and of the World. Such is the relevant irrelevance of the traditional (theism-atheism) perspective on the problem of God. Heidegger's thinking, in the final analysis, reawakens not only the question of Being but also the question of God. His insights make valuable contributions to the contemporary reflection on the question of God.

The question of God in Heidegger's thinking, in spite of its seemingly "destructive" dimensions, shows the need for a radical rethinking of the notion (and meaning) of God; it inspires and prepares, though indirectly, a new way of discerning and looking at the relation of the human being to a living God. The truly divine God, then, is not the fixed object of intellectual speculation but rather the ultimate mystery of the superabundance of aliveness (of Life); prayer and dancing can be meaningful only before the truly meaningful divine God.

A Critical Assessment

T he following reflections indicate, though briefly, some limits and
limitations of the question of God in Heidegger's philosophy.
These observations deepen the "critique" included in this study.

A genuine thought is not merely an intellectual insight; it is
also the mirroring of the depth as well as the breadth of the thinker
and the "matter" (*Sache*) of thinking. This is the reason for the contemporary interest in a "living" thought, in that kind of thinking that
leads to a commitment and discloses a (if not the) meaning of the
World and of the human being. Heidegger leaves open the question
of option, of personal choice about the meaning of God; he is not
examining the nature and function of commitment in facing the question of God. He seems to retain an attitude of indifference toward
the "success" of his philosophy with regard to the problem of God
even though he characterized his thought in an interview (in 1948)
as a "waiting for God."[1] In a sense Heidegger's phenomenology can
be regarded as the result of a very profound but also highly "abstract"
way of thinking, as an original and yet "historical" (rooted in the
tradition) exploration of the problem of Being. The very expression
of thought on Being is difficult; it requires a new vocabulary and a
new way of speaking that often borders on bursting the boundaries
(tests the ultimate limits) of language. The task of thinking the truth
of Being is demanding and yet rewarding at the same time. Is Hei-

degger's thought really understood today? Only time will be able to give the right answer to this question. Thought "demands time, much time, its time. It has time," he said in a conversation in 1969.[2] He wondered, in the same conversation, whether his works were really read and understood. Heidegger emphasizes the difficulty of finding the appropriate language to speak of Being and of God. Language hides within itself the "treasures of all the sciences."[3] The "wrecked" relation to Being, Heidegger claims, is the root of our incongruous relationship to language.[4]

The continual insistence on the indifference (neutrality) of the ontological questioning toward any anthropological or theological interpretation of human existence can give the impression of a more abstract and detached way of thinking and of a "lifeless" view of the World, of a purely hypothetical experiment of thought. It may seem sometimes that Heidegger's meditations ignore or (at least) neglect some relevant aspects of human thinking and knowing. A purely intellectual view is an abstraction and not a primordial mode of disclosure; the human being as such, the thinker, is engaged in life. The different kinds of knowing and the nature of human commitment as a response to the "situations" and demands of life should not be regarded as completely irrelevant to the ontological problematic; the mode of being ("dwelling") in the World, the experience of living, is part of human thinking. The comprehension of the meaning of Being cannot be detached (at least not entirely) from the interpretation of beings and especially from the hermeneutics of human existence (from the multidimensionality of the human being). Heidegger himself, then, rightly calls attention to the existentiell grounding of the existential analysis and to the historical dimensions (and roots) of the question of Being and of the question of God.

It should be recognized that the question of God in Heidegger's thinking shows clearly the limits as well as the limitations of his philosophy. Heidegger follows his own way of thinking and leaves aside many relevant aspects of the philosophical problematic involved in his thought. He does not enter into a reflection on the nature and meaning of the different dimensions of human existence (community, personal encounter as a source of thinking, significance of the phenomenon of religious experience, epistemological and even ontological potentials of the relation to the "other," creation of meanings and values); he seems to underestimate the philosophical significance of the anthropological questions, the weight of the possible (though limited) ontological contribution of the ontic levels of experience.

Contemporary philosophy can benefit from paying more attention to the other "human sciences" (existential psychology and psychotherapy, psychoanalysis, genetic psychology, depth psychology), from the dialogue with and the reflection on the scientific understanding of the World.[5] The exploration of the fullness of human presence, of the I-Thou relationship (as it can be seen in M. Buber, G. Marcel, E. Levinas), and the analysis of contemporary social issues should not be alien (and not even of secondary interest only) to a philosophy that is being characterized by the understanding of finitude, of the human "dwelling" in the World. The openness to the "other," it can be suggested quite readily, is (or at least may be) connected with the openness to Being, with the essence of human freedom. However, these limitations (and thus even the failure to explore fully the ontological significance of the relation to the "other") of Heidegger's phenomenology can be viewed as the result of the fidelity to the unique task of Heidegger's thinking, to the limits set by the question of Being (as the demand of the fullness of attention to Being itself). It is important to see the different dimensions of a problem. Nevertheless, it is even more crucial to discern the primordiality and the uniqueness of the ontological problematic (of the nature of the ontological comprehension) and thus to keep to the boundaries (the limits) of the different kinds of thinking and knowing. The apparent limitations (the shortcomings) of Heidegger's thinking indicate that he is very much alert to the depth as well as to the limits (boundaries) of the ontological interpretation of beings and of the entire question of Being.

The main difficulty in understanding Heidegger's thinking, it should be clearly recognized, lies in the interpretation of Being as essentially finite. For Heidegger, Being is not supratemporal (not the same as Hegel's Absolute) but historical and finite; it "needs" (*braucht*) and uses man (it is not "something" for itself without relation to man) as the "There" of its manifestation, as its "shepherd."[6] Its manifestations (the epochs of its destiny) are in time. Such is the burden of all human understanding and of philosophy as well. The consciousness of finitude in Heidegger's thinking is the ground for unfolding, for discerning the mystery of Being, and for retaining a sense of the "mystery" of the "divine." Heidegger's meditation on the mystery of Being can take its right "place" in the history of those philosophical insights and questions that ultimately do not merely put asunder (divide) but also "gather together" (unite) the different trends of thought.[7]

The recognition of the boundaries (set by the nature of the

task of thinking as focused on the question of Being) and of the limitations (the shortcomings, failures, one-sidedness of perspectives and claims, unexplored issues, such as openness to the "other" and value of commitment) is an integral part of grasping Heidegger's way of thinking; they are included in the analysis of his views on the question of God. Heidegger remarked in a seminar on Hegel: "When you see my limits, you have understood me."[8] Thus even the critical assessment and the indication of the need to go "beyond" Heidegger's way of thinking may be seen as endemic to his pathway of thought.

What is the final (philosophical and even theological) value of the "storytelling" way to God, of the "storytelling" perspective on the question of God? Is there a more radical, a more profound function of the "storytelling" explanation (of the tracing back of the origin of beings to a highest being) than the one claimed by Heidegger? Is the nature of "storytelling" more symbolic than ontic? Are the great myths (primordial, original "storytellings") not, in the final analysis, ways of interpreting ultimate reality and meaning (the final horizon of transcendence)? Can "storytelling" function as an ultimate attempt to speak, at least symbolically, of that which cannot be spoken of; to try to think (even beyond metaphysics) even that which cannot be thought of in the same way as beings and things? The great myths and the primordial symbols incorporate as well as transcend mere "storytelling" about beings; they bring (call) forth thoughts; they give "something" to think about to the "teller" and by the listener. The idea of demythologization (the critique of the "storytelling," metaphysical approach to the question of God) in SZ does not examine (nor does it preempt the raising of) these questions; their development and resolution, however, are quite significant for the openness of thinking about the question of God with and beyond Heidegger.

What relation does the notion of God in Heidegger have to the God of faith, of religious experience, of theology? The attention to this question, especially at the end of this study, discloses the final limitation of his perspective on the notion of God. It would be inadequate to claim that the idea of God in Heidegger, especially in the third phase of its development, has no relation to (that it shares nothing in common with) the God of religious faith.[9] Heidegger's laconic though puzzling remarks about the "divine" God as well as his distantiation from the theological aspects of the notion of God severely limit his capacity to make further distinctions regarding the idea of God. It should be kept in mind, however, that the notion of God in the earlier as well as in the later Heidegger entails a two-directional relationship. On the one hand, it relates to the status of the notion of Being; on the other, at the same time, it relates to the theological (even the Biblical) idea of God. The discovery of the ontological difference implies the "rejection" (critique) of the metaphysical conceptualization of God because of the separation of the notion of Being from the notion of God. The reexamination of Cartesian metaphysics in SZ is a good example. The meditative, postmetaphysical (and even poetic) thinking of the difference as such (that is, of the essential nature of the ontological difference), of the truth of Being as such, and the recovery of the primordial nature of language allow for (and introduce) a new concern with the nature of the "divine" God due to the new, deeper grasp of beings, of Being, and of language; they shed a new light on the notion and on the entire question of God. The meditations on Hölderlin, Heraclitus, Hegel, and Nietzsche (in Heidegger's lecture courses) provide good examples.

What is the significance of the two-directional relationship of the notion of God for the understanding of the final status of the question of God in Heidegger? Heidegger's reflections include some suggestions for but not a final, adequate description of the ("new") idea of God, of the transmetaphysical perspective on the question of God. The reintroduction of the word *God* into the "constellation" and thinking of Being, and into the new understanding of language, it can be suggested, may have created some additional difficulties for the final assessment of Heidegger's thinking. Many of his claims about the question of God, nevertheless, remain quite clear. Because of the relationship of the question of God to the question of Being even after the separation of these two notions from each other, it is still possible and worthwhile to ask what is the nature of this relationship according to the indication of HB (that is, that one first ought to clarify Being, then the Holy, then the essence of divinity; then, and only then, it becomes possible to think what the word *God* ought to name). There are no adequate guidelines in Heidegger's works for accomplishing this task; his remarks and suggestions do not explain how to "redefine" God after and in the light of the more primordial comprehension of Being (*Ereignis*, Appropriation) according to his later development (ZD). The interpretations of Hölderlin's poetry and the reflections on Heraclitus' doctrine of logos, for instance, are helpful but not sufficient for grasping the full measure of the reopening of the question of God after SZ. The insights into how God should not be thought of are valuable; they, however, remain incomplete; they indicate primarily a "negative idea" of the ("new") theological difference (they spell out more what it is not). These difficulties, however, should not obscure the fact that the essential claim by Heidegger remains valid: The meditative (listening, poetic) thinking of Being opens up the parameters for the consideration of the question of God. This idea (the "opens up") may be regarded as the new articulation of the earlier claim (SZ) that the ontological difference is more primordial than the decision about the nature and the possibility of a theological difference. The thinking of the essential nature of the ontological difference precedes and in some way decides the horizon (the possible parameters) for considering the theological difference. The comprehension of the truth of Being lays the foundation for the understanding and the interpretation of the different regions of particular beings. This language, however, is inadequate (it cannot speak of God as not a being; it cannot articulate fully the meaning of Being); at the end, then, even phenomenology is left behind. At the limits of language (at the end of philosophy) the experience of attentive thinking represents the final alternative as the preparation for the advent of a more primordially speaking language and thought. The recommendation to keep silence about God, according to the insights of ID, therefore, remains valid.[10]

What is the relationship of the "new" idea about God (as surmised from the context of the attentive thinking of Being) to the theological, religious notion of God? The basic and most persistent claim made by Heidegger about God as discernibly meaningful in the ontological "constellation" is that there is a more truly "divine" God before whom human beings may pray, sing, and dance (that human beings can relate only to this possible, more "divine" God). This concern with the "divinity" of God, however, is qualified (though not preempted) by Heidegger's rejection of the ontotheological (religious) notion of God (including the God of the prophets of the Hebrew Bible). Nevertheless, for instance, in PT, religious existence is understood by Heidegger as a life based on faith (a mode of being-in-the-World); his lectures on Nietzsche as well as his other works establish a clear distinction between the cultural, social phenomenon of Christianity and the essence of Christian faith. Moreover, as Heidegger can recognize it, there is a difference between the theological, speculative conception of God (the main target of criticism by Heidegger) and the ultimately not objectifiable (ineffable) religious relationship (faith) with the mystery of the living God (situated within the horizon of the openness of the philosophy of Being). The theological (thus for Heidegger, metaphysical) speculation about God represents only one (and perhaps not the best) type of articulation of a living (praying, singing, dancing) relationship with a divinely transcendent God. Heidegger's laconic references to a more "divine" God relate to that notion of God that is rooted (ultimately) in religious faith; the God of a genuine religious "experience" (of those who dare to believe) is not simply an object of thought (as in theology and metaphysics) but a "partner" in dialogue, prayer, and song.

In the final analysis, Heidegger's way of thinking retains a sense of wonder about the mystery called "God" in spite of the radicality of his questioning about Being and about God. His basic conviction that "we know only *questioningly*,"[11] therefore, is not the sign of skeptical hyperreflection, but a manifestation of the dynamics of the sense of wonder as the source of philosophizing. Questioning emptied of the sense of wonder, he would agree, is no longer genuine thinking. It may be, however, that his methodology stretches to its ultimate limit the power of questioning. The recapturing of the sense of wonder about Being does not extinguish but rather reawakens the question of God, the sense of wonder about the sacred, divine horizon of human living. Heidegger's meditation on Being, then, is able to say "something" about God; the deeper comprehension of the truth of Being leads to the rethinking of the question as well as of the "place" of God in the search for knowledge and wisdom.

Notes

Part 1

Chapter 1

[1] *Gelassenheit,* 2d ed. (Pfullingen: Neske, 1960), pp. 23 (*der Weg zum Nahen ist der schwerste*), 27 (*totale Gedankenlosigkeit*), 45 (*Denken . . . In-die-Nähe-kommen zum Fernen*) (hereafter: G). See also *Holzwege,* 4th ed. (Frankfurt am Main: Klostermann, 1963), pp. 245–46 (*Naheliegendes gibt zu denken*) (hereafter: HW).

[2] "So gibt es denn zwei Arten von Denken, die beide jeweils auf ihre Weise berechtigt und nötig sind: das rechnende Denken und das besinnliche Nachdenken" (G, p. 15). See also G, p. 14.

[3] Some important references in this regard: *Was heisst Denken?* 2d ed. (Tübingen: Niemeyer, 1961), pp. 85 (*Bedenklichste*), 86 (*Gabe*), 92 (*Dank, An-dacht*), 93 (*der ursprüngliche Dank*), 94 (*Gabe, der eigentliche Dank*), 158 (*Andenken*). (Hereafter: WD); *Aus der Erfahrung des Denkens,* 2d ed. (Pfullingen: Neske, 1965), pp. 9 (*Zumutung des Seyns*), 11 (*Gedanken kommen zu uns*), 19 (*Denken—Andenken*) (hereafter: ED). For a description of the Heideggerian notion of thinking (*Denken*), see: William J. Richardson, *Heidegger: Through Phenomenology to Thought,* Phaenomenologica, vol. 13 (The Hague: Nijhoff, 1963), pp. 476–81; Samuel IJsseling, *Heidegger. Denken en Danken—Geven en Zijn* (Antwerp: De Nederlandsche Boekhandel, 1964), pp. 75–85. This later study gives a clear explanation of the relationship between thinking and thanking. For a most comprehensive analysis and interpretation of Heidegger's way of thought, see Henri Birault, *Heidegger et l'expérience de la pensée* (Paris: Gallimard, 1978).

[4] The important relationship between thinking and Being is clearly expressed by Heidegger in: *Über den Humanismus,* 6th ed. (Frankfurt am Main: Klostermann, 1964) (hereafter: HB); *Was ist Metaphysik?* 8th ed. (Frankfurt am Main: Klostermann, 1960) (hereafter: WM). The following quotations can give a short explanation of the Heideggerian idea about thinking. "Das Denken ist des Seins, insofern das Denken, *vom Sein* ereignet, dem Sein gehört. Das Denken ist zugleich *Denken des Seins,* insofern das Denken, dem Sein gehörend, auf das Sein hört" (HB, p. 7). My emphasis. See also HB, pp. 46–47. "ist das wesentliche Denken ein *Ereignis des Seins* (*event of*

Being)" (WM, p. 47). My emphasis. For the multidimensionality (*Mehrdimensionalität*) of thinking, see HB, p. 6. The nature and the implications of "essential thinking" according to Heidegger are examined briefly in George Kovacs, "Phenomenology and the Art of Teaching," *Journal of Thought*, 14 (1979): 194–98.

⁵This idea represents a focal point in Heidegger's development. Further clarification can be found in a text of Heidegger entitled "La fin de la philosophie et la tâche de la pensée." It was published originally in *Kierkegaard vivant*, Colloque organisé par l'Unesco à Paris du 21 au 23 avril 1964 (Paris: Gallimard, 1966), pp. 165–204 (hereafter: KV). The German text is included in Martin Heidegger, *Zur Sache des Denkens* (Tübingen: Niemeyer, 1969), pp. 61–80 (hereafter: SD). See also his remarks in "Only a God Can Save Us: *Der Spiegel*'s Interview with Martin Heidegger," trans. Maria P. Alter and John D. Caputo, *PhilosophyToday*, 20 (1976): 279 (hereafter: IH). See also Heidegger's *Zur Bestimmung der Philosophie*: 1. *Die Idee der Philosophie und das Weltanschauungs problem*. 2. *Phänomenologie und transzendentale Wertphilosophie*, Gesamtausgabe Bd. 56/57 (Frankfurt am Main: Klostermann, 1987), pp. 7–11, 12 (catastrophe of philosophy), 63 (death of philosophy) (hereafter: BP).

⁶The "epochal mittence of Being," as concise terminology, is an expression of the Heideggerian interpretation of Being as mittence (*Geschick*), event (*Ereignis*), as history (*Geschichte, Epoche des Seins*), and as eschatological (*Eschatologie des Seins—die letzte seines Geschickes*). The epochal mittence of Being, therefore, is understood as the epochal manifestation of Being that comes from Being and *is* history (in the ontological sense). This history leads to the reversal (*die Kehre*), to a new era (*Epoche*) of Being. This change can take place only through the discovery of the forgottenness of Being (*Seinsvergessenheit*) *as* the forgottenness of the ontological difference (*Vergessehneit des Unterschiedes des Seins zum Seienden*) (cf. especially: HW, pp. 336, 337). The destiny and the essence (*Wesen*) of man are understood by Heidegger as staying in the lighting-process of Being (*Lichtung des Seins*), as "guarding" the essence of Being in its truth in the midst of beings (*das Wesen des Seins in seine Wharheit zu wahren*). The expression "epochal mittence of Being" is found almost verbatim in Heidegger (*Epoche des Seinsgeschickes, Geschick des Seins, das epochale Wesen seines Geschickes, Geschick eines Geschickes, ereignet sich Sein in seine Epoche*). I consider this as an essential expression, and because of this I indicate some helpful references in this regard. These references are as follows: HB, pp. 27 (*Phase der Geschichte des Seins, seinsgeschictliches Geschick des Seins*), 46 (*Sein als Geschick des Denkens*), 47 (*Geschick des Seins*); HW, pp. 245 (*Metaphysik—eine Epoche der Geschichte des Seins selbst*), 295 (*Weltalter als Geschick beruht im Sein*), 310 (*Geschick, Licht des Seins*), 311 (*epochale Wesen des Seins*), 312 (*das Epochale des Seins, Epoche des Seins*), 342 (*Epoche des Seins*), 301–2 (*Eschatologie des Seins*); *Der Satz vom Grund*, 3d ed. (Pfullingen: Neske, 1965), 97 (*Epoche des Seins*), 98 (*Geschichk des Seins*), 108 (*Seinsgeschichte ist das Geschick des Seins*, explains "schicken"), 120 (*die Geschichte des Seins als Geschick*), 146 (man is in the *Lichtung des Seins*, in a *Geschick des Seins*), 154 (*Epochen des Seingeschickes*) (hereafter:

SG); *Nietzsche,* 2 vols. (Pfullingen: Neske, 1961), vol. 1, p. 451 (*Geschichte—Grundmacht des Seins); vol.* 2, pp. 28 (*Geschichte ist Geschichte des Seins*), 383 (*Epoche der Geschichte des Seins*), 386 (*Geschichte als Sein*), 389 (*seinsgeschichtliches Denken*), 481 (*Metaphysik—eine Epoche der Geschichte des Seins*), 485 (*Geschichte, Sein, Ereignis*), 489 (*Seinsgeschichte ist das Sein selbst*) (hereafter: N, 1, and N, 2, respectively); *Vorträge und Aufsätze,* 3 parts, 3d ed. (Pfullingen: Neske, 1967), part 1, p. 24 (*Geschick*), part 3, p. 48 (*Geschick*) (hereafter: VA, 1, and VA, 2, and VA, 3, respectively); *Die Technik und die Kehre* (Pfullingen: Neske, 1962), pp. 38 (*Geschick des Seins*), 39 (*das Geschickliche eines Geschickes des Seins, das Wesen des Seins und das Wesen des Menschen*), 40–41 (*Kehre, Gefahr, Licht*), 42 (*Epoche des Seins*), 43 (*ereignet sich Sein in seine Epoche*) (hereafter: TK). For an interpretation of some of these terms see: W. J. Richardson, *Heidegger: Through Phenomonology to Thought,* pp. 533–34 (mittence of Being, epochs of mittence), 435 and 493 (*Geschick,* mittence), 614 (*Ereignis,* event).

[7]IH, p. 281. In this context Heidegger calls attention to the special significance of his understanding of the nature of thinking as developed in WD.

Chapter 2

[1]An insightful meditation on the meaning of philosophy for Heidegger can be found in his *Was ist das—die Philosophie?* 4th ed. (Pfullingen: Neske, 1966) (hereafter: WP). For Heidegger's emphasis on the Western nature of philosophy, see, for example, his concise remarks in *Heraklit:* 1. *Der Anfang des abendländischen Denkens (Heraklit).* 2. *Logik: Heraklits Lehre Vom Logos,* Gesamtausgabe Bd. 55 (Frankfurt am Main: Klostermann, 1979), pp. 3, 41–42, 98 (hereafter: H). See also BP, pp. 7–12, and his *Vom Wesen der Wahrheit: Zu Platons Höhlengleichnis und Theätet,* Gesamtausgabe Bd. 34 (Frankfurt am Main: Klostermann, 1988), pp. 13–16. (Hereafter: WWP).

[2]For a balanced comparison of Hegel and Heidegger, see: Alphonse De Waelhens, *Chemins et Impassess de l'Ontologie Heideggerienne: À propos de Holzwege* (Louvain: Nauwelaerts, 1953), pp. 43–44; Alphonse De Waelhens, "Identité et différence: Heidegger et Hegel," *Revue Internationale de Philosophie,* 14 (1960): 221–37. Cf. also Jacques Taminiaux, *Le regard et l'excédent* (The Hague: Nijhoff, 1977), pp. 116–155. Heidegger's interpretation of Hegel's philosophy is clearly expressed in his *Hegels Phänomenologie des Geistes,* Gesamtausgabe Bd. 32 (Frankfurt am Main: Klostermann, 1980) (hereafter: HP).

[3]HP, pp. 4, 16, 53–56, 59, 106, 140–46.

[4]The lecture courses on Nietzsche contain several reflections in this regard. Heidegger says about Hegel: "Die Geschichte der Philosophie ist keine Sache der Historie, sondern der Philosophie. Die erste philosophische Geschichte der Philosophie ist diejenige Hegels; er hat sie nicht als Werk gestaltet, sondern nur in seinen Jenenser, Heidelberger und Berliner Vorlesungen vorgetragen. Die Hegelsche Geschichte der Philosophie ist bisher

die einzige philosophische geblieben und wird es bleiben, bis die Philosophie in eninem noch wesentlich ursprünglicheren Sinne aus ihrer eigensten Grundfrage her geschichtlich denken muss" (N, 1, p. 450). The references to Hegel are an example of the historical dimension of Heidegger's way of thinking.

[5]See, for instance: HW, pp. 13, 324, 342; *Einführung in die Metaphysik,* 3d ed. (Tübingen: Niemeyer, 1966), pp. 12, 42, 140 (hereafter: EM); *Wegmarken* (Frankfurt am Main: Klostermann, 1967), p. 370 (hereafter: W); H. pp. 83–84, 361.

[6]Heidegger describes the meaning of the destruction of metaphysics in *Sein und Zeit,* 10th ed. (Tübingen: Niemeyer, 1963), pp. 19–27 (hereafter: SZ). The later Heidegger reflects on this passage and emphasizes the positive meaning of the destruction in WP, p. 22: "Destruktion heist: unser Ohr öffnen, freimachen für das, was sich uns in der Überlieferung als Sein des Seienden zuspricht. Indem wir auf diesen Zuspruch hören, gelangen wir in die Entsprechung."

[7]Cf. Otto Pöggeler, *Der Denkweg Martin Heideggers* (Pfullingen: Neske, 1963), pp. 46, 132–42. The following texts of Heidegger clearly indicate the central significance of his claim that Being (*das Sein*) is not a (particular) being (*das Seiende*): *Metaphysische Anfangesgründe der Logik im Ausgang von Leibniz,* Gesamtausgabe Bd. 26 (Frankfurt am Main: Klostermann, 1978), pp. 184–85 (hereafter: ML); HP, p. 32; WM, pp. 30–31. Throughout this study *das Sein* is rendered as "Being" and *das Seiende* as "being" in order to indicate clearly the distinction (ontological difference) between them. Regarding some important reasons for this translation of these key terms, see W. J. Richardson, *Heidegger: Through Phenomenology to Thought,* pp. 4–14. The term "to-be" is also used as a helpful variant for "Being." This allows for emphasizing the verbal sense of *Sein,* especially in reference to *Dasein.* The term *sein* is rendered as "being" (in the verbal sense) and also as "to-be." Richardson's work develops a clear and most incisive analysis of the relationship between the early phase and the later period of Heidegger's thought; it includes Heidegger's letter to Richardson regarding his own understanding of this issue (pp. viii–xxiii).

[8]For some interesting examples of this, see Max Müller, *Existenzphilosophie im geistigen Leben der Gegenwart,* 3d enlarged ed. (Heidelberg: Kerle, 1964), pp. 239–49.

[9]"Im Gedanken des Willens zur Macht vollendet sich zuvor das metaphysische Denken selbst. Nietzsche, der Denker des Gendankens vom Willen zur Macht, ist der *letzte Metaphysiker* des Abendlandes" (N, 1, p. 480).

[10]"Das Stehen in der Lichung des Seins nenne ich die Ek-sistenz des Menschen." (HB, p. 13). "Der Mensch west so, dass er das Da', das heisst die Lichtung des Seins, ist" (HB, p. 15). "Die Lichtung selber aber ist das Sein" (HB, p. 20). "*Das Lichtung-lose des Seins ist die Sinnlosigkeit des Seienden im Ganzen*" (N, 2, p. 26). For a clear explanation of the lighting-process (*Lichtung*), see also: KV, pp. 190–94; SD, pp. 71–74.

[11]Cf. EM, pp. 6–10, and WP, pp. 18–30.

[12]"Je mehr wir uns der Gefahr nähern, um so heller beginnen die Wege ins Rettende zu leuchten, um so fragender werden wir. Denn das Fragen ist die Frömmigkeit des Denkens" (TK, p. 36).

[13]SZ, pp. 38–39. Only the meditative reading and study of Heidegger's writings can lead to the right, comprehensive understanding of his philosophy. However, the following works, in addition to the ones already mentioned, can be valuable helps in grasping his thought: Walter Biemel, *Martin Heidegger: An Illustrated Study*, trans. J. L. Mehta (New York-London: Harvest Book, Harcourt Brace Jovanovich, 1976); Werner Marx, *Heidegger and the Tradition*, trans. Theodore Kisiel and Murray Greene (Evanston, Ill.: Northwestern University Press, 1971); Jean Beaufret, *Dialogue avec Heidegger: I. Philosophie Grecque* (Paris: Minuit, 1973); Jean Beaufret, *Dialogue avec Heidegger: II. Philosophie Moderne* (Paris: Minuit, 1973); Jean Beaufret *Dialogue avec Heidegger: III. Approche de Heidegger* (Paris: Minuit, 1974); Friedrich Wilhelm von Hermann, *Die Selbstinterpretation Martin Heideggers* (Meisenheim am Glan: Verlag Anton Hain, 1964); Thomas Sheehan, ed., *Heidegger: The Man and the Thinker* (Chicago: Precedent Publishing, 1981); Vincent Vycinas, *Earth and Gods: An Introduction to the Philosophy of Martin Heidegger* (The Hague: Nijhoff, 1961); Thomas A. Fay, *Heidegger: The Critique of Logic* (The Hague: Nijhoff, 1977); J. L. Mehta, *Martin Heidegger: The Way and the Vision* (Honolulu: University of Hawaii Press, 1976); Maurice Corvez, *La Philosophie de Heidegger*, 2d ed. (Paris: Presses Universitaires de France, 1966); Otto Pöggeler, *Philosophie und Politik bei Heidegger*, 2d ed., with "Nachwort" (Freiburg-Munich: Verlag Karl Alber, 1974); Herbert Spiegelberg, *The Phenomenological Movement: A Historical Introduction*, Phaenomenologica vol. 5/6, 3d rev. and enlarged ed. (The Hague: Nijhoff, 1982).

[14]"Der Mensch aber ist nicht nur ein Lebewesen, das neben anderen Fähigkeiten auch die Sprache besitzt. Vielmehr ist die Sprache das Haus des Seins, darin wohnend der Mensch ek-sistiert, indem er der Wharheit des Seins, sie hütend, gehört" (HB, pp. 21–22). "Das Sein kommt, sich lichtend, zur Sprache. Es ist stets unterwegs zu ihr" (HB, p. 45).

Chapter 3

[1]"Jeder Denker denkt nur einen *enizigen* Gedanken" (N, 1, p. 475). This phrase can (and ought to) be applied to Heidegger. The meaning of Being, the meaning of the ontological difference—this is the one and the *"unique"* thought of his philosophy. This same view is emphasized in the following insightful studies: Albert Dondeyne, "La différence ontologique chez M. Heidegger," *Revue Philosophique de Louvain*, 56 (1958): 35–62, 251–93; M. Müller, *Existenzphilosophie im geistigen Leben der Gegenwart*, p. 17; A. De Waelhens, *Chemins et Impasses de l'Ontologie Heideggerienne*, p. 5

[2]Mircea Eliade, *Le Sacré et le Profane* (Paris: Gallimard, 1965), p. 181.

[3]For a general view of the problem of God today, see Claude Tresmontant, *Comment se pose aujourd'hui le problème de l'existence de Dieu?* (Paris: Seuil, 1966).

[4]The quotation that follows gives the next phrase too as we read it in Maurice Merleau-Ponty, *Éloge de la philosophie et autres essais* (Paris: Gallimard, 1965), p. 50: "Il est frappant de constater qu'aujourd'hui on ne prouve plus guère Dieu, comme le faisaient saint Thomas, saint Anselme ou Descartes. Les preuves restent d'ordinaire sous-entendues et l'on se borne à réfuter la négation de Dieu, soit en cherchant dans les philosophies nouvelles quelque fissure par où puisse reparaître la notion toujours supposée de l'Être nécessaire, soit, au contraire, si décidément ces philosophies la mettent en question, en les disqualifiant brièvement comme *atheisme.*"

[5]See, for instance: Pierre Thévenaz, *What Is Phenomenology? and Other Essays*, ed. with an intro. by James M. Edie, trans. James M. Edie, Charles Courtney, and Paul Brockleman (Chicago: Quadrangle Books, 1962), p. 145 (God is beyond metaphysics); William A. Luijpen, *Phenomenology and Metaphysics* (Pittsburgh: Duquesne University Press, 1965), pp. 156–64; William A. Luijpen, *Phenomenology and Atheism* (Pittsburgh: Duquesne University Press, 1964).

[6]Heidegger gives a concise description of the "indigent time" (needy time) (*dürftige Zeit*) in *Erläuterungen zu Hölderlins Dichtung*, 3d ed. (Frankfut am Main: Klostermann, 1963), p. 44; "die Zeit der entflohenen Götter und des kommenden Gottes. Das ist die dürftige Zeit, weil sie in einem gedoppelten Mangel und Nicht steht: im Nichtmehr der entflohenen Götter und im Nochnicht des Kommenden" (hereafter: HD). See also HW, p. 253.

[7]This idea is emphasized by Walter Schulz, *Der Gott der neuzeitlichen Metaphysik*, 3d ed. (Pfullingen: Neske, 1957), p. 111.

Chapter 4

[1]A few but significant works in this regard: Heinrich Ott, *Denken und Sein: Der Weg M. Heideggers und der Weg der Theologie* (Zollikon: Evangelisher Verlag, 1959); Joseph Möller, *Existenzialphilosophie und katholische Theologie* (Baden-Baden: Verlag für Kunst und Wissenschaft, 1952); John Macquarrie, *An Existentialist Theology: A Comparison of Heidegger and Bultmann*, foreword by Rudolf Bultmann (London: SCM Press, 1965); James M. Robinson and John B. Cobb, Jr., eds., *The Later Heidegger and Theology* (New York and London: Harper and Row, 1963); Alfred Jäger, *Gott: Nochmals Martin Heidegger* (Tübingen: J. C. B. Mohr-Paul Siebeck, 1978), esp. pt. 1; Richard Kearney and Joseph S. O'Leary, eds., *Heidegger et la question de Dieu* (Paris: Grasset, 1980), esp. pp. 145–67; 194–237; 248–70; Otto Pöggeler, ed., *Heidegger: Perspectiven zur Deutung seines Werks* (Cologne-Berlin: Kiepenheuer-Witsch, 1969), pp. 54–77; 140–217; Heinrich Ott, "Die Bedeutung von Martin Heideggers Denken für die Methode der Theologie," in Vittorio Klostermann,

ed., *Durchblichke: Martin Heidegger zum 80. Geburtstag* (Frankfurt am Main: Klostermann, 1970), pp. 27–38. Heidegger presents a clear and masterful description of his understanding of the relationship between philosophy and theology in his *Phänomenologie und Theologie* (Frankfurt am Main: Klostermann, 1970) (hereafter: PT).

²In this context, the term "relatedness to" stands for Heidegger's *"Sein zu,"* which means "being-toward" (*being* as a verb and also as the noun *Being*). The issue at hand, then, is the ontological status of human existence's relationship to God (*Gottesverhältnis des Daseins*), the clarification of the meaning of transcendence. See the entire passage in Heidegger's *Vom Wesen des Grundes,* 4th ed. (Frankfurt am Main: Klostermann, 1955), p. 39 (hereafter: WG).

³This remark is made because the philosophical thought of Heidegger can be characterized as a godless thought. A summary reflection on this aspect of Heidegger's philosophy can be found in W. J. Richardson, "Heidegger and God—and Professor Jonas," *Thought,* 40 (1965): 13–40, esp. 29–30, 40 ("The question is not how Heidegger comes to God, but how God comes to Heidegger. . . . The voice of a radically transcendent God comes not out of Being—a phenomenologist's Being—but breaks into this kingdom from without."). See also the remarks by François Fédier regarding Heidegger's "atheism" in his essay "Heidegger et Dieu," in R. Kearney and J. S. O'Leary, eds., *Heidegger et la question de Dieu,* pp. 37–38. Cf. also H. Birault, *Heidegger et l'expérience de la pensée,* p. 339.

Chapter 5

¹W. J. Richardson, *Heidegger: Through Phenomenology to Thought,* p. xxviii.

²This study, in the appropriate parts, shall indicate the number of references in Heidegger's writings in question.

³This issue belongs to the central concern of this research; it is analyzed according to its implications for the new understanding of the problem of God. A discussion regarding the possibility of the theological difference in Heidegger's thinking can be found in: M. Müller, *Existenzphilosophie im geistigen Leben der Gegenwart,* pp. 63–72; O. Pöggeler, *Der Denkweg Martin Heideggers,* pp. 158–63, 260–67.

⁴"Die Gottesfrage steht von Anfang an über dem Denkweg Heideggers" (O. Pöggeler, *Der Denkweg Martin Heideggers,* p. 261).

⁵See, for example: WG, pp. 39, 42; *Identität und Differenz,* 3d ed. (Pfullingen: Neske, 1957), pp. 33, 35–37 (hereafter: ID); HB, pp. 19, 26, 36–37, 39.

⁶"Die Entgötterung ist der Zustand der Entscheidungslosikeit über den Gott und die Götter" (HW, p. 253).

⁷*Der Feldweg,* 3d ed. (Frankfurt am Main: Klostermann, 1962), pp. 5, 7 (hereafter: F).

[8]Karl Löwith, *Heidegger: Denker in dürftiger Zeit*, 3d. and rev. ed. (Göttingen: Vandenhoeck and Ruprecht, 1965), p. 112.

[9]O. Pöggeler, *Der Denkweg Martin Heideggers*, p. 217.

[10]SZ, pp. 10, 229, 427 (note 1).

[11]"Ist das gott-lose Denken, das den Gott der Philosophie, den Gott als Causa sui preisgeben muss, dem göttlichen Gott vielleicht näher" (ID, p. 71).

[12]"Der Satz: Das Wesen des Menschen beruht auf dem in-der-Welt-sein, enthält auch keine Entscheidung darüber, ob der Mensch im theologisch-metaphysischen Sinne ein nur diesseitiges oder ob ein jenseitiges Wesen sei." "Mit der existenzialen Bestimmung des Wesen des Menschen ist deshalb noch nichts über das 'Dasein Gottes' oder sein 'Nicht-sein', ebensowenig über die Möglichkeit oder Unmöglichkeit von Göttern entschieden" (HB, p. 36).

[13]See: HB, p. 37; WG, p. 39 (n. 56); ML, p. 211.

[14]O. Pöggeler, *Der Denkweg Martin Heideggers*, pp. 262, 266. The foundational significance of Heidegger's insights on truth for the understanding of his works is emphasized by H. Birault, *Heidegger et l'expérience de la pensée*, pp. 445–527.

[15]There are several indications in this regard in: N, 1, pp. 321–24; HW, p. 246. See also about this: Friedrich Nietzsche, *Also sprach Zarathustra* (Stuttgart: Reclam, 1972), pp. 34–35; ID, pp. 70–71. These last two passages clearly indicate some enlightening relationships between Nietzsche and Heidegger regarding the nature of metaphysics and the notion of God.

Chapter 6

[1]W. Schulz, *Der Gott der neuzeitlichen Metaphysik*, pp. 28, 49–56.

[2]Ibid., p. 26.

[3]HP, pp. 140–46, 180–84; ID, pp. 51, 55, 68–72; HW, pp. 178–87; 198–204, 239–40. For a lucid examination of the historical aspects of Heidegger's thought with emphasis on metaphysics, see Odette Laffoucrière, *Le Destin de la Pensée et "la Mort de Dieu" selon Heidegger*, Phaenomenologica vol. 24 (The Hague: Nijhoff, 1968).

[4]Edmund Husserl, "Philosophy as Rigorous Science," included in Edmund Husserl, *Phenomenology and the Crisis of Philosophy*, trans. with an intro. by Quentin Lauer (New York: Harper and Row, 1965), p. 89. See also: pp. 87–93, 108–12.

[5]Ibid., p. 112.

[6]Edmund Husserl, *Ideas: General Introduction to Pure Phenomenology*, vol. 1 of *Ideen*, trans. W. R. Boyce Gibson (London: Allen and Unwin, 1969), pp. 176–77.

[7]Ibid., pp. 113–14.

[8]Robert Sokolowski, *The Formation of Husserl's Concept of Constitution*, Phaenomenologica vol. 18 (The Hague: Nijhoff, 1964), p. 139. Cf. also: pp. 133–39, 196–99. This work is a clear exposition of Husserl's theory of constitution

and an excellent introduction to his entire thought. Regarding the notion of constitution see also: Pierre Thévenaz, *What Is Phenomenology? and Other Essays*, p. 50; Paul Ricoeur, *Husserl: An Analysis of His Phenomenology*, trans. Edward G. Ballard and Lester E. Embree (Evanston, Ill.: Northwestern University Press, 1967), p. 9; E. Husserl, *Phenomenology and the Crisis of Philosophy*, p. 112; E. Husserl, *Cartesian Meditations: An Introduction to Phenomenology*, trans. Dorion Cairns (The Hague: Nijhoff, 1977), p. 26.

[9]Quentin Lauer, *Phenomenology: Its Genesis and Prospect* (New York: Harper and Row, 1965), pp. 85–86, speaks of the indifference of Husserl's philosophy toward God and suggests, "Had Husserl read Saint Augustine he might have concluded that I can constitute a world and thus realize subjectivity only because I am an 'image' of the Creator-God. The fact that he did not so conclude is not a proof that he *denied* it, but simply that in cutting himself off from history he could scarcely be complete even as a phenomenologist."

[10]E. Husserl, *Ideas: General Introduction to Pure Phenomenology*, p. 174.

[11]Ibid., p. 174.

[12]Ibid., p. 157.

[13]Ibid., p. 236. Rudolf Boehm, *Vom Gesichtspunkt der Phänomenologie: Husserl-Studien*, Phaenomenologica vol. 26 (The Hague: Nijhoff, 1968), pp. 72–105, includes an insightful discussion of the meaning of this passage and examines the difficulties involved in interpreting this issue in Husserl's thought (see esp. pp. 92–105). Alexander Pfänder, an associate of Husserl, claims to find the meaning of God through a special type of contemplation as it is suggested in Alexander Pfänder, *Phenomenology of Willing and Motivation*, trans. with an intro. and supplementary essays by Herbert Spiegelberg (Evanston, Ill.: Northwestern University Press, 1967), p. xxiii. Eugen Fink, *De la phénoménologie*, with a preface by E. Husserl, trans. Didier Franck (Paris: Editions de Minuit, 1974), p. 197, indicates that the problem of God is not situated outside the horizon of phenomenological work. These references illustrate the divergent phenomenological perspectives on Husserl's concern with the idea of God and other related metaphysical questions. Heidegger, Sartre, Merleau-Ponty, and Max Scheler deal significantly with the question of God.

[14]WM, p. 42 ("Warum ist überhaupt Seiendes und nicht vielmehr Nichts?"). See also EM, pp. 1–7.

[15]R. Boehm, *Vom Gesichtspunkt der Phänomenologie: Husserl-Studien*, pp. 104–5.

[16]Adelgundis Jaegerschmid, "Die letzten Jahre Edmund Husserls (1936–1938)," *Stimmen der Zeit*, Bd. 199 (1981): 130. Regarding Husserl's personal convictions about God, see also: Adelgundis Jaegerschmid, "Gespräche mit Edmund Husserl 1931–1936," *Stimmen der Zeit*, Bd. 199 (1981): 49, 43, 56. These two articles include the information relevant to the discussion at hand in this paragraph of our study.

[17]Q. Lauer, *Phenomenology: Its Genesis and Prospect*, p. 125.

[18]Ibid., pp. 146–47. See also E. Husserl, *Ideas: General Introduction to Pure Phenomenology*, pp. 150–53, 158–64.

[19]See, for instance, W. A. Luijpen, *Phenomenology and Metaphysics*, pp. 179, 182, 185–90.

[20]*Vom Wesen der Wahrheit*, 4th ed. (Frankfurt am Main: Klostermann, 1961), pp. 8–9 (hereafter: WW).

[21]Throughout this study the term *"Dasein"* is rendered as "There-being" in order to retain the special Heideggerian, ontological meaning of this term. This translation indicates the relatedness of human reality (existence) to Being as well as the sense of presence (awareness), the mode of "to-be" that distinguishes it from all other beings. This translation also allows for richer linguistic possibilities in rendering Heidegger's original language and his play on words (for example, man is the "There," the presence and manifestation of Being; human existence is ontological, related to Being, to the "is"). For some other considerations for this translation, see W. J. Richardson, *Heidegger: Through Phenomenology to Thought*, p. 34 (note 17). Occasionally (mainly in Parts III–V of this study), however, the terms "human existence," "human reality," "existence," and "human being" are also used for rendering *Dasein*; whenever the usage of these terms would compromise clarity (or consistency of terminology) *"Dasein"* is added in parentheses.

[22]"Heidegger kann die Gottesfrage neu stellen, weil nach seiner Erfahrung nicht die Gottheit Gottes, sondern nur das metaphysisch gedachte Wesen Gotes widerlegt ist" (O. Pöggeler, *Der Denkweg Martin Heideggers*, p. 262).

Conclusion

[1]In addition to the studies already indicated in note 1, chapter 4, and note 3, chapter 6, see the followig works: Henri Birault, "La foi et la pensée d'aprés Heidegger," *Philosphies Chrétiennes: Recherches et Débats*, vol. 10, no. 4 (Paris: Fayard, 1955), pp. 108–32; Henri Birault, "De l'être, du divin et des dieux chez Heidegger," *L' existence de Dieu*, 2d ed. (Tournai: Casterman, 1963), pp. 49–76; Bernard Welte, "La question de Dieu dans la pensée de Heidegger," *Les études philosophiques*, 19 (1964): 69–84; Maurice Corvez, "La place de Dieu dans l'ontologie de Martin Heidegger," *Revue Thomiste*, 53 (1953): 287–320; Helmut Danner, *Das Göttliche und der Gott bei Heidegger* (Meisenheim am Glan: Verlag Anton Hain, 1971); Jean Beaufret, *Dialogue avec Heidegger: III. Approche de Heidegger*, pp. 91–107; Hans Köchler, *Skepsis und Gesellechaftskritik im Denken Martin Heideggers* (Meisenheim am Glan: Verlag Anton Hain, 1978), pp. 29–81; Jean-Dominique Robert, "La critique de l'onto-théologie chez Heidegger," *Revue Philosophique de Louvain*, 78 (1980): 533–52.

[2]The following works include especially significant and comprehensive explanations by Heidegger in this regard: *Die Grundprobleme der Phänomenologie*, Gesamtausgabe Bd. 24 (Frankfurt am Main: Klostermann, 1975) (hereafter: GP); ML; HP; H. See also: *Prolegomena zur Geschichte des Zeitbegriffs*, Gesamtausgabe Bd. 20 (Frankfurt am Main: Klostermann, 1979)

(hereafter: PZ); *Logik: Dei Frage nach der Wahrheit,* Gesamtausgabe Bd. 21 (Frankfurt am Main: Klostermann, 1976) (hereafter: LW); *Phänomenologische Interpretation von Kants Kritk der reinen Vernunft,* Gesamtausgabe Bd. 25 (Frankfurt am Main: Klostermann, 1977) (hereafter: PK); *Aristoteles: Metaphysik IX 1–3: Vom Wesen und Wirklichkeit der Kraft,* Gesamtausgabe Bd. 33 (Frankfurt am Main: Klostermann, 1981) (hereafter: AM); *Hölderlins Hymnen "Germanien" und "Der Rhein,"* Gesamtausgabe Bd. 39 (Frankfurt am Main: Klostermann, 1980) (hereafter: HH); *Grundbergriffe,* Gesamtausgabe Bd. 51 (Frankfurt am Main: Klostermann, 1981) (hereafter: GB); *Hölderlins Hymne "Andenken,"* Gesamtausgabe Bd. 52 (Frankfurt am Main: Klostermann, 1982) (hereafter: HA); *Phänomenologische Interpretationen zu Aristoteles: Einführung in die phänomenologische Forschung,* Gesamtausgabe Bd. 61 (Frankfurt am Main: Klostermann, 1985) (hereafter: PA); *Beiträge zur Philosophie: Vom Ereignis,* Gesamtausgabe Bd. 65 (Frankfurt am Main: Klostermann, 1989) (hereafter: BE).

Part 2

[1]"Das Sein des Seienden 'ist' nicht selbst ein Seiendes. Der erste philosophische Schritt im Verständnis des Seinsproblems besteht darin, nicht μῦϑόν τινα διηγεῖσϑαι(Plato, *Sophistes* 242c), 'keine Geschichte erzählen', d.h. Seindes als Seindes nicht durch Rückführung auf ein anderes Seinedes in seiner Herkunft zu bestimmen, gleich als hätte Sein den Charakter eines möglichen Seienden" (SZ, p. 6). The word *demythologization* is not found in SZ, even though the preceding passage seems to include and suggests its meaning as explained by these reflections. SZ indicates that the Christian definition of the essence of man has been "detheologized" (*enttheologisiert*) in modern times (p. 49) and refers to the Cartesian notion of God as the most perfect being and as a mere "ontological title" (*ein rein ontologischer Titel*) (p. 92). The term *demythologization* is being used in these reflections in order to emphasize the questioning (rethinking and "criticizing") attitude of SZ toward the traditional approach to the philosophical problem of God; it epitomizes several phenomenological insights and their implications regarding the metaphysical concept of a supreme being. For some important aspects of Heidegger's understanding of the words *myth* and *logos,* see: WD, pp. 6–7; H, pp. 278, 292, 319–48, 396 (on how to think the authentic meaning of the word *logos*). An insightful discussion of the problem of demythologization in the context of theology can be found in Walter Strolz, *Menschsein als Gottesfrage* (Pfullingen: Neske, 1965), pp. 196–206.

[2]See, for instance: HB, pp. 17 (SZ and *die Kehre*), 19 (*Ek-sistenz, Exsistenz*), 22–24 (*"es gibt" Sein*), 29 (*Ek-sistenz*), 31 (SZ is valid even today as a preparation for the Being-question), 41 (SZ as the thinking of Being), 42 (dwelling as to-be-in-the-World); KV, pp. 173–74, 204 (SZ and the later Heidegger); WM, p. 9 (SZ and the overcoming of metaphysics); *Unterwegs zur Sprache,* 3d ed. (Pfullingen: Neske, 1965), p. 122 (SZ and the later Heidegger) (hereafter:

US). The publication of Heidegger's works in the *Gesamtausgabe* reinforces the unity and the continuity of his thought; it shows that, to a significant extent, "all is there" in the early works, specially in SZ. See, for example: GP, pp. 24–25, 71–75, 220, 389–90; ML, pp. 171–95, 197, 203, 215, 268; SD, pp. 9, 30, 34, 77, 90.

³"Vorwort" (Letter to Richardson, April 1962), in W. J. Richardson, *Heidegger: Through Phenomenology to Thought*, p. xxii.

⁴The references to God are: SZ, pp. 10, 24, 28, 49, 92, 95, 190, 199, 269, 275, 427. The reference to "divine" is in SZ, p. 291. There are other, often quite significant and indirect, references (or at least relationships) to the problem of God in SZ; they are substantial elements of the process of demythologization as shown in this study.

Chapter 7

¹SZ, p. 6. Heidegger gives a concise explanation of the meanings of and of the close relationship between the words *myth* and *logos* in the early Greek thinkers in WD, pp. 6–7. The original "unity" of myth and logos, however, is lost in the course of history. Regarding the ground of mythology according to Heidegger see, for instance, GP, p. 331.

²"Das Fragen dieser Frage (Seinsfrage) ist als *Seins*modus eines Seienden selbst von dem her wesenhaft bestimmt, wonach in ihm gefragt ist—vom Sein. Dieses Seiende, das wir selbst je sind und das unter anderem die Seinsmöglichkeit des Fragens hat, fassen wir terminologisch als *Dasein*" (SZ, p. 7).

³"Die ausdrückliche und durchsichtige Fragestellung nach dem Sinn vom Sein verlangt ein vorgängige angemessene Explikation eines Seienden (Dasein) hinsichtlich seines Seins" (SZ, p. 7).

⁴"*Das 'Wesen' des Daseins liegt in seiner Existenz*" (SZ, p. 42). "Das 'Wesen' dieses Seinden liegt in seinem Zu-sein" (SZ, p. 42). *Sein und Zeit*, Gesamtausgabe Bd. 2 (Frankfurt am Main: Klostermann, 1977), p. 56 (marginal note d) reinforces the ontological meaning of "Zu-sein" ("drive-to-be") by stating, "dass es zu seyn 'hat'; Bestimmung!" (hereater: SZG). The rendering of "Zu-sein" as "drive-to-be," then, intends to emphasize the ontological "drive" (thrust, relationship) of There-being (existence) toward Being; it indicates an ontological (existential) dynamism (structure) and not a (merely) moral imperative. Thus Being is always an issue (a matter of concern) for There-being; this is what this being is all about. See SZ, pp. 41–42: "Als Seiendes dieses Seins ist es seinem eigenen Sein überantwortet. Das *Sein* ist es, darum es diesem Seienden je selbst geht." Cf. also SZG, p. 56 (marginal note c). There-being is its own potentiality; it relates to its Being (chooses, achieves itself in its Being) as its ownmost (most authentic) potentiality (*Möglichkeit*). The essential qualities of existence (the basic ways of "to-be" of There-being; its ontological potentialities, choices) are called by SZ the "existentials" (*Existenzialien*). The term "existentiality" (*Existenzialität*) (of the existence of There-being) stands for the ontological

constitution (*Seinsverfassung*) of existence (Being is always an issue for it) and for the interconnection (as well as for the systematic description) of its structures (existentials; the essential qualities of existence). See SZ, pp. 43–44. The term "facticity" (*Faktizität*) refers to those qualities of existence that are given and not chosen; it includes "thrownness" (*Geworfenheit*) as well as "being-in-the-world" (SZ, pp. 56, 135). The fundamental analysis of There-being (*Analyse des Daseins, Analytik des Daseins, Daseinsanalytik, existenziale Analytik*) according to SZ is ontological in nature; it is essentially different from the (mere) ontic, existentiell (anthropological, psychological, biological) descriptions of human reality (SZ, pp. 45–52). The word "existence" (*Existenz*, later written as "*Ek-sistenz*," ek-sistence), then, in Heidegger's sense, refers to the ontological constitution (Being-comprehension; special relation to Being) of There-being (*Dasein*); its meaning differs substantially from the traditional sense of *existentia*, for which Heidegger uses the term *Vorhandensein* (the mode of "to-be" of things, the existence of mere things as fixed objects or entities), as well as from *Zuhandensein* (the mode of "to-be" of instruments). There-being is described additionally with the terms *transcendence* and *freedom*.

⁵"Dem Dasein gehört nun aber gleichrusprünglich—also Konstituens des Existenzverständnisses—zu: ein Verstehen des Seins alles nicht daseinsmässigen Seienden. Das Dasein hat daher den dritten Vorrang als ontisch-ontologische Bedingung der Möglichkeit aller Ontologien. Das Dasein hat sich so als das vor allem anderen Seienden ontologisch primär zu Befragende erwiesen" (SZ, p. 13).

⁶"Die exsitenziale Analytik ihrerseits aber ist letzlich *existenziell* d.h. *ontisch* verwurzelt" (SZ, p. 13). Heidegger insists definitively that without an existentiell comprehension the analysis of existentiality remains groundless: "Ohne ein existenzielles Verstehen bleibt doch alle Analyse der Existenzialität bodenlos" (SZ, p. 312).

⁷Alphonse De Waelhens, *Existence et Signification*, 2d ed. (Louvain-Paris: Nauwelaerts, 1967), p. 117. De Waelhens italicizes this passage. See also Alphonse De Waelhens, "Nature humain et compréhension de l'être," *Revue Philosophique de Louvain*, 59 (1961): 672–82.

⁸"Die *Theologie* sucht nach einer ürsprünglicheren, aus dem Sinn des Glaubens selbst vorgezeichneten und innerhalb seiner verbleibenden Auslegung des Seins des Menschen zu Gott" (SZ, p. 10).

⁹SZ, p. 49. Cf. also ID, p. 51.

¹⁰SZ, p. 5.

¹¹SZ, pp. 10, 11.

¹²SZ, p. 15.

¹³SZ, pp. 19, 326, 327, 376, 436.

¹⁴"*Sein ist das transcendens schlechthin*" (SZ, p. 38). See also SZG, p. 51 (marginal note a).

¹⁵"Die Transzendenz des Daseins ist eine ausgezeichnete, sofern in ihr die Möglichkeit und Notwendigkeit der radikalsten *Individuation* liegt" (SZ, p. 38).

Chapter 8

¹SZ, p. 51.

²SZ, p. 46.

³SZ, p. 48–49. See also Heidegger's *Ontologie: Hermeneutik der Faktizität,* Gesamtausgabe Bd. 63 (Frankfurt am Main: Klostermann, 1988), pp. 21–29 (hereafter: OH).

Chapter 9

¹Cf. A. De Waelhens, *Existence et Signification,* pp. 96, 98, 100, 101. For a more profound study of this problem, see also A. De Waelhens, *La philosophie et les expériences naturelles,* Phaenomenologica vol. 9 (The Hague: Nijhoff, 1961), esp. pp. 107–21.

²A most valuable and revealing statement of this issue can be found in E. Husserl, "Nachwort zu meinen *Ideen zu einer reinen Phänomenologie und phänomenolgischen Philosophie,*" *Jahrbuch für Philosophie und phänomenologische Forschung,* 11 (Halle: Niemeyer, 1930), 551: We will prove "dass eine transzendentale Phänomenologie meines Sinnes in der Tat den universalen Problemhorizont der Philosophie umspannt und dafür die Methodik bereit hält; dass sie also wirklich alle vom knokreten Menschen aus zu stellenden Fragen, darunter auch alle sogenannten Metaphysischen, in ihrem Felde hat, soweit sie überhaupt einen möglichen Sinn haben—den allerdings erst diese Phänomenologie ursprünglich zu gestalten und kritisch zu begrenzen berufen ist." This passage is quoted and insightfully examined by A. De Waelhens, *Existence et Signification,* pp. 105–7. Husserl gives the following warning against any misunderstanding of his thought on this issue in his *Cartesian Meditations,* p. 156: "Finally, lest any misunderstanding arise, I would point out that, as already stated, phenomenology indeed *excludes every naive metaphysics* that operates with absurd things in themselves, but *does not exclude metaphysics as such.*" See also E. Husserl, *Ideas: Introduction to Pure Phenomenology* p. 46 (phenomenology is the precondition of all metaphysics "which would aspire to be a *science*").

³Cf. A. De Waelhens, *Chemins et Impasses de l'Ontologie Heideggerienne,* p. 28.

⁴"Das In-der-Welt-sein ist zwar eine a priori notwendige Verfassung des Daseins, aber längst nicht ausreichend, um dessen Sein voll zu bestimmen" (SZ, p. 53). "Der Satz: das Wesen des Menschen beruht auf dem In-der-Welt-sein, enthält auch keine Entscheidung darüber, ob der Mensch im theologisch-metaphysischen Sinne ein nur diesseitiges Wesen sei" (HB, p. 36). See also WG, pp. 39, 42.

⁵A clear and insightful explanation of the notion of the World in SZ can be found in Walter Biemel, *Le concept du monde chez Heidegger* (Louvain-Paris: Nauwelaerts-Vrin, 1950), esp. pp. 130, 154, 157, 160, 162, 165.

⁶SZ, pp. 54, 53, 56. The terms "to-be-in-the-World" and "being-in-the-World" are interchangeable renderings of "In-der-Welt-sein."

⁷"Im Erkennen gewinnt das Dasein einen neuen *Seinsstand* zu der im Dasein je schon entdeckten Welt . . . Erkennen ist ein im In-der-Welt-Sein fundierter Modus des Daseins" (SZ, p. 62).

⁸SZ, pp. 63, 64–65 (World, phenomenon, nature), 70–71.

⁹SZ, p. 76. The term *Umwelt* (environment) means the world around us; it refers to the beings (things) surrounding everyday There-being that are other than (not like) There-being.

¹⁰A summary description of these concepts can be found in W. J. Richardson, *Heidegger: Through Phenomenology to Thought*, pp. 56–59. The term *Weltlichkeit* (translated as "worldliness"; it may also be rendered as "worldness" or as "worldhood") is an ontological concept (an existential structure). The term *Worumwillen* is translated in the following reflections as "whereunto" and also (less frequently) as "for-the-sake-of-which."

¹¹SZ, p. 82.

¹²SZ, p. 86.

¹³SZ, p. 87 (be-deuten).

¹⁴SZ, pp. 89–100.

¹⁵SZ, p. 92.

¹⁶"Herstellung zu Vorhandenem, bzw. Herstellungsunbedürftigkeit machen den Horizont aus, innerhalb dessen 'Sein' verstanden wird" (SZ, p. 92).

¹⁷SZ, p. 93.

¹⁸SZ, p. 94.

¹⁹"Er hat die Meinung verfestigt, das vermeintlich strengste ontische *Erkennen* eines Seienden sei auch der mögliche Zugang zum primären Sein des in solcher Erkenntnis entdeckten Seienden" (SZ, p. 100).

²⁰PT, pp. 13–33, esp. pp. 27–33.

²¹"Wer die Theologie, sowohl diejenige des cristlichen Glaubens als auch diejenige der Philsophie, aus gewachsener Herkunft erfahren hat, zieht es heute vor, im Bereich des Denkens von Gott zu schweigen" (ID, p. 51).

Chapter 10

¹"Alle Seinsstrukturen des Daseins, mithin auch das Phänomen, das auf diese Wer-frage antwortet, sind Weisen seines Seins. Ihre ontologische Charakteristik ist eine existenziale" (SZ, p. 114). The term *Mitsein* is rendered in the following reflections as "with-being" and also as "to-be-with" and as "being-with." These interchangeable translations allow for some helpful linguistic flexibilities; they emphasize the existential (ontological) structure of coexistence, of human encounter.

²"Die Klärung des In-der-Welt-seins zeigte, dass nicht zunächts 'ist' und auch nie gegeben ist ein blosses Subjekt ohne Welt. Und so ist am Ende ebensowenig zunächst ein isoliertes Ich gegeben ohne die Anderen" (SZ, p. 116).

[3]"Dieses Seiende ist weder vorhanden noch zuhanden, sondern ist *so, wie das freigebende Dasein selbst—es ist auch und mit da*" (SZ, p. 118).

[4]"Die Welt des Daseins ist *Mitwelt.* Das In-Sein ist *Mitsein* mit Anderen. Das innerweltliche Ansichsein dieser ist *Mitdasein*" (SZ, p. 118). The term *Mitwelt* is rendered in this analysis as "common World"; it may be translated also (more literally) as "with-World" and as "World-with."

[5]SZ, p. 122 (*eigentliche Verbundenheit*).

[6]"Als Mitsein 'ist' daher das Dasein wesenhaft umwillen Anderer. Das muss als existenziale Wesensaussage verstanden werden" (SZ, p. 123).

[7]"Im Seinsverständnis des Daseins liegt schon, weil sein Sein Mitsein ist, das Verständnis Anderer. . . . Das Sichkennen gründet in dem ursprünglich verstehenden Mitsein" (SZ, p. 123–24).

[8]SZ, pp. 126–30.

[9]*Das Man ist ein Existenzial und gehört als ursprüngliches Phänomenon zur positiven Verfassung des Daseins. Es hat selbst wieder verschiedene Möglichkeiten seiner daseinsmässigen Konkretion*" (SZ, p. 129). See also SZ, p. 128.

[10]A. De Waelhens, *La Philosophie de Martin Heidegger*, 5th ed. (Louvain-Paris: Nauwelaerts, 1967), pp. 77–78. The philosophical insights and the existential psychology (logotherapy) of Viktor E. Frankl show quite powerfully that the many concrete situations (each moment) of life offer unique possibilities for the realization of (experiential, creative, and attitudinal) values and meanings. See the following works of V. E. Frankl: *The Doctor and the Soul: From Psychotherapy to Logotherapy*, 2d expanded ed. (New York; Bantam, 1971), pp. 34–36, 21–140; *The Will to Meaning: Foundations and Applications of Logotherapy* (New York: New American Library, Plume Books, 1970), pp. 55, 61; *Anthropologische Grundlagen der Psychotherapie* (Bern-Stuttgart-Vienna: Verlag Hans Huber, 1975), pp. 241–317; *Die Sinnfrage in der Psychotherapie* (Munich: R. Piper & Co. Verlag, 1981), pp. 77–141; *Der Wille zum Sinn*, 4th ed. (Bern-Stuttgart-Vienna: Verlag Hans Huber, 1982), pp. 81–118; *Man's Search for Meaning: An Introduction to Logotherapy*, 3d newly revised and enlarged ed. (New York: Simon and Schuster, Touchstone Books, 1984), pp. 103–53. The main related issue at stake here, however, is the right understanding of the difference and of the relationship between phenomenology and existential psychotherapy (logotherapy). An analysis of the phenomenological roots of existential psychotherapy (with special attention to the logotherapy of V. E. Frankl) can be found in George Kovacs, "Phenomenology and Logotherapy," in Sandra A. Wawrytko, ed., *Analecta Frankliana: The Proceedings of the First World Congress of Logotherapy (1980)* (Berkeley, Calif.: Institute of Logotherapy Press, 1982), pp. 33–45. See also the following studies by George Kovacs: "The Philosophy of Death in Viktor E. Frankl," *Journal of Phenomenological Psychology*, 13 (1982): 197–209; "Der Sinn der Arbeit," in Alfried Längle, ed., *Wege zum Sinn: Logotherapie als Orientierungshilfe: Für Viktor E. Frankl* (Munich: R. Piper & Co. Verlag, 1985), pp. 91–100; "Viktor E. Frankl's 'Place' in Philosophy," *International Forum for Logotherapy*, 8 (1985): 17–21.

[11]ML, pp. 238–55, especially 241–45. Gabriel Marcel suggests that Heidegger neglects the exploration of the fullness of the I-Thou relationship; he seems to claim that the "openness to the other" is absent in Heidegger. See Gabriel Marcel, "Ma relation avec Heidegger," in (collected vol.) *Gabriel Marcel et la pensée allemande: Nietzsche, Heidegger, Ernst Bloch*, Cahier N. 1 (1979), Présence de Gabriel Marcel (Paris: Aubier, 1979), pp. 35 (the notion of intersubjectivity in SZ), 36 (no interest in the openness to the "other"), 38 (the absence of true openness to the "other," the neglect of the "other" as a person). The validity of Marcel's claim, however, cannot be assessed without keeping in mind the nature and the ontological task of Heidegger's analysis of There-being's relation to the "other." Marcel's view may be in conflict with the existential notion of the relation to the "other" (and with the phenomenon of "to-be-with") in SZ. Karl Jaspers is quite critical of Heidegger's philosophy in this regard; he sees "solipsism" and the lack of "communication" in Heidegger's notion of human existence. See Karl Jaspers, *Notizen zu Martin Heidegger* (Munich: R. Piper & Co. Verlag, 1978), pp. 33–34, 56, 147, 197, 247, 261. Martin Buber sees Heidegger's notion of existence as "monological" and as knowing nothing of "any essential relation with others." See Martin Buber, *Between Man and Man*, trans. Ronald Gregor Smith, with an intro. by Maurice S. Friedman and an Afterword by the author on "The History of the Dialogical Principle," trans. Maurice S. Friedman (New York: Macmillan, 1969), pp. 168, 174. The examination of these (in several respects questionable) interpretations of Heidegger's thought would go beyond the scope of this study.

[12]The notion of the "other" as a revelation and the significance of this view for the problem of God are examined in Emmanuel Levinas, *Totalité et Infini: Essai sur l'Extériorité*, Phaenomenologica vol. 8, 2d ed. (The Hague: Nijhoff, 1965), pp. 21–22, 29–30, 50–51. The following works of Martin Buber are especially significant for the problem of God: *Ich und Du* (Cologne: Hegner, 1972), esp. pp. 91–160; *Between Man and Man* (for instance), pp. 36, 44, 64, 73, 209; *Eclipse of God: Studies in the Relation between Religion and Philosophy*, trans. by Maurice S. Friedman, Eugene Kamenka, Norbert Guterman, and I. M. Lask (New York; Harper and Row, 1952). For a comprehensive study of Buber's philosophy, see Maurice S. Friedman, *Martin Buber: The Life of Dialogue* (New York: Harper Torchbooks, 1960). A critical examination of Buber's thought on modern atheism and on the question of God can be found in George Kovacs, "Atheism and the Ultimate Thou," *International Journal for Philosophy of Religion*, 5 (1974): 1–15. For some foundational insights of Gabriel Marcel see, for instance, his *Essai de philosophie concrète* (Paris: Gallimard, 1967).

[13]This remark emphasizes the significance of the philosophical (especially of the phenomenological) assessment of the concept of God and of the analysis of human relationships in the works of Sigmund Freud, Carl G. Jung, Leopold Szondi, and others. The logotherapy of Viktor E. Frankl and its contributions to the question of ultimate reality and meaning are discussed in George Kovacs, "Ultimate Reality and Meaning in Viktor E. Frankl," *Ulti-*

mate Reality and Meaning, 5 (1982): 118–39. The description of human existence as expression and the philosophy of the body in Merleau-Ponty make valuable contributions to the analysis of the relation to the "other," to the exploration of the human mode of being in the World. See more about this in George Kovacs, "The Personalistic Understanding of the Body and Sexuality in Merleau-Ponty," *Review of Existential Psychology and Psychiatry*, 18 (1982–83): 207–17.

[14]Rudolf Otto, *The Idea of the Holy*, trans. John W. Harvey from the 9th ed. of *Das Heilige* (first published in 1917) (London: Unwin, Pelican Books, 1959), especially pp. 21, 39 (the notion of the "wholly other"—"Ein begriffener Gott ist kein Gott."), 47, 133, 156 (the knowledge of God in Luther), 193 (religion as an offspring of history as the manifestation of the Holy).

[15]Cf. Heinrich Ott, "What Is Systematic Theology?" in J. M. Robinson and J. B. Cobb, Jr., eds., *The Later Heidegger and Theology*, pp. 77–111. See also the following writings by Heinrich Ott: *Denken und Sein: Der Weg M. Heideggers und der Weg der Theologie*; "Die Bedeutung von Martin Heideggers Denken für die Methode der Theologie," in Vittorio Klostermann, ed., *Durchblicke: Martin Heidegger zum 80: Geburtstag*, pp. 27–38; *Das Reden vom Unsagbaren: Die Frage nach Gott in unserer Zeit* (Stuttgart-Berlin: Kreuz Verlag, 1978).

[16]W. Schulz, *Der Gott der neuzeitlichen Metaphysik*, p. 52, refers to the "closeness" between the notion of God and the notion of Being in Heidegger as well as in modern metaphysics; he speaks, in this context, of the entire modern metaphysics as a "disguised theology" (*eine verkappte Theologie*). W. Schulz indicates that modern philosophy originates from the Christian tradition of thought; he is explaining Heidegger's philosophy from the point of view of the problem of God (p. 26). A more helpful and comprehensive discussion of this problem can be found in M. Müller, *Existenzphilosophie im geistigen Leben der Gegenwart*, pp. 63–70 (Heidegger and the problem of God), 45–47 (Being and God), 232–35 (Heidegger's relationship to Christianity), 228–31 (the Judaic-Christian understanding of Being and the interpretation of Being in Heidegger).

Chapter 11

[1]Cf. Hans-Georg Gadamer, "Vom Zirkel des Verstehens," in Günther Neske, ed., *Martin Heidegger zum siebzigsten Geburtstag: Festshcrift* (Pfullingen: Neske, 1959), pp. 24–34.

[2]SZ, p. 131.

[3]The rendering of the term *Rede* as "logos" and the translation of the term *Befindlichkeit* as "disposition" are adopted from W. J. Richardson, *Heidegger: Through Phenomenology to Thought*, pp. 66 (logos), 64 (disposition).

[4]SZ, pp. 135 and 139 (*Befindlichkeit*), 143–44 (*Verstehen*), 161 and 165 (*Rede*).

⁵*"Ihre Absicht ist eine fundamentalontologische"* (SZ, p. 131).

⁶The use of the term *principle* and its expansion into the *principle of demythologization*, as formulated by this study, are intended to "propose" and to think the thought of Heidegger. An essay, as Heidegger likes to insist, should always be an event, an experience of thinking.

⁷SZ, p. 136–37.

⁸SZ, pp. 134–38.

⁹SZ, pp. 143–45.

¹⁰SZ, p. 146.

¹¹SZ, p. 162 ("Redend spricht sich Dasein *aus*, nicht weil es zunächst als 'Inneres' gegen ein Draussen abgekapselt ist, sondern weil es als In-der-Welt-sein verstehend schon 'draussen' ist").

¹²W. J. Richardson, *Heidegger: Through Phenomenology to Thought*, p. 68.

¹³SZ, p. 162.

¹⁴"Die befindliche Verständlichkeit des in-der-Weltseins *spricht sich als Rede aus*. Das Bedeutungsganze der Verständlichkeit *kommt zu Wort*. Den Bedeutungen wachsen Worte zu" (SZ, p. 161).

¹⁵SZ, pp. 131, 142, 151, 161.

¹⁶W. J. Richardson, *Heidegger: Through Phenomenology to Thought*, p. 69.

¹⁷SZ, pp. 132 ("Der Ausdruck "Da" meint die wesenhafte Erschlossenheit."), 133 ("es selbst die Lichtung *ist*" and *"Das Dasein ist seine Erschlossenheit"*). See also SZG, p. 177 (marginal notes a, b, and c).

¹⁸SZ, p. 131.

¹⁹Some important texts of Heidegger in this regard include: WG, pp. 27, 39, 42; ID, pp. 67, 69, 70; SG, pp. 43, 53, 55, 169; EM, p. 5; WM, p. 19 (the ontotheological essence of philosophy); WW, p. 8 (consequence for the notion of truth).

²⁰SZ, pp. 138, 171 (*Sehen entdeckt das Sein, Wahrheit als reine Anschauung*). See also OH, pp. 47–49.

²¹"Das Verstehen macht in seinem Entwurfcharakter existenzial das aus, was wir die *Sicht* des Daseins nennen. Die mit der Erschlossenheit des Da existenzial seiende Sicht *ist* das Dasein glechursprügnlich . . . Die Sicht, die sich primär und im ganzen auf die Existenz bezieht, nennen wir die *Durchsichtigkeit"* (SZ, p. 146).

²²SZ, p. 147.

²³SZ, p. 159.

²⁴SZ, p. 176.

²⁵SZ, p. 179.

²⁶SZ, p. 180. See also PT.

²⁷"*Sinn ist das durch Vorhabe, Vorsicht und Vorgriff strukturierte Woraufhin des Entwurfs, aus dem her etwas als etwas verständlich wird*. . . . Sinn ist ein Existenzial des Daseins, nicht eine Eigenschaft, die am Seienden haftet, 'hinter' ihm liegt oder als 'Zwischenreich' irgendwo schwebt. Sinn 'hat' nur das Dasein, sofern die Erschlossenheit des In-der-Wel-seins durch das in ihr entdeckbare Seiende 'erfüllbar' ist. *Nur Dasein kann daher sinnvoll oder sinnlos sein"* (SZ, p. 151).

Chapter 12

¹SZ, p. 183.
²SZ, pp. 190-91.
³SZ, pp. 188-89.
⁴SZ, p. 185.
⁵"*Das Wovor der Angst ist die Welt als solche.* . . . Wenn sich demnach als das Wovor der Angst das Nichts, das heisst die Welt als solche herausstellt, dann besagt das: *wovor die Angst sich angstät, ist das In-der-Welt-sien selbst.*" And again: "die Angst erschliesst als Modus der Befindlichkeit allererst die *Welt als Welt.* Das beduetet jedoch nicht, dass in der Angst die Weltlichkeit der Welt begriffen wird." (SZ, p. 187).

⁶"Die Überlassenheit des Daseins an es selbst zeigt sich ursprünglich konkret in der Angst. Das Sich-vorweg-sein besagt voller gefasst: *Sich-vorweg-im-schon-sein-in-einer-Welt.* . . . Existenzialität ist wesenhaft durch Faktizität bestimmt." And in the last paragraph of this same page: "Das Sein des Daseins besagt: Sich-vorweg-sein-in-(der-Welt) als Sein-bei (innerweltlich begegnendem Seienden). Dieses Sein erfüllt die Bedeutung des Titles *Sorge,* der rein ontologisch-existenzial gebraucht wird" (SZ, p. 192). See also SZ, pp. 188-96.

⁷SZ, p. 190 (note 1).

⁸The philosophy of the *insecuritas humana* is emphasized by Peter Wust, *Ungewissheit und Wagnis* (Salzburg: Pustet, 1937). CF. also the following works by P. Wust: *Die Dialektik des Geistes* (Augsburg: B. Filser, 1928); *Naivität und Pietät* (Tübingen: J. C. B. Mohr, 1925); *Im Sinnkreis des Ewigen* (Graz: Styria, 1954); *Die Auferstehung der Metaphysik* (Leipzig: Meiner, 1920). See also: W. T. Cleve, *Denken und Erkennen: Ein Weg in die Philosophie nach Peter Wust* (Emsdetten: Lechte, 1952); Gabriel Marcel, "Peter Wust on the Nature of Piety," in his *Being and Having: An Existentialist Diary,* trans Katherine Farrer (New York: Harper and Row, 1965), pp. 213-36; Wilhelm Steinberg, *Grundfragen des menschlichen Seins: Eine Einführung in die philosophische Anthropologie* (Munich-Basel: E. Reinhardt, 1953).

⁹"Die ontologische elementare Ganzheit der Sorgestruktur kann nicht auf ein ontishches 'Urelement' zurückgeführt werden, so gewiss *das Sein nicht aus Seiendem 'erklärt' werden kann.* Am Ende wird sich zeigen, dass die Idee von Sein überhaupt ebensowenig 'einfach' ist wie das Sein des Daseins" (SZ, p. 196). My emphasis; it identifies the translated (quoted) portion of this text. See also: SZ, pp. 200, 209 ("Ontologische Interpretation des Daseins bedeutet jedoch nicht ontisch Zurückgehen auf ein anderes Seiendes."), 212, 207 ("Sein nicht durch Seiendes erklärt werden kann"), 303. See also: AM, pp. 21-26; ML, pp. 85, 184 ("Sein ist früher als das Seiende"), 185 ("Sein ist nicht das Seiende, und sein Erfasstwerden liegt nicht in der Ordnung des Erfassens des Seienden. So ist am Ende das Sein sehr wohl früher bezüglich des Erfasstseins in einem weiten Sinne, vor allem Erfassen des Seienden").

¹⁰SZ, p. 199 (note 1).
¹¹SZ, pp. 211-12.
¹²SZ, p. 218.

[13]"Die Aussage ist *wahr*, bedeutet: sie entdeckt das Seiende an ihm selbst. Sie sagt aus, sie zeigt auf, sie 'lässt sehen' (ἀπόφανσις) das Seiende in seiner Entdecktheit. *Wahrsein (Wahrheit)* der Aussage muss verstanden werden als *entdeckend-sein*" (SZ, p. 218).

[14]"Ein *entdeckendes Sein zum* realen Seienden selbst" (SZ, p. 218). The significance of this passage is emphasized by A. De Waelhens, *La Philosophie de Martin Heidegger*, p. 102 (note 5).

[15]SZ, p. 219.

[16]SZ, p. 230.

[17]"Entdeckend ist das Dasein" (SZ, p. 220).

[18]*Dasein ist 'in der Wahrheit'* " (SZ, p. 221). This passage continues as follows: "Diese Aussage hat ontologischen Sinn. Sie meint nicht, dass das Dasein ontisch immer oder auch nur je 'in alle Wahrheit' eingeführt sei, sondern dass zu seiner existenzialen Verfassung Erschlossenheit seines eigensten Seins gehört."

[19]SZ, pp. 218; 222; N, 1, pp. 341 (the total structure of the World), 349 (beings-in-their-totality as chaos). For a more lengthy explanation see also O. Pöggeler, *Der Denkweg Martin Heidegger*, p. 113.

[20]SZ, p. 226.

[21]SZ, p. 221.

[22]SZ, p. 222.

[23]*Alle Wahrheit ist gemäss deren wesenhafter daseinsmässiger Seinsart relativ auf das Sein des Daseins*" (SZ, p. 227).

[24]SZ, p. 227.

[25]"Zum Sein und Seinkönnen des Daseins als In-derWelt-sein gehört wesenhaft die Erschlossenheit und das Entdecken" (SZ, p. 228).

[26]*Warheit 'gibt es' nur, sofern und solange Dasein ist.* Seiendes ist nur *dann* entdeckt und nur *solange* erschlossen, als überhaput Dasein *ist*" (SZ, p. 226).

[27]SZ, p. 227.

[28]SZ, p. 229.

[29]"Auch die 'Allgemeingültigkeit' der Wahrheit ist lediglich darin verwurzelt, dass das Dasein Seiendes an ihm selbst entdecken und freigeben kann" (SZ, p. 227).

[30]SZ, pp. 245 (*Sein zum Ende*), 248 (*Tod: eine ausgezeichnete Möglichkeit des Daseins*), 250 (*Tod: die Möglichkeit der schlechthinnigen Daseinsunmöglichkeit*), 262 (*die Möglichkeit als die der Unmöglichkeit der Existenz überhaupt*), 263 (*Möglichkeit eigentlicher Existenz*), 264 (*Freiwerden, die Möglichkeit als ganzes Seinkönnen zu existieren*), 265 (*Tod beansprucht das Dasein in der vollen Eigentlichkeit seiner Existenz*), 266 (*ontologische Möglichkeit eines eigentlichen Ganzseinkönnens des Daseins, Freiheit zum Tode*). See also Heidegger's *Kant und das Problem der Metaphysik*, 4th expanded ed. (Frankfurt am Main: Klostermann, 1973), pp. 222–23, 229, 231, 239 (hereafter: KM). This existential, ontological interpretation of death is quite significant for understanding the problem of God in Heidegger's thought because the "definition" of man as finite and temporal existence represents a "self-definition," an understanding of finitude and of temporality without a relation to God. Therefore, Heidegger leaves aside There-being's

relation to God. The apparent cancellation of the religious dimension of There-being, in this context, is a consequence of his views (concepts) of transcendence, of finitude, and of existence. It should be emphasized, however, that Heidegger's thought as a whole remains open toward the possibility of a "questioning faith" and toward the divine. These issues shall be examined in the rest of this study. A summary explanation of some aspects of these concerns can be found in O. Pöggeler, *Der Denkweg Martin Heideggers*, pp. 168, 178, 193–94.

³¹For some insightful reflections regarding Heidegger's hermeneutics of facticity see Hans-Georg Gadamer, *Le problème de la conscience historique* (Louvain-Paris: Publications Universitaires de Louvain-Nauwelaerts, 1963), pp. 39–49. See also OH, pp. 14–20.

³²SZ, p. 10.

³³SZ, p. 427 (note 1).

³⁴The ecstatic notion of temporality shall be examined in Chapter 13 of this study. See also: W. Biemel, *Le concept du monde chez Heidegger*, pp. 130–36; W. J. Richardson, *Heidegger: Through Phenomenology to Thought*, pp. 86–88; Hildegard Feick, *Index zu Heideggers "Sein und Zeit,"* 2d rev. ed. (Tübingen: Niemeyer, 1968), p. 17 (*Ekstasen der Zeitlichkeit*).

Chapter 13

¹SZ, pp. 240, 245, 248, 250, 263, 264, 266.

²"Je unverhüllter diese Möglichkeit verstanden wird, um so reiner dringt das Verstehen vor in die Möglichkeit *als die der Unmöglichkeit der Existenz überhaupt*" (SZ, p. 262). The term *Möglichkeit* may be rendered as "potentiality" as well as "possibility." The term *Unmöglichkeit* may be rendered as "impossibility" as well as "impotence." "Potentiality" and "impotence" indicate more forcefully the meaning intended by Heidegger. See also SZ, pp. 306 (*Möglichkeit der Unmöglichkeit der Existenz; schlechthinnige Nichtigkeit des Daseins*), 250 (*die Möglichkeit der schlechthinnigen Daseinsunmöglichkeit*). For a more comprehensive and critical examination of Heidegger's contributions to the contemporary awareness of death, see George Kovacs, "Man and Death: An Existential-Phenomenological Approach," *Proceedings of the American Catholic Philosophical Association*, 47 (1973): 183–90.

³SZ, p. 259.

⁴SZ, p. 251, states quite clearly: "Das Dasein ihm selbst wesenhaft erschlossen ist und zwar in der Weise des Sich-vorweg. Diese Strukturmoment der Sorge hat im Sein zum Tode seine ursprünglichste Konkretion." SZ, p. 252, concludes, "*Das Sterben gründet hinsichtlich seiner ontologischen Möglichkeit in der Sorge.*" SZG, p. 335 (marginal note a) reinforces this latter passage by adding: "Aber die Sorge west aus der Wahrheit des Seyns." See also SZ, p. 259: "Das Sein zum Tode gründet in der Sorge."

⁵SZ, pp. 251, 263, 266, 306. For an examination of the status of the

question of immortality in contemporary thanatology, see George Kovacs, "Death and the Question of Immortality," *Death Education*, 5 (1981): 15–24.

[6]SZ, pp. 296–97.

[7]"Nunmehr ist mit der Erschlossenheit die ursprünglichste, weil *eigentliche* Wahrheit des Daseins gewonnen" (SZ, p. 297). And the beginning of the paragraph preceding this passage says, "Die Entschlossenheit ist ein ausgezeichneter Modus der Erschlossenheit des Daseins." See also SZ, p. 263 (*Vereinzelung, Tod—eine Weise des Erschliessens des 'Da'*).

[8]SZ, pp. 251, 263, 266.

[9]SZ, pp. 277 (*existenzial verstandene Gewissensruf*), 279 (*das Gewissen als eine im Dasein selbst liegende Bezeugung seines eigensten Seinkönnens*), 298 (*Entschlossenheit, Entschluss*).

[10]SZ, pp. 276–77.

[11]SZ, pp. 278 (*keiner Zuflucht zu nichtdasiensmässigen Mächten*), 269 (theological interpretations of conscience, *Gottesbewusstsein, Gottesbeweise*), 291 (*Ausfluss der göttlichen Macht*).

[12]"Es '*ist*' nur in der Seinsart des Daseins und bekundet sich als Faktum je nur mit und in der faktischen Existenz" (SZ, p. 269). And the next paragraph of the same page states: "Das Gewissen gibt 'etwas' zu verstehen, es *erschliesst*. . . . Der Gewissensruf hat den Charakter des *Anrufs* des Daseins auf sein eigenstes Selbstseinkönnen und das in der Weise des *Anrufs* zum eigensten Schuldigsein."

[13]"Die formal existenziale Idee des 'schuldig' bestimmen wir daher also: Grundsein für ein durch ein Nicht bestimmtes Sein—das heisst *Grundsein einer Nichtigkeit*" (SZ, p. 283). "*Das Dasein ist als solches schuldig*" (SZ, p. 285). "Zum *Sein* des Daseins gehörend, als Schuldigseinkönnen. . . ." (SZ, p. 306).

[14]SZ, p. 288 (*Bereitschaft für das Angerufenwerden*).

[15]SZ, pp. 265 (death and the authenticity of There-being), 308 (*eigentliche Entschlossenheit zur Wierderholung ihrer selbst*). "Die Entschlossenheit 'hat' nicht lediglich einen Zusammenhang mit dem vorlaufen als einem anderen ihrer selbst. *Sie birgt das eigentliche Sein zum Tode in sich als die mögliche existenzielle Modalität ihrer eigenen Eigentlichkeit*" (SZ, p. 305).

[16]SZ, pp. 297 (*Sichentwerfen auf das eigenste Schuldigsein*), 301 (anthropology), 306 (note 1: theological interpretation).

[17]"Hat das *In-der-Welt-sein* eine höhere Instanz seines Seinkönnens als seinen *Tod*?" (SZ, p. 313).

[18]SZ, pp. 375 (*Geschichtlichkeit*), 376 (*zeitlich*).

[19]"Das sich verstehende Dasein selbst" (SZ, p. 325). See also SZ, p. 324.

[20]SZ, pp. 325–28 (the three ecstases). A concise explanation of the ecstatic structure of temporality can be found in W. J. Richardson, *Heidegger: Through Phenomenology to Thought*, pp. 85–89.

[21]SZ, pp. 348, 365.

[22]"Netzwerk von Formen, das von einem weltlosen Subjekt einem Material übergestülpt wird" (SZ, p. 366).

[23]"Wenn kein *Dasein* existiert, ist auch keine Welt 'da'" (SZ, p. 365).

[24]SZ, p. 374 (*sein eigenes Sein als Erstreckung, "Zwischen"*).

[25]"*Das eigentliche Sein zum Tode, das heisst die Endlichkeit der Zeitlichkeit, ist der verborgene Grund der Geschichtlichkeit des Daseins*" (SZ, p. 386).

[26]SZ, p. 395 (*die Blässe eines überzeitlichen Musters*).

[27]"In der Entschlossenheit ist die Gegenwart aus der Zerstreuung in das nächst Besorgte nicht nur zurückgeholt, sondern wird in der Zukunft und Gewesenheit gehalten. Die in der eigentlichen Zeitlichkeit gehaltene, mithin *eigentliche Gegenwart* nennen wir den *Augenblick*" (SZ, p. 338). See also SZ, pp. 410, 427. For a brief but clear explanation of the term *Augenblick* see J. Macquarrie, *An Existentialist Theology: A Comparison of Heidegger and Bultmann*, p. 194.

[28]SZ, pp. 423-24.

[29]SZ, p. 431.

[30]SZ, p. 427 (note 1).

[31]SZ, pp. 436-37.

[32]W. Biemel, *Le concept du monde chez Heidegger*, pp. 160-65.

Conclusion

[1]This absence of a more comprehensive elaboration renders difficult the task of understanding the nature as well as the significance of the problem of God in Heidegger's thinking (especially in SZ). Regarding this "absence" see also A. De Waelhens, *La Philosophie de Martin Heidegger*, pp. 103, 358, 360.

[2]A brief but insightful explanation of this issue can be found in M. Müller, *Existenzphilosophie im geistigen Leben der Gegenwart*, pp. 43 (ontic contingence and ontological contigence), 211 (transcendence).

[3]W. J. Richardson, "Heidegger and God—and Professor Jonas," *Thought*, 40 (1965): 30, 31, 40.

[4]"Bei der ersten Entfaltung des Gedankens der ewigen Wiederkunft des Gleichen, wie bei allen grossen Gedanken, im ersten Anbruch alles Wesentliche da ist, aber unentfaltet belibt" (N, 1, p. 337). See also SG, p. 124 (*Ungedachte*).

Part 3

[1]"Die Eile des Herausbringens und die Angst des Zuspätkommens fallen hier schon deshalb weg, weil es zum Wesen jeder echten Philosophie gehört, dass sie von ihren Zeitgenossen notwendig missverstanden wird. Sogar sich selbst gegenüber muss der Philosoph aufhören, sein eigener Zeitgenosse zu sein. Je wesentlicher und umwälzender eine philosophische Lehre ist, um so mehr bedarf sie erst der Heranbildung jener Menschen und Geschlechter,

die sie aufnehem sollen" (N, 1, p. 269). See also: N, 1, pp. 404, 490–10. According to Nietzsche's insight in his *Beyond Good and Evil* (Chicago: Regnery, 1966), p. 227: "The greatest events and thoughts (and the greatest thoughts are the greatest events) are comprehended most slowly. The generations which are their contemporaries do not experience, do not 'live through' them—they live alongside them."

²"Die Grunderfahrungen des Denkers entstammen . . . geschehen aus der wesenden Wharheit des Seins . . ." (N, 2, p. 239).

³US, pp. 121 (*um meinenen Denkweg im Namenlosen zu lassen*), 99 (*Das Bleiben im Denken ist der Weg*); WW, p. 24; WP, pp. 20–29.

⁴Heidegger's acceptance and interpretation of the distinction between the earlier phase and the later development of his thought can be found in his "Vorwort" (Letter to Richardson, 1962), in W. J. Richardson, *Heidegger: Through Phenomenology to Thought*, p. xxii; for Richardson's explanation of the "two Heideggers," see ibid., pp. 229–45, 623–28. Insightful presentations and interpretations of this change in Heidegger's development can be found in: Otto Pöggeler, ed., *Heidegger: Perspektiven zur Deutung seines Werks* (esp. pp. 11–54); Samuel IJsseling, *Heidegger: Denken en Danken—Geven en Zijn*, p. 38; Alphonse De Waelhens, "Reflections on Heidegger's Development: A Propos of a Recent Book," *International Philosophical Quarterly*, 5 (1965): 475–502 (esp. 496–97, 499, 501–2).

⁵"Vorwort" (Letter to Richardson, 1962), in W. J. Richardson, *Heidegger: Through Phenomenology to Thought*, p. viii.

⁶*Kants These über das Sein* (Frankfurt am Main: Klostermann, 1963) (hereafter: KS).

⁷*Die Frage nach dem Ding: Zum Kants Lehre von den transzendentalen Grundsätzen* (Tübingen: Niemeyer, 1962) (hereafter: FD).

⁸*Platons Lehre von der Wahrheit: Mit einem Brief über den "Humanismus,"* 2d ed. (Bern: Francke, 1954) (hereafter: PW).

⁹In VA, 1, pp. 63–93.

¹⁰The following numbers indicate the number of times the word *God* occurs in these works: 6 in KM (pp. 8, 23, 166, 200, 204, 237); 15 in KS (pp. 8, 9, 12, 13, 14, 21); 28 in FD (pp. 4, 18, 29, 36, 38, 84, 86, 87, 91, 92, 131); 17 in EM (pp. 5, 6, 68, 78, 103, 147); 2 in WW (p. 2); 2 in PW (pp. 20, 48); 12 in WG (pp. 25, 27, 29, 39, 51); 6 in WM (pp. 19, 20, 39); 48 in HD (pp. 9, 12, 21, 27, 28, 41, 44, 48, 50, 52, 53, 58, 61, 66, 67, 68, 70, 71, 73, 99, 104, 108, 141).

Chapter 14

¹KM, p. 188 (*Wiederholung*). See also SZ, p. 385 (*Wiederholung—ausdrückliche Überlieferung*). The term re-petition (*Wiederholung*) expresses the radicality of Heidegger's rethinking of the great philosophers; it is a way of appropriating the tradition creatively (KM, pp. 267–68).

[2]KM, p. 200. For an explanation of the development of Heidegger's interpretation of Kant, see: PK, p. 431; Hansgeorg Hoppe, "Wandlungen in der Kant-Auffassung Heideggers," in Vittorio Klostermann, ed., *Durchblicke*, pp. 284–311; KM, pp. 243–68.

[3]KM, pp. 199, 201.

[4]KM, pp. 5, 9, 200.

[5]KM, p. 200.

[6]KM, p. 202.

[7]KM, pp. 203–4.

[8]KM, pp. 209–11.

[9]"Die Endlichkeit im Dasein nicht als vorhandene Eigenschaft, sondern als das ständige, obzwar meist verborgene Erzittern alles Existierenden" (KM, p. 231). "Ursprünglicher als der Mensch ist die Endlichkeit des Daseins in ihm" (KM, p. 222).

[10]KM, p. 8. See also: EM, p. 80; HW, pp. 184, 209, 246; FD, pp. 74, 85–86, 92.

[11]KS, p. 9; FD, pp. 84–86, 91–92; KM, pp. 8, 201, 230–31; ID, pp. 47, 57, 69, 72; EM, pp. 137, 147—just to mention a few passages.

[12]KS, p. 9.

[13]"Dass das Sein als Grund bestimmt ist, hält man bis zur Stunde für Selbstverständlichste; und doch ist es das Fragwürdigste" (KS, p. 9).

[14]"Positio, ponere heisst: setzen, stellen, legen, liegen, *vor*liegen, zum Grunde liegen" (KS, p. 9). See also: KS, pp. 12, 33, 36.

[15]KS, pp. 30–36. See esp. p. 35.

[16]KS, pp. 34–35. See also: EM, pp. 11, 41; WD, pp. 85, 143.

[17]"Sein kann nicht *sein*. Würde es sein, bleibe es nicht mehr Sein, sonder wäre ein Seiendes" (KS, p. 35).

[18]"Im unscheinbaren 'ist' verbirgt sich alles Denkwürdige des Seins. Das Denkwürdigste darin bleibt jedoch, dass wir bedenken, ob 'Sein,' ob das 'ist' selbst sein kann, oder ob Sein niemals 'ist' und dass gleichwohl wahr bleibt: Es gibt Sein" (KS, p. 35). Heidegger meditates on the "es gibt" in his conference "Zeit und Sein" (given in Freiburg, on January 31, 1962, published in SD, pp. 1–26). See also KV, pp. 167–204 and SD, pp. 61–80.

[19]KS, p. 35.

[20]KS, p. 35.

[21]FD, pp. 84–86. See also EM, pp. 134, 147.

[22]FD, pp. 91–92. See also FD, pp. 18, 36, 58, 69, 71.

[23]FD, pp. 74–75. The term *dechristianization* is my expression in this context; Heidegger speaks of the emergence of natural knowledge.

[24]FD, pp. 78, 80, 81.

[25]FD, p. 82.

[26]FD, p. 18. See also: EM, p. 109; KM, pp. 230–231.

[27]"Und wenn gar das Unmögliche möglich wäre, ein Geschaffensein des Menschen rational nachzuweisen, dann wäre durch die Kennzeichnung des Menschen als eines ens creatum nur wieder das Faktum seiner Endlichkeit

erwiesen, aber nicht das Wesen derselben aufgewiesen und dieses Wesen als Grundverfassung des Seins des Menschen bestimmt" (KM, p. 213).

[28]KM, p. 237.

[29]KM, pp. 23–24, 29–31.

[30]See, for instance: KM, pp. 122–27; EM, p. 157 (*fragend wissen*). The following reflections will show the importance of this aspect of Heidegger's philosophy.

Chapter 15

[1]Some basic reflections on faith and thinking in Heidegger can be found in: Henri Birault, "La foi et la pensé d'apres Heidegger," *Philosophies Chrétiennes: Recherches et Débats*, vol. 10, no. 4 (Paris: Fayard, 1955), pp. 108–32; O. Pöggeler, *Der Denkweg Martin Heideggers*, pp. 193–95. We will consider this question from the point of view of the problem of God. The separation of faith and thinking (philosophy) is a basic characteristic of Heidegger's thought. See, for instance: HW, pp. 70, 75, 325, 342 ("Der Glaube hat im Denken keinen Platz"), 246 (this passage suggests a relationship between thinking and believing); WD, pp. 103–4, 100 ("Die Unbedingtheit des Glaubens und die Fragwürdigkeit des Denkens sind zwei abgründig verschiedene Bereiche"); N, 1, pp. 238–39; WM, p. 20; WW, p. 9; EM, pp. 5–6, 109, 147.

[2]EM, pp. 14, 15.

[3]EM, p. 1 ("Warum ist überhaupt Seiendes und nicht vielmehr Nichts?"). This passage may also be rendered as "Why is there (any) being at all and not rather nothing?" The main issue under discussion is the understanding of the essential (ontological) nature of the difference between Being and being(s). See also: WM, p. 42; EM, pp. 1–7, 21 ("Warum ist überhaupt das Seiende?"), 22 ("Grund der Entscheidung für das Seiende gegen das Nichts"), 24 ("was ist im Unterschied zum Seienden—das Sein?"), 25 ("das Sein des Seienden"). Regarding the "place" and the function of the ontological difference in Heidegger's thought as a whole, see George Kovacs, "The Ontological Difference in Heidegger's *Grundbegriffe*," *Heidegger Studies*, 3/4 (1987/1988): 61–74.

[4]"Die Vorfrage steht hier überhaupt nicht ausserhalb der Grundfrage, sondern sie ist das im Fragen der Grundfrage gleichsam glühende Herdfeuer, der Herd alles Fragens" (EM, p. 32). See also: EM, p. 28; VA, 1, p. 63.

[5]"Fragen: Wie steht es um das Sein?—das besagt nichts Geringeres als den Anfang unseres geschichtlich-geistigen Daseins *wieder-holen*, um ihn in anderen Anfang zu verwandeln" (EM, p. 29). See also EM, pp. 11, 39.

[6]EM, pp. 30, 28. See also EM, pp. 39 ("der zerstörte Bezug zum Sein als solchem ist der eigentliche Grund für unser gesamtes Missverhältnis zur Sprahce"), 62–63.

[7]EM, p. 33 (*geschichtliches Fragen*). See also VA, 1, pp. 63, 64, 70 ("Die Überwindung der Metaphysik wird seinsgeschichtlich gedacht").

[8]"Erschwerung des geschichtlichen Daseins und damit im Grunde des Seins schlechthin ist vielmehr der echte Leistungssin der Philosophie. Erschwerung gibt den Dingen, dem Seienden, das Gewicht zurück (das Sein)" (EM, p. 9). "Philosophie . . . ist ein Geschehnis, das sich jederzeit neu das Sein (in seiner ihm zugehörigen Offenbarkeit) erwirken muss" (EM, p. 65).

[9]EM, p. 31.

[10]EM, pp. 2–3. See also: N, 2, p. 448 (*Grund, Gott*); ID, p. 69 (*Sein als Grund, das Seiende das Gegründete, das höchste Seiende das Begründende*).

[11]EM, p. 5. See also: EM, p. 4 (*Seiendes als Gründendes*); ID, p. 69. For a more limited discussion of the diversity between philosophical thinking and faith-knowledge (the main issue at stake in the following reflections), see George Kovacs, "Philosophy and Faith in Heidegger," *Proceedings of the American Catholic Philosophical Association*, 54 (1980): 135–43.

[12]EM, p. 5.

[13]"Wer auf dem Boden solchen Glaubens steht, der kann zwar das Fragen unserer Frage in gewisser Weise nach- und mitvollziehen, aber er kann nicht eigentlich fragen, ohne sich selbst als einen Gläubigen aufzugeben mit allen Folgen dieses Schrittes" (EM, p. 5). Ralph Manheim's translation in Martin Heidegger, *An Introduction to Metaphysics* (Garden City, N.Y.: Doubleday, Anchor Books, 1961), p. 6.

[14]"Aber andererseits ist jener Glaube, wenn er sich nicht ständig der Möglichkeit des Unglaubens aussetzt, auch kein Glauben, sondern eine Bequemlichkeit und ein Verabredung mit sich, künftig an der Lehre als einem irgendwie Überkommenen festzuhalten" (EM, p. 5). R. Manheim's translation in M. Heidegger, *An Introduction to Metaphysics*, p. 6.

[15]"Das ist dann weder Glauben noch Fragen, sondern Gleichgültigkeit, die sich nunmehr mit allem, vielleicht sogar sehr interessiert, beschäftigen kann, mit dem Glauben ebenso wie mit dem Fragen" (EM, p. 5). R. Mannheim's translation in M. Heidegger, *An Introduction to Metaphysics*, p. 6.

[16]EM, p. 6. See also: WD, p. 110; N, I, p. 350; N, 2, pp. 58–59, 131–32. For a summary presentation of Heidegger's thought on this issue, see also O. Pöggeler, *Der Denken Martin Heideggers*, pp. 192–94.

[17]"Durch vermeintliche Auffrischung mit Hilfe der Philosophie könne eine Theologie gewinnen oder gar ersetzt und dem Zeitbedürfnis schmackhafter gemacht werden" (EM, p. 6).

[18]"Es daraufhin wagen, das Unausschöpfbare dieser Frage durch die Enthüllung dessen, was sie zu fragen fordert, auszuschöpfen, durchzufragen. Wo dergleichen geschieht, ist Philosophie" (EM, p. 6).

[19]"*Wie steht es um das Sein?*" (EM, p. 25). Heidegger's other way of asking the same question is "Welches ist der Sinn von Sein" (EM, p. 32). When Heidegger explains the meaning of this question he uses these expressions: "Wie steht es mit dem Sein?"; "Worin liegt und besteht das Sein?"; "Wie und wem offenbart sich das Sein?" (EM, p. 26). He likes to say: "Aber wo steckt das Sein? Steckt es überhaupt irgendwo?" (EM, p. 27). These expressions reveal Heidegger's meditation on the Being-question. See EM, pp. 25–32. "Die

φύσις ist das Sein selbst, kraft dessen das Seiende erst beobachtbar wird und bleibt." Such an understanding of "nature" had been disclosed to the Greeks "aufgrund einer dichtend-denkenden Grunderfahrung des Seins. . . ." (EM, p. 11). See also: EM, pp. 10, 16, 17, 20 (*Dichten und Denken*), 63, 74, 127, 156; WM, pp. 44, 45, 47, 50. "Philosophieren . . . ist ausser-ordentliches Fragen nach dem Ausser-ordentlichen" (EM, p. 10). For Heidegger's understanding of philosophy see WP, pp. 20–23, 29–30.

[20]"Dass jemand die Sätze, die das Dogma der katholischen Kirche aussagt, glaubt, ist Sache des Einzelnen und steht hier nicht in Frage" (EM, p. 109). See also: EM, pp. 137 and 147 (these passages give the reasons for Heidegger's attitude toward the Christian and the metaphysical interpretations of Being and human existence); FD, pp. 18, 84–86; HB, pp. 24, 36; WG, pp. 39 (note 56), 42 (note 59); N, 1, pp. 349–53; N, 2, pp. 131–32 (the Christian interpretation of beings, the basic difference between Christian faith and philosophy).

[21]See, for instance: EM, pp. 137, 147; HW, pp. 19, 50; WM, p. 20. The Heideggerian view of Being goes beyond the metaphysical interpretation of beings as beings. This "going beyond" the metaphysical way of understanding beings is a "going toward" a more original (primordial) understanding of the meaning of Being. This is the source of the "atheistic" dimension of the Heideggerian questioning. Heidegger's insight (the Being-question) calls attention to the strength and to the weakness of metaphysical thinking. Some reflections about these can be found in O. Pöggeler, *Der Denkweg Martin Heideggers*, pp. 46 (the basic insight of Heidegger on the failure of metaphysics), 94 (the why-question of metaphysics), 137 (beings and the notion of God in metaphysics), 168 (the metaphysical notion of transcendence, the theological notion of transcendence). M. Müller, *Existenzphilosophie im geistigen Leben der Gegenwart*, p. 125, gives a concise explanation of the strength and of the limitation of classical metaphysics: "Die klassische Metaphysik als Ontologie entfunkionalisiert das Seiende durch eine restlose Funktionalisierung von Wesen, Sein und Gott. Sie fragt erstmalig und wirklich nach dem Seienden als Seienden. Das ist ihre Grösse. Sie kahn aber nicht die Fragen nach dem Wesen des Wesens, nach dem Sein des Seins, nach der Göttlichkeit des Gottes, entfalten. Das ist ihre Grenze." See also M. Müller, *Existenzphilosophie im geistigen Leben der Gegenwart*, pp. 120–24, 137–39.

[22]EM, p. 6.

[23]EM, p. 5. See note 14 for German text and translation references.

[24]Johannes B. Metz, "Unbelief as a Theological Problem," *Concilium*, 6 (1965): 35. See also J. B. Metz, "Der Unglaube als theologisches Problem," *Salesianum*, 27 (1965): 286–302.

[25]Karl Rahner, *Im Heute Glauben* (Einsiedeln: Benziger, 1965), pp. 24–25 (*Bezweifelbarkeit—bedauerliche Eigenschaft des Glaubens der Pilger*), 28 (*Gefährdetheit des Glaubens*). The human being, and thus even the believer, is a questioning, critical being. K. Rahner clearly claims that faith can coexist with questioning in his *The Practice of Faith* (New York: Crossroad, 1983), p. 229:

"Absolute commitment in faith can certainly coexist with critical enquiry about that faith in any specific individual, and the two do not have to be mutually exclusive—even though considerable theoretical and practical difficulties are inherent in a coexistence of this kind."

[26]Rudolph Bultmann, "Erziehung und christlicher Glaube," in Günther Neske, ed., *Martin Heidegger zum siebzigsten Geburtstag: Festschrift* (Pfullingen: Neske, 1959), p. 176.

[27]Bultman, *Martin Heidegger*, pp. 177, 178.

[28]Thomas Langan, *The Meaning of Heidegger: A Critical Study of an Existentialist Phenomenology*, 2d paperback ed. (New York: Columbia University Press, 1967), p. 209. For more reflection on this issue, see O. Pöggeler, *Der Denkweg Martin Heideggers*, pp. 91 (*Wahrheit und Dasein sind faktisch*), 93 (*Transcendenz des Daseins, Gottesverhältnis des Daseins*), 128 (*Heidegger spricht von Nietzsche als von dem letzten leidenschaftlich den Gott suchenden deutschen Philosophen*), 206–7 (*die Gotteserfahrung in Heidegger*).

[29]M. Müller, *Existenzphilosophie im geistigen Leben der Gegenwart*, pp. 46–48 (with note 1). See also the reflections of the same author on the difference between the comprehension of Being (*Seinsverständnis*) and faith-understanding (*Glaubensverständnis*), pp. 232–33, 237, 256.

[30]"Die christliche Erfahrung ist etwas so ganz anderes, dass sie es gar nicht nötig hat, mit der Philosophie in Konkurrenz zu treten." (From: Hermann Noack, "Gespräch mit Martin Heidegger" as quoted in Pöggeler, *Der Denkweg*, p. 194.) See also: WM, p. 20; WD, pp. 103–4 (faith as faith needs no other foundation); HW, p. 343; N, 1, p. 385 (faith for Nietzsche).

[31]M. Müller, *Existenzphilosophie im geistigen Leben der Gegenwart*, p. 46. Heidegger emphasizes the difference between the ontical explanation and the ontological understanding of beings. He acknowledges, however, a possible directive and corrective function of ontology in the clarification of fundamental concepts of theology. See his PT, p. 27.

[32]See: EM, p. 6 (*fragen; wagen*); N, 1, pp. 457–58 (*Antwort: nur der allerletzte Schritt des Fragens selbst*); ED, pp. 15 (the dangers of thinking), 17 (*Wer gross denkt, muss gross irren*).

[33]R. Otto, *The Idea of the Holy*, pp. 39, 47.

[34]Paul Ricoeur, "Sciences humaines et conditionnement de la foi," in *Dieu aujourd'hui: Recherches et Débats*, collected vol. (Bruge: Desclée de Brouwer, 1965), p. 140 (*Le chrétien: adversaire de l'absurde, prophete du sense*). For a philosophical reflection on the structure and meaning of (Christian) faith, see Joseph Pieper, *Über den Glauben: Ein philosophischer Traktat* (München: Kösel Verlag, 1962). For a theological and philosophical meditation on the contemporary aspects of the knowledge of God and Christian faith, see W. Strolz, *Menschsein als Gottesfrage: Wege zur Erfahrung der Inkarnation*, pp. 143–48, 152–225.

[35]For a concise explanation of the "circle of understanding" and of "the unity of meaning," see Hans-Georg Gadamer, "Vom Zierkel des Verstehens," in G. Neske (ed.), *Martin Heidegger zum siebzigsten Geburtstag: Festschrift*, pp.

24–34, 28, 30. Heidegger analyzes the nature of theology and the relationship of theology to philosophy in his PT, p. 15–33. Some critical reactions to Heidegger's position on faith and philosophy can be found in: Francis Guibal, *. . . et combien de dieux nouveaux: Approches contemporaines. 1. Heidegger* (Paris: Aubier-Montaigne, 1980), pp. 19–30, 125–66; Paul Ricoeur, *La métaphore vive* (Paris: Seuil, 1975), pp. 388–98.

Chapter 16

[1]"Das Sein selbst den in ihm verwahrten Unterschied von Sein und Seiendem erst dann in seiner Wahrheit lichten kann, wenn der Unterschied selbst sich eigens ereignet" (VA, 1, p. 70). See also: WW, p. 26 (*Wahrheit des Seins und nicht nur des Seienden*); N, 2, pp. 207 (*Wir stehen in der Unterschied von Seiendem und Sein*), 208 (*Onto-logie*), 346 (*Sein als Sein*), 353 (*Sein als Ausbleiben*), 358 (*das Wesen des Denkens*), 369 (*Nihilismus als Geschick des Seins*), 485 (*Ereignis*), 486 (*Lichtung*), 489 (*Die Seinsgeschichte ist das Sein selbst*); VA, 2, p. 72 (*Lichtung*).

[2]"Wharheit des Seins . . . Grund aller Metaphysik" (WM, p. 16). "Die Überwindung ist die Über-lieferung der Metaphysik in ihre Wahrheit" (VA, 1, p. 71). "Die überwundene Metaphysik verschwindet nicht. Sie kehrt gewandelt zurück and bleibt als der fortwaltende Unterschied des Seins zun Seienden in der Herrschaft" (VA, 1, p. 64). See also: VA, 1, pp. 63, 65, 68, 83, 86–87; WP, pp. 20–23.

[3]VA, 3, pp. 66–67; HD, pp. 87–89; WW, p. 23.

[4]WW, pp. 27 (*Wandlung des Bezugs zum Sein*). Some concise descriptions of the nature of thinking by Heidegger can be found in: WM, pp. 43, 47 (*wesentliches Denken: ein Ereignis des Seins*), 49 (*wesentliches Denken: der Widerhall der Gunst des Seins; die menschliche Antwort auf das Wort der lautlosen Stimme des Seins*), 50 (*Denken: gehorsam der Stimme des Seins*); WW, p. 24 (*Denken: die Gelassenheit der Milde*); VA, 2, p. 13 (*warten*); EM, p. 151 (*fragen: warten*); G, pp. 34 (*nicht von uns bei uns*), 35 (*das Schwierige*), 37 (*warten*), 62 (*Andenken*); WD, pp. 51 (*Denken als Hand-Werk*), 68 (*Mehrdeutigkeit als Element des Denkens*), 93 (*Dank*), 94 (*Dank*), 103 (*Geheiss*), 158 (*Andenken*).

[5]EM, pp. 137, 147. See also PW, pp. 35, 49, and WWP, p. 15.

[6]WG, p. 39 (note 56).

[7]WG, p. 42 (note 59).

[8]WG, p. 39.

[9]WG, pp. 25–27.

[10]WG, pp. 29, 31, 32, 35.

[11]"Der ursprüngliche Entwurf der Möglichkeiten des Daseins" (WG, p. 39).

[12]WG, pp. 13, 48–49.

[13]"Weil 'Grund' ein transzendentaler Wesenscharakter des *Seins überhaupt* ist, deshalb gilt vom *Seienden* der Satz des Grundes Zum Wesen des Seins aber gehört Grund, weil es Sein (nicht Seiendes) nur gibt in der Transzendenz als dem weltentwerfend befindlichen Gründen" (WG, p. 51).

[14]WG, pp. 54, 43.

[15]*Die Freiheit is der Ursprung des Satzes vom Grunde*" (WG, p. 51). See also WG, pp. 43, 49.

[16]WG, pp. 50, 48–49.

[17]"Ontologische Interpretation des Seins in und aus der Transcendenz des Daseins heisst aber doch nicht ontische Ableitung des Alls des nicht-daseins-mässigen Seienden aus dem Seienden qua Dasein" (WG, p. 42). For more reflection on this, see also O. Pöggeler, *Der Denkweg*, pp. 92–93.

[18]WM, pp. 19–20. See also: KS, p. 9; *Zur Seinsfrage*, 2d ed. (Frankfurt am Main: Klostermaann, 1959), pp. 18, 25 (hereafter: SF).

[19]The rendering of the term *Nichts* as "Non-being" is adopted from W. J. Richardson, *Heidegger: Through Phenomenology to Thought*, p. 196 (note 6). This translation emphasizes the ontological (Being) dimension of the question about "nothing"; it is more descriptive than the commonly used word *nothing*.

[20]"In der Angst in eins mit dem Seienden im Ganzen" (WM, p. 33). See also WM, p. 32. This study uses "beings-in-the-ensemble" as well as "beings-in-their-totality" for rendering Heidegger's "das Seiende im Ganzen"; it uses "totality of beings" for rendering Heidegger's "das Ganze des Seienden." The difference between "das Seiende im Ganzen" and "das Ganze des Seienden" is explained by Heidegger in WM, pp. 27, 28. The importance of the difference at stake in these two expressions is examined in Albert Dondeyne, "La différence ontologique chez M. Heidegger," *Revue Philosophique de Louvain*, 56 (1958): 262 (note 29).

[21]"In der hellen Nacht des Nichts der Angst ersteht erst die ursprüngliche Offenheit des Seienden als eines solchen: dass es Seiendes ist—und nicht Nichts" (WM, p. 34). Translated by W. J. Richardson in his *Heidegger: Through Phenomenology to Thought*, p. 197.

[22]"Das Nichts ist die Ermöglichung der Offenbarkeit des Seienden als eines solchen für das menschliche Dasein" (WM, p. 35). See also WM, p. 34, W. J. Richardson's translation, p. 198.

[23]"Das Nichts bleibt nicht das unbestimmte Gegenüber für das Seiende, sondern enthüllt sich als zugehörig zum Sein des Seienden" (WM, p. 39). "Das Nichts gibt nicht erst den Gegenbegriff zum Seienden her, sondern gehört ursprünglich zum Wesen selbst" (WM, p. 35).

[24]WM, p. 38 ("Platzhalter des Nichts"). See also SF, p. 38.

[25]WM, pp. 40, 41. See also EM, pp. 1, 24, 25.

[26]"Warum ist überhaupt Seiendes und nicht vielmehr Nichts?" (WM, p. 42).

[27]"Im Sein des Seienden geschieht das Nichten des Nichts" (WM, p. 35). Richardson's translation in his *Heidegger: Through Phenomenology to Thought*, p. 201.

[28]"Das Nichts . . . enthüllt sich als zugehörig zum Sein des Seienden" (WM, p. 39). Richardson's translation in his *Heidegger*, p. 201.

[29]"Das Nichts als das Andere zum Seienden ist der Schleier des Seins" (WM, p. 51).

[30]"Das reine Sein und das Reine Nichts ist also dasselbe" (Wissenschaft der Logic I, Buch WW III, S. 74, as quoted in WM, p. 39).

[31]"Weil das Sein selbst im Wesen endlich ist und sich nur in der Transcendenz des in das Nichts hinausgehaltenen Daseins offenbart" (WM, p. 40).

[32]WM, pp. 35, 38.

[33]WM, p. 41: "Das menschliche Dasein kann sich nur zu Seiendem verhalten, wenn es sich in das Nichts hineinhält."

[34]WM, p. 40.

[35]WM, p. 38.

[36]WM, p. 29. See also WM, pp. 28–31.

[37]"Über das Nichts spricht sich die Metaphysik von altersher in einem freilich mehrdeutigen Satz aus: ex nihilo nihil fit, aus Nichts wird Nichts" (WM, p. 38). Regarding "Non-being," see note 19.

[38]"Das Nichts wird jetz der Gegenbegriff zum eigentlich Seienden, zum summum ens, zu Gott als ens increatum" (WM, p. 39).

[39]WM, p. 40. The significance of this Heideggerian insight is emphasized by Alphonse De Waelhens, Phénoménologie et Vérité, 2d ed. (Louvain-Paris: Nauwelaerts, 1965), p. 89. A fine description of the ontological difference in the context of Nonbeing and of the phenomenon of anxiety can be found in John C. Sallis, "La différence ontologique et l'unité de la pensée de Heidegger," Revue Philosophique de Louvain, 65 (1967): 192–206.

[40]SZ, pp. 212–30.

[41]WW, p. 8; PW, pp. 20, 44, 48.

[42]WW, p. 9. See also SZ, p. 229.

[43]WW, pp. 7–9.

[44]WW, p. 12. See also W. Biemel, Le concept du monde chez Heidegger, p. 121.

[45]"Das Wesen der Wahrheit ist die Freiheit" (WW, p. 12). See also: WG, pp. 44, 50, 53, 54; WM, p. 41.

[46]"Sich einlassen auf das Offene und dessen Offenheit, in die jegliches Seiende hereinsteht, das jene glechsam mit sich bringt" (WW, p. 14). Richardson's translation in his Heidegger: Through Phenomenology to Thought, p. 216.

[48]"Wahreit ist die Entbergung des Seienden, durch die eine Offenheit west" (WW, p. 16). Richardson's translation in his Heidegger, p. 217.

[49]WW, pp. 18–19.

[50]WW, pp. 19–30.

[51]"Dasein nicht nur ek-sistiert, sondern zugleich in-sistiert " (WW, p. 21). About the Heideggerian transition from "existence" to "ek-sistence", see, for instance, O. Pöggeler, Der Denkweg Martin Heideggers, pp. 173–75.

[52]WW, pp. 19 (Un-warheit, Geheimnis), 22 (Irre, Irrtum). The term errance is Richardson's translation, Heidegger, p. 224.

[53]PW, pp. 44, 48. See also EM, p. 147, and WWP, p. 93.

[54]PW, pp. 40–42.

[55]PW, pp. 35, 38, 49.

[56]PW, pp. 48, 51; HB, p. 36; WG, p. 39; WM, pp. 43–44 (explains the

metaphysical understanding of beings and the problem of Being). See also A. De Waelhens, *Phenomenologie et Verité*, p. 133 (with note 1).

[37]PW, pp. 37, 44, 45.

[38]PW, p. 51. See also WW, pp. 27, 48–49; SF, pp. 17, 18–25. A concise explanation of the Heideggerian characterization and usage of the term *metaphysics* can be found in M. Müller, *Existenzphilosophie im geistigen Leben der Gegenwart*, p. 51 (with note 1).

[39]PW, pp. 51–52. See also: BE, pp. 57, 179; Fridolin Wiplinger and Martin Heidegger, *Von der Un-Verborgenheit: F. Wiplingers Bericht von einem Gespräch mit M. Heidegger: Aufgezeichnet von Ekkehard Fräntzki* (Pfaffenweiler: Centaurus-Verlagsgesellschaft, 1987), pp. 6, 7, 56.

Chapter 17

[1]HB, p. 5; HD, p. 122; HW, p. 253. See also B. Allemann, *Hölderlin et Heidegger*, trans. F. Fédier (Paris: Presses Universitaires de France, 1959), pp. 135–42.

[2]HD, pp. 37–38, 44. See also: HW, pp. 61, 70, 252–53, 272–73, 294; G, p. 33; EM, pp. 29, 34, 47, 110.

[3]HD, pp. 26, 27, 28, 34–55, 40, 66 (*das Heilige zu sagen, zu nennen*), 70 (*das Unmittelbare, Vermittlung, das Heilige das Wort wird*), 74 (*Das Wort is das Ereignes des Heiligen, Bereitschaft für das Heilige*), 116.

[4]For instance, the "Holy" is mentioned in HD 115 times (see: pp. 18, 26, 47, 52, 61, 62, 63, 64, 65, 66, 67, 68, 69, 70, 71, 72, 73, 74, 82, 83, 98, 99, 100, 101, 104, 107, 108, 116, 118, 119, 139, 140, 142), the "gods" 97 times, and the "demigod" 20 times.

[5]HD, pp. 47–75.

[6]HD, pp. 58–59, 69.

[7]HD, pp. 64, 65, 67.

[8]"Das Heilige verschenkt das Wort und kommt selbst in dieses Wort. Das Wort ist das Eriegnis des Heiligen" (HD, p. 74).

[9]HD, pp. 51, 52, 57.

[10]HD, pp. 61 (*das Heilige als das Un-nahbare*), 62 (*das Heilige kommend sich enthüllt*), 64 (*Kommen des Heiligen*), 65 (*Unmittelbarkeit des Heiligen, die Art ihrer Gegenwart ist das Kommen*), 58 (*Heiligkeit* as the essence of "nature" in Hölderlin), 141 (*Heiligkeit des Gotes*).

[11]"Indem das Heilige das Wort wird, kommt sein innerstes Wesen ins Wanken" (HD, p. 70). "Das Unmittelbare wird so zu einem Mittelbaren" (HD, p. 70).

[12]"Das Heilige 'älter denn die Zieten' und 'über die Götter' gründet in seinem Kommen einen anderen Anfang einer anderen Geschichte. Das Heilige entscheidet anfänglich zuvor über die Menschen und über die Götter, ob sie sind und wer sie sind und wan sie sind" (HD, pp. 73–74). See also HD, pp. 84, 101.

[13]HD, pp. 57 (*die älteste Zeit*), 73 (*Jetz; älter denn die Zeiten; dieses Kommen des Heiligen allein gibt die "Zeit"*).

[14]"Das Wort ist das Eriegnis des Heiligen." (HD, p. 74).

[15]HD, pp. 73–74, 101, 61 (*"das Einstige"*).

[16]"Das ursprünglich Heile aber verschenkt durch seine Allgegenwart jedem Wirklichen das Heil seiner Verweilung" (HD, p. 61). See also HD, pp. 84–85 (*wohnen*).

[17]"Das Heilige setz alles Erfahren asu seiner Gewöhnung heraus und entzieht ihm so den Standort. Also ent-stezend ist das Heilige das Entsetzliche selbst" (HD, p. 61–62). See a similar description of the Holy in R. Otto, *The Idea of the Holy*, pp. 26–36.

[18]HD, pp. 119 (poetical dwelling), 140 (*Götter zu Gast kommen und Menschen eine Behausung bauen können*), 116 (*heiligt, Wohnstatt*). For the "demigod" (*Halbgott*), see HD, pp. 98, 99, 105, 107, 108, 109, 118, 123, 139.

[19]HD, pp. 27 (*Gott fehlt, Gottlosigkeit*), 28 (*Fehl des Gottes*), 44 (*die Zeit der entflohenen Götter und des kommenden Gottes, die dürftige Zeit*); HW, pp. 248–53 (*Wegbleiben des Gottes, die Spuren der entflohenen Götter, die Spur des Heiligen*); G, p. 33 (flight of the gods).

[20]HD, p. 72.

[21]HD, pp. 57 (nature), 63 (powers of the gods).

[22]HD, p. 63.

[23]HD, pp. 66–67 (*Gesang, Mittlerschaft*).

[24]HD, p. 67.

[25]"Der Wesenstand des Dichters gründet nicth in der Empfängnis des Gottes, sondern in der Umpfängnis durch das Heilige" (HD, p. 67). And in the next paragraph: "Die Seele des Dichters . . . erbevt von Erinnerung, will sagen, von der Erwartung dessen, was zuvor geschah; das ist das Sich-öffnen des Heiligen."

[26]"Eine Helle entbreitet sich den vereinzelten Seelen jener dichter, die vom Heiligen umfangen ihm zugehören. . . . Jene Dichter stehen dann selbst offen im Offenen. . . ." (HD, p. 62).

[27]HD, pp. 39, 73–74.

[28]HD, pp. 21, 27, 28, 44, 48, 50, 52, 53, 66, 67, 70, 71, 141.

[29]HD, p. 50.

[30]HD, p. 52.

[31]HD, p. 53.

[32]HD, p. 54.

[33]"Das Heilige ist nicht, weil es göttlich ist, sondern das Göttliche ist göttlich, weil es in seiner Weise 'heilig' ist. . . ." (HD, p. 58).

[34]HD, pp. 66, 67, 70.

[35]HD, p. 72.

[36]O. Pöggeler, *Der Denkweg Martin Heideggers*, pp. 217, 214.

[37]O. Pöggeler, *Der Denkweg*, p. 234.

[38]HD, pp. 35, 51, 58, 59. *Cf.* also: O. Pöggeler, *Der Denkweg*, p. 214; W. J. Richardson, *Heidegger: Through Phenomenology to Thought*, p. 424.

[39]HD, pp. 62, 67.

[40]M. Müller, *Existenzphilosophie im geistigen Leben der Gegenwart*, p. 92.

[41]B. Allemann, *Hölderlin et Heidegger*, pp. 137, 152. *Cf.* also: Reuben Guilead, *Être et Liberté: Une étude sur le dernier Heidegger* (Louvain-Paris: Nauwelaerts, 1965), p. 118; Joseph Sadzik, *Esthétique de Martin Heidegger* (Paris: Editions Universitaires, 1963), p. 195.

[42]HW, pp. 252, 253.

[43]HD, p. 73. See also HD, pp. 74, 35, 38, 51, 64.

[44]"Bleibt nicht nur das Heilige als die Spur zur Gottheit verborgen, sondern sogar die Spur zum Heiligen, das Heil, scheint ausgelöscht zu sein" (HW, p. 272). See also HW, pp. 70, 248, 253.

[45]HW, pp. 246, 248, 249, 250–53, 272, 294. See also BE, p. 437.

[46]HB, pp. 26, 33, 35–37, 51–53, 57, 70–71; VA, 2, pp. 23–24, 51–52, 73–74; TK, pp. 43, 45, 46; ID, pp. 51–52, 57, 70–71.

[47]"Wir ohne eine zureichende Besinnung auf die Sprache niemals wahrhaft wissen, was die Philosophie als das gekennzeichnete Ent-sprechen, was die Philosophie als eine ausgezeichnete Weise des Sagens ist" (WP, p. 30).

Chapter 18

[1]N, 1, pp. 457–58.

[2]N, 2, p. 329.

[3]N, 2, p. 44. See also HB, pp. 5, 45, 47, 29.

[4]WP, p. 28.

[5]HB, p. 22.

[6]HB, p. 29. See also p. 25.

[7]HB, p. 45.

[8]KV, pp. 174, 196, 197.

[9]For instance: in the short lecture *Die Kehre* (TK) the term *God* appears four times in a significant context; in HB twenty-seven times; in ID twenty-six times. Heidegger's dialogues with Hölderlin and Nietzsche are the most eloquent expressions of the "place" of the word *God* in the language of Being. See also BE, pp. 410–417 (Being, God, man).

[10]TK, pp. 38, 39, 45.

[11]For an examination of Heidegger's entire philosophy of technology, see John Loscerbo, *Being and Technology: A Study in the Philosophy of Martin Heidegger*, Phaenomenologica vol. 82 (The Hague: Nijhoff, 1981).

[12]J. Loscerbo, *Being and Technology*, p. 146. The term *enframing* is the translation of *Gestell* by David F. Krell in Martin Heidegger, *Basic Writings: From Being and Time (1927) to The Task of Thinking (1964)*, ed. and intro. David Farrell Krell (New York: Harper and Row, 1977), p. 285.

[13]TK, p. 38.

[14]TK, p. 39.

[15]TK, p. 41.

[16]TK, p. 43.

[17]TK, p. 42.

[18]TK, p. 43.

[19]TK, p. 43.

[20]TK, p. 45. See also BE, pp. 437–440 (Being is not above God; God is not above Being).

[21]VA, 3, pp. 75, 74, 73, 71; TK, p. 47.

[22]TK, p. 46.

[23]TK, p. 44.

[24]TK, p. 46.

[25]"Ob Gott Gott ist, ereignet sich aus der Konstellation des Seins und innerhalb ihrer" (TK, p. 46).

[26]"Ob der Gott lebt oder tot bleibt, entscheidet sich nicht durch die Religiosität der Menschen und noch weder durch theologische Asprationen der Philosophie und der Naturwisseschaft" (TK, p. 46).

[27]HB, pp. 10, 13, 17, 19, 20, 26, 33, 34, 35, 36, 37, 39, 41. In *Die Kehre* the term *God* is used four times (TK, pp. 45, 46). HB uses the word *Holy* six times and the term *divinity* three times.

[28]"Das Denken vollbringt den Bezug des Seins zum Wesen des Menschen" (HB, p. 5).

[29]"Was ihm selbst vom Sein übergeben ist" (HB, p. 5).

[30]"Zum Sein innerhalb des Bezugs des Seins zum Menschenwesen" (HB, p. 21).

[31]"Der Mensch ist vielmehr vom Sein selbs in die Wahrheit des Seins 'geworfen,' dass er, dergestalt ek-sistierend, die Warheit des Seins hüte, damit im Lichte des Seins das Seiende als das Seinde, das es ist, erscheine" (HB, p. 19). See also HB, p. 25.

[32]HB, p. 13. See also pp. 24, 29.

[33]HB, p. 25 (*Nähe zum Sein*). See also p. 29 (*Nachbar des Seins*).

[34]"Das Sein ist weiter denn alles Seiende und ist gleichwohl dem Menschen näher als jedes Seiende, sei dies ein Fels, ein Tier, ein Kunstwerk, eine Maschine, sei es ein Engel oder Gott" (HB, pp. 19–20).

[35]"Doch das Sein—was ist das Sein? Es ist Es selbst. Dies zu erfahren und zu sagen, muss das künftige Denken lernen. Das 'Sein'—das ist nicht Gott und nicht ein Weltgrund" (HB, p. 19).

[36]HB, p. 35.

[37]HB, p. 36.

[38]HB, p. 26.

[39]HB, pp. 36–37. See also p. 26.

[40]"Keineswegs für den Theismus entschieden haben. Theistisch kann es so wenig sein wie atheistisch" (HB, p. 37).

[41]"Nicht auf Grund einer gleichgültigen Haltung, sondern aus der Achtung der Grenzen, die dem Denken als Denken gesetzt sind und zwar durch das, was sich ihm als das Zu-denkende gibt, durch die Wahrheit des Seins" (HB, p. 37). See also BE, pp. 412–17 (the last God and the truth of Being).

[42]"Das denken überwindet die Metaphysik nicht, in dem es sie, noch höher hinaufsteigend, übersteigt und irgendwo aufhebt, sondern indem es zurücksteigt in die Nähe des Nächsten" (HB, p. 37).

[43]This view of Heidegger's position regarding the question of God is emphasized and adopted by F. Guibal, in his *et combien de dieux nouveaux: Approchees contemporaines. 1. Heidegger*, p. 166, 133–52.

[44]WP, pp. 28, 30, 24, 23.

[45]WP, pp. 7 (medieval philosophy), 16 (cause, ground).

[46]VA, 2, p. 57 (*Fehl Gottes, Fülle des Gewesenen*).

[47]VA, 2, p. 71.

[48]VA, 2, pp. 74, 51, 57.

[49]VA, 2, p. 51 (*der Gott, entzieht*).

[50]VA, 2, pp. 23–24.

[51]"Wer ist der Gott? Vielleicht ist diese Frage zu schwehr für den Menschen and zu voreilig" (VA, 2, p. 73).

[52]The term *God* occurs twenty-seven times in this essay.

[53]ID, p. 51. See also pp. 52, 53, 55, 57, 70.

[54]ID, p. 51 ("im Bereich des Denkens von Gott zu schweigen").

[55]ID, p. 70 ("Zu diesem Gott kann der Mensch weder beten, noch kann er ihm opfern. Vor der Causa sui kann der Mensch weder aus Scheu ins Knie fallen, noch kann er vor diesem Gott musizieren und tanzen"). The issue at stake here is quite close to Nietzsche's concern in his *Thus Spoke Zarathustra*, trans. R. J. Hollingdale (Baltimore, Md.: Penguin Books, 1971), p. 68: "I should believe only in a God who understood how to dance."

[56]"Demgemäss ist das gott-lose Denken, das den Gott der Philosophie, den Gott als Causa sui preisgeben muss, dem göttlichen Gott vielleicht näher. Dies sagt hier nur: Es ist freier für ihn, als es die Onto-Theo-Logik wahrhaben möchte" (ID, p. 71).

[57]US, p. 200 (*erscheinen lassen, lichtend-verbergend frei-geben*). See also: US, pp. 111, 213–215; SF, p. 29.

[58]"La fin de la philosophie et la tâche de la pensée," KV, pp. 167–204.

Conclusion

[1]WG, pp. 39 (note 56), 42 (note 59); HB, pp. 35, 36 (*Indifferenz*), 37, 24 (*Sein ist das transcendens schlechthin*); SF, pp. 17–18 (*Transcendenz*, its meanings). "Die Transcendenz des Daseins ist vielmehr gedacht als das Öffnen und Offenhalten jenes 'transcendens schlechthin,' welches das Sein ist" (O. Pöggeler, *Der Denkweg Martin Heideggers*, p. 168.) "Heidegger klammert dagegen ein mögliches Gottesverhältnis des Menschen erst einmal aus und bestimmt die Existenz aus sich selbst heraus als endlich und zeitlich, so dass sie zur faktischen Existenz wird" (Pöggeler, *Der Denkweg*, p. 168; see also pp. 91–94). For a concise explanation of the Heideggerian notion of transcendence, see M. Müller, *Existenzphilosophie im geistigen Leben der Gegenwart*,

p. 211. A brief analysis of the contemporary aspects of the theological consequences of the philosophical crisis of the God-question can be found in W. H. van de Pol, "Auf dem Weg zu einem verantworteten Gottesglauben," *Stimmen der Zeit*, Bd. 180 (1967), Heft 10: 236–38.

[2]"Und wenn gar das Unmögliche möglich wäre, ein Geschaffensein des Menschen rational nachzuweisen, dann wäre durch die Kennzeichnumg des Menschen als eines ens creatum nur wieder das Faktum seiner Endlichkeit erwiesen, aber nicht das *Wesen* derselben aufgewiesen und dieses Wesen *als Grundverfassung* des Seins des Menschen bestimmt" (KM, p. 213). My emphasis. The importance of the *way* of understanding finitude is indicated very clearly by Heidegger. For a brief exposition of the various ways of understanding finitude, see Eugen Fink, *Sein, Wahrheit, Welt: Vor-Fragen zum Problem des Phäenomen Begriffs*, Phaenomenologica vol. 1 (The Hague: Nijhoff, 1958), pp. 54–65, esp. p. 59.

[3]Pierre Trotignon, *Heidegger: Sa vie, son oeuvre: Avec un exposé de sa philosophie* (Paris: Presses Universitaires de France, 1965), pp. 38–39.

[4]See: HW, pp. 202–4 (distinguishes between the political-cultural-historical form of Christianity and the Christianity of the New Testament; differentiates between Christianity and Christian life as such; knows the difference between theology and faith; unbelief as a consequence of Nihilism); WM, p. 24 (speaks of the Pauline notion of theology); EM, p. 147 (distinguishes between the act of faith and thinking; speaks of the Christian, metaphysical interpretation of the Being of beings); WD, pp. 103–4 (distinguishes between Christian faith and thinking as questioning); US, pp. 75–76 (the meaning of Christianity and that of Christianness as essential questions); N, 2, pp. 38 (distinguishes between the Christian notion of God and the Nietzschean interpretation of the Christian view of God), 421–27 (speaks of Christianity as a phenomenon of culture, that is, as *Kulturchristentum*, and as faith, that is, as *Christlichkeit des Glaubens*).

[5]This may be examined by analyzing the Heideggerian interpretation of the Nietzschean idea of the "death of God." In this context Heidegger speaks of the various forms of atheism. He says that Nietzsche's atheism (the idea of the death of the "moral" and "cultural" God, the concern with the question of God as a question and as an outcry for the living God, the evaluation of Nietzsche as a *Gottsucher*) is something quite different from the atheism of those who simply deny God for the reason of not finding him in the "test tube" (the superficial atheists). Nietzsche, according to Heidegger, should not be viewed as a "half-Christian" characterized by a "romantic" search for God (the "sentimental" atheist). For these ideas, see: N, 1, pp. 321–24, 183; N, 2, pp. 58–59, 78, 131–34, 426–27; HW, pp. 202–4, 234–35, 239. Finally, Heidegger speaks of those who cannot seek God because they do not think (they gave up the possibility of faith). See: HW, p. 246; N, 1, p. 322.

[6]SF, p. 30. See also: SF, pp. 26 (*die Sprache der Metaphysik*), 36 (*die ursprünglichen Seinserfahrungen*), 42 (*des andenkende Denken*).

[7]"Wir versuchen, auf die Stimme des Seins zu hören" (WP, p. 28). See

also: F, p. 4 (*Zuspruch des Feldwegs, hören können, Hörige, schwerhörig für seine Sprache bleiben*); WD, pp. 164–65 (*Das Denken baut erst im fragenden Gang seinen Weg*).

Part 4

¹That is, as of the end of March 1989. The complete list (including the dates of the university lecture courses) of all his works published in the *Gesamtausgabe* as of this time as well as the list of his writings (including the dates of their composition) published in his lifetime are included in the Bibliography at the end of this study. Regarding Heidegger's guidelines for the editing and publication of his writings in the *Gesamtausgabe*, see Friedrich-Wilhelm von Herrmann, "Die Edition der Vorlesungen Heideggers in seiner Gesamtausgabe letzter Hand," *Heidegger Studies*, 2 (1986): 153–72.

Chapter 19

¹PA, p. 196.
²PA, p. 197.
³PA, p. 197.
⁴PA, p. 197.
⁵PA, p. 197.
⁶PA, p. 197.
⁷PA, p. 199.
⁸PA, p. 196.
⁹PZ, pp. 109–10.
¹⁰Maurice Merleau-Ponty, *Phénoménolgie de la perception* (Paris: Gallimard, 1972), p. ii.
¹¹PZ, p. 122.
¹²PZ, p. 391 (*keine versteckte Theologie*).
¹³PZ, p. 233.
¹⁴PZ, pp. 200, 201.
¹⁵PZ, p. 207.
¹⁶PZ, pp. 180, 181.
¹⁷PZ, p. 6.
¹⁸PZ, p. 4.
¹⁹PZ, p. 6.
²⁰PZ, p. 3.
²¹GP, p. 28.
²²GP, pp. 15–18, 29, 466–67.
²³GP, p. 58.
²⁴AM, p. 46.

[25]AM, pp. 46–47.

[26]AM, p. 129.

[27]AM, p. 158.

[28]HH, pp. 97–100.

[29]HH, p. 100.

[30]HH, p. 95.

[31]HH, p. 95.

[32]HH, p. 95.

[33]HH, p. 101.

[34]HH, p. 174.

[35]HH, p. 263.

[36]HH, p. 210; HA, pp. 140–41.

[37]HH, p. 220.

[38]HH, p. 210.

[39]*Hölderlins Hymne "Der Ister,"* Gesamtausgabe Bd. 53 (Frankfurt am Main: Klostermann, 1984) (hereafter: HI).

[40]HA, pp. 13, 24.

[41]HA, p. 165.

[42]HA, p. 178.

[43]HA, pp. 133, 100–102.

[44]HA, p. 134.

[45]HI, p. 173.

[46]HA, pp. 132–33.

[47]Martin Heidegger and Eugen Fink, *Heraklit* (Frankfurt am Main: Klostermann, 1970) (hereafter: HS).

[48]H, pp. 228, 3, 41–42, 156.

[49]HS, pp. 259–60. Cf. also Heidegger's comprehensive meditation on the historical destiny (transformation) and essence of truth in his lecture course at Freiburg (Winter Semester, 1942–1943), published as *Parmenides,* Gesamtausgabe Bd. 54 (Frankfurt am Main: Klostermann, 1982) (hereafter: P).

[50]H, p. 296.

[51]H, p. 180.

[52]H, pp. 355, 356.

[53]H, p. 375.

[54]H, pp. 396, 377.

[55]H, p. 341. See also BE, pp. 437–40 (God is not above Being; Being is not above God).

[56]H, pp. 74, 13, 209, 318.

[57]H, pp. 367, 373, 13.

Chapter 20

[1]ML, p. 177.

[2]ML, pp. 170, 276–77; GP, pp. 423–29.

³ML, pp. 211–13.
⁴ML, p. 275.
⁵ML, p. 217.
⁶GP, pp. 425–26.
⁷GP, p. 425.
⁸LW, p. 143.
⁹SZ, p. 38.
¹⁰An examination of Heidegger's contribution to the question of ultimate meaning can be found in George Kovacs, "Values and Limitations of Heidegger's Approach to the Question of Ultimate Meaning," *Ultimate Reality and Meaning*, 11 (1988): 119–21. For a study of the interpretation of the ultimate meaning of transcendence in Heidegger and V. E. Frankl, see George Kovacs, "The Meaning of Transcendence in Frankl and Heidegger," *International Journal of Philosophy and Psychotherapy: HSIN* (forthcoming). See also George Kovacs, "Heidegger and Marx," *Documentation sur l'Europe Centrale* (Université de Louvain), 16 (1978): 209–16. For an examination of the ultimate meaning of human work and self-transcendence, see George Kovacs, "Phenomenology of Work and Self-Transcendence," *Journal of Value Inquiry*, 20 (1986): 195–207. For additional reflections on the search for ultimate meaning, see George Kovacs, "The Search for Meaning in Albert Camus," *Ultimate Reality and Meaning* 10 (1987): 121–39.
¹¹ML, p. 85.
¹²ML, pp. 211, 241–45.
¹³ML, p. 211.

Chapter 21

¹*Die Grundbegriffe der Metaphysik: Welt-Endlichkeit-Einsamkeit*, Gesamtausgabe Bd. 29/30 (Frankfurt am Main: Klostermann, 1983) (hereafter: GM).
²*Grundfragen der Philosophie: Ausgewählte "Probleme" der "Logik,"* Gesamtausgabe Bd. 45 (Frankfurt am Main: Klostermann, 1984), p. 188 (hereafter: GL). See also P.
³GM, p. 198. See also: GL, pp. 212, 213; and Heidegger's lecture course at Freiburg (Summer Semester, 1930), published as *Vom Wesen der menschlichen Freiheit: Einleitung in die Philosophie*, Gesamtausgabe Bd. 31 (Frankfurt am Main: Klostermann, 1982), p. 130 (hereafter: WF).
⁴PZ, p. 230.
⁵PZ, pp. 231–51.
⁶ GP, pp. 422–23, 234–38; PZ, pp. 250–91; ML, pp. 222–23.
⁷GP, pp. 422, 420; ML, pp. 212–13, 238.
⁸ML, p. 239.
⁹SZ, pp. 83–88; PZ, pp. 275–76.
¹⁰GP, pp. 316, 420; ML, p. 211; PZ, pp. 182, 206–7, 291, 391.
¹¹GP, p. 140.

[12]GP, pp. 145, 148, 162–63.
[13]GP, pp. 167–68.
[14]GP, p. 170.
[15]GP, pp. 168–69.
[16]GP, p. 168.
[17]GP, p. 213.
[18]GP, p. 214.
[19]GP, pp. 215, 214.
[20]GP, p. 215.

Chapter 22

[1]PZ, pp. 410 (love), 387 (friendship), 201 and 391 (goal of existential analysis). See also pp. 434, 394.
[2]GP, pp. 225–38.
[3]GP, pp. 194–95.
[4]GP, p. 76.
[5]ML, pp. 241, 243.
[6]ML, pp. 241–43.
[7]ML, p. 214.
[8]ML, p. 211.
[9]Martin Buber, *Between Man and Man* (New York: Macmillan, 1969), p. 174.
[10]Ibid., p. 179.

Chapter 23

[1]Martin Heidegger, *Vier Seminare* (Frankfurt am Main: Klostermann, 1977), p. 24 (hereafter: VS).
[2]ML, p. 85.
[3]VS, pp. 47–49. Heidegger italicizes the quoted expression. For an examination of the essential nature (radicality) and function of the onto-logical difference in Heidegger's thought, see George Kovacs, "The Onto-logical Difference in Heidegger's *Grundbegriffe*," *Heidegger Studies*, 3/4 (1987/1988): 61–74.
[4]ML, p. 10. An analysis of Heidegger's rethinking of the essence of philosophy can be found in George Kovacs, "Philosophy as Primordial Science (*Urwissenschaft*) in the Early Heidegger," *Journal of the British Society for Phenomenology* (forthcoming).

Part 5

[1]The destiny of the question of God in Heidegger is the same as the destiny of his philosophy as a whole: a way and not a final opus. See the

description of his writings as "Wege—nicht Werke" in *Frühe Schriften*, Gesamtausgabe Bd. 1 (Frankfurt am Main: Klostermann, 1978), p. 437 (hereafter: FS). Cf. also SZ, p. 345 (*der existenziale Sinn des Hoffens*).

[2]"Fragen können heisst: warten können, sogar ein Leben long" (EM, p. 157).

[3]"Das Denken zieht Furchen in den Acker des Seins." (US, p. 173). See also: WP, pp. 24–26 (*Erstaunen*); TK, pp. 40 (*dem Sein und dessen Anspruch zu entsprechen*), 41 (*der Mensch als der Hirt des Seins*), 44 (*Im 'ist' wird 'Sein' ausgesprochen*); SF, pp. 27–28 (*Sein—Mensch*).

[4]*Schellings Abhandlung über das Wesen der menschlichen Freiheit (1909)*, ed. Hildegard Feick (Tübingen: Niemeyer, 1971), p. 175 (hereafter: SA).

Chapter 25

[1]See, for instance: ID, pp. 51, 70–71; HW, pp. 70, 202–4; HB, pp. 36–37; TK, pp. 45–46; *Aus der Erfahrung des Denkens*, Gesamtausgabe Bd. 13 (Frankfurt am Main: Klostermann, 1983), p. 154 (*Also ist Gott nicht tot*) (hereafter: EDG); BE, pp. 417, 438.

[2]FS, p. 438.

Chapter 26

[1]Stefan Schimansky, "On Meeting a Philosopher," *Partisan Review*, 15 (1948): 511.

[2]Richard Wisser, ed., *Martin Heidegger im Gespräch* (Freiburg-Munich: Verlag Karl Alber, 1970), p. 51.

[3]*Hebel—der Hausfreund*, 3d ed. (Pfullingen: Neske, 1965), p. 25 (hereafter: HF).

[4]EM, p. 39 (*der zerstörte Bezug zum Sein, Missverhältnis zur Sprache*). See also: SA, p. 175; HF, p. 41; US, pp. 214–15, 267; EDG, p. 33. A comprehensive, clear explanation of Heidegger's understanding of language can be found in Hans Jaeger, *Heidegger und die Sprache* (Bern-Munich: Francke Verlag, 1971).

[5]Heidegger rightly recognized the historical role of the natural sciences; his university lecture courses (as published in the *Gesamtausgabe*, e.g., WF) confirm that he perceived the nature and the value of the sciences more profoundly than his critics seem to be willing to admit. For an insightful dialogue between Heidegger and the natural sciences, see, C. F. v. Weizsäcker, "Heidegger und die Naturwissenschaft," in Hans-Georg Gadamer, Werner Marx, and Carl Friedrich von Weizsäcker, *Heidegger: Freiburger Universitätsvorträge zu seinem Gedeneken*, ed. Werner Marx (Freiburg-Munich: Verlag Karl Alber, 1977), pp. 63–86. Some further reflec-

tions on the scientific understanding of the World can be found in George Kovacs, "Nueva Imagen del Hombre: Ontogénesis y Filogénesis," *Ciencia y Fé*, 15 (1959): 303–24. See also George Kovacs, "Una nueva génesis humana: Ingeniería Genética y Ética," *Mensaje* (Santiago, Chile), 16 (1978): 91–98.

[6]VS, pp. 108–9 (*Endlichkeit des Seins, Hirt des Seins, das Sein braucht den Menschen als das Da seiner Offenbarkeit, das Sein nicht ohne seine Beziehung zum Dasein*). Cf. also O. Pöggeler, *Der Denkweg Martin Heideggers*, p. 289. See also BE, pp. 11, 26, 32, 413, 415, 439.

[7]For further study of Heidegger's "place" in the history of philosophy, see: Walter Schulz, "Über den philosophiegeschichtlichen Ort Martin Heideggers," *Philosophische Rundschau*, 1 (1953–1954): 65–93, 211–32; O. Pöggeler (ed.), *Heidegger: Perspektiven zur Deutung seines Werks*; H.-G. Gadamer, W. Marx, and C. F. v. Weizsäcker, *Heidegger: Freiburger Universitätsvorträge zu seinem Gedneken*. For valuable information on Heidegger's biography and work, see Günther Neske (ed.), *Erinnerung an Martin Heidegger*, collected volume (Pfullingen: Neske, 1977).

[8]Hannah Arendt, Jean Beaufret, Medard Boss, et al., *Dem Andenken Martin Heideggers: Zum 26.Mai 1976* (Frankfurt am Main: Klostermann, 1977), p. 21. Regarding Heidegger's recognition of the limitations of philosophical communication (especially in public), see, for instance, his *Zollikoner Seminare* (Frankfurt am Main: Klostermann, 1987), pp. 303, 313. A critical assessment of the thinking of Being by Heidegger in relation to the realm of human interaction (and thus to political life) and an examination of some endemic limitations of his thought can be found in George Kovacs, "On Heidegger's Silence," *Heidegger Studies*, 5 (1989): 135–51.

[9]H. Danner, *Das Göttliche und der Gott bei Heidegger*, p. 175, seems to conclude that the notion of God in Heidegger has nothing in common with the God of Christian (religious) faith (cf. also pp. 69–178). H.-G. Gadamer, "Sein, Geist, Gott" (in H.-G. Gadamer, W. Marx, C. F. v. Weizsäcker, *Heidegger: Freiburger Universitätsvorträge zu seinem Gedenken*, pp. 43–62), however, among others, suggests a more open-ended interpretation of Heidegger on this issue.

[10]ID, p. 51. Cf. also HB, pp. 45–47.

[11]EM, p. 157 (*fragend*).

Bibliography

This bibliography includes only books and articles cited in this study.

Works by Heidegger

The following lists identify the writings of Heidegger according to the editions used in this study. These two lists together include almost all (with the exception of some "minor" items) his published works. However, because of the publication of all his writings in the *Gesamtausgabe* now in progress, no list of Heidegger's works can be complete at this time.

Works published outside the *Gesamtausgabe*

This list, in addition to the editions used in this study, indicates the dates or at least the range of dates of the composition (in parentheses after the title) and the dates or at least the range of dates of the first publication (in parentheses at the end of each entry) of these writings. They are listed according to the (approximate) order of their *first publication*.

A detailed chronology (composition, publication, public presentation) of each item in these works (many of them contain several essays written at different times) can be found in the seminal work by W. J. Richardson, *Heidegger: Through Phenomenology to Thought* (pp. 675–80 list Heidegger's works in the order of composition and of publication; pp. 663–71 give the listing of his lecture courses and seminars at Marburg and Freiburg) and in the three-volume bibliography by Hans-Martin Sass: *Heidegger-Bibliographie* (Meisenheim am Glan: Verlag Anton Hain, 1968); *Materialien zur Heidegger-Bibliographie 1917–1972* (Meisenheim am Glan: Verlag Anton Hain, 1975); *Martin Heidegger: Bibliography and Glossary* (Bowling Green, Ohio: Philosophy Documentation Center, Bowling Green State University, 1982). Many of Heidegger's earlier (shorter) writings that were published separately are now available also in the *Gesamtausgabe* (see, for instance, vols. 1 and 13).

Frühe Schriften (1914–16). Frankfurt am Main: Klostermann, 1972. (1914–17).

Sein und Zeit (1927). 10th ed. Tübingen: Niemeyer, 1963. (1927).

Kant und das Problem der Metaphysik (1927–29). 4th expanded ed. (with: "Davoser Vorträge" and "Davoser Disputation"). Frankfurt am Main: Klostermann, 1973. (1929).

Vom Wesen des Grundes (1928). 4th ed. Frankfurt am Main: Klostermann, 1955. (1929).

Was ist Metaphysik? (1929; "Nachwort" added to the 4th ed., 1943; "Einleitung" added to the 5th ed., 1949). 8th ed. Frankfurt am Main: Klostermann, 1960. (1929).

Die Selbstbehauptung der deutschen Universität (1933). Breslau: Korn, 1933. (1933).

Vom Wesen der Wahrheit (1930). 4th ed. Frankfurt am Main: Klostermann, 1961. (1943).

Erläuterungen zu Hölderlins Dichtung (1943, 1936, 1939, 1943). 3d ed. Frankfurt am Main: Klostermann, 1963. (1944, 1937, 1941, 1943).

Platons Lehre von der Wahrheit (1940): Mit einem Brief über den "Humanismus" (1946). 2d ed. Bern: Francke, 1954. (1942; 1947).

Über den Humanismus (1946). 6th ed. Frankfurt am Main: Klostermann, 1964. (1947).

Der Feldweg (1949). 3d ed. Frankfurt am Main: Klostermann, 1962. (1949).

Holzwege (1935–46). 4th ed. Frankfurt am Main: Klostermann, 1963 (1950).

Der Ursprung des Kunstwerkes (1935; with "Zusatz" in 1956; includes "Zur Einführung" by Hans-Georg Gadamer). Stuttgart: Philipp Reclam, 1965. (1935, 1960).

Einführung in die Metaphysik (lecture course at Freiburg, Summer Semester, 1935). 3d ed. Tübingen: Niemeyer, 1966. (1953).

Aus der Erfahrung des Denkens (1947). 2d ed. Pfullingen: Neske, 1965. (1954).

Was heisst Denken? (lecture course at Freiburg, Winter Semester, 1951–52 and Summer Semester, 1952). 2d ed. Tübingen: Niemeyer, 1961. (1954).

Vorträge und Ausätze (1936–1953). 3 parts. 3d ed. Pfullingen: Neske, 1967. (1954).

Was ist das—die Philosophie? (1955). 4th ed. Pfullingen: Neske, 1966. (1956).

Zur Seinsfrage (1955). 2d ed. Frankfurt am Main: Klostermann, 1959. (1955).

Der Satz vom Grund (lecture course at Freiburg, Winter Semester, 1955–56; lecture, 1956). 3d ed. Pfullingen: Neske, 1965. (1957).

Identität und Differenz (1957). 3d ed. Pfullingen: Neske, 1957. (1957).

Hebel—der Hausfreund (1957). 3d ed. Pfullingen: Neske, 1965. (1957).

"Grundsätze des Denkens" (1958). In: *Jahrbuch für Psychologie und Psychotherapie*, 6 (1958): 33–41.

Wegmarken (1929–62). Frankfurt am Main: Klostermann, 1967. (1929–64).

"Vom Wesen und Begriff der *Physis*, Aristoteles Physik B 1" (1939). In: *Wegmarken*, pp. 309–71. (1958).

Gelassenheit (1955; 1944–45). 2d ed. Pfullingen: Neske, 1960. (1959).

Unterwegs zur Sprache (1950–59). 3d ed. Pfullingen: Neske, 1965. (1959).

"Hegel und die Griechen" (1958). In: *Wegmarken*, pp. 255–72. (1960).

Nietzsche (1936–46). 2 vols. Pfullingen: Neske, 1961. (1961).

Die Frage nach dem Ding: Zu Kanst Lehre von den transzendentalen Grundsätzen (lecture course at Freiburg, Winter Semester, 1935–36). Tübingen: Niemeyer, 1962. (1962).

Kants These über das Sein (1962). Frankfurt am Main: Klostermann, 1963. (1962).

Die Technik und die Kehre (1953, 1949). Pfullingen: Neske, 1962. (1954, 1962).

"Vorwort" (Letter to William J. Richardson, April 1962). In: W. J. Richardson, *Heidegger: Through Phenomenology to Thought*. Phaenomenologica vol. 13. The Hague: Nijhoff, 1963, pp. viii–xxiii (German original and English translation by W. J. Richardson). (1963).

"Aus der letzten Marburger Vorlesung" (1928). In: *Wegmarken*, pp. 373–95. (1964).

"La fin de la philosophie et la tâche de la pensée" (1964).Translated by Jean Beaufret and François Fédier. In: *Kierkegaard vivant* (collected volume). Colloque organisé par l'Unesco à Paris du 21 au 23 avril 1964. Paris: Gallimard, 1966, pp. 165–204. (1966).

Zur Sache des Denkens (1962–64). Tübingen: Niemeyer, 1969. (1963–68).

Phänemonologie und Theologie (1927, 1964). Frankfurt am Main: Klostermann, 1970. (1969).

"Colloque Cassirer-Heidegger" (Davos, Spring 1929. Rédaction: Dr. O. F. Bollnow et Dr. J. Ritter). In: Ernst Cassirer—Martin Heidegger, *Débat sur le Kantisme et la philosophie (Davos, mars 1929) et autres textes de 1929–1931*. Presented by Pierre Aubenque. Translated from the German by P. Aubenque, J.-M. Fataud, and P. Quillet. Paris: Beauchesne, 1972, pp. 28–51. (some portions of this text, 1960–69).

Die Kunst und der Raum: L'art et l'espace (1969). St. Gallen: Erker, 1969. (1969).

Martin Heidegger: Zum 80. Geburtstag von siner Heimatstadt Messkirch (1949–64). Frankfurt am Main: Klostermann, 1969. (1949–69).

"Martin Heidegger im Gespräch" (1969). In: *Martin Heidegger im Gespräch* (collected volume). Edited by Richard Wisser. Freiburg-Munich: Verlag Karl Alber, 1970, pp. 67–77. (1970).

Heraklit (seminar at Freiburg, Winter Semester, 1966–67; with Eugen Fink). Frankfurt am Main: Klostermann, 1970. (1970).

Schellings Abhandlung über das Wesen der menschilichen Freiheit (1809) (lecture course at Freiburg, Summer Semester, 1936). Edited by Hildegard Feick. Tübingen: Niemeyer, 1971. (1971).

Vier Seminare (1966, 1968, 1969, 1973). Translated from the French (proceedings of the seminars) by Curd Ochwadt. Frankfurt am Main: Klostermann, 1977. (parts of the text, 1969, 1976).

"Only a God Can Save Us: *Der Spiegel*'s Interview with Martin Heidegger" ("Nur noch ein Gott kann uns retten," *Der Spiegel*, issue N. 23, May 31, 1976, 193–219; date of the interview: September 23, 1966). Translated by Maria P. Alter and John D. Caputo. In: *Philosophy Today*, 20 (1976): 267–84.

Denkerfahrungen (1910–76). Edited by Hermann Heidegger. Frankfurt am Main: Klostermann, 1983. (1910–76).

Die Selbstbehauptung der deutschen Universität (1933) and *Das Rektorat 1933/1934* (1945). Edited by Hermann Heidegger. Frankfurt am Main: Klostermann, 1983. (1933 and 1983).

"Das Wesen der Philosophie" (1940–45). In: *Jahresgabe der Martin Heidegger Gesellschaft*, 1987, 23–30. (1987).

Zollikoner Seminare: Protokolle (1959–69), *Gespräche* (1961–72), *Briefe* (1947–71). Edited by Medard Boss. Frankfurt am Main: Klostermann, 1987. (1987).

Wiplinger, Fridolin, and Heidegger, Martin. *Von der Un-Verborgenheit: Fridloin Wiplingers Bericht von einem Gespräch mit Martin Heidegger* (1972). Aufgezeichnet von Ekkehard Fräntzki. Pfaffenweiler: Centaurus-Verlagsgesellschaft, 1987. (1987).

Works published in the *Gesamtausgabe*

This is a complete list of all the works published so far (that is, as of the end of March 1989) in the *Gesamtausgabe*. They are listed according to their chronology of *publication* in this edition. The dates of the university lecture courses and the dates (or at least the range of dates) of composition of the essays are indicated in parentheses after the title of each volume.

Die Grundprobleme der Phänomenologie (lecture course at Marburg, Summer Semester, 1927). Gesamtausgabe vol. 24. Edited by Friedrich-Wilhelm von Herrmann. Frankfurt am Main: Klostermann, 1975.

Wegmarken (1919–64). Gesamtausgabe vol. 9. Edited by Friedrich-Wilhelm von Herrmann. Frankfurt am Main: Klostermann, 1976.

Logik: Die Frage nach der Wahrheit (lecture course at Marburg, Winter Semester, 1925–26). Gesamtausgabe vol. 21. Edited by Walter Biemel. Frankfurt am Main: Klostermann, 1976.

Sein und Zeit (1927). Gesamtausgabe vol. 2. Edited by Friedrich-Wilhelm von Herrmann. Frankfurt am Main: Klostermann, 1977.

Holzwege (1935–46). Gesamtausgabe vol. 5. Edited by Friedrich-Wilhelm von Herrmann. Frankfurt am Main: Klostermann, 1977.

Phänomenologische Interpretation von Kants Kritik der reinen Vernunft (lecture course at Marburg, Winter Semester, 1927–28). Gesamtausgabe vol. 25. Edited by Ingtraud Görland. Frankfurt am Main: Klostermann, 1977.

Frühe Schriften (1912–16). Gesamtausgabe vol. 1. Edited by Friedrich-Wilhelm von Herrmann. Frankfurt am Main: Klostermann, 1978. (Includes some important notes by Heidegger on the *Gesamtausgabe*.)

Metaphysische Anfangsgrüde der Logik im Ausgang von Leibniz (lecture course at Marburg, Summer Semester, 1928). Gesamtausgabe vol. 26. Edited by Klaus Held. Frankfurt am Main: Klostermann, 1978.

Prolegomena zur Geschichte des Zeitbegriffs (lecture course at Marburg, Summer Semester, 1925). Gesamtausgabe vol. 20. Edited by Petra Jaeger. Frankfurt am Main: Klostermann, 1979.

Heraklit. 1: Der Anfang des abendländischen Denkens (Heraklit). 2: Logik: Heraklits Lehre vom Logos (two lecture courses at Freiburg: Summer Semester, 1943, and Summer Semester, 1944). Gesamtausgabe vol. 55. Edited by Manfred S. Frings. Frankfurt am Main: Klostermann, 1979.

Hegels Phänomenologie des Geistes (lecture course at Freiburg, Winter Semester, 1930–31). Gesamtausgabe vol. 32. Edited by Ingtraud Görland. Frankfurt am Main: Klostermann, 1980.

Hölderlins Hymnen "Germanien" und "Der Rhein" (lecture course at Freiburg, Winter Semester, 1934–35). Gesamtausgabe vol. 39. Edited by Susanne Ziegler. Frankfurt am Main: Klostermann, 1980.

Erläuterungen zu Hölderlins Dichtung (1936–68). Gesamtausgabe vol. 4. Edited by Friedrich-Wilhelm von Herrmann. Frankfurt am Main: Klostermann, 1981.

Aristoteles, Metaphysik IX 1–3: Vom Wesen und Wirklichkeit der Kraft (lecture course at Freiburg, Summer Semester, 1931). Gesamtausgabe vol. 33. Edited by Heinrich Hüni. Frankfurt am Main: Klostermann, 1981.

Grundbegriffe (lecture course at Freiburg, Summer Semester, 1941). Gesamtausgabe vol. 51. Edited by Petra Jaeger. Frankfurt am Main: Klostermann, 1981.

Vom Wesen der menschlichen Freiheit: Einleitung in die Philosophie (lecture course at Freiburg, Summer Semester, 1930). Gesamtausgabe vol. 31. Edited by Hartmut Tietjen. Frankfurt am Main: Klostermann, 1982.

Hölderlins Hymne "Andenken" (lecture course at Freiburg, Winter Semester, 1941–42). Gesamtausgabe vol. 52. Edited by Curd Ochwadt. Frankfurt am Main: Klostermann, 1982.

Parmenides (lecture course at Freiburg, Winter Semester, 1942–43). Gesamtausgabe vol. 54. Edited by Manfred S. Frings. Frankfurt am Main: Klostermann, 1982.

Aus der Erfahrung des Denkens (1910–76). Gesamtausgabe vol. 13. Edited by Hermann Heidegger. Frankfurt am Main: Klostermann, 1983.

Die Grundbegriffe der Metaphysik: Welt-Endlichkeit-Einsamkeit (lecture course at Freiburg, Winter Semester, 1929–30). Gesamtausgabe vol. 29/30. Edited by Friedrich-Wilhelm von Herrmann. Frankfurt am Main: Klostermann, 1983.

Einführung in die Metaphysik (lecture course at Freiburg, Summer Semester, 1935). Gesamtausgabe vol. 40. Edited by Petra Jaeger. Frankfurt am Main: Klostermann, 1983.

Die Frage nach dem Ding: Zu Kants Lehre von den transzendentalen Grundsätzen (lecture course at Freiburg, Winter Semester, 1935–36). Gesamtausgabe vol. 41. Edited by Petra Jaeger. Frankfurt am Main: Klostermann, 1984.

Grundfragen der Philosophie: Ausgewählte "Probleme" der "Logik" (lecture course at Freiburg, Winter Semester, 1937–38). Gesamtausgabe vol. 45. Edited by Friedrich-Wilhelm von Herrmann. Frankfurt am Main: Klostermann, 1984.

Hölderlins Hymne "Der Ister" (lecture course at Freiburg, Summer Semester, 1942). Gesamtausgabe vol. 53. Edited by Walter Biemel. Frankfurt am Main: Klostermann, 1984.

Unterwegs zur Sprache (1950–59). Gesamtausgabe vol. 12. Edited by Friedrich-Wilhelm von Herrmann. Frankfurt am Main: Klostermann, 1985.

Phänomenologische Interpretationen zu Aristoteles: Einführung in die phänomenologische Forschung (early Freiburg lecture course, Winter Semester, 1921–22). Gesamtausgabe vol. 61. Edited by Walter Bröcker and Käte Bröcker-Oltmanns. Frankfurt am Main: Klostermann, 1985.

Nietzsche: Der Wille zur Macht als Kunst (lecture course at Freiburg, Winter Semester, 1936–37). Gesamtausgabe vol. 43. Edited by Bernd Heimbüchel. Frankfurt am Main: Klostermann, 1985.

Nietzsche: Der europäische Nihilismus (lecture course at Freiburg, Second Trimester, 1940). Gesamtausgabe vol. 48. Edited by Petra Jaeger. Frankfurt am Main: Klostermann, 1986.

Nietzsches metaphysische Grundstellung im abendländische Denken: Die ewige Wiederkehr des Gleichen (lecture course at Freiburg, Summer Semester, 1937). Gesamtausgabe vol. 44. Edited by Marion Heinz. Frankfurt am Main: Klostermann, 1986.

Seminare (1951–1973). Gesamtausgabe vol. 15. Edited by Curd Ochwadt. Frankfurt am Main: Klostermann, 1986.

Zur Bestimmung der Philosophie (early Freiburg lecture courses): 1. *Die Idee der Philosophie und das Weltanschauungsproblem* (War Emergency Semester, January 25–April 16, 1919); 2. *Phänomenologie und transzendentale Wertphilosophie* (Summer Semester, 1919); mit einer Nachschrift der Vorlesung "Über das Wesen der Universität und des akademischen Studiums" (Summer Semester, 1919; notes taken by Oskar Becker). Gesamtausgabe vol. 56/57. Edited by Bernd Heimbüchel. Frankfurt am Main: Klosterman, 1987.

Schelling: Vom Wesen der menschlichen Freihiet (1809) (lecture course at Freiburg, Summer Semester, 1936). Gesamtausgabe vol. 42. Edited by Ingrid Schüssler. Frankfurt am Main: Klostermann, 1988.

Ontologie: Hermeneutik der Faktizität (early Freiburg lecture course, Summer Semester, 1923). Gesamtausgabe vol. 63. Edited by Käte Bröcker-Oltmanns. Frankfurt am Main: Klostermann, 1988.

Vom Wesen der Wahrheit: Zu Platons Höhlengleichnis und Theätet (lecture course at Freiburg, Winter Semester, 1931–32). Gesamtausgabe vol. 34.

Edited by Hermann Mörchen. Frankfurt am Main: Klostermann, 1988.
Beiträge zur Philosophie: Vom Ereignis (1936–38). Gesamtausgabe vol. 65. Edited by Friedrich-Wilhelm von Herrmann. Frankfurt am Main: Klostermann, 1989.

Other Works Cited

Allemann, Beda. *Hölderlin et Heidegger.* Translated from the German by François Fédier. Paris: Presses Universitaires de France, 1959.
Arendt, Hannah; Beaufret, Jean; Boss, Médard et al. *Dem Andenken Martin Heideggers: Zum 26. Mai 1976* (collected volume). Frankfurt am Main: Klostermann, 1977.
Beaufret, Jean. *Dialogue avec Heidegger: I. Philosophie Grecque.* Paris: Minuit, 1973.
———. *Dialogue avec Heidegger: II. Philosophie Moderne.* Paris: Minuit, 1973.
———. *Dialogue avec Heidegger: III. Approche de Heidegger.* Paris: Minuit, 1974.
Biemel, Walter. *Le concept du monde chez Heidegger.* Louvain-Paris: Nauwelaerts-Vrin, 1950.
———. *Martin Heidegger: An Illustrated Study.* Translated from the German by J. L. Mehta. New York and London: Harcourt Brace Jovanovich, 1976.
Birault, Henri. "La foi et la pensée d'aprés Heidegger," *Philosophies Chrétiennes: Recherches et Débats* (collected volume), vol. 10, no. 4. Paris: A. Fayard, 1955, pp. 108–32.
———. "De l'être, du divin et des dieux chez Heidegger," *L'existence de Dieu* (collected volume). 2d ed. Tournai: Casterman, 1963, pp. 49–76.
———. *Heidegger et l'expérience de la pensée.* Paris: Gallimard, 1978.
Boehm, Rudolf. *Vom Gesichtspunkt der Phänomenologie: Husserl-Studien.* Phaenomenologica vol. 26. The Hague: Nijhoff, 1968.
Buber, Martin. *Eclipse of God: Studies in the Relation between Religion and Philosophy.* Translated by Maurice S. Friedman, Norbert Guterman, Eugene Kamenka, and I. M. Lask. New York: Harper and Row, 1952.
———. *I and Thou.* Translated by Ronald Gregor Smith. 2d ed. New York: Charles Scribner's Sons, 1958.
———. *Between Man and Man.* Translated by R. G. Smith, with an Introduction by Maurice S. Friedman and an Afterward by the author on "The History of the Dialogical Principle" in Maurice S. Friedman's translation. New York: Macmillan, 1969.
———. *Ich und Du.* Cologne: Hegner, 1972.
Bultmann, Rudolf. "Erziehung und christlicher Glaube," *Martin Heidegger*

zum siebzigsten Geburtstag: Festschrift. Edited by Günther Neske. Pfullingen: Neske, 1959, pp. 175–79.

Cassirer, Ernst, and Heidegger, Martin. *Débat sur le Kantisme et la philosophie (Davos, March 1929) et autres textes de 1929–1931.* Presented by Pierre Aubenque. Translated from the German by P. Aubenque et al. Paris: Beauchesne, 1972.

Cleve, W. T. *Denken und Erkennen: Ein Weg in die Philosophie nach Peter Wust.* Emsdetten: Lechte, 1952.

Corvez, Maurice. "La place de Dieu dans l'ontologie de Martin Heidegger," *Revue Thomiste,* 53 (1953): 287–320.

————. *La Philosophie de Heidegger.* 2d ed. Paris: Presses Universitaires de France, 1966.

Danner, Helmut. *Das Göttliche und der Gott bei Heidegger.* Meisenheim am Glan: Verlag Anton Hain, 1971.

Dondeyne, Albert. "La différence ontologique chez M. Heidegger," *Revue Philosophique de Louvain,* 56 (1958): 35–62, 251–93.

Dieu aujourd'hui: Recherches et Débats. Collected volume. Bruge: Desclée de Brouwer, 1965.

L'Existence de Dieu. Collected vol. 2d ed. Tournai: Casterman, 1963.

Eliade, Mircea. *Le Sacré et le Profane.* Paris: Gallimard, 1965.

Fay, Thomas A. *Heidegger: The Critique of Logik.* The Hague: Nijhoff, 1977.

Fédier, François. "Heidegger et Dieu," *Heidegger et la question de Dieu* (collected volume). Edited by Richard Kearny and Joseph S. O'Leary. Paris: Grasset, 1980, pp. 37–45.

Feick, Hildegard. *Index zu Heideggers "Sein und Zeit."* 2d rev. ed. Tübingen: Niemeyer, 1968.

Fink, Eugen. *Sein, Wahrheit, Welt. Vor-Fragen zum Problem des Phänomen-Begriffs.* Phaenomenologica vol. 1. The Hague: Nijhoff, 1958.

————. *De la Phénoménologie.* Preface by Edmund Husserl. Translated from the German by Didier Franck. Paris: Minuit, 1974.

Frankl, Viktor E. *The Will to Meaning: Foundations and Applications of Logotherapy.* New York: New American Library–Plume Books, 1970.

————. *The Doctor and the Soul: From Psychotherapy to Logotherapy.* 2d expanded ed. New York: Bantam, 1971.

————. *Anthroplogische Grundlagen der Psychotherapie.* Bern-Stuttgart-Wien: Verlag Hans Huber, 1975.

————. *Der Wille zum Sinn.* 4th ed. Bern-Stuttgart-Wien: Verlag Hans Huber, 1982.

————. *Die Sinnfrage in der Psychotherapie.* München: R. Piper & Co. Verlag, 1981.

————. *Man's Search for Meaning: An Introduction to Logotherapy.* 3d, newly revised and enlarged ed. New York: Simon and Schuster, Touchstone Books, 1984.

Friedman, Maurice S. *Martin Buber: The Life of Dialogue.* New York: Harper Torchbooks, 1960.

Gadamer, Hans-Georg. "Zur Vorgeschicte der Metaphysik," *Anteile: Martin Heidegger zum 60. Geburtstag.* Edited by Vittorio Klostermann. Frankfurt am Main: Klostermann, 1950, pp. 51–79.

_____. "Vom Zirkel des Verstehens," *Martin Heidegger zum siebzigsten Geburtstag: Festschrift.* Edited by Günther Neske. Pfullingen: Neske, 1959, pp. 24–34.

_____. *Le problème de la conscience historique.* Louvain-Paris: Publications Universitaires Nauwelaerts, 1963.

_____. "Sein, Geist, Gott," in Hans-Georg Gadamer, Werner Marx, and Carl-Friedrich von Weizsäcker, *Heidegger: Freiburger Universitätsvorträge zu seinem Gedenken.* Edited by Werner Marx. Freiburg-Munich: Verlag Karl Alber, 1977, pp. 43–62.

Guibal, Francis. . . .*et combien de dieux nouveaux: Approches contemporaines: 1. Heidegger.* Paris: Aubier-Montaigne, 1980.

Guilead, Reuben. *Être et Liberté: Une étude sur le drenier Heidegger.* Paris-Louvain: Nauwelaerts, 1965.

Herrmann, Friedrich Wilhelm von. *Die Selbstinterpretation Martin Heideggers.* Meisenheim am Glan: Verlag Anton Hain, 1964.

_____. "Die Edition der Vorlesungen Heideggers in seiner Gesamtausgabe letzter Hand," *Heidegger Studies,* 2 (1986): 153–72.

Hoppe, Hansgeorg. "Wandlungen in der Kant-Auffassung Heideggers," *Durchblicke: Martin Heidegger zum 80. Geburtstag.* Edited by Vittorio Klostermann. Frankfurt am Main: Klostermann, 1970. pp. 284–317.

Husserl, Edmund. "Nachwort zu meinen *Ideen zu einer reinen Phänomenologie und phänomenologischen Philosophie,*" *Jahrbuch für Philosophie und phänomenologische Forschung,* 11 (Halle: Niemeyer, 1930), newly edited by Marly Biemel in Husserl's *Gesammelte Werke,* vol. 5. The Hague: Nijhoff, 1952, pp. 138–162.

_____. *Ideas: General Introduction Pure Phenomenology.* Vol. 1 of *Ideen.* Translated by W. R. Boyce Gibson. London: Allen and Unwin, 1969.

_____. *Phenomenology and the Crisis of Philosophy.* Includes Husserl's "Philosophy as Rigorous Science" (pp. 71–147) and "Philosophy and the Crisis of European Man" (pp. 147–92). Translated with an Introduction by Quentin Lauer. New York: Harper and Row, 1965.

_____. *Cartesian Meditations: An Introduction to Phenomenology.* Translated by Dorion Cairns. The Hague: Nijhoff, 1977.

IJsseling, Samuel. *Heidegger: Denken en Danken—Geven en Zijn.* Antwerp: Neerlandsche Boeckhandel, 1964.

Jaeger, Hans. *Heidegger und die Sprache.* Bern-Munich: Francke Verlag, 1971.

Jaegerschmid, Adelgundis. "Gespräche mit Edmund Husserl 1931–1936," *Stimmen der Zeit,* Bd. 199 (1981), Heft 1, 48–58.

_____. "Die letzten Jahre Edmund Husserls (1936–1938)," *Stimmen der Zeit,* Bd. 199 (1981), Heft 2, 129–38.

Jäger, Alfred. *Gott: Nochmals Martin Heidegger.* Tübingen: J. C. B. Mohr (Paul Siebeck), 1978.

Jaspers, Karl. *Notizen zu Martin Heidegger*. Edited by Hans Saner. Munich-Zürich: R. Piper & Co. Verlag, 1978.

Kearney, Richard and O'Leary, Joseph Stephen (eds.). *Heidegger et la question de Dieu*. Paris: Grasset, 1980.

Klostermann, Vittorio (ed.). *Anteile: Martin Heidegger zum 60. Geburtstag*. Frankfurt am Main: Klostermann, 1950.

————. *Durchblicke: Martin Heidegger zum 80. Geburtstag*. Frankfurt am Main: Klostermann, 1970.

Kovacs, George. "Man and Death: An Existential-Phenomenological Approach," *Proceedings of the American Catholic Philosophical Association*, 47 (1973): 183–90.

————. "Atheism and the Ultimate Thou," *International Journal for Philosophy of Religion*, 5 (1974): 1–15.

————. "Nueva Imagen del Hombre: Ontogénesis y Filogénesis (En el Centenario de Darwin)," *Ciencia y Fé*, 15 (1959): 303–24.

————. "Una nueva génesis humana: Ingeniería Genética y Etica," *Mensaje* (Santiago, Chile), 26 (1977): 91–98.

————. "Heidegger and Marx," *Documentation sur l'Europe Centrale* (Université de Louvain), 16 (1978): 209–16.

————. "Phenomenology and the Art of Teaching," *Journal of Thought*, 14 (1979): 194–98.

————. "Philosophy and Faith in Heidegger," *Proceedings of the American Catholic Philosophical Association*, 54 (1980): 135–43.

————. "Death and the Question of Immortality," *Death Education*, 5 (1981): 15–24.

————. "Ultimate Reality and Meaning in Viktor E. Frankl," *Ultimate Reality and Meaning*, 5 (1982): 118–39.

————. "Phenomenology and Logotherapy," *Analecta Frankliana: Proceedings of the First World Congress of Logotherapy (1980)*. Edited by Sandra A. Wawrytko. Berkeley, Calif.: Institute of Logotherapy Press, 1982, pp. 33–45.

————. "The Philosophy of Death in Viktor E. Frankl," *Journal of Phenomenological Psychology*, 13 (1982): 197–209.

————. "The Personalistic Understanding of the Body and Sexuality in Merleau-Ponty," *Review of Existential Psychology and Psychiatry*, 18 (1982–1983): 207–17.

————. "Der Sinn der Arbeit," *Wege zum Sinn: Logotherapie als Orientierungshilfe: Für Viktor E. Frankl*. Edited by Alfried Längle. Serie Piper vol. 387. Munich: R. Piper & Co. Verlag, 1985, pp. 91–100.

————. "Viktor E. Frankl's 'Place' in Philosophy," *International Forum for Logotherapy*, 8 (1985): 17–21.

————. "Values and Limitations of Heidegger's Approach to the Question of Ultimate Meaning," *Ultimate Reality and Meaning*, 11 (1988): 119–21.

————. "Phenomenology of Work and Self-Transcendence," *Journal of Value Inquiry*, 20 (1986): 195–207.

_____. "The Meaning of Transcendence in Frankl and Heidegger," *International Journal of Philosophy and Psychotherapy: HSIN*, (forthcoming).

_____. "The Search for Meaning in Albert Camus," *Ultimate Reality and Meaning*, 10 (1987): 121–39.

_____. "The Ontological Difference in Heidegger's *Grundbegriffe*," *Heidegger Studies*, 3/4 (1987/1988): 61–74.

_____. "Philosophy as Primordial Science (*Urwissenschaft*) in the Early Heidegger," *Journal of the British Society for Phenomenology* (forthcoming).

_____. "On Heidegger's Silence," *Heidegger Studies*, 5 (1989): 135–51.

Köchler, Hans. *Skepsis und Gesellschaftskritik im Denken Martin Heideggers*. Meisenheim am Glan: Verlag Anton Hain, 1978.

Laffoucrière, Odette. *Le Destin de la Pensée et "La Mort de Dieu" selon Heidegger*. Phaenomenologica vol. 24. The Hague: Nijhoff, 1968.

Langan, Thomas. *The Meaning of Heidegger: A Critical Study of an Existentialist Phenomenology*. 2d paperback printing. New York: Columbia University Press, 1965.

Längle, Alfried (ed.). *Wege zum Sinn: Logotherapie als Orientierungshilfe: Für Viktor E. Frankl*. Serie Piper vol. 387. Munich: R. Piper & Co. Verlag, 1985.

Lauer, Quentin. *Phenomenology: Its Genesis and Prospect*. New York: Harper and Row, 1965.

Levinas, Emmanuel. *Totalité et Infini: Essai sur l'Extériorité*. Phaenomenologica vol. 8. 2d ed. The Hague: Nijhoff, 1965.

Loscerbo, John. *Being and Technology: A Study in the Philosophy of Martin Heidegger*. Phaenomenologica vol. 82. The Hague: Nijhoff, 1981.

Löwith, Karl. *Heidegger: Denker in dürftiger Zeit*. 3d revised ed. Göttingen: Vandenhoeck & Ruprecht, 1965.

Luijpen, William A. *Phenomenology and Atheism*. Pittsburgh: Duquesne University Press, 1964.

_____. *Phenomenology and Metaphysics*. Pittsburgh: Duquesne University Press, 1965.

Macquarrie, John. *An Existentialist Theology: A Comparison of Heidegger and Bultmann*. Foreword by Rudolf Bultmann. London: SCM Press, 1965.

Marcel, Gabriel. *Being and Having: An Existentialist Diary*. Translated by Katherine Farrer. New York: Harper and Row, 1965.

_____. "Peter Wust on the Nature of Piety," *Being and Having: An Existentialist Diary*. Translated by Katherine Farrer. New York: Harper and Row, 1965. pp. 213–36.

_____. *Essai de philosophie concrète*. Paris: Gallimard, 1967.

_____. "Ma relation avec Heidegger," *Gabriel Marcel et la pensée allemande: Nietzsche, Heidegger, Ernst Bloch*. Cahier N. 1 (1979), Présence de Gabriel Marcel. Paris: Aubier, 1979, pp. 25–38.

_____, et al. *Gabriel Marcel et la pensée allemande: Nietzsche, Heidegger, Ernst Bloch*. Cahier N. 1 (1979), Présence de Gabriel Marcel. Paris: Aubier, 1979.

Marx, Werner. *Heidegger and the Tradition*. Translated from the German by

Theodore Kisiel and Murray Greene. Evanston, Ill.: Northwestern University Press, 1971.

————(ed.). Gadamer, Hans-Georg; Marx, Werner; and Weizsäcker, Carl-Friedrich von. *Heidegger: Freiburger Universitätsvorträge zu seinem Gedenken*. Freiburg-Munich: Verlag Karl Alber, 1977.

Mehta, J. L. *Martin Heidegger: The Way and the Vision*. Honolulu: University of Hawaii Press, 1976.

Merleau-Ponty, Maurice. *Éloge de la philosophie et autres essais*. Paris: Gallimard, 1965.

————. *Phénoménologie de la perception*. Paris: Gallimard, 1972.

Metz, Johannes B. "Unbelief as a Theological Problem," *Concilium*, 6 (1965): 32–42.

————. "Der Unglaube als theologisches Problem," *Salesianum*, 27 (1965): 286–302.

Möller, Joseph. *Existenzialphilosophie und katholische Theologie*. Baden-Baden: Verlag für Kunst und Wissenschaft, 1952.

Müler, Max. *Existenzphilosophie im geistigen Leben der Gegenwart*. 2d enlarged and revised ed. Heidelberg: Kerle, 1964.

Neske, Günther (ed.). *Martin Heidegger zum siebzigsten Geburtstag: Festschrift*. Pfullingen: Neske, 1959.

————. *Erinnerung an Martin Heidegger*. Collected volume. Pfullingen: Neske, 1977.

Nietzsche, Friedrich. *Beyond Good and Evil*. Translated by Marianne Cowan. Chicago: Regnery, 1966.

————. *Thus Spoke Zarathustra*. Translated by R. J. Hollingdale. Baltimore, Md.: Penguin Books, 1971.

————. *Also sprach Zarathustra*. Stuttgart: Reclam, 1972.

Noack, Hermann. "Gespräch mit Martin Heidegger," *Anstösse* (Berichte aus der Arbeit der Ev. Akademie Hofgeismar), 1 (1954), 30–37.

Ott, Heinrich. *Denken und Sein: Der Weg Martin Heideggers und der Weg der Theologie*. Zollikon: Evangelischer Verlag, 1959.

————. "What Is Systematic Theology?" *The Later Heidegger and Theology*. Edited by James M. Robinson and John B. Cobb, Jr. New York: Harper and Row, 1963, pp. 77–111.

————. "Die Bedeutung von Martin Heideggers Denken für die Methode der Theologie," *Durchblicke: Martin Heidegger zum 80. Geburtstag*. Edited by Vittorio Klostermann. Frankfurt am Main: Klostermann, 1970, pp. 27–38.

————. *Das Reden vom Unsagbaren: Die Frage nach Gott in unserer Zeit*. Stuttgart-Berlin: Kreuz Verlag, 1978.

Otto, Rudolf. *The Idea of the Holy*. Translated by John W. Harvey from the 9th German edition of *Das Heilige* (first published in 1917). London: Pelican Books, 1959.

Pfänder, Alexander. *Phenomenology of Willing and Motivation*. Translated by

Herbert Spiegelberg, with an Introduction and supplementary essays by H. Spiegelberg. Evanston, Ill: Northwestern University Press, 1967.

Pieper, Joseph. *Über den Glauben: Ein philosophischer Traktat.* Munich: Kösel Verlag, 1962.

Pöggeler, Otto. *Der Denkweg Martin Heideggers.* Pfullingen: Neske, 1963.

_____(ed.). *Heidegger: Perspektiven zur Deutung seines Werks.* Cologne-Berlin: Kiepenheuer & Witsch, 1969.

_____. *Philosophie und Politik bei Heidegger.* 2d ed. with a "Nachwort." Freiburg-Munich: Verlag Karl Alber, 1974.

Pol, H. W. Van de. "Auf dem Weg zu einem verantworteten Gottesglauben," *Stimmen der Zeit,* Bd. 180 (1967), Heft 10, 236–38.

Rahner, Karl. *Im Heute Glauben.* Einsiedeln: Benziger, 1965.

_____. *The Practice of Faith: A Handbook of Contemporary Spirituality.* Edited by Karl Lehmann and Albert Raffelt. New York: Crossroad, 1983.

Richardson, William J. *Heidegger: Through Phenomenology to Thought.* Preface by Martin Heidegger. Phaenomenologica vol. 13. The Hague: Nijhoff, 1963.

_____. "Heidegger and God—and Profesor Jonas," *Thought,* 40 (1965): 13–40.

Ricoeur, Paul. "Sciences humaines et conditionnements de la foi," *Dieu aujourd'hui: Recherches et Débats.* Collected vol. Bruge: Desclée de Brouwer, 1965, pp. 136–46.

_____. *Husserl: An Analysis of His Phenomenology.* Translated by Edward G. Ballard and Lester E. Embree. Evanston, Ill: Northwestern University Press, 1967.

_____. *La métaphore vive.* Paris: Seuil, 1975.

Robert, Jean-Dominique. "La critique de l'onto-théologie chez Heidegger," *Revue Philosophique de Louvain,* 78 (1980): 533–52.

Robinson, James M., and Cobb, John B., Jr. (eds.). *The Later Heidegger and Theology.* New York: Harper and Row, 1963.

Sadzik, Joseph. *Esthétique de Martin Heidegger.* Paris: Éditions Universitaires, 1963.

Sallis, John C. "La différence ontologique et l'unité de la pensée de Heidegger," *Revue Philosophique de Louvain,* 65 (1967): 192–206.

Schimansky, Stefan. "On Meeting a Philosopher," *Partisan Review,* 15 (1948): 506–9.

Schulz, Walter. "Über den philosophigeschichtlichen Ort Martin Heideggers," *Philosophische Rundschau,* 1 (1953–1954): 65–93, 211–32.

_____. *Der Gott der neuzeitlichen Metaphysik.* 3d ed. Pfullingen: Neske, 1957.

Sheehan, Thomas (ed.). *Heidegger: The Man and the Thinker.* Chicago: Precedent Publishing, 1981.

Sokolowski, Robert. *The Formation of Husserl's Concept of Constitution.* Phaenomenologica vol. 18. The Hague: Nijhoff, 1964.

Spiegelberg, Herbert. *The Phenomenological Movement: A Historical Introduction.* Phaenomenologica vol. 5/6. 3d revised and enlarged ed. The Hague: Nijhoff, 1982.

Steinberg, Wilhelm. *Grundfragen des menschlichen Seins: Eine Einführung in die philosophische Anthroplogie.* Munich-Basel: E. Reinhardt, 1953.

Strolz, Walter. *Menschsein als Gottesfrage: Wege zur Erfahrung der Inkarnation.* Pfullingen: Neske, 1965.

Taminiaux, Jacques. *Le regard et l'excédent.* Phaenomenologica vol. 75. The Hague: Nijhoff, 1977.

Thévenaz, Pierre. *What Is Phenomenology? and Other Essays.* Edited with an Introduction by James M. Edie, translated by J. M. Edie, Charles Courtney, and Paul Brockelman. Chicago: Quadrangle Books, 1962.

Tresmontant, Claude. *Comment se pose aujourd'hui le problème de l'existence de Dieu?* Paris: Seuil, 1966.

Trotignon, Pierre. *Heidegger: Sa vie, son oeuvre: Avec un exposé de sa philosophie.* Paris: Presses Universitaires de France, 1965.

Vycinas, Vincent. *Earth and Gods: An Introduction to the Philosophy of Martin Heidegger.* The Hague: Nijhoff, 1961.

Waelhens, Alphonse De. *Chemins et Impasses de l'Ontologie Heideggerienne: À propos de Holzwege.* Louvain: Nauwelaerts, 1953.

—————. "Identité et différence: Heidegger et Hegel," *Revue Internationale de Philosophie,* 14 (1960): 221–37.

—————. *La philosophie et les expérience naturelles.* Phaenomenologica vol. 9. The Hague: Nijhoff, 1961.

—————. "Nature humaine et compréhension de l'être," *Revue Philosophique de Louvain,* 59 (1961): 672–82.

—————. "Reflections on Heidegger's Development: A Propos of a Recent Book," *International Philosophical Quarterly,* 5 (1965): 475–502.

—————. *Phénomenologie et Verité.* 2d ed. Louvain-Paris: Nauwelaerts, 1965.

—————. *La Philosophie de Martin Heidegger.* 5th ed. Louvain-Paris: Nauwelaerts, 1967.

—————. *Existence et Signification.* 2d ed. Louvain-Paris: Nauwelaerts, 1967.

Wawrytko, Sandra A. (ed.). *Analecta Frankliana: The Proceedings of the First World Congress of Logotherapy (1980).* Berkeley: Calif.: Institute of Logotherapy Press, 1982.

Weizsäcker, Carl-Friedrich von. "Heidegger und die Naturwissenschaft," in H.-G. Gadamer, W. Marx, and C. F. v. Weizsäcker, *Heidegger: Freiburger Universatätsvorträge zu seinem Gedenken.* Edited by W. Marx. Freiburg-Munich: Verlag Karl Alber, 1977, pp. 63–86.

Welte, Bernard. "La question de Dieu dans la pansée de Heidegger," *Les études philosophiques,* 19 (1964): 69–84.

Wiplinger, Fridolin, and Heidegger, Martin. *Von der Un-Verborgenheit: F. Wiplingers Bericht von einem Gespräch mit M. Heidegger: Aufgezeichnet von Ekkehard Fräntzki.* Pfaffenweiler: Centaurus-Verlagsgesellschaft, 1987.

Wisser, Richard (ed.). *Martin Heidegger im Gespräch*. Freiburg-Munich: Verlag Karl Alber, 1970.

Wust, Peter. *Die Auferstehung der Metaphysik*. Leipzig: Meiner, 1920.

_____. *Naivität und Pietät*. Tübingen: J. C. B. Mohr, 1925.

_____. *Dialektik des Geistes*. Augsburg: B. Filser, 1928.

_____. *Ungewissheit und Wagnis*. Salzburg: Pustet, 1937.

_____. *Im Sinnkreis des Ewigen*. Graz: Styria, 1954.

English Translations of Heidegger's Works Briefly Cited

An Introduction to Metaphysics (Einführung in die Metaphysik). Translated by Ralph Manheim. Garden City, N.Y.: Doubleday, Anchor Books, 1961.

"Preface" ("Vorwort," Letter to William J. Richardson, April 1962). In: William J. Richardson, *Heidegger: Through Phenomenology to Thought*. Phaenomenologica vol. 13. The Hague: Nijhoff, 1963, pp. viii–xxiii (German original and English translation by W. J. Richardson).

"Only a God Can Save Us: Der *Spiegel*'s Interview with Martin Heidegger" ("Nur noch ein Gott kann uns retten," *Der Spiegel*, issue No. 23, May 31, 1976, 193–219; date of the interview: September 23, 1966). Translated by Maria P. Alter and John D. Caputo. In: *Philosophy Today*, 20 (1976): 267–84.

Basic Writings: From Being and Time (1927) to the Task of Thinking (1964). Edited and introduced by David Farrell Krell. New York: Harper and Row, 1977.

Extensive bibliographies of works by and about Heidegger in English can be found in Thomas Sheehan (ed.), *Heidegger: The Man and the Thinker* (Chicago: Precedent Publishing, 1981), pp. 277–346. A list of the currently available English translations of Heidegger's writings published in the *Gesamtausgabe* is included in *Heidegger Studies*, 5 (1989): 216. For an extensive and detailed bibliographical guide to Heidegger (listings of his works, of translations into various languages, and of secondary literature up to 1982), see the three volumes by Hans-Martin Sass: *Heidegger-Bibliographie* (Meisenheim am Glan: Verlag Anton Hain, 1968); *Materialien zur Heidegger-Bibliographie 1917–1972* (Meisenheim am Glan: Verlag Anton Hain, 1975); *Martin Heidegger: Bibliography and Glossary* (Bowling Green, Ohio: Philosophy Documentation Center, Bowling Green State University, 1982).

Index

Italicized page numbers indicate more substantial discussion or definition of terms.
Heidegger's writings are identified by the symbols used in this study.